New features for the 2014 edition

This year, the number of wines tasted has again increased dramatically, soaring over the 20,000 mark. A total 3,000 wines representing the wine regions of France and Europe feature in the 2014 edition, highlighting stiff competition to secure a place in the guide. This is not only due to the extensive range and quality of France's wine regions but also to the fact that wines from neighbouring countries have ramped up their presence.

In fact, this is one of the major features of our 2014 edition for which we have selected some remarkable Italian and Spanish wines as well as a few offerings from other countries. Our greatest innovation this year, though, is the QR codes you can scan with your mobile phone, giving you instant access to all wines from each appellation available on our website (***www.gilbertgaillard.com***).

Enjoy!

Gilbert & Gaillard

CONTENTS

11th edition
The International Exhibition
of Mediterranean Wines and Spirits
Montpellier - France
24, 25, 26 February 2014
VINISUD
Passionately Mediterranean
Reserved for professionals
www.vinisud.com

HOW TO USE THIS GUIDE

THE ORDER OF THE WINES :

We have chosen to present wines by region (Alsace, Beaujolais…), then by appellation with each company or château listed in alphabetical order, and finally by tasting scores in descending order.

INDEX: There are two indexes at the back of the book: one for wines and producers (page 462) and one for appellations (page 520)

WINE SCORES :

Our tasting notes are scored on a 100 point scale, which gives enough range to evaluate every characteristic that we taste in a wine. Below are the different levels that make up this scoring:

95-100/100 : an outstanding wine, when a great "terroir" meets exceptional winemaking expertise.

90-94/100 : a superlative wine combining finesse, complexity and remarkable winemaking.

85-89/100 : a wine of extremely high standard, which we enjoyed for its typicity and character.

80-84/100 : a quality wine combining balance, structure and neatness for a pleasurable wine drinking experience.

75-79/100 : a wine deemed acceptable.

70-74/100 : a wine with defects, unacceptable.

65-69/100 : a wine with major defects, inadmissible.

50-64/100 : unacceptable wine, not worthy for sale.

Note : wines scoring less than 75/100 are not included in our publications.

THE COLOUR OF THE WINES :

- ▼ Red wine
- ▼ Dry white wine
- ▼ Rose wine
- ▼ Sweet white wine
- ▼ sparkling brut or extra-brut
- ▼ sparkling brut rose
- ▼ Liqueur wine
- ▼ Brandy
- ▼ Appetiser

PRICING :

Most of the wines in the guide have a price. All along the guide, we replaced the price of each wine by symbols that are explained below.

0 to 9.99 € = Price: ❍ - 10 to 19.99 € = Price: ❍❍
20 to 49.99 € = Price: ❍❍❍ - 50 to 99.99 € = Price: ❍❍❍❍
More than 100 € = Price: ❍❍❍❍❍

SPECIFIC CONDITIONS

Bordeaux - P. 71-109

1er Cru Classé du Médoc 1855 or 1er Cru Classé de Sauternes 1855: First Classed Growth 1855
2e Cru Classé du Médoc 1855 or 2e Cru Classé de Sauternes1855: Second Classed Growth 1855
3e Cru Classé du Médoc 1855: Third Classed Growth 1855
4e Cru Classé du Médoc 1855: Fourth Classed Growth 1855
5e Cru Classé du Médoc 1855: Fifth Classed Growth 1855
1er Grand Cru Classé de Saint-Émilion A:
First Classed Growth A category
1er Grand Cru Classé de Saint-Émilion B:
First Classed Growth B category
Cru Classé: Classed Growth

OTHER FEATURES

ORG: Organic wine
CONV: in the process of converting to organic production
FUTURES: 2012 Bordeaux en primeur, released for sale 2014

PRESENTATION

QRcode: scan it with your mobile phone and access all the wines in the appellation available on our website (www.gilbertgaillard.com)

Appellation:
After the first presentation tier (by wine region), the wines are grouped by appellation.

Moulis

CHÂTEAU BISTON-BRILLETTE

Cru Bourgeois du Médoc

▼ Vintage 2010 Price: ○○ — 89/100

▼ Château Biston 2010 Price: ○○ — 88/100

CHÂTEAU GRANINS GRAND-POUJEAUX

▼ Vintage 2010 Price: ○○ — 89/100

CHÂTEAU LAGORCE BERNADAS

▼ Vintage 2010 Price: ○○ — 87/100

CHÂTEAU MALMAISON

▼ Vintage 2010 Price: ○○ — 89/100

COUBRIS JLC

▼ Domaine de Lagorce de la Mouline 2010
Price: ○ — 88/100

Wine colour :
this is a red wine (also see page 7)

Cellaring capacity:
Enjoying this wine at its peak:

- Drink now
- Drink now or keep
- Keep

GILBERT & GAILLARD medals

Note : 90/100 and +

Note : 80-89/100

Note : 75-79/100

Choosing wines effortlessly

AWARD WINING WINES

Chandon de Briailles
Château Beauregard Mirouze
Château Belgrave
Château Bellegrave
Château Biston-Brillette
Château Cabezac
Château Canet
Château Cantenac
Château Chevalier Saint-Georges
Château Croque Michotte
Château d'Anglès
Château de Brégançon
Château de la Baume
Château de la Chaize
Château de Lastours
Château de l'Ille
Château de Santenay
Château de Targé
Château de Valmer
Château de Vaucouleurs
Château de Villars Fontaine
Château des Anglades
Château des Coccinelles
Château des Peyregrandes
Château d'Orschwihr
Château du Donjon
Château du Galoupet
Château du Glana
Château Fonbadet
Château Fortia
CChâteau La Tour de By
Domaine Canet Valette
Domaine Casabianca
Domaine Champagnon
Domaine Coste-Caumartin
Domaine Daniel Reverdy et fils...

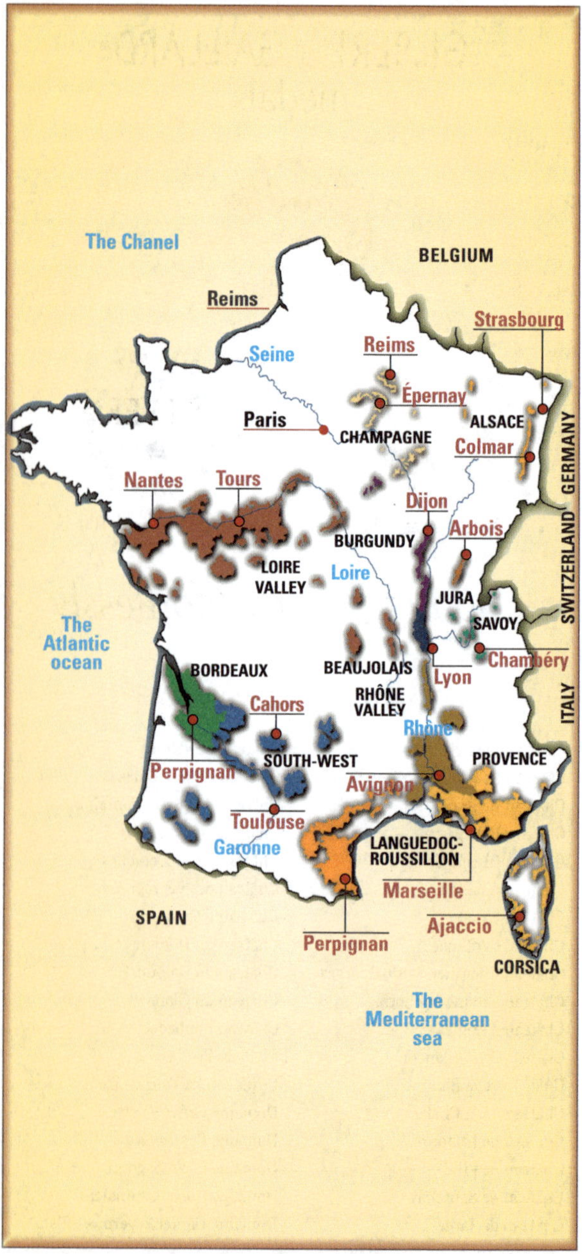
The Chanel
BELGIUM
Reims
Strasbourg
Reims
Seine
Épernay
Paris
ALSACE
CHAMPAGNE
Colmar
GERMANY
Nantes
Tours
Dijon
Arbois
BURGUNDY
LOIRE VALLEY
Loire
SWITZERLAND
JURA
The Atlantic ocean
SAVOY
Chambéry
BORDEAUX
BEAUJOLAIS
Lyon
RHÔNE VALLEY
Cahors
ITALY
Rhône
SOUTH-WEST
PROVENCE
Perpignan
Avignon
Toulouse
Garonne
LANGUEDOC-ROUSSILLON
Marseille
SPAIN
Ajaccio
Perpignan
CORSICA
The Mediterranean sea

BRIEF OVERVIEW OF THE FRENCH WINE REGIONS

France has a dozen wine regions spread over virtually the entire country, with the exception of the north-east where the climate is cool and damp. Whilst southern vineyards (Languedoc-Roussillon, Provence, South-West, Bordeaux) cover vast swathes of land, northern vineyards (Alsace, Champagne, Burgundy) must contend with adverse weather, particularly spring frosts, which confines them to the sunniest, most sheltered hillside sites. This explains their elongated shape which follows the landform.

ALSACE

Vines cover around 13,500 hectares split between Haut-Rhin and Bas-Rhin. The region has a distinct continental climate with relatively harsh winters and hot summers. Frequent morning fog promotes the development of botrytis cinerea, a microscopic fungus that produces the great late harvest and noble rotted sweet wines. Alsace is unusual in that it states the grape varietal on the label: Riesling, Gewurztraminer, Tokay-Pinot gris, Muscat, Sylvaner, Pinot blanc and Pinot noir. The best vineyard sites (50) have been promoted to Alsace Grand Cru status. Although white wines are the dominant style, red wines are worthy of note and are made locally from Pinot noir. The eternally successful Crémant d'Alsace also deserves a specific mention.

BORDEAUX

Vines occupy just over 100,000 hectares here and produce nearly 6 million hectolitres. Red wines, made from the Merlot, Cabernet-Sauvignon and Cabernet Franc grape varieties are the most ubiquitous here. Some of them, like Médoc, Saint-Emilion, Pomerol and Fronsac, boast remarkable ageing capacity. Others, such as Bordeaux, Bordeaux Supérieur, Côtes de Blaye and Côtes de Bourg, are more supple and round, making them suitable for early drinking. The region's dry white wines are also noteworthy (Graves, Pessac-Léognan, Entre-Deux-Mers...) as are the sweet white wines (Sauternes, Sainte-Croix-du-Mont, Loupiac...) made from Sauvignon, Sémillon and Muscadelle. Crémant de Bordeaux, a sparkling wine made with regional grape varieties, also deserves special notice. The region is home to more than fifty controlled appellations providing endless cellar door opportunities!

BURGUNDY

This region covers 25,000 hectares and is spread over three departments - Yonne, home of the great Chablis, Côte d'Or, famous for its superlative red and white wines from Côte de Nuits and Côte de Beaune, and Saône-et-Loire where Côte Chalonnaise in the north leads into the Mâcon area in the south. The region's total output is 1.3 million hectolitres: 58% is white (principal grape variety: Chardonnay) and 42% red (principal grape variety: Pinot noir). Burgundy plays host to 96 controlled appellations arranged in a well-defined quality pyramid: regional, village, Premier Cru, Grand Cru.

BEAUJOLAIS

Beaujolais extends southwards from Burgundy and boasts its own distinctive personality. Red wines are made here from Gamay, a varietal which imparts floral, fruity and spicy aromas. In addition to the Beaujolais and Beaujolais Villages appellations, the region also has ten growths: Saint-Amour, Juliénas, Chénas, Moulin à Vent, Fleurie, Chiroubles, Morgon, Brouilly, Côte de Brouilly and Régnié. There is also white Beaujolais.

CHAMPAGNE

Champagne boasts 33,000 hectares under vine. Vineyards grow on chalky hillside sites and are therefore very fragmented. The area can be subdivided into four zones, each one home to a different varietal range: Montagne de Reims (where Pinot noir reigns supreme), Côte des Blancs with its southern extension, Sézannais (Chardonnay territory), the Marne Valley (where Pinot Meunier dominates) and Côte des Bars (where Pinot noir is the majority varietal). Such diversity enables Champagne to produce extremely different wine styles: 'blancs de blancs' with fragrances of flowers, hazelnut and pastries; more powerful 'blancs de noirs' with distinctive fruity aromas; blended 'bruts', prestige vintage 'cuvées'.... A range of wine styles and also vineyard sites to search out.

JURA AND SAVOY

The two regions have little actually in common but people generally assimiSeine late the two as being home to mountain wines. In Jura, vines are planted on the Revermont, hillsides overlooking the plains of the Saône, facing Côte d'Or. The region has a western aspect and is planted to a specific varietal range with grapes called Trousseau (reds), Poulsard or Ploussard (rosés) and Savagnin (whites). The area is home to two highly unusual wines: 'vin jaune' and 'vin de paille'. Jura wines come under a variety of appellations: Côtes du Jura, l'Etoile, Arbois, Arbois-Pupillin... As for Savoy, it produces primarily white wines from Jacquere and in some places Roussette (also called Altesse). The red and rosé wines are drawn from Gamay and Mondeuse. Try with regional specialities (fish, cooked cold pork meats, cheese-based specialities...).

LANGUEDOC-ROUSSILLON

With more than 350,000 hectares under vine, Languedoc-Roussillon is home to France's largest wine region. An active drive to upgrade quality has led to a complete overhaul of the area over the past twenty years. The region can be subdivided nowadays into three main categories of wine: appellation wines -Coteaux du Langue-doc, Saint-Chinian, Faugères, Minervois, Corbières, Limoux, Côtes du Roussillon, Collioure...- which are grown on hillside sites and made from Mediterranean grape varieties (Grenache, Syrah, Mourvedre, Cinsault, Carignan...); regional wines, mostly varietals, made from grapes not native to the region (Merlot, Cabernet-Sauvignon, Chardonnay...). The dessert wines - Muscats, Rivesaltes, Maury or Banyuls - also deserve a special mention because they are astounding and in some cases can prove to be truly sumptuous.

PROVENCE

The Provence wine region covers the Bouches-du-Rhône and Var departments as well as two minute enclaves in the Nice area. Over 80% of the wines are rosé although Provence also provides some very noteworthy red and white wines. The varietal range is Mediterranean with Grenache, Mourvedre, Syrah and Cinsault forming its backbone and local, minor occurrences of Cabernet Sauvignon (particularly in Coteaux d'Aix and Coteaux Varois). Corsica boasts its own specific varietal range dominated by Nieluccio, Scia-carello and Vermentino.

THE SOUTH-WEST

Is perhaps France's most diverse wine region. From the Dordogne to the Pyrenees, the Atlantic to the Rouergue, wine lovers are offered a vast array of wines to choose from. Bergerac, the vineyards of Lot, including the famous Cahors, the middle Garonne region, Gascony, Béarn, the Basque country... Red wines mingle with rosés, dry whites, sweet wines and in some places, such as Gaillac, sparklers. Wines are made here from local varieties, some of them native only to the region, which lend them their unique characteristics: Fer Servadou, Auxerrois, Tannat, Negrette, En de l'El, Arrufiac... The wines are often robust and pair with traditional South-West dishes: foie gras, cassoulet...

THE LOIRE VALLEY

Is a galaxy unto itself, where you can wend your way along its reaches without ever tiring of it. As a rule the region is sub-divided into four areas with clear-cut differences: upriver are wines from the Centre, a vague term used to describe white appellation wines, Sauvignon territory (Sancerre, Pouilly Fumé...). Tou-raine follows on with its appellations - Touraine, Chinon, Bourgueil, Vouvray, Montlouis.... Red wines, rosés, dry whites, sweet, sparkling - diversity is the area's calling card. It is in Anjou, too, the third stretch of the valley where the subsoil is chalky in Saumur and switches to granite in the Layon area. And the last port of call: the Nantes region, dry white wine country (Muscadet and Gros Plant).

THE RHÔNE VALLEY

Is France's second-largest appellation wine region, after Bordeaux. In the north, which is planted to Syrah (reds) and Viognier (whites), vines 'cling' to the river, whilst in the south, where the Mediterranean climate prevails, they open out onto wide expanses. A broad range of grape varieties (Grenache, Syrah, Viognier, Marsanne, Roussanne...) forms the basis of the region's appellation pyramid: Côtes du Rhône, Côtes du Rhône Villages and growths (Gigondas, Châteauneuf-du-Pape, Vac-queyras, Tavel...). In addition to these are the peripheral regions: Côtes du Ventoux, Côtes du Luberon, Costières de Nîmes... A majestic chain of vineyards, threaded together by the Rhône, which is capable of catering for the most catholic tastes and everyone's purse.

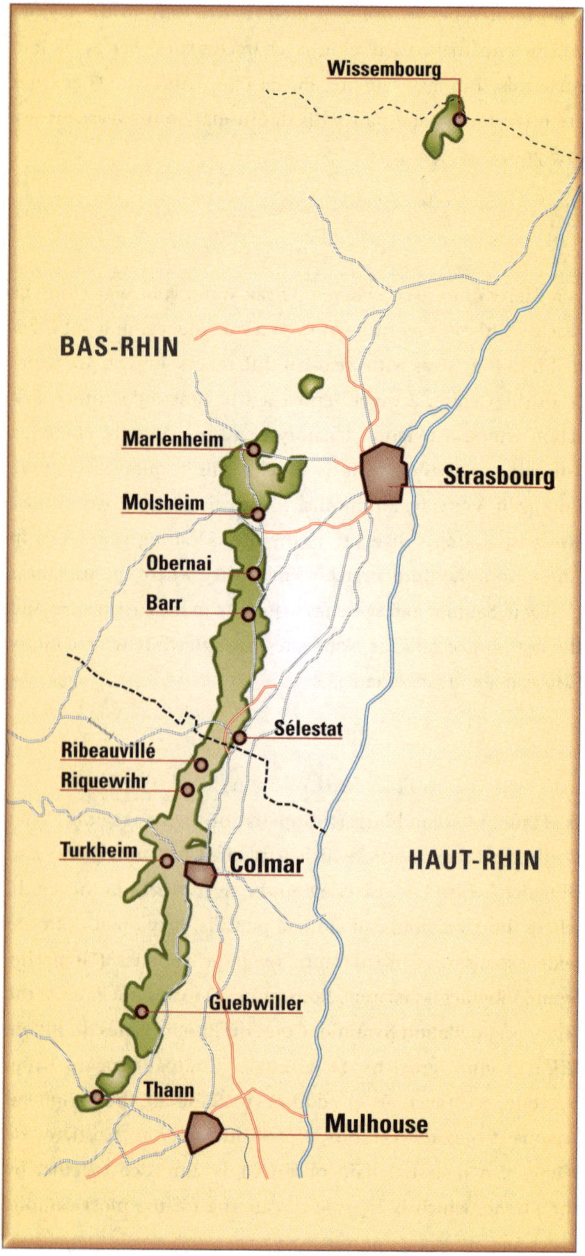
Wissembourg
BAS-RHIN
Marlenheim
Strasbourg
Molsheim
Obernai
Barr
Sélestat
Ribeauvillé
Riquewihr
Turkheim
Colmar
HAUT-RHIN
Guebwiller
Thann
Mulhouse

ALSACE

ONE OF FRANCE'S BEST KEPT SECRETS

Alsace has long been famous as one of the most food and wine-loving regions in the whole of France. Its wines are capable of creating unsuspected harmonies and providing flavours that complement each other. What for example is the secret alchemy that brings pikeperch (zander) together with Riesling, foie gras with Tokay-Pinot Gris, Munster cheese with Gewurztraminer and kugelhopf with Crémant? An extraordinary diversity to discover.

The Alsace wine-growing area stretches for about 100 kms along the western section of the Vosges mountains from Marlenheim to Thann, with a small northern enclave at Wissembourg. It is at the northern limit of the vine-growing area and white grape varieties are therefore in the majority. 14,000 hectares of vines are laid out at altitudes of between 200 and 400 m and yield an annual average of 150 million bottles. The wine-growing area has a generally south or south-east aspect. This is the perfect location for following the famous Alsace Wine Route. But most importantly, it enables the vines to take advantage of a maximum amount of sunshine in the growing and ripening period. In addition, its position means it enjoys a remarkable microclimate: «A warm temperature band showed up on the slopes and half-way up the hills, where the temperature is 1 to 1.5° higher than on the lower or upper slopes. This band is not located exactly on the south-facing slopes, but in general on the steepest slope» (Claude Sittler, 1990). On the other hand, the Alsace wine-growing soils are characterised by a great geological diversity that is probably unique in French vine growing. The vine has colonised chalk, marly-chalk, sandy-clay, clayey-loam, gypseous, volcanic sandstone, schistous, granitic and granitic gneiss soils. As we will see, some grape varieties are happier in particular types of soil.

THE GRAPE VARIETIES OF ALSACE-A DISTINCTIVE FAMILY

THE WINES OF ALSACE: including the grand crus - are made from a single type of grape, except for Crémant which can be blended from several separate varieties. However the specific nature of the Alsace varieties remains essential for producing very distinctive wines. All knowledgeable wine lovers know that there are 7 original grape varieties and can list them without thinking. Here they are in more detail, together with another, less well-known member of the family, but one equally worth considering.

• **Sylvaner** • this variety, one of the best-known in Alsace, was discredited years ago because of high yields. If it is handled well and if its late ripening is carefully taken into account, it can produce a wine that is remarkable for its lightness, is lively and thirst-quenching and has aromas of young fruit or flowers.

• **Riesling** • this is one of the greatest white grape varieties in the world. On sandy-clay soils the «gentle aromatic» - as it is sometimes called - gives a dry and elegant wine of distinction, the colour of crystal, with delicate fruit (orange peel and exotic fruits) and with floral and mineral (flinty) hints. It has surprising finesse, power, balance and length on the palate. It can ripen at relatively low temperatures and its vintage years mature perfectly.

• **Gewürztraminer** • the most aromatic grape variety grown in the area, it is used to make the most famous of the Alsace wines on marly-chalk soils. It comes from a selection of the most aromatic Savagnin Rose or Traminer varieties. The wine, full of vigour, well-rounded, with a powerful structure, offers great complexity. In it are found scents of acacia, lily, rose, carnation, honey, cardamom, spices (gewürz = spicy), cinnamon, clove, pepper, lychee, grapefruit and quince. This superb and generous wine is capable of maturing marvellously. The finest vintages bestow upon the wine a touch of sweetness.

• **Muscat** • this gives an aromatic wine that is heady yet dry and which is nothing like the Muscats from the south. It has inimitable fruit and flower aromas with a veritable explosion of acacia, box, rosewood and geranium.

• **Pinot Blanc** • this variety, which gives of its best on a loamy soil, gives a soft, supple wine full of freshness and with subtle aromatic hints. It has become one of the basic varieties of Crémant d'Alsace.

• **Pinot Gris** • this is the proper name of the Alsace Tokay (Grauer Tokayer). It is happy in deep soils and clayey-loam conglomerates. Its powerful, well-structured, even opulent wine is very long on the palate and releases aromas of dried fruit, fruit tree wood, undergrowth and game, where a hint of smoked meat can be detected. It is most certainly one of Alsace's greatest wines.

• **Pinot Noir** • this is Alsace's only red wine grape variety. Perfect when it has found a sandy or chalky soil, it is made into rosé or red wine. The latter, which has the characteristic colour of claret, develops flavours of small red fruits where the cherry dominates.

• **Klevener** • this variety of the former Traminer or Savagnin Rose gives a full-bodied and well-balanced wine. Under the decree of 4th February 1997, only the communes of Bougheim, Getwiller, Heiligenstein and Obernai can use the name «Klevener de Heiligenstein».

WHAT ARE THE PRODUCTION CONDITIONS?

Alsace wines normally show the grape variety on the label and are made 100% from that grape. A blend of two or more varieties is called Edelzwicker. The appellation wines have a yield per hectare of 8,000 litres with a minimum alcohol level of 8.5°. The production conditions for the 50 Grands Crus reduce the yield to 6,000 litres/hectare with 10° minimum for Riesling and Muscat, and 12° for Gewürztraminer or Pinot Gris. Their areas have been set out by the I.N.A.O. (the National Institute for Appellations d'Origine) on the basis of very strict geological and climatic criteria. The «Vendange tardive» (late harvest) and the «Sélection de grains nobles» (selection of superior over-ripe grapes), which have been official Alsace specialities since 1984, have won a place in the hearts of all wine lovers.

«Vendange tardive» is only practised on the Gewürztraminer, Pinot Gris, Riesling and Muscat grapes, both for Vin d'Alsace A.C. and for the Grands Crus. Harvesting when they are overripe increases the available sugar within the berry, especially if it has begun to be covered with the noble rot. The wines then reach the pinnacle of their development and are real masterpieces. The «Sélections de grains nobles» are harvested by hand, with successive pickings of grapes affected by botrytis cinerea. The resulting concentration gives a powerful wine with complex aromas that is exceptionally long on the palate and has an unparalleled long life.

The Crémant d'Alsace sparkling wines, the vast majority of which are white, are produced by the traditional method of a second fermentation in the bottle. They are made from one or more grape varieties (Pinot Blanc, Riesling, Pinot Gris and occasionally Chardonnay). Crémant Rosé is made from the Pinot Noir. Strict production conditions that are very close to those for the Vin d'Alsace appellation and an irreproachable quality have been the basis of the success of the Crémants. Wonderful grands crus The fame of Alsace wine was initially built upon the sure foundation of its grape varieties. But connoisseurs, and even more so the winemakers themselves, have long recognised that such and such a wine from such and such a place was better than a commune's general production. In a deliberate move, the producers therefore decided to put those parcels of land that for centuries had been the glory of Alsace wine back onto their pedestal. If we leaf through the fact sheets of the terroirs where the 50 current Grands Crus are produced, we immediately see that these thousand-year old vineyards cover all the steepest slopes of the hills sheltering them from cold winds that these are very often in the shape of a bowl, a crescent or an arc that encourages exposure to the sun; that there is little topsoil; that the wine-growing parcels are located on gravel that both warms the soil and gives good drainage; and that thanks to a specific micro-climate, rainfall is low. This is effectively the jewel in the crown of Alsace wine. By taking this step, Alsace has not only gone back to its roots, but rediscovered its best wines.

REVIEW OF RECENT VINTAGES

• **2009** • Exceptional grape health and maturity gave rise to wines high in alcohol but that retain a satisfactory level of acidity. They are perfumed and can be enjoyed when young. The fine weather in October allowed an excellent Vendange Tardive and Sélections de Grains Nobles for late-harvest wines.

• **2010** • 20 percent volume decrease on 2009 yet abundant fruit and freshness. A vintage for pleasure.

• **2011** • Drought in the spring and rainfall at the start of the summer yielded a fruity, ripe vintage with low acidity. The wines will be early-drinking, except for the superlative sites which always produce wines with ageability.

• **2012** • Despite a somewhat disrupted growth cycle, this vintage is well balanced. The Crémant wines are remarkable, and the Pinots (whether Pinot Blanc, Pinot Gris or Pinot Noir) are excellent. The other grape varieties do not stand out to the same degree, but are very respectable all the same.

THREE APPELLATIONS FOR ONE REGION

A.C. VIN D'ALSACE

These wines must be bottled in the area of production and in the slender bottle characteristic of Alsace wine. They are available in all the authorised grape varieties. This is unique in France and ratified by the I.N.A.O., taking account of both the actual history of the rebuilding of the Alsace vine-growing area post phylloxera and of a Rhine tradition. They have been part of the great A.C. family since 1962.

A.C. ALSACE GRAND CRU

Only four grape varieties are permitted for the A.C. Alsace Grand Cru: Gewürztraminer, Riesling, Muscat and Pinot Gris. The label must include A.C. Alsace Grand Cru and show the locality, the grape variety and the year. Twenty-five localities were selected in 1983. Then in 1992, the National Institute for Appellations d'Origine ratified the definition of 25 new parcels. From that time, Alsace has prided itself on a new appellation made up of 51 Grands Crus. The wines produced in these areas have rare elegance and great finesse, and also power, quality and distinction. The best years give wines that can be laid down for a long time.

A.C. CRÉMANT D'ALSACE

Created in 1976, this has been given an unprecedented welcome by wine-lovers, as Crémant d'Alsace is the top appellation sparkling wine drunk in France, ahead of Clairette de Die. It is made by 500 producers who put nearly 20 million bottles on the market. It has the particular feature of being able to blend the various recommended grape varieties which must all come from the regional appellation area.

• • •

ALSACE

Alsace auxerrois

DOMAINE JEAN-MARIE KOEHLY +33 3 88 82 09 77

▼ Vintage 2011 Price:O 87/100

VICTOR LORANG ET FILS +33 3 89 27 05 29

▼ Cuvée Vierge 2011 Price:O 85/100

Alsace gewurztraminer

DOMAINES SCHLUMBERGER +33 3 89 74 27 00

▼ Les Princes Abbés 2011 Price:OO 89/100

CAVE VINICOLE DU VIEIL ARMAND +33 3 89 76 73 75

▼ Vendanges Tardives 2009 Price:OO 92/100

CHÂTEAU D'ORSCHWIHR +33 3 89 74 25 00

▼ Bollenberg 2011 Price:O 89/100

CLOS DES TERRES BRUNES +33 3 89 47 90 70

▼ Jean Siegler Vieilles Vignes 2011 Price:OO 87/100

DOMAINE ANDRÉ BLANCK ET SES FILS +33 3 89 78 24 72

▼ Altenbourg 2012 Price:O 88/100

DOMAINE DES MARRONNIERS +33 3 88 08 93 20

▼ Vendanges Tardives 2010 Price:OOO 88/100

DOMAINE PAUL SPANNAGEL ET FILS +33 3 89 27 01 70

▼ Steinbruchreben - Vieilles Vignes 2011 Price:OO 90/100

DOMAINES SCHLUMBERGER +33 3 89 74 27 00

▼ Cuvée Anne - SGN 2009 Price:OOOO 96/100

EDMOND RENTZ +33 3 89 47 90 17

▼ Le Bourg 2011 Price:O 87/100

Alsace - *Alsace Gewurztraminer*

FRÉDÉRIC MALLO & FILS +33 3 89 73 61 41

CV ▼ Frédéric Mallo Cuvée Saint-Jacques 2009 Price:○ 85/100

HAEGELIN BERNARD +33 3 89 76 14 62

BIO ▼ Bernard Haegelin Cuvée Catherine 2011 Price:○ 88/100

JEAN-LOUIS SCHOEPFER +33 3 89 80 71 29

▼ Vintage 2011 Price:○ 78/100

MAISON HUMBRECHT +33 3 89 49 62 97

BIO ▼ Jean 2010 Price:○○ 91/100

Alsace Grand Cru gewurztraminer

DOMAINES SCHLUMBERGER +33 3 89 74 27 00

▼ Kessler 2007 Price:○○○ 93/100

DOMAINE ANDRÉ BLANCK ET SES FILS +33 3 89 78 24 72

▼ Vendanges Tardives 2009 Price:○○ 91/100

FRÉDÉRIC MALLO & FILS +33 3 89 73 61 41

CV ▼ Frédéric Mallo Rosacker 2008 Price:○○ 86/100

BESTHEIM & CHÂTEAUX +33 3 89 49 09 29

▼ Bestheim Zinnkoepflé 2010 Price:○○ 89/100

CAVE DE RIBEAUVILLÉ +33 3 89 73 61 80

▼ Altenberg de Bergheim 2010 Price:○○ 94/100

DOMAINE ANDRÉ BLANCK ET SES FILS +33 3 89 78 24 72

▼ Schlossberg 2012 Price:○○ 91/100

DOMAINE HORCHER +33 3 89 47 93 26

▼ Sporen 2011 Price:○○ 91/100

DOMAINE JEAN-MARIE KOEHLY +33 3 88 82 09 77

▼ Gloeckelberg 2010 Price:○ 88/100

DOMAINES SCHLUMBERGER +33 3 89 74 27 00

▼ Cuvée Christine - VT 2008 Price:○○○ 95/100

EDMOND RENTZ +33 3 89 47 90 17

▼ Froehn 2011 Price:○○ 93/100

FRÉDÉRIC MALLO & FILS +33 3 89 73 61 41

CV ▼ Mandelberg - Cuvée Justine - 50 cl 2008 Price:○○ 92/100

Alsace Grand Cru muscat

DOMAINE PIERRE FRICK +33 3 89 49 62 99

BIO ▼ Steinert - Vendanges Tardives 2009 Price:○○○ 91/100

Alsace Grand Cru pinot gris

PAUL SCHNEIDER +33 3 89 41 50 07

▼ Pfersigberg 2010 Price:○○ 89/100

DOMAINE PAUL SPANNAGEL ET FILS +33 3 89 27 01 70

▼ Paul Spannagel Kaefferkopf 2011 Price:○○ 92/100

DOMAINES SCHLUMBERGER +33 3 89 74 27 00

▼ Kitterlé 2008 Price:○○○ 94/100

PAUL SCHNEIDER +33 3 89 41 50 07

▼ Steinert 2009 Price:○○ 91/100

Alsace Grand Cru riesling

DOMAINES SCHLUMBERGER +33 3 89 74 27 00

▼ Saering 2008 Price:○○ 94/100

DOMAINE DES MARRONNIERS +33 3 88 08 93 20

▼ Wiebelsberg 2011 Price:○○ 91/100

▼ Moenchberg 2011 Price:○○ 90/100

FRÉDÉRIC MALLO & FILS +33 3 89 73 61 41

CV▼ Rosacker - Vendanges Tardives - 50 cl 2009 Price:○○ 90/100

BESTHEIM & CHÂTEAUX +33 3 89 49 09 29

▼ Bestheim Wiebelsberg 2009 Price:○ 87/100

CAVE VINICOLE DU VIEIL ARMAND +33 3 89 76 73 75

▼ Château Ollwiller Vieilles Vignes 2009 Price:○○ 88/100

Alsace - *Alsace Grand Cru Riesling*

DOMAINE AIMÉSTENTZ +33 3 89 80 63 77

BIO Grand Cru Sommerberg 2011 Price:OO 90/100

DOMAINE ANDRÉ BLANCK ET SES FILS +33 3 89 78 24 72

Schlossberg 2012 Price:O 89/100

DOMAINE DES MARRONNIERS +33 3 88 08 93 20

Kastelberg 2011 Price:OO 91/100

DOMAINE JEAN SIPP +33 3 89 73 60 02

Jean Sipp 2010 Price:OO 87/100

DOMAINE JOSEPH SCHARSCH +33 3 88 38 30 61

CV Altenberg de Wolxheim 2011 Price:OO 89/100

DOMAINE PAUL SPANNAGEL ET FILS +33 3 89 27 01 70

Paul Spannagel Wineck Schlossberg 2011 Price:OO 89/100

DOMAINES SCHLUMBERGER +33 3 89 74 27 00

Kessler 2008 Price:OO 94/100

EDMOND RENTZ +33 3 89 47 90 17

Schoenenbourg 2009 Price:OO 89/100

FRÉDÉRIC MALLO & FILS +33 3 89 73 61 41

CV Frédéric Mallo Rosacker 2009 Price:O 92/100

PAUL SCHNEIDER +33 3 89 41 50 07

Eichberg 2011 Price:OO 88/100

ROBERT FALLER ET FILS +33 3 89 73 60 47

Faller Geisberg 2010 Price:OOO 87/100

Alsace klevener de Heiligestein

BESTHEIM & CHÂTEAUX +33 3 89 49 09 29

Bestheim Réserve 2011 Price:O 88/100

Alsace muscat

JEAN-LOUIS SCHOEPFER +33 3 89 80 71 29

Vintage 2011 Price:O 83/100

Alsace pinot blanc

DOMAINE ANDRÉ BLANCK ET SES FILS +33 3 89 78 24 72

André Blanck Vintage 2012 Price:O — 85/100

JEAN-LOUIS SCHOEPFER +33 3 89 80 71 29

Vintage 2010 Price:O — 82/100

MAISON HUMBRECHT +33 3 89 49 62 97

BIO Laura 2010 Price:OO — 86/100

Alsace pinot gris

DOMAINES SCHLUMBERGER +33 3 89 74 27 00

Les Princes Abbés 2011 Price:O — 89/100

CLOS DES TERRES BRUNES +33 3 89 47 90 70

Jean Siegler Vieilles Vignes 2011 Price:OO — 85/100

BESTHEIM & CHÂTEAUX +33 3 89 49 09 29

Bestheim Réserve 2011 Price:O — 85/100

CLOS DES TERRES BRUNES +33 3 89 47 90 70

Jean Siegler Vendanges Tardives 2009 Price:OO — 88/100

DOMAINE ANDRÉ BLANCK ET SES FILS +33 3 89 78 24 72

Clos Schwendi 2012 Price:O — 87/100

DOMAINE HORCHER +33 3 89 47 93 26

Sélection 2011 Price:O — 86/100

DOMAINE JEAN SIPP +33 3 89 73 60 02

Vintage 2005 Price:OOO — 92/100

DOMAINE PIERRE FRICK +33 3 89 49 62 99

BIO Rot - Murlé 2011 Price:OO — 88/100

DOMAINES SCHLUMBERGER +33 3 89 74 27 00

Cuvée Clarisse - SGN 2009 Price:OOOO — 96/100

HAEGELIN BERNARD +33 3 89 76 14 62

BIO Bernard Haegelin Bollenberg 2011 Price:O — 89/100

Alsace - *Alsace Pinot gris*

JEAN-LOUIS SCHOEPFER +33 3 89 80 71 29

▼ Vintage 2011 Price:❍ 82/100

VICTOR LORANG ET FILS +33 3 89 27 05 29

▼ Cuvée Vierge 2011 Price:❍❍ 86/100

Alsace pinot noir

CAVE DE RIBEAUVILLÉ +33 3 89 73 61 80

▼ Vieilles Vignes - Réserve 2009 Price:❍ 82/100

CAVE VINICOLE DU VIEIL ARMAND +33 3 89 76 73 75

▼ Château Ollwiller Pinot Noir 2009 Price:❍ 87/100

JEAN-LOUIS SCHOEPFER +33 3 89 80 71 29

▼ Vintage 2011 Price:❍ 84/100

MAISON CHARLES WANTZ +33 3 88 08 90 44

▼ Rouge d''Ottrott 2010 Price:❍ 83/100

VICTOR LORANG ET FILS +33 3 89 27 05 29

▼ Cuvée Prestige - Vieilli en fût de chêne 2011 Price:❍ 83/100

Alsace riesling

CAVE DE RIBEAUVILLÉ +33 3 89 73 61 80

▼ Terroirs - Réserve 2009 Price:❍ 86/100

CHÂTEAU D'ORSCHWIHR +33 3 89 74 25 00

▼ Bollenberg 2011 Price:❍ 88/100

DOMAINE AIMÉSTENTZ +33 3 89 80 63 77

BIO ▼ Neufeld 2011 Price:❍ 88/100

DOMAINE DES MARRONNIERS +33 3 88 08 93 20

▼ Andlau 2011 Price:❍ 87/100

DOMAINE HORCHER +33 3 89 47 93 26

▼ Sélection 2011 Price:❍ 84/100

DOMAINE JEAN-MARIE KOEHLY +33 3 88 82 09 77

▼ Lieu-dit Hahnenberg 2010 Price:❍ 87/100

DOMAINES SCHLUMBERGER	+33 3 89 74 27 00
▼ Les Princes Abbés 2010 Price:❍	88/100
EDMOND RENTZ	+33 3 89 47 90 17
▼ Les Alouettes 2011 Price:❍	85/100
FRÉDÉRIC MALLO & FILS	+33 3 89 73 61 41
CV▼ Réserve Spéciale 2009 Price:❍	87/100
HAEGELIN BERNARD	+33 3 89 76 14 62
BIO ▼ Bernard Haegelin Bollenberg 2011 Price:❍	89/100
MAISON HUMBRECHT	+33 3 89 49 62 97
BIO ▼ Clémence 2010 Price:❍❍	87/100

Alsace sylvaner

DOMAINE PIERRE FRICK	+33 3 89 49 62 99
BIO ▼ Bergweingarten 2007 Price:❍❍	90/100
MAISON CHARLES WANTZ	+33 3 88 08 90 44
▼ Domaine Charles Wantz Vieilles Vignes 2009 Price:❍	83/100

Crémant d'Alsace

BESTHEIM & CHÂTEAUX	+33 3 89 49 09 29
▼ Bestheim Brut Price:❍	86/100
▼ Bestheim Brut rosé Price:❍	84/100
▼ Bestheim Brut Prestige Price:❍❍	90/100
JEAN-LOUIS SCHOEPFER	+33 3 89 80 71 29
▼ Brut Price:❍	86/100

Other Alsace

CLOS DES TERRES BRUNES	+33 3 89 47 90 70
▼ Vintage 2011 Price:❍	86/100

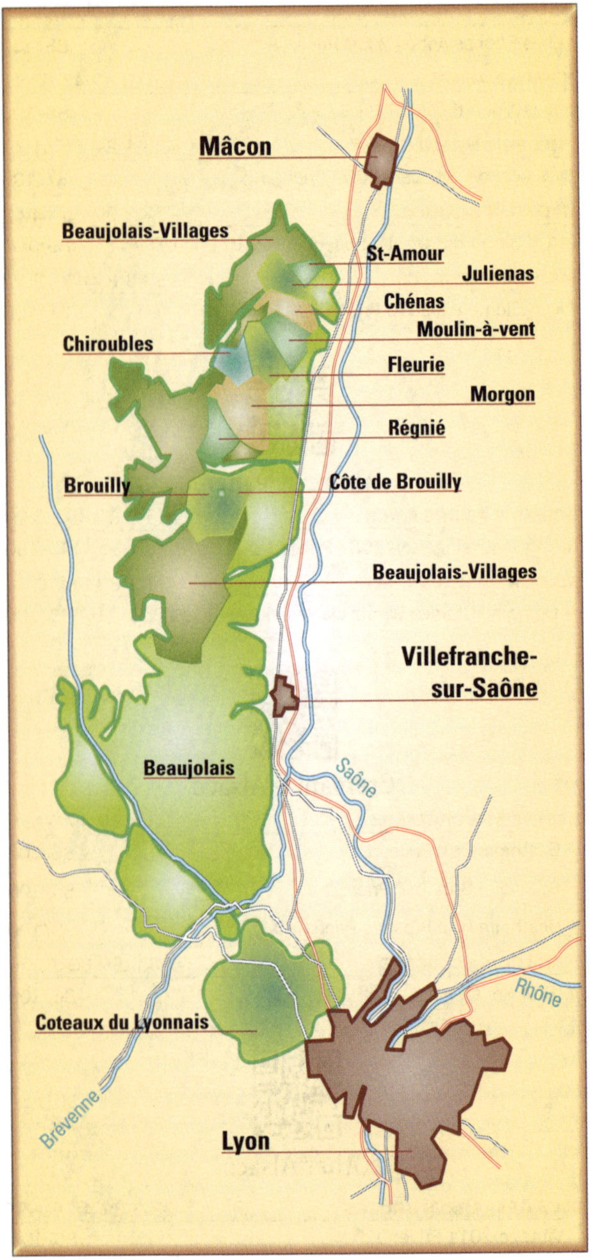
Mâcon
Beaujolais-Villages
St-Amour
Julienas
Chénas
Moulin-à-vent
Chiroubles
Fleurie
Morgon
Régnié
Brouilly
Côte de Brouilly
Beaujolais-Villages
Villefranche-sur-Saône
Beaujolais
Saône
Rhône
Coteaux du Lyonnais
Brévenne
Lyon

BEAUJOLAIS

A WINE REGION WITH A STORY TO TELL

The Beaujolais wine region lies to the east of central France. It takes its name from the small town of Beaujeu. It starts off below Macon, in Burgundy, and stretches south, virtually down to the northern gateway to Lyon. The vast majority of its wines are red with a few rosés, though a small proportion of white wines are also produced in the north. Beaujolais wines boast a distinctive aromatic personality derived from a unique combination of the three fundamental elements of winegrowing: grape varietals, terroir and climate.

The region's flagship wines are of course its growths: Brouilly, Chénas, Chiroubles, Côte de Brouilly, Fleurie, Juliénas, Morgon, Moulin à Vent, Regnié and Saint-Amour (see map), which are situated in the northern reaches of the area. The southern part of the region is largely devoted to a generic Beaujolais appellation, further sub-divided into two more tiers, Beaujolais-Villages and Beaujolais Supérieur.

This is where the archetypal characteristics of the Gamay varietal bloom. The granite soils, intermingled with shale and sandstone, form a perfect environment for it. Isolated pockets of soil with a slightly different make-up provide the substance for the distinctive personalities of the growths: higher clay content in Juliénas; manganese-rich granite in Chénas; silica and granite intermingled in the Fleurie appellation area; granite and 'green horn' shale on the slopes of Mount Brouilly... (A.C. Côte de Brouilly). When these characteristics are combined with the craftsmanship of the winegrower, each Beaujolais growth achieves its fullest expression. Some of the region's proudest standard bearers are featured over the next few pages of this book.
The neighbouring wine region, Coteaux du Lyonnais, is often considered to be part of Beaujolais: since Roman times, it has

traditionally been the vine growing garden of Lyon. Gamay reigns supreme here on granite soils, comprised chiefly of metamorphic and sedimentary rock. Classed as A.C. wines since 1984, red Coteaux du Lyonnais are made in the same way as Beaujolais, though a balance of wines are also rosé, and occasionally white.

GRAPE VARIETALS: «Gamay noir à jus blanc», or black Gamay with white juice, for the reds (the vast majority) and the balance of rosés. Chardonnay for the tiny proportion of whites, though also some Pinot blanc and Aligoté in the Coteaux du Lyonnais area.

WINE STYLES: generic Beaujolais are soft, fruit-driven reds for quaffing; the growths are more complex and the better vintages of Morgon and Moulin à Vent can even be cellared. The rosés are in their prime when young, as are the whites, which are acidulous, vigorous wines. Both are delicious served as appetisers or with soft, fresh goat's cheese.

REVIEW OF RECENT VINTAGES

• **2009** • A superb vintage thanks to exceptional weather. The 2009 harvest produced wines with many good qualities - they are structured, well developed, ripe, fruity and not heavy. The Beaujolais and Beaujolais Villages wines can be enjoyed now, while the vintage crus have good potential for aging.

• **2010** • Low quantity caused by millerandage yet nevertheless a vintage boasting fruit and faultless structure after a hot, dry September.

• **2011** • A strange growing season like everywhere else in France with a hot spring and unsettled weather in the summer until late August which saved the day. The berries were small and often very healthy with normal cluster weight. The wines should be destined for an honourable future.

• **2012** • Yields were low due to climatic disturbances, but the general quality is good thanks to a dry spell at the beginning of September that encouraged ripening. A fruity vintage that is not likely to go down in history, but is nonetheless very well made.

THE BEAUJOLAIS APPELLATIONS

A.C. BEAUJOLAIS AND BEAUJOLAIS SUPÉRIEUR

OVERVIEW: the vineyard runs north to south over a stretch of land 90 kilometres long and 15 kilometres wide. Covering three

cantons and 55 towns and villages, it starts off in Leynes, below Macon, and extends southwards to the canton of Abresle. The boundaries of this entire region are etched by the river Arlais in the north, the Monts du Lyonnais range in the west, the Saône in the east and by another river, the Turdine, in the south.
Virtually all of the wines classed as AC Beaujolais and Beaujolais Supérieur are made south of Villefranche-sur-Saône.
The vast majority of the wines are red, drawn from the Gamay varietal. The whites, drawn from Chardonnay, account for just 2% of overall production. The minimum alcohol requirement for Beaujolais is 10%, which is raised to 11% for Beaujolais Supérieur.
Most of the wines are sold as 'nouveau' and three-quarters of these are sold via shipping companies.
CLIMATE AND SOILS: there are two types of soils. In the north, they are crystalline, granite with traces of manganese. In the southern section, they are comprised of sedimentary rocks and are predominantly calcareous clay. The vineyards are planted on hillside sites along the myriad rivers which provide drainage for the region. In the northern reaches, home to the growths, the ground is shallow and permeable. Most wines classed as AC Beaujolais are grown in the southern part of the region. The temperate climate has a pronounced continental influence, with potentially harsh winters and hot summers. The Beaujolais hills shield the vineyard from westerly winds and with their east and south facings, the vines clock up a good deal of sunlight hours.
WINE STYLES: Beaujolais wines are neither crushed nor destemmed prior to vinting. Whole clusters enter the vats and ferment inside the skins producing fresh, fruit-forward, lively wines for quaffing. Their ruby-red hue with purple-blue tints and fragrance of small red fruit (red currant, blackcurrant, raspberry…) reward early drinking. Everyday home cooking and cooked cold pork meats are perfect drinking partners.

A.C. BEAUJOLAIS-VILLAGES

OVERVIEW: the appellation area covers 39 towns and villages in the Rhône departments and a further eight in Saône-et-Loire. The appellation runs from Leynes in the north to Denicé. Village names to look for are Odenas, Montmelas, Vauxrenard, Rivolet, Saint-Lager… This particular wine region also embraces nine of the ten Beaujolais growths. The soils here are crystalline and are predominantly formed of shale and granite which is where Gamay flourishes. The alcohol requirement for Beaujolais-Villages is 10.5%. They account for a quarter of the entire region's output. Fact: although winegrowers are entitled to state the name of their village on the label, very few actually do.

WINE STYLES: they display a cherry-red hue and fragrances of red fruit, predominantly strawberry and blackcurrant. Occasionally they exude notes of leather, spices or game. They are also more robust than AC Beaujolais wines. These fruit-driven, lively, well-balanced, round wines are smooth and harmonious and can be drunk young or laid down. Saveloy cooked in brioche, grilled chitterlings sausage, coq au vin, red meat, Lyon cheeses, suckling pig, stew, grilled chicken… are all dishes that enhance these qualities.

A.C. BROUILLY

OVERVIEW: the most southerly and extensive of the Beaujolais growths. The vineyard encircles Brouilly hill, through Saint-Lager, Cercié, Quincié, Odenas, Saint-Etienne-la-Varende and Charentay. There were vines growing on the southern slopes of the hill as far back as the 4th century and up until the 17th century the wines were drunk locally. It is sometimes dubbed 'the wine of love'. Several different soil profiles can be found here. In Saint-Etienne-la-Varende, Quincié and Odenas, sandy clay soils rest on granite. On limestone marl bedrock, the soil is formed of limestone, silica and sandstone stones. On one hillside facing due south in Cercié, 22 hectares of vines are entitled to carry the 'pisse vieille' label which is the only climatically distinct site recognised in Brouilly.

WINE STYLES: Brouilly are well-structured wines. They are soft, delicate, lively wines which are firm, robust, powerful and fruity. They are also harmonious, round and have relatively good vinosity with pleasant tannins. They display an intense ruby-style hue and fragrances of blueberry, blackberry, fresh grapes, kirsch, cherry and mineral notes. Brouilly partners well with red meats, barbecues, cooked cold pork meats and goat's cheeses.

A.C. CHÉNAS

OVERVIEW: this growth takes its name from the oak trees that were the area's original inhabitants. The appellation extends over Chénas and La-Chapelle-de-Guinchay in the Rhône and Saône-et-Loire departments. Situated between Juliénas and Saint-

Amour in the north and Moulin-à-Vent in the south, it is one of Beaujolais' smallest growths. The greater part of the appellation overlooks the Mauvaise valley. Due to the area's microclimate, the grapes are harvested earlier than in other parts of the region. In the upper reaches of the appellation, the soils are granite and as they descend towards the valley floor the ground turns into clay silica. The surface soil is littered with stones and as a whole the soils are meagre and light. Fact: the local co-operative winery produces roughly half of total output.

WINE STYLES: Chenas has a deep hue and floral fragrances, predominantly peony, rose and violet. As it ages, it sometimes develops spicy, woody notes. The wines have bouquet, they are soft, fleshy, voluptuous and warm. They have elegant, long-lasting tannins which mellow with age. They exude a more marked bouquet than Juliénas and tend to be more similar in style to Moulin-à-Vent. Their average cellar life is 5 to 8 years. La-Chapelle-de-Guinchay tends to produce softer wines. An expression often used to describe them is of 'bunches of flowers resting on a basket of velvet'. They deserve to be paired with roasted red meats, meat served with a sauce, quail, pigeons with peas, cheeses, veal cutlets with chestnuts…

A.C. CHIROUBLES

OVERVIEW: 50 kilometres north of Lyon, the Chiroubles appellation is situated west of Fleurie and north of Morgon. Planted on terraces creating a bowl formation, this growth boasts the highest elevation in Beaujolais (between 250 to 400 m). The hillsides planted to vines act as a natural barrier. Consequently, the temperature range is greater than in the other growths. The soils are meagre, permeable and homogeneous, comprising shallow granite sand.

WINE STYLES: Chiroubles are ethereal, brilliant, light, soft wines which have a pleasant bouquet, are lively and easy drinking. They are also elegant, delicate, well-balanced with very discrete tannins, which earns them a reputation as 'feminine' wines. They could be described as archetypal Beaujolais with their light vermilion hue, fragrances of violet, peony, lily-of-the-valley, iris, raspberry and woodland fruits. They are also some of the quickest-maturing wines in Beaujolais and should be drunk young. An expression often used to describe them is that they 'caress you inside'. Serve with rabbit terrine in aspic, grilled meats, cooked cold pork meats, grilled or chitterlings sausages, poultry, white meats, lamb shoulder, Charolais cheeses…

A.C. CÔTE DE BROUILLY

OVERVIEW: the wine growing area climbs the steep slopes of the Brouilly hills, around Saint-Lager, Quincié, Cercié and Odenas. Vines can be traced back here to the 4th and 5th centuries which means that this AC lays a claim to being Beaujolais' oldest appellation; it also claims to be protected by the Virgin. Located in its midst is the chapel of Nôtre-Dame-du Raisin, which was inaugurated in 1857 and since then has hosted an annual pilgrimage. The soils in Côte de Brouilly have truly definable characteristics: crystalline and volcanic rocks known as Brouilly 'blue stone'. Shale and diorite also known as 'green horn'.

WINE STYLES: Côte-de-Brouilly display a deep ruby-red hue and fragrances of fresh grapes, red fruit (raspberry, blueberry), kirsch, iris and notes of vanilla. They are flavoursome, have well-balanced mellowness and vinosity. They are robust, ample, fleshy and have good structure. They are long on the palate and well-balanced with elegant tannins. Their ageing capacity is greater than for Brouilly and they can even be firm when young. Because of their structure, they can be paired with red meats, either roasted or served with a sauce, rib steak with marrow, poultry (goose, duck, Bresse chicken), grilled chitterlings sausage, rabbit stew, cheese tart…

A.C. FLEURIE

OVERVIEW: the Fleurie appellation covers just one village of the same name, which is adjacent to Chiroubles, Morgon and Moulin-à-Vent. The vineyard has a south-east and north-west aspect, and whilst some vines are located on steep inclines, others occupy more gentle slopes. The soils are meagre and are formed of crystal granite with a smattering of clay in the eastern portion of the appellation. Around the chapel of the Black Virgin, on the steepest summits of the appellation, they become skeletal whereas those below the village have a higher clay content. INAO has identified thirteen different climate types within the appellation area: Les Côtes, Le Bon Cru, La Roilette, Les Moriers, Les Roches, Les Garants, Poncié, Montgenas, La Chapelle des Bois, La Madone, Grille Midi, Champagne and La Joie du Palais. Fact: a large share of the wines are made by the local co-operative winery.

WINE STYLES: Fleurie displays a deep cherry-red hue and fragrances of peach, red fruit like blackcurrant, floral notes with iris, violet and rose. Occasionally they are slightly spicy. The wines are fleshy, elegant, velvety, fruit-driven and feminine. Wines grown in the upper reaches of the appellation are more delicate and aromatic whilst those drawn from the lower slopes have more structure. If Moulin-à-Vent is considered to be the 'king' of Beaujolais then, by the same measure, Fleurie is the 'queen' of the growths. The wines can be laid down. Serve with chitterlings sausage, duck with cherries, leg of lamb, white meats and poultry.

A.C. JULIÉNAS

OVERVIEW: this growth is situated in the far northern part of the region and embraces Juliénas, Juillé and Emeringes in the Rhône and Pruzilly in Saône-et-Loire. It is located between Chénas in the south and Saint-Amour in the north-west. Juliénas grows at the crux of two contrasting worlds: Chardonnay territory in the Mâcon region, and Gamay in Beaujolais. The vines have south-west and north-west exposure and are sheltered from the northerly and easterly winds.

They are planted on soils made up of shale and granite with pockets of clay. The western portion of the appellation is granite with some manganese, whilst in the east, the soils are deeper and have greater clay content.

WINE STYLES: Juliénas displays a deep hue and its fragrances are predominantly peony, violet, red fruit (red currant, wild strawberry, raspberry), cinnamon, blackcurrant and vine peach. Occasionally spicy notes can be detected. The wines are generous, well-structured, powerful, rich and virile and, apart from the odd exception, they should be drunk when aged between two to five years. However, wines grown in Juillé and Emeringes mature earlier, whilst those drawn from more clayey soils need longer to reveal their full potential. Enjoy with red meats, either roasted or served with a sauce, barbecues, poultry or coq au vin.

A.C. MORGON

OVERVIEW: this Beaujolais growth encircles Villié-Morgon, 25 km from Mâcon and from Villefranche-sur-Saône. Its boundaries are formed by Chiroubles and Fleurie in the north and Régnié in the south-west. The appellation area is criss-crossed with streams travelling west to east. It is the most extensive Beaujolais growth, along with Brouilly. The appellation has even lent its name to a verb: a young Beaujolais with similar characteristics to a Burgundy is said 'to morgon'. The soils are formed of altered, friable crystalline rocks, dubbed 'rotten earth'. The granite in this particular area is intermingled with clay and sand. The ground is manganoan and pyritic which is said to enhance a wine's ageing capacity.

WINE STYLES: Morgon has a distinctive garnet-red hue and fragrances of stone fruits (apricot, peach, cherry, plum), kirsch, pear drops, strawberry, red currant, blackcurrant and raspberry. In hot years, aromas of very ripe fruit develop. The wines are hearty, full-bodied, fleshy and robust, particularly those from the Côte de Py, which tend to display the hallmark depth of a Morgon. These are some of the region's best laying-down wines and they need time to express their full potential. Some growers, however, have opted for early-drinking alternatives.

Since 1985, Morgon has been divided into six climatically distinct sites: Les Charmes (well-structured wines), Corcelettes, Côte du Py (extremely robust, laying down wines), Douby (softer on the palate), Les Grands Crus (round, pleasant, aromatic) and Les Micouds (middle of the road). Morgon pairs well with sirloin steak, meat served with a sauce (pheasant), game, coq au vin, mutton stew, duck with onions, or a leg of lamb.

A.C. MOULIN À VENT

OVERVIEW: this growth takes its name from an old 15th century windmill. It embraces Chénas (Rhône) and Romanèche-Thorins (Saône-et-Loire) and is adjacent to Juliénas, Fleurie and Chénas. Moulin à Vent boasts five site-specific vineyards: Grand Carquelin, Champ de la Cour, Les Thorins, La Roche and Rochegrès. The first four are located in the vicinity of the windmill, whilst the latter one is situated in the upper portion of the appellation, on the border with Fleurie. The vines are planted on rolling hills facing east. The soils are formed of friable pink granite (known locally as 'gore'), rich in manganese oxide, which is said to impart Moulin à Vent wines their hallmark characteristics.

Wine styles: they display a ruby-red hue and fragrances of red fruit (cherries) and floral notes, predominantly iris, violet and rose. As they age, they develop aromas of ripe red fruits, spices, truffle, musk, sometimes even game. Moulin à Vent wines are concentrated, full-bodied, powerful, robust and rich in tannins. They are considered to be the most suitable laying-down wines. They have garnered a reputation as being as graceful as Beaujolais and as prestigious as Burgundy. Enjoy with beef casserole, roasted red meats, game or cheeses.

A.C. RÉGNIÉ

OVERVIEW: Beaujolais' most westerly growth. It embraces Régnié-Durette and Latignié, 25 km north-west of Villefranche-sur-Saône, and was the last Beaulolais growth to be officially recognised. Prior to that, the local wines were ranked top amongst Beaujolais-Villages. The vineyard unfolds gently down towards the floor of the Ardières valley. To the north-west, mount Avenas acts a natural barrier for the vines. The soils, which are light and poor, are made up of pink granite, relatively rich in minerals and containing clay in parts.

WINE STYLES: Régnié wines are fruity, quaffing wines. They are well-balanced, pleasant and mature well, with delicate tannins. Their cherry-red hue, fragrances of red (raspberry, red currant, blackcurrant) and black fruits (blueberries, blackberries), occasionally ripe peach, floral (honeysuckle) and spicy notes, reward early drinking. Serve with grilled red meats, chitterlings sausage, ham in parsley aspic, knuckle of ham, hot dried sausage, potato tart or cheeses.

A.C. SAINT-AMOUR

OVERVIEW: Beaujolais' most northerly growth, located in Amour-Bellevue. The village is said to derive its name from Amor (subsequently Saint-Amateur), a Roman soldier who survived a massacre and then sought refuge in Gaul where he later became a missionary. The village was thus named after him.

The appellation area, which is situated on the border with Mâcon, is also home to white Beaujolais and Saint-Véran (from Chardonnay). Set against the backdrop of mount Bessay, the terroir here is formed of limestone though also granite with patches of shale and sandstone. The terrain is clay-silica scattered with stones and rocky debris.

WINE STYLES: the area produces two styles of wines: powerful, voluptuous wines with good structure, fat and harmony, for cellaring. These are relatively tannic with an intense hue ranging from crimson to garnet-red, exuding fragrances of apricot, peach, apple, crushed strawberries, raspberry and peony. Alternatively, it produces wines destined for early drinking, fleshy, soft, light and elegant which conjure up aromas of kirsch, spices and floral notes (mignonette). Each style suits different foods, ranging from red to white meat, cooked cold pork meats and cheeses.

A.C. COTEAUX DU LYONNAIS

OVERVIEW: covering an extensive 48 towns and villages, this appellation stretches westwards along the right banks of the Rhone. It occupies a strip of land 40 km long by 30 km wide and is sandwiched between Beaujolais in the north and the Côtes-du-Rhône in the south. The vines are planted on hillside and plateaux sites facing east or south-east. The lion's share of the wines are red, with a balance of whites making up the remaining 5%.
WINE STYLES: red Coteaux du Lyonnais boast a cherry-red hue and fragrances of raspberry and cherry. They are light, fruity wines for quaffing, best enjoyed when served with cooked cold pork meats (chitterlings sausages, paté, hot dried sausage), poultry, roasted or braised red meats, stew, roast poultry and cheeses. The whites have a yellow hue with hints of green and develop aromas of citrus fruit, grapefruit and exotic fruits. They are the perfect match for pike quenelles. The rosés are fresh, intense, fruity and elegant wines, which are great as thirst-quenchers.

• • •

BEAUJOLAIS

Beaujolais

DOMAINE DU VISSOUX +33 4 74 71 79 42

▼ Pierre-Marie Chermette Les Griottes 2012 Price:❍ 87/100

DOMAINES PIRON +33 4 74 69 10 20

CV ▼ Domaine de La Chanaise 2011 Price:❍ 86/100

MAISON COQUARD +33 4 74 71 11 59

▼ Clochemerle Vintage 2012 Price:❍ 83/100

Brouilly

DOMAINE COMTE DE MONSPEY +33 4 26 47 02 62

▼ Vieilles Vignes 2012 Price:❍ 87/100

TERROIRS ORIGINELS +33 4 74 69 53 86

▼ Robert Perroud L'Enfer des Balloquets 2011 Price:❍❍ 86/100

DOMAINE BERTRAND +33 4 74 66 85 96

▼ Vintage 2011 Price:❍ 87/100

DOMAINE COMTE DE MONSPEY +33 4 26 47 02 62

▼ Cuvée du Commandeur 2009 Price:❍❍ 90/100

DOMAINE DE TANTE ALICE +33 4 74 66 89 33

▼ Vintage 2011 Price:❍ 86/100

TERROIRS ORIGINELS +33 4 74 69 53 86

▼ Robert Perroud Pollen 2011 Price:❍❍ 86/100

VINS DE PIZAY +33 4 74 66 26 10

▼ Château de Saint Lager Vintage 2012 Price:❍ 89/100

Detailed instructions are featured at the start of the book.

Chénas

ANITA & ANDRÉ KUHNEL +33 4 74 04 22 59

▼ Anita et André Kuhnel Prix Bacchus 2011 Price:○ 88/100

DOMAINES PIRON +33 4 74 69 10 20

CV ▼ Domaine Piron-Lameloise Quartz 2011 Price:○○ 90/100

TERROIRS ORIGINELS +33 4 74 69 53 86

▼ Pascal Aufranc Vignes de 1939 2011 Price:○○ 87/100

Chiroubles

DOMAINE HUBERT DESMURES +33 4 74 69 86 15

▼ Vintage 2011 Price:○ 87/100

Côte de Brouilly

DOMAINE DU BARON DE L\'ECLUSE +33 4 74 03 40 29

▼ Vieilles Vignes 2010 Price:○ 82/100

▼ Vintage 2011 Price:○ 87/100

DOMAINE DU PAVILLON DE CHAVANNES +33 4 74 04 35 01

▼ Cuvée des Ambassades 2011 Price:○ 86/100

Prices mentioned in this book are guideline and can vary depending on point of sale. The shops, wineries or publisher can in no way be held responsible for this.

Fleurie

DOMAINE COMTE DE MONSPEY +33 4 26 47 02 62

▼ Comte de Monspey Le Débuché 2011 Price:❍ 87/100

DOMAINE DU VISSOUX +33 4 74 71 79 42

▼ Pierre-Marie Chermette Poncié 2012 Price:❍❍ 89/100

DOMAINE GAGET +33 4 74 04 20 75

▼ La Madone 2011 Price:❍❍ 88/100

Morgon

DOMAINE GAGET +33 4 74 04 20 75

▼ Côte du Py - Cuvée Joseph - Elevé en Fûts de Chêne 2011

Price:❍❍ 89/100

+33 4 74 04 20 75

▼ Côte du Py 2011 Price:❍ 88/100

DOMAINES PIRON +33 4 74 69 10 20

CV ▼ Domaine de la Chanaise Vintage 2011 Price:❍ 87/100

JOËL LACOQUE +33 4 74 69 16 52

▼ Cuvée Marie Jeanne - Côte du Py 2009 Price:❍❍ 87/100

DOMAINE MARIE ANTOINETTE +33 4 74 69 15 10

▼ Domaine de Fond Chatonne - Vieilles Vignes 2011

Price:❍ 86/100

▼ Cuvée Château Gaillard - Vieilles Vignes 2010

Price:❍ 88/100

DOMAINES PIRON +33 4 74 69 10 20

CV ▼ Côte du Py 2011 Price:❍❍ 92/100

JOËL LACOQUE +33 4 74 69 16 52

▼ Côte du Py 2011 Price:❍ 87/100

MAISON COQUARD +33 4 74 71 11 59

▼ Epices et Cannelle 2012 Price:○ 86/100

TERROIRS ORIGINELS +33 4 74 69 53 86

▼ Laurent Gauthier Grand Cras - Vieilles Vignes 2011
Price:○○ 88/100

VINS DE PIZAY +33 4 74 66 26 10

▼ Château de Pizay Vintage 2012 Price:○ 90/100

Moulin à Vent

DOMAINE DE LA FOND MOIROUX +33 4 74 67 47 48

CV ▼ Domaine Fond Moiroux Vintage 2010 Price:○○ 87/100

DOMAINE MORTET +33 3 85 35 55 51

▼ Vintage 2011 Price:○ 84/100

ANITA & ANDRÉ KUHNEL +33 4 74 04 22 59

▼ Anita et André Kuhnel Reine de Nuit 2012 Price:○ 89/100

DOMAINE COMTE DE MONSPEY +33 4 26 47 02 62

▼ Comte de Monspey Les Honneurs 2011 Price:○ 87/100

DOMAINE DE FORETAL +33 4 74 69 90 45

▼ Vintage 2011 Price:○ 88/100

DOMAINE DE LA FOND MOIROUX +33 4 74 67 47 48

CV ▼ Gros Vosges 2009 Price:○○ 90/100

DOMAINE MORTET +33 3 85 35 55 51

▼ Vintage 2010 Price:○ 86/100

TERROIRS ORIGINELS +33 4 74 69 53 86

▼ Gérard Charvet La Réserve d'Amélie 2011 Price:○○ 87/100

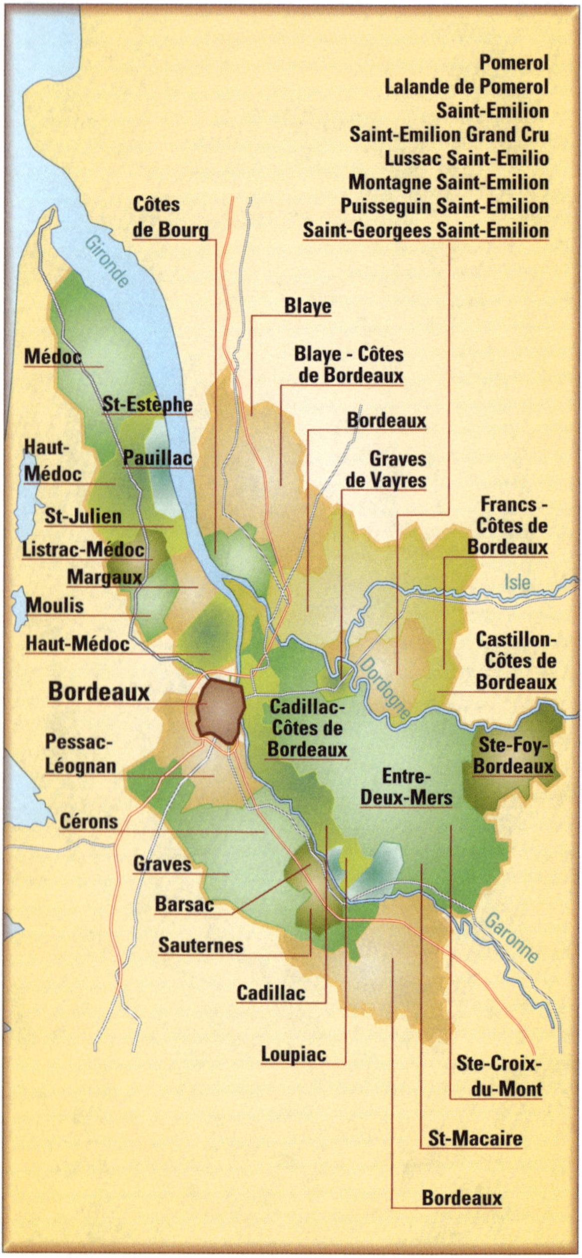

Pomerol
Lalande de Pomerol
Saint-Emilion
Saint-Emilion Grand Cru
Lussac Saint-Emilio
Montagne Saint-Emilion
Puisseguin Saint-Emilion
Saint-Georgees Saint-Emilion
Côtes de Bourg
Gironde
Blaye
Médoc
Blaye - Côtes de Bordeaux
St-Estèphe
Bordeaux
Haut-Médoc
Pauillac
Graves de Vayres
St-Julien
Francs - Côtes de Bordeaux
Listrac-Médoc
Margaux
Isle
Moulis
Haut-Médoc
Castillon-Côtes de Bordeaux
Dordogne
Bordeaux
Cadillac-Côtes de Bordeaux
Pessac-Léognan
Ste-Foy-Bordeaux
Entre-Deux-Mers
Cérons
Graves
Barsac
Garonne
Sauternes
Cadillac
Loupiac
Ste-Croix-du-Mont
St-Macaire
Bordeaux

BORDEAUX

A LAND OF SUPERLATIVE QUALITY AND DIVERSITY

No other wine region in the world sparks as much passion as Bordeaux. Ask around and you won't find a single wine lover who does not have well-formed opinions about Bordeaux wines, how they taste, their varieties, their unrivalled terroirs and even their prices.

With its 120,000 hectares (300,000 acres) under AC-classed vines, the Bordeaux wine region is the revered behemoth of French wine growing, though its boundaries fit snugly within a single department. Four components factor into the quality of this unparalleled wine region. Firstly, a favoured vineyard site along the Gironde plateau, on gently undulating land. A climate particularly conducive to wine growing, marked by maritime influences rising off the Atlantic which combine with a matrix of distinct local traits (incline, topography, aspect) to form a myriad of microclimates. Once these then partner up with all the various soil types, they form the third component which will determine the 'terroirs' most suitable for producing quality wines. Last comes a range of noble grape varieties painstakingly selected through trial and error by the people who care (grape growers, wine makers...), whose labour can in many ways be considered the fifth component of Bordeaux's success.

So here you have the tremendous alchemy of the Bordeaux wine region. And as these components do not work in unison, the result is a cornucopia of styles, sufficiently numerous to form territorial entities with their own distinct personalities.

LE MÉDOC

Situated between the Gironde estuary and the Atlantic Ocean, the Médoc peninsula, meaning 'middle land' in local patois, is

Bordeaux's prodigy with prestigious names such as Margaux or Pauillac... Here, a combination of sandy, stony and clay soils - the famous 'graves' or gravel - deposited by the Garonne over thousands of years, retain heat during the day before gradually releasing it. They also regulate drainage.
The Médoc is primarily home to Cabernet-Sauvignon, a late-ripening varietal renowned for its tannins and powerful blackcurrant aromas, dominating its fellow varietals, Merlot, Cabernet Franc and Petit-Verdot (not extensively planted). The area covers eight appellations: six 'communal' appellations, Listrac, Moulis, Margaux, Pauillac, Saint-Estèphe and Saint-Julien, and two 'sub-regions', Médoc to the far north and Haut-Médoc at the southern end.

LES GRAVES

This area is situated south of Bordeaux, extending south-east of the Médoc with similar soil types, in addition to which are sand, clay, shelly sand (limestone with shells), and sometimes even quartz and quartzite. The land is home to two red wine appellations, Pessac-Léognan on the outskirts of Bordeaux, to the north (an AC since 1987 embracing all the Graves classed growths), and Graves, in the south. Wines from the northern part are well-structured, powerful reds with a deep hue and good cellaring capacity, whilst in the south the wines tend to be lighter and more delicate on the palate. All of them are drawn from the same red varietals grown in the Médoc. However, both the northern and southern parts also have the capacity to produce powerful, mouth-filling whites, with a delicate bouquet and extensive ageing potential. They are drawn from Semillon, a productive, hardy varietal well-suited to oak ageing, and Sauvignon, a lively, aromatic varietal.

THE REALMS OF THE SWEET WINES

South of the Graves, this area straddling the Garonne river is home to the sweet wines: Loupiac and Sainte-Croix-du-Mont along the right bank, Sauternes, Barsac and Cérons along the left bank.... These prestigious appellations are fortunate to have a climate conducive to producing a microscopic fungus - botrytis cinerea - which develops by sucking water out from inside the grapes, hence concentrating sugars in the wines. Vintages where the wines fully express all the rich, subtle aromas imparted by the fungus are occasionally referred to as 'botrytised' years. These outstanding wines can only be drawn from three varietals -

Semillon (70%), Sauvignon (25%) and Muscadelle (5%) - in that order, though the latter varietal, whilst highly aromatic on gravely and calcareous clay soils, is not widely planted because it does not always ripen easily.

THE LIBOURNE AREA

Fanning out from the northern banks of the Dordogne, with the town of Libourne as its focal point, this area is primarily a red wine region where Bordeaux's most ubiquitous grape variety (Merlot with 53.5%) is by far the most predominant. Here it produces a clutch of world-famous wines like Canon-Fronsac, Fronsac, Pomerol, Lalande de Pomerol and the highly celebrated Saint-Emilion Grand Cru... Though slightly less renowned, Montagne-Saint-Emilion, Lussac and Puisseguin offer enticing alternatives. These particular vineyard sites provide this varietal with extremely varied soil types based on a backbone of clay (calcareous clay, clay-gravel, clay-sand...) where it forms a perfect partnership with Cabernet Franc (or Bouchet), yielding generous, racy, powerful wines with subtle aromas.

CÔTES-DE-BORDEAUX WINES

Although this region is geographically extensive, the wines it produces are not as heterogeneous as one might imagine. They share a similar landscape, consisting of hilly slopes of clay-limestone soils along the banks of the Dordogne and the Garonne, as well as a south to southeast orientation -another feature they have in common is they are excellent value for money.

Côtes-de-Bordeaux is made up of seven appellations. In the north, on the right bank of the Gironde, across from Médoc, lie the vineyards of Blaye, Côtes-de-Bourg and Blaye Côtes-de-Bordeaux, which produce red wines that are rustic yet agreeable. Further south are two appellations around the town of Libourne: Francs Côtes-de-Bordeaux and Castillon Côtes-de-Bordeaux to the east, entirely dev oted to reds, and Graves-de-Vayres to the west, which produces interesting reds and whites. South of this lies Cadillac Côtes-de-Bordeaux, which stretches along the Garonne River from Bordeaux to Langon. Benefiting from very good conditions, today these vineyards produce quality wines that are highly appreciated by demanding consumers. The unique Carménère grape is still grown here, a variety that produces excellent wines with a rich taste and deep colour, with a structure that is rather similar to Cabernet Franc.

ENTRE-DEUX-MERS

Set between the Garonne and the Dordogne, this is Bordeaux's most extensive wine growing region, stretching almost 30 kilometres wide and a good 60 km long. Home of the dry whites (primarily Entre-Deux-Mers), this area is now governed by strict regulations. To be entitled to appellation status, the wines must be drawn from 70% Semillon, Sauvignon and Musca-delle and no more than 30% Merlot Blanc or 10% Ugni blanc, Mauzac and Colombard.

WINE STYLES

The red wines are evidently blends (chiefly Cabernets and Merlot). They are well-structured and tannic, with intense aromas of blackcurrant and are often able to withstand the test of time. The most prestigious appellations are all of the above and much more, displaying incomparable finesse and exceptional complexity.

The dry whites, which more often than not are also blends (Semillon-Sauvignon), cover a range of styles. White Bordeaux and Entre-Deux-Mers are lively, floral, fruity wines, in their prime when young. Graves and Pessac-Léognan have a longer life span due to a more ample structure, often enhanced by oak-ageing. Lastly come the sweet whites, legally required to come from the Semillon, Sauvignon and Muscadelle trio, which no longer need an introduction: Sauternes, Barsac, Cérons, Loupiac and Sainte-Croix-du-Mont acquired star status aeons ago. In good years, their structure keeps them fresh and young after decades in the bottle.

REVIEW OF RECENT VINTAGES

• **2005** • All the credentials of a great wine, greatly helped by near-perfect weather. The reds and dry whites are aromatic, harmonious and typically Bordeaux; the sweet wines are proving to be very promising.

• **2006** • Both a classic and uneven vintage, lacking the concentration of the 2005s yet still promising in terms of balance and elegance.

• **2007** • Although the summer was mediocre, the autumn was magnificent. The red wines are soft, moderately concentrated and have a bouquet of ripe fruit. They can be drunk when young. The dry white wines are excellent, and the dessert wines amazing.

• **2008** • With a relatively cool August and a sunny end of September, 2008 was a rather mixed year, producing red wines that are fruity, lively and elegant, not without a certain power. The whites are very fresh, and the dessert wines moderately rich.

• **2009** • An exceptional, monumental vintage, particularly for the red wines. Bordeaux reds have never before reached such concentration. They are powerful, complete and deep. The Grands Crus will age well, while the humbler wines can be enjoyed already. The dry whites and dessert wines are full-bodied, sometimes perhaps a bit overly so, but there are also some excellent examples that are balanced with freshness.

• **2010** • Record concentrations due to the drought that prevailed throughout the summer. The 2010 vintage broke all previous records for phenolic concentration and alcoholic strength. However, unlike 2009, August stayed relatively cool thus ensuring slightly higher acidity levels, particularly in the Cabernets. Vintage 2010 saw successful wines when power and concentration took a back seat to freshness and the purity of the fruit.

• **2011** • after a warm, dry spring, July and August were unsettled leading to an inconsistent vintage. Some successful dry and sweet whites. The reds are a more mixed bunch with two main taste profiles: enjoyable, fruity and fairly full-bodied wines and another group showing more pronounced tannins and a measure of dryness on the finish.

• **2012** • In contrast to 2011, the spring was disrupted by precipitation and slow flowering, with the weather improving only in mid-July. The dry white wines are well made, while the dessert wines are decent without being excellent, and the reds are variable (particularly in Médoc). However, the wines are generally pleasant, with mature tannins and well-defined fruit.

LES APPELLATIONS BORDELAISES

A.C. BARSAC

OVERVIEW: AC Barsac is grown in and around the town of Barsac on the left bank of the Garonne. All wines produced within AC Barsac can be labelled as Sauternes, however this only works one way.

WINE STYLES: Traditionally, Barsacs are considered to be moderately lighter than Sauternes, perhaps because the soil has greater sand and clay content and the terrain is marginally flatter. As a rule of thumb, Barsacs display a characteristically beautiful golden colour, running the gamut from pale gold for the youngest to deep amber for the most mature. They exude a full, deep nose.

On the palate, they develop flavours of acacia honey, the flesh of white peach, almond, toast and above all botrytised grapes which, over time, mellow and become more complex and harmonious. Enjoy with baked sole fillets in a creamy hollandaise sauce, smoked salmon, or chocolate cake.

BLAYE AOC

OVERVIEW: The vineyards of Blaye are located on the right bank of the Gironde, around 50 kilometres northwest of Bordeaux. The vineyards stretch over a large area of 6,000 hectares (of which 90% are planted with red varieties) and are cultivated by 700 winegrowers. The Blaye AOC produces still red wines.

WINE STYLES: These red wines are quite smooth, with a bouquet of spices, prune and ripe fruit that can develop over time to give musky hints. They develop an attractive brick-red colour during ageing.

BLAYE CÔTES-DE-BORDEAUX AOC

OVERVIEW: This winegrowing area shares the same territory as Blaye AOC, separated from the Médoc by the Gironde estuary. The Blaye Côtes-de-Bordeaux reds are mainly produced from Merlot and have a deep colour and fruity notes. They are pleasant, easy-drinking wines that go well with meat and cheese. The Blaye Côtes-de- Bordeaux whites are principally made from Sauvignon, giving them their pale yellow colour, nose of citrus and broom, as well as a nice bite and long finish, making them intensely subtle wines. These whites are ideal for an apéritif or with seafood.

WINE STYLES: Blaye Côtes-de-Bordeaux AOC wines are typically more delicate that those of Blaye AOC, as the grapes can be markedly different. The dominant aromas are white flowers, yellow fruits and broom. They can be served with seafood.

AC BORDEAUX

OVERVIEW: AC Bordeaux covers the entire Gironde department, with the exception of wetlands, valley floors and the sandy soils of the Landes woodlands. It applies only to red wines (dry whites are governed by a specific dry Bordeaux appellation). Legally, they can only be made from Cabernet-Sauvignon, Cabernet Franc, Merlot, Malbec, Petit Verdot and Carmenere. Four different soil types form the Bordeaux appellation area: marshlands (recent alluvial soils edging the Garonne and the Dordogne), gravely soils made up of gravel and quartz, calcareous clay earth,

extremely widespread on hillside sites, and 'boulbenes' (loamy soils characteristic of the Entre-Deux-Mers plateaux). The wines are made traditionally in temperature-controlled stainless steel or lined concrete tanks. They can be aged in oak but this is optional.
WINE STYLES: As a rule of thumb, red AC Bordeaux wines boast a fine cherry-red colour, they are well-balanced, harmonious and fruity, not overly robust and reward early drinking.

AC BORDEAUX SEC

OVERVIEW: Grown in the same area as red Bordeaux, dry Bordeaux are made from Semillon, Sauvignon and Muscadelle.
WINE STYLES: They offer floral, fruity fragrances, are relatively fat and rarely woody. At their best when served young, with seafood, fish and poultry.

AC BORDEAUX SUPÉRIEUR

OVERVIEW: The AC Bordeaux Supérieur fits within the Bordeaux appellation area and can be used for reds and whites, both dry and sweet. There are two major differences between the two: Bordeaux Supérieur has lower yields and a higher minimum alcohol content than Bordeaux. However the varietal range for the reds is identical: Cabernet-Sauvignon, Cabernet Franc, Merlot, Malbec, Petit Verdot, Carmenere; and for the whites: Semillon, Sauvignon and Muscadelle.
WINE STYLES: They are more robust and fuller wines than 'basic' Bordeaux. Bordeaux Supérieur wines have red fruit (raspberry) and black fruit (blackcurrant) aromas, with a dash of vanilla for the oak-aged wines. They pair well with sirloin steak cooked over a fire of vine twigs, pan-fried Bayonne ham and roast beef with shallot chutney.
The sweet white wines are rich in alcohol and sugar with scents of honey, acacia, plum and tobacco. They make perfect appetisers or accompaniments to white meat and foie gras.

AC BORDEAUX HAUT-BENAUGE

OVERVIEW: The Haut-Benauge region is set like a lone island amidst the sea of Entre-Deux-Mers vines. Its soils are calcareous clay and clay-silica. The Bordeaux-Haut-Benauge appellation applies only to sweet white wines which account for one third of the area's output: Semillon, Sauvignon and Muscadelle.
WINE STYLES: The dry white wines display a pale yellow hue with hints of green. They are soft, supple, fruity, easy-drinking wines. Predominant aromas are flinty and floral notes.

AC BORDEAUX ROSÉ

OVERVIEW: Bordeaux's rosé wines are labelled under the regional appellations Bordeaux Rosé and Bordeaux Clairet. They can produced anywhere in the Gironde department, providing the land is suitable for wine growing. They are drawn from the same varietals as red wines. Bordeaux rosés are briefly macerated (for 10-18 hours) to impart some colour and are then run off and bottled shortly after.

WINE STYLES: Fresh, fruity wines rewarding early drinking, the rosés are lighter than the Clairets. Fragrances of blackcurrant, redcurrant, raspberry and strawberry intermingle with caramel, orange peel and grapefruit... Try as an appetiser or with fish or cooked cold pork meats.

AC BORDEAUX CLAIRET

OVERVIEW: Bordeaux Clairets, blended from Cabernet-Sauvignon, Cabernet Franc, Merlot, Malbec, Petit Verdot and Carmenere, are vinted in the same way as the rosés. However, because they macerate for longer (24 to 36 hours), their colour is deeper and tannin content higher. Some of them spend a short period in oak.

WINE STYLES: The Clairets display fruit (peach, raspberry, redcurrant, strawberry, lychee) and floral aromas (seringa, rose, orange blossom) with a hint of primary bud aromas. They are more appropriate for a meal time, served with cooked cold pork meats, kebabs, grilled fish...

AC CADILLAC CÔTES-DE-BORDEAUX

OVERVIEW: Cadillac AOC, located to the north of Loupiac on the right bank of the Garonne, produces white dessert wines. Until 1973, Cadillac was part of the Premières Côtes-de-Bordeaux appellation. Today, 22 districts have the right to claim this AOC, but many winegrowers continue to use Premières Côtes-de-Bordeaux AOC. The wines are produced from Sémillon, Sauvignon and Muscadelle.

WINE STYLES: These wines are elegant, aromatic, fruity and full. They are good apéritif wines, but also go well with foie gras and sweet-and-sour dishes such as caramelised pork.

AC CANON-FRONSAC

OVERVIEW: In the Libourne area only two villages are entitled to carry the Canon-Fronsac appellation - Fronsac and Saint-Michel-de-Fronsac - and even then, the grapes can only come from specific vineyard sites. The vines (Cabernet-Sauvignon, Cabernet Franc, Merlot and Malbec) are planted on hillside sites where the soils are calcareous clay or clay-sand on a limestone bedrock.

WINE STYLES: Canon-Fronsac wines (exclusively reds) are on the whole deeply-coloured, fat, fleshy wines whilst at the same time revealing suppleness and elegance with a delicate, slightly spicy flavour and a distinctive bouquet. With good cellaring potential, they develop aromas of red fruits, pepper, spices and truffle. They pair well with marinated or roast meats, preserved duck or goose, poultry and pears cooked in wine.

AC CASTILLON CÔTES-DE-BORDEAUX

OVERVIEW: Some 40 kilometres east of Bordeaux, on the northeast border of the Gironde region, Castillon is known for the battle in 1453 that brought an end to the Hundred Years' War. There are nine districts that have the right to claim the appellation. The area benefits from a favourable climate for growing grapes. The soils are rich in iron and limestone and lie on clay-limestone or limestone slopes. The grape varieties used are Merlot, Cabernet Sauvignon, Cabernet Franc and Malbec.

WINE STYLES: The wines resemble those around Saint-Émilion, although they are less tannic and need to age for several years in order to soften. They have an intense colour and are structured, powerful, balanced and fleshy. They develop aromas of prune, spices and animal notes. They pair well with red meat, either barbecued or prepared with a sauce, game and strong cheeses.

AC CÉRONS

OVERVIEW: this appellation covers around 120 hectares in Cérons, Illats and Podensac on the left bank of the Garonne, thirty or so kilometres south-east of Bordeaux. Set within the Graves appellation area, it only produces sweet wines from Semillon, Sauvignon and Muscadelle grapes harvested when overripe and picked in batches as they ripen.

WINE STYLES: Cérons is an elegant sweet wine, perhaps slightly lighter and vigorous than Sauternes. It is a good match for foie gras, white meat served in a sauce or blue cheeses (Roquefort).

AC CÔTES DE BLAYE

OVERVIEW: This area fits within the AC Blaye region, looking out over the Gironde to the Médoc. It only produces white wines and these must legally be blended from at least two varietals, usually Colombard, with a balance of Semillon, Sauvignon or Muscadelle.

WINE STYLES: As a rule, wines entitled to use the Côtes de Blaye appellation tend to be more refined than those labelled AC Blaye, mainly because the varietal range can be noticeably different. Predominant aromas are white blossom, yellow fruit and broom. Food pairings include fish or seafood.

AC CÔTES DE BORDEAUX SAINT-MACAIRE

OVERVIEW: This appellation lies to the extreme southeast of Cadillac Côtes-de-Bordeaux AOC over some ten districts (including Saint-Macaire) on the right bank of the Garonne. Only whites (dessert and dry wines) made from Sémillon, Sauvignon, Sauvignon Gris and Muscadelle can be labelled with this AOC. Both the dry and moelleux dessert wines are produced from grapes harvested at a late stage of ripening. The liquoreux dessert wines are produced from overripe grapes affected by noble rot.

WINE STYLES: These sweet wines, more or less botrytised depending on the year, are subtle, quite full-bodied yet soft, and best drunk when young. They have a bouquet with notes of honey, acacia and tobacco. They can be drunk as an apéritif and also pair well with white meat and foie gras.

AC CÔTES-DE-BOURG

OVERVIEW: This appellation sits on the right bank of the Dordogne, near the confluence with the Garonne, some 30 kilometres northeast of Bordeaux. It spreads over the district of Bourg-sur-Gironde. The hillsides generally have clay-limestone or clay-gravel soils. The vineyards along the banks of the Gironde estuary are particularly well protected from freezing due to the influence of the Atlantic Ocean. This area is often called 'Gironde's Little Switzerland' for its green, hilly landscapes. Its red wines are made from Cabernet Sauvignon, Cabernet Franc, Merlot and Malbec. Its whites are made from Sémillon, Sauvignon, Muscadelle, Merlot Blanc and Colombard.

WINE STYLES: Côtes-de-Bourg wines are mainly red. The whites were once used as the base wine for making Cognac. Today some of them are distilled into Fine de Bordeaux, a brandy that received recognition in 1974. The red wines are robust, well-structured and highly aromatic, with a deep, brilliant purple colour. They have surprising roundness and velvety tannins. They pair wonderfully with poultry, roast beef with boletus mushrooms or leg of lamb.

AC CÔTES DE CASTILLON

OVERVIEW: Located 40 kilometres east of Bordeaux, along the north-east border of Gironde, Castillon is famous for the 1453 battle which ended the 100 Years' War. Nine towns and villages are entitled to use the appellation. The area is blessed with a climate conducive to wine growing. The soils are rich in iron and limestone on hillside sites of calcareous clay or just clay. The wines are blended from the varietals Merlot, Cabernet-Sauvignon, Cabernet Franc and Malbec.

WINE STYLES: The wines are similar in style to the Saint-Emilion satellite appellations although they tend to be less tannic and take a few years to mellow. Their hue is intense and they are well-constituted, powerful, well-balanced and fleshy. They develop aromas of prunes, spices and animal notes. They are suitable partners for red meats either grilled or served with a sauce, game or mature cheeses.

AC CRÉMANT DE BORDEAUX

OVERVIEW: Crémants are sparkling wines which can be made anywhere within the Bordeaux appellation area from both the red and white varietals used in Gironde. They are made using the traditional method with secondary fermentation in the bottle after a blend of sugar and yeasts has been added.

WINE STYLES: Crémants can generally divided into three different styles: 'blancs de blancs' made from Semillon, Sauvignon and Muscadelle, Crémant Rosé made from red Bordeaux varietals and blended white Crémant, a combination of red and white varietals. With their pale yellow colour, Crémants are usually fresh and lively. They can be served as appetisers, or with fish, shellfish, white meats, cheeses or desserts.

AC ENTRE-DEUX-MERS

OVERVIEW: this extensive appellation should actually be called 'Entre-Deux-Rivières' (or between two rivers) as it sits between the Dordogne and the Garonne. It produces white wines only, from Sauvignon, Semillon and Muscadelle, with just over 2,000 hectares on-stream. Red wines grown here are labelled as Bordeaux or Bordeaux Supérieur.

WINE STYLES: these are dry, fresh, fruity wines which have become rounder over the past few years. Characteristic aromas of citrus fruit (lemon, grapefruit), peach and occasionally exotic fruit (lychee) are present. Try with seafood or fish.

AC ENTRE-DEUX-MERS HAUT-BENAUGE

OVERVIEW: The Entre-Deux-Mers Haut-Benauge region is set like a lone island amidst the sea of Entre-Deux-Mers vines; only a clutch of villages producing dry white wines are entitled to use it. The appellation applies only to white wines which account for one third of the area's output. Varietals used are Sauvignon, Semillon and Muscadelle.

WINE STYLES: These dry white wines display a pale yellow hue with hints of green. They are soft, supple, fruity, easy-drinking wines. They develop aromas of flint and floral notes. They can be served either as an appetiser or with seafood or grilled fish.

AC FRANCS-CÔTES DE BORDEAUX

OVERVIEW: This appellation extends east from Puisseguin-Saint-Émilion and Lussac-Saint-Émilion. It covers the districts of Francs, Saint-Cibard and Tayac. In the valleys, the soils are clay, and the hillsides have clay-limestone soil over marly or limestone subsoils. The red grape varieties are Cabernet Sauvignon, Cabernet Franc, Merlot, Malbec, Petit Verdot and Carménère. The white varieties are Sémillon, Sauvignon and Muscadelle.

WINE STYLES: The red wines have a rich colour and are opulent and full-bodied, characterised by harmonious tannins. They have notes of red fruits (red currant) and spices, with woody notes when young that evolve over time to aromas of game and leather. The dry white wines are fat and complex with floral, woody fragrances. The dessert wines, which are produced only when the harvest and weather allow, are powerful, fat, well balanced and endowed with an attractive wealth of aromas.

AC FRONSAC

OVERVIEW: Set within the Libourne region, this appellation embraces Fronsac, La Rivière, Saint-Germain-la-Rivière, Saint-Michel-de-Fronsac, Saint-Aignan, Saillans and Galgon. Soil types range from modern alluvium along the marshland bordering the Dordogne and the Isle to calcareous clay and clay-sand. Only wines blended from Cabernet-Sauvignon, Cabernet Franc, Merlot and Malbec are made here.

WINE STYLES: As a general rule, Fronsac wines are deeply-coloured (vermilion red or deep ruby hue, occasionally turning a topaz shade with age), fat, fleshy and well-balanced, though at the same time supple and delicate with a distinctive flavour and bouquet. They are laying-down wines which develop aromas of pepper, spices and truffle.

AC GRAVES

OVERVIEW: The extensive region of Graves, which runs parallel with the banks of the Garonne, is Bordeaux's oldest wine growing area. AC Graves wines hail primarily from the stretch of land between La Brède and Langon, encircling the Barsac and Sauternes appellations. In 1987, it parted company with AC Pessac-Léognan in the north which embraces all the classed growths. The gravel-strewn outcrops near Bordeaux and sandy gravel soils further south are home to vineyards blessed with a particularly mild climate. The red wines are blended from Merlot; Cabernet-Sauvignon, Cabernet Franc, Petit Verdot and Malbec. The whites from Semillon, Sauvignon and Muscadelle.

WINE STYLES: The red wines are supple, elegant, well-structured, delicate and well-balanced with an enticing bouquet (red berries, violet, liquorice, peach). They generally mature harmoniously and pair well with roast white meats (veal, lamb) and cheeses (brie, coulommiers). The white wines, which bear the tell-tale characteristics of Bordeaux wines and are amongst the best the region has to offer, are dry, elegant, fleshy, lively wines that linger on the palate and boast a layered aromatic profile: honey, wax, muscat and acacia blossom when they are made from Semillon; more predominant citrus and exotic fruits when Sauvignon is the backbone varietal. Enjoy with shellfish, fish and white meats served with a sauce.

AC GRAVES DE VAYRES

OVERVIEW: This diminutive appellation situated near Libourne, along the left bank of the Dordogne, embraces just two villages: Vayres and Arveyres. It is entirely surrounded by the northern section of the Entre-Deux-Mers appellation.

WINE STYLES: The wines display a ruby-red hue and are delicate and elegant with a supple, well-balanced tannic structure. They are equally suited to early drinking and laying down. They boast fragrances of cherry, redcurrant, blackcurrant, strawberry and notes of liquorice, leather and vanilla. Whites made predominantly from Sauvignon are dry with a pleasant bouquet, brimming with freshness on the palate. The sweet whites, drawn from over-ripe Semillon grapes, display an attractive straw-yellow hue. On the palate, they are generous and overwhelmingly supple. The scale of production remains, however, boutique.

AC GRAVES SUPÉRIEURES

OVERVIEW: This AC produces sweet white wines from Semillon, Sauvignon and Muscadelle. Minimum natural sugar content in the must is 221g/l and alcoholic strength must be in excess of 13.5%. Wine making practices are identical to those in Sauternes.
WINE STYLES: Graves Supérieures are sweet white wines with a distinctive bouquet and great length on the palate. Golden yellow in colour, they display a characteristic balance between acidity and sweetness with toasted, honey notes and occasionally dried fruit. They partner well with fresh or pan-fried foie gras and desserts.

AC HAUT-MÉDOC

OVERVIEW: The regional Haut-Médoc appellation forms the southern part of the Medoc peninsula. It covers 29 towns and villages from Blanquefort in the south as far as Saint-Seurin-de-Cadourne in the north, including the communal appellations Saint-Estèphe, Pauillac, Saint-Julien, Moulis, Listrac-Médoc and Margaux. Dotted throughout the region are the star-studded châteaux producing some of the world's greatest wines.
The region is home to five classed growths, hundreds of Bourgeois growths producing some of Bordeaux's finest wines and five co-operative wineries. The soil make-up comprises gravel from the Quaternary era, deposited by the Garonne and shaped into outcrops. The temperate climate is strongly defined by the Atlantic and the nearby estuary. The wines are made traditionally at controlled temperatures and subsequently aged in oak for 12 to 18 months.
WINE STYLES: Blended from Cabernet-Sauvignon, Cabernet Franc, Merlot, Malbec, Petit Verdot and Carmenere, the wines are elegant, with great finesse and a layered bouquet. They are reasonably robust and perfectly suited to laying down. They conjure up aromas of ripe red fruit, notes of roasted coffee, mild spices (liquorice, vanilla...) and sweet pepper, sometimes prune. They pair well with Normandy-style veal cutlets, roast meats or game.
CLASSED GROWTHS:
Château La Lagune (3rd growth),
Château La Tour Carnet (4th growth),
Château Camensac, Château Cantemerle and Château Belgrave (all three 5th growths).

AC LALANDE-DE-POMEROL

OVERVIEW: The Lalande-de-Pomerol appellation area embraces just two villages, Lalande-de-Pomerol itself and Néac, situated

north of Saint-Emilion and Pomerol. In fact, only a tiny river, the Barbanne, separates them from Pomerol. Soil types range from clay and clay-gravel in the east to gravel in the north and north-east, and sand in the western reaches. Vines thrive here in hot sunny climes, blessed with sufficient rainfall. Red varietals: Merlot, Cabernet-Sauvignon, Cabernet Franc and Malbec.
WINE STYLES: Deeply coloured red wines, powerful and velvety with a pleasant mouthfeel. Predominant aromas are truffle, violet and undergrowth. They are a good match for roast beef, duck and unfermented cheeses.

AC LISTRAC-MÉDOC

OVERVIEW: Officially recognised in 1957, Listrac is the youngest of the six communal appellation areas in Haut-Médoc.It is also the furthest away from the Gironde estuary, set on the border between the wine growing areas of Medoc and its woodlands. The soils are either gravely or calcareous clay. The nearby ocean and the estuary provide a temperate climate.
WINE STYLES: The wines are all of a consistent standard. Deeply coloured, tannic and well-structured, they display a virile, fleshy personality. Predominant aromas are ripe red and black fruit, vanilla or caramel, roasted coffee, dark chocolate and spices. They can be served with beef casserole or preserved duck. There are no classed growths within this communal appellation.

AC LOUPIAC

OVERVIEW: This appellation is situated 40 km from Bordeaux along the right bank of the Garonne, near Sainte-Croix-du-Mont. The vines are planted on hillside sites where the soils are either calcareous clay or clay-sand. This south-facing area is blessed with a microclimate conducive to the onset of noble rot. Varietals for blending are Semillon, Sauvignon and Muscadelle.
WINE STYLES: Loupiac are fruity wines with a well-balanced mellowness. They are delicate, elegant, firm and generous, developing aromas of crystallised fruit (apricot), honey and gingerbread. They pair well with roast duck or duck breasts.

AC LUSSAC-SAINT-EMILION

OVERVIEW: Lussac-Saint-Emilion is one of Saint-Emilion's four satellite appellations. Set in the village of Lussac, it is a red-wine only appellation. The wines are grown on average 10-hectare plots by around a hundred growers. The vineyards are planted on plateaux and hillside sites where soil types are calcareous clay in the south eastern portion and gravely in the west, though there are pockets of sand and clay. The wines are blended from Merlot, Cabernet Franc, Cabernet-Sauvignon, Malbec and Carmenère.

WINE STYLES: Lussac's hallmark character traits are sourced in its 'terroir'. The wines display a distinctively intense colour, finesse and generosity. They are well-balanced, full and suitable for laying down. They can be paired with grilled or roast meats and game.

AC MARGAUX

OVERVIEW: Situated on a plateau 6 km long by 2 km wide, the appellation encompasses five villages (Margaux, Cantenac, Soussans, Arsac and Labarde). It is not only the most extensive appellation in the Haut-Médoc, it is also the most southerly.

The core of the appellation is in Cantenac and Margaux along a string of prime hillock sites. The vineyards are planted on a plateau of gravel flanked by gravely outcrops. They in fact boast the deepest layer of gravel throughout the whole of the Médoc and have the stoniest soils.

WINE STYLES: These delicate, refined wines are rich, subtle and elegant. They are reputedly the Medoc's most 'feminine' wines. Their aromas cover a broad spectrum, predominantly violet, rose and raspberry. Recommended pairings include venison fillet, rack of lamb, hare or roast partridge, morels in puff pastry, sweetbreads and veal cutlets with chanterelles. In fact, they enhance all red meats and mild flavoured game.

CLASSED GROWTHS:

First growth: *Château Margaux.*

Second growths: *Château Brane-Cantenac, Château Dufort-Viviens, Château Lascombes, Château Rauzan-Gassies, Château Rauzan-Ségla.*

Third growths: *Château Boyd-Cantenac, Château Kirwan, Château d'Issan, Château Giscours, Château Malescot Saint-Exupéry, Château Cantenac-Brown, Château Palmer, Château Ferrière, Château Desmirail, Château Marquis d'Alesme Becker.*

Fourth growths: *Château Prieuré-Lichine, Château Pouget, Château Marquis de Terme.*

Fifth growths: *Château Dauzac, Château du Tertre.*

AC MÉDOC

OVERVIEW: AC Médoc is situated in the northern part of Médoc, around the towns and villages north of Saint-Seurin-de-Cadourne. Interspersed amongst the calcareous clay soils are less frequent occurrences of gravel. The temperate climate is strongly defined by the Atlantic ocean and the nearby estuary. The wines are made traditionally at controlled temperatures. They are matured for varying periods of time either under oak or in tanks.

WINE STYLES: AC Médoc is a red-wine only appellation. The wines display a brilliant cherry-red hue. On both the nose and the palate they have distinctive fruit aromas (blackcurrant, red fruit). These superbly round, delicate, supple wines tend to mature well. They can be enjoyed from an early age and served with grilled sirloin steak, cooked cold meats and cheeses.

AC MONTAGNE SAINT-EMILION

OVERVIEW: Of the four Saint-Emilion satellite appellations, this AC has the greatest acreage. Its soil type is quite similar to that of nearby Saint-Emilion: calcareous clay hillside sites on a subsoil of limestone, clay-silica or loam. The wines are blended from Merlot, Cabernet Franc, Cabernet-Sauvignon, Malbec and Carmenere.
WINE STYLES: With a hue of varying intensity, these wines are fresh, powerful, rich and mild. Tannins are quite present but the wines remain supple and display extremely pleasant characteristic floral, fruity notes. They partner with game and poultry served in a sauce.

AC MOULIS

OVERVIEW: Situated on the left bank of the Gironde, in Haut-Médoc, the Moulis appellation area embraces seven villages (Moulis, Listrac-Médoc, Lamarque, Arcins, Avensan, Castelnau-de-Médoc, Cussac-Fort-Médoc). Forty or so wine growers share the appellation and 14 of those boast Bourgeois growth status. The vines grow on outcrops studded with gravel of Pyrenean origin or deposited by the Garonne.
WINE STYLES: The wine boasts great finesse and an elegant bouquet supported by a strong framework and good length. An intense ruby-red colour, it is both seductive yet virile. For some, it is the epitome of a Médoc, with the potential finesse of Margaux, the complexity of a Saint-Julien and the strength of a Pauillac. Their tannin content makes Moulis capable of considerable longevity. They exude aromas of prunes and leather as well as spicy and vanilla notes. They can be served with stew, casseroles, sirloin steak with a shallot sauce, leg of mutton…

AC PAUILLAC

OVERVIEW: Pauillac is a Médoc communal appellation. It boasts an impressive concentration of top-flight wines with three of the five First Growths within its boundaries (Lafite, Latour and Mouton-Rothschild). The vines are planted on a virtually unbroken ridge stretching from Saint-Julien in the south to Saint-Estèphe in the north. Only a few hundred metres of m arshland separate them from the waters of the Gironde estuary. The soils are gravely with sandy deposits, providing superb drainage. The nearby ocean and estuary define a warm temperate climate.

WINE STYLES: Pauillac's red wines, whose principal varietal is Cabernet-Sauvignon, are some of the Médoc's most concentrated wines. Rich and complex, they have a well-structured, harmonious body bolstered by a fine tannic structure. They are robust, elegant, distinguished wines with a great ability to age. They develop fragrances of raspberry, blackcurrant, rose, violet, iris, cedar and cigar box. Enjoy with Pauillac lamb, roast wood pigeon, rack of veal with chanterelles.

CLASSED GROWTHS:

First Growths: *Château Lafite Rothschild, Château Latour, Château Mouton Rothschild.*

Second Growths: *Château Pichon-Longueville (Baron), Château Pichon-Longueville (Comtesse de Lalande).*

Fourth Growth: Château Duhart-Milon-Rothschild.

Fifth Growths: *Château Batailley, Château Haut-Batailley, Château Clerc Milon, Château Croizet-Bages, Château Grand-Puy Ducasse, Château Grand-Puy Lacoste, Château Haut-Bages Libéral, Château Lynch-Bages, Château Lynch-Moussas, Château Pédesclaux, Château Pontet-Canet, Château d'Armailhac.*

AC PESSAC-LÉOGNAN

OVERVIEW: Pessac-Léognan, which was given its own appellation in 1987, is set in the heart of Graves country. It embraces ten towns and villages south of Bordeaux (Pessac, Talence, Villemanve d'Ornon, Léognan, Martillac, Mérignac, Gradignan, Cadaujac, Canéjan, Saint-Médard d'Eyrans). The terrain forms gravel outcrops and has good drainage. Bordered by pine forests then the ocean to the west and the Garonne to the east, the Graves region enjoys an extremely mild climate.

The wines are made traditionally at controlled temperatures. The reds are aged in oak as are the whites which are both fermented and matured under oak, almost invariably on the lees.

WINE STYLES: Pessac-Léognan scales the quality heights with elegant, complex wines. Displaying a highly attractive garnet-red hue, they show concentration and structure and are blessed with a finely woven texture, spanning a broad range of aromas. Ripe fruit, spices (pepper, liquorice) and humus aromas intermingle with smoky, chocolaty notes. The white wines are dry, vigorous, elegant, fleshy wines, velvety on the palate exuding an extremely refined bouquet (honey, acacia flowers, butter, dried fruit (peach, apricot), crystallised citrus fruit). The reds pair with roast poultry

and meat served in a sauce; the whites with shellfish, pike served with a butter sauce... Both red and white Pessac-Léognan are wines for laying down and will keep for between 5 to 20 years.
CLASSED GROWTHS:
First growth (Official 1855 Classification): *Château Haut-Brion.*
Classed growths: *Château Bouscaut, Château Carbonnieux, Domaine de Chevalier, Château Couhins, Château Couhins-Lurton, Château de Fieuzal, Château Haut-Bailly, Château La Mission Haut-Brion, Château La Tour Haut-Brion, Château Latour Martillac, Château Laville Haut-Brion, Château Malartic-Lagravière, Château Olivier, Château Pape-Clément, Château Smith Haut-Lafitte.*

AC POMEROL

OVERVIEW: Pomerol is a village situated near Libourne. The hillsides of Saint-Emilion roll down to Pomerol ending in a plateau carved into terraces which gently descend towards the valley floor. The soils are predominantly gravel interspersed with layers of clay. The subsoil however is shot through with a kind of iron-rich sandstone called 'iron dross' which in some cases imparts very distinctive characteristics to the wines.
Despite the fact that Pomerol is one of the most renowned and popular wines in the world, it has no official classification.
WINE STYLES: Pomerol wines are rich in colour, powerful and brimming with body, roundness and generosity, though they also boast finesse and an overwhelmingly rich bouquet. Red fruit, truffle and violet form the backbone of its aromatic range. Pomerol is an all-rounder which can be paired with all sorts of food, including foie gras. It sits nicely alongside dishes such as roast beef en croûte, jugged hare, lamprey in a red wine sauce, mushrooms and most cheeses.

AC PUISSEGUIN-SAINT-EMILION

OVERVIEW: This is one of Saint-Emilion's four satellite appellations, with a total 120 growers, one third of whom belong to the local co-operative. The soil is primarily calcareous clay with a rocky, stony subsoil. A large proportion of the vineyards enjoy a south, south-east aspect and a dry microclimate. The wines grown here are red, drawn from Merlot, Cabernet Franc (or Bouchet) Cabernet-Sauvignon and very occasionally Malbec.
WINE STYLES: Puisseguin-Saint-Emilion wines have good depth of colour. They are powerful, well-constituted, delicate, harmonious wines. The more mature wines pair well with white meat whilst the younger versions are better suited to red meat and game.

AC SAINTE-CROIX-DU-MONT

OVERVIEW: Situated 45 km south-south-east of Bordeaux, this appellation sits on the opposite bank of the Garonne to Sauternes. The soils are calcareous clay in type with fossils set on a subsoil of limestone or gravel. The vines are planted on plateaux or hillside sites. The wines are blended from Semillon, Sauvignon and Muscadelle.

WINE STYLES: These sweet wines are fruity, rich and elegant with a well-balanced mellowness. They have a high sugar and alcohol content. They pair with melon, roast chicken or quenelles.

AC SAINTE-FOY-BORDEAUX

OVERVIEW: Set in the north-eastern corner of Gironde, this appellation embraces 19 towns and villages. Sainte-Foy-Bordeaux produces dry and sweet white wines and reds. Red wines are blended from Cabernet-Sauvignon, Cabernet Franc, Merlot, Malbec and Petit Verdot and white wines primarily from Semillon, Sauvignon and Muscadelle.

WINE STYLES: The red wines have good depth of colour and can be supple or robust. Depending on how they are made, they are either suitable for early drinking or should be kept. They display aromas of red fruit, undergrowth, leather and notes of vanilla. The dry whites are round with a touch of acidity, exuding discrete, appealing fragrances. The sweet whites show a pale yellow hue, finesse and mellowness, with scents of honey, linden and muscat.

AC SAINT-EMILION

OVERVIEW: Saint-Émilion is near the town of Libourne to the east of the Gironde. It dates back to the end of the 13th century, when Emilianus, a monk from Brittany, settled there. Saint-Émilion was a winegrowing region well before Médoc. Although Médoc is made up of very large estates, several hundred small winegrowers cultivate the vineyards of Saint-Émilion. The appellation consists of eight districts: Saint-Émilion, Saint-Christophe-des-Bardes, Saint-Étienne-de-Lisse, Saint-Hippolyte, Saint-Laurent-des-Combes, Saint-Pey-d'Armens, Saint-Sulpice-de-Faleyrens and Vignonet, as well as part of Libourne. As the topography of the area is varied, the grapes produce very different wines depending on the orientation and location of the vines. Saint-Émilion has four main types of terroir: a limestone plateau near the town, a large terrace of siliceous-clay gravel stretching in the direction of

Libourne, clay-limestone hillsides and valleys, and the sand and gravel plain of the Dordogne valley, which produces lighter wines.
WINE STYLES: Saint-Émilion produces only reds, which are plum-coloured and reputed for their generous, warm, powerful character and opulent bouquet. Saint-Émilion AOC wines are nonetheless less full-bodied than Saint-Émilion grands crus. The main aromas are red fruit jam, spices and coffee. It pairs well with lamprey à la bordelaise, duck casserole or goose confit.

AC SAINT-ÉMILION GRAND CRU

OVERVIEW: Produced in the same winegrowing area as Saint-Émilion AOC, the grand crus are found on the best terrains: the clay-limestone hillsides, the plateau or the gravel terrace. Its wines are produced according to strict rules: a maximum yield of 46 hectolitres per hectare (in contrast with 53 for other Saint-Émilion wines), a minimum natural level of alcohol (11.5° in contrast with 11°) and final tasting before authorization. The crus classés concern only Saint-Émilion Grand Cru AOC.
CRUS CLASSÉS: Saint-Émilion is ranked to distinguish premiers grands crus classés and grands crus classés. This ranking is reviewed every ten years. All these wines belong to the Saint-Émilion Grand Cru appellation, however not all the wines of this AOC are grands crus classés. Within the premiers grands crus classés, there are two categories, A and B.

GRANDS CRUS CLASSES :
Château l'Arrosée, Château Fleur Cardinale, Château Monbousquet, Château Balestard la Tonnelle, Château La Fleur Morange, Château Moulin du Cadet, Château Barde-Haut, Château Fombrauge, Clos de l'Oratoire, Château Bellefont-Belcier, Château Fonplégade, Château Pavie Decesse, Château Bellevue, Château Fonroque, Château Peby Faugères*, Château Berliquet, Château Franc Mayne, Château Petit Faurie de Soutard, Château Cadet-Bon, Château Grand Corbin, Château de Pressac*, Château Capdemourlin, Château Grand Corbin-Despagne, Château le Prieuré, Château le Chatelet, Château Grand Mayne, Château Quinault l'Enclos*, Château Chauvin, Château les Grandes Murailles, Château Ripeau, Château Clos de Sarpe, Château Grand-Pontet, Château Rochebelle, Château la Clotte, Château Guadet, Château Saint-Georges-Cote-Pavie, Château la Commanderie, Château Haut-Sarpe, Clos Saint-Martin, Château Corbin, Clos des Jacobins, Château Sansonnet, Château Côte de Baleau, Couvent des Jacobins, Château la Serre, Château la Couspaude, Château Jean Faure, Château Soutard, Château Dassault, Château Laniote, Château Tertre Daugay, Château Destieux, Château Larmande Château la Tour Figeac,*

Château la Dominique, Château Laroque, Château Villemaurine, Château Faugères, Château Laroze, Château Yon-Figeac, Château Faurie de Souchard, Clos la Madeleine, Château de Ferrand*, Château la Marzelle.*

* Châteaux promoted in 2012

AC SAINT-ESTÈPHE

OVERVIEW: This is the most northerly of the six Haut-Médoc communal appellations. Set on gravely outcrops with a stony limestone, and occasionally clayey subsoil, it is a red-wine only appellation. The five 1855 classed growths account for just 20% of overall production, underscoring the crucial role of the Bourgeois growths and the lesser wine growers, at the root of the area's diverse wine styles.

WINE STYLES: As a rule, Saint-Estèphe wines tend to have great depth of colour and a robust structure which does not compromise their finesse. They have a full tannic structure and cover a broad aromatic spectrum. They are robust, though not unpleasantly so, and are extremely well-suited to cellaring. Ripe red fruit and spices are the predominant aromas. Serve with large game, roast meat or meat served in a sauce, and a choice of cheeses.

CLASSED GROWTHS:

Second growths: *Château Cos d'Estournel, Château Montrose.*

Third growth: *Château Calon-Ségur.*

Fourth growth: *Château Lafon-Rochet.*

Fifth growth: *Château Cos Labory.*

AC SAINT-GEORGES SAINT-EMILION

OVERVIEW: This is the smallest of the Saint-Emilion satellite appellations and in fact most growers sell their wines as Montagne-Saint-Emilion. The vineyards are located exclusively along rolling hillsides and face south or south-west. The range of varietals is traditional with Merlot, Cabernet Franc, Cabernet-Sauvignon, Malbec and Carmenere.

WINE STYLES: The consistency of the terrain is mirrored in the quality of the wines. They display an intense crimson hue, are fruity and gain complexity as they mature. They are well-constituted, mild, fat and boast velvety tannins. They enhance red meat and game.

AC SAINT-JULIEN

OVERVIEW: Saint-Julien sits within a rectangle, 5 km long by 3.5 km wide, south of Pauillac. Roughly three-quarters of Saint-Julien wines are made by its 11 classed growths. Outcrops of

gravel from the Quaternary era deposited by the Garonne are home to its vineyards, as are silica-type soils to the west. The nearby ocean and the estuary provide a mild temperate climate.
WINE STYLES: Saint-Julien wines display an intense colour. They are subtle, well-balanced, elegant and show great length on the palate with a delicate, tell-tale bouquet. With their aromas of red fruit, mild spices, leather, vanilla... they boast a considerable ability to age. Enjoy with red meat, game, duck...
CLASSED GROWTHS:
Second growths: *Château Léoville Las Cases, Château Léoville-Poyferré, Château Léoville-Barton, Château Gruaud-Larose, Château Ducru-Beaucaillou.*
Third growths: *Château Lagrange, Château Langoa-Barton.*
Fourth growths: *Château Talbot, Château Saint-Pierre, Château Beychevelle, Château Branaire-Ducru.*

AC SAINTE-FOY-BORDEAUX

OVERVIEW: Located in the east of the Gironde region and covering 19 districts, the appellation of Sainte-Foy-Bordeaux produces dry and sweet white wines as well as reds. The red varieties used are Cabernet Sauvignon, Cabernet Franc, Merlot, Malbec and Petit Verdot. The main white varieties are Sémillon, Sauvignon and Muscadelle.
WINE STYLES: The red wines are rich in colour, smooth and full-bodied. Depending on the vinification method, they can be drunk when young or can be kept. They have a bouquet of red fruits, undergrowth, leather and notes of vanilla. The dry whites are round and slightly acidic and have subtle, flattering aromas. The dessert wines are pale yellow in colour, with a delicate and mild palate with scents of honey, lime flower and Muscat.

AC SAUTERNES

OVERVIEW: Sauternes, considered to be one of the greatest sweet white wines in the world, comes from an area located in the southern part of the Graves. This regional appellation embraces 5 villages: Sauternes, Fargues, Bommes, Preignac and Barsac. The cold waters of the river Ciron, which cuts through Sauternes, flow into the warmer Garonne, producing the autumn mists which envelop the vineyard in the evening and linger until the following morning. These climatic conditions are conducive to the formation of noble rot. Soil make-up is extremely varied, covering the gamut from gravel, to clay, silica and limestone or all four simultaneously. Subsoil is primarily clay though patches of limestone or gravel are also present. The wines are made from white varietals prone to 'Botrytis cinerea' (noble rot) such as Semillon (80% of the blend), Sauvignon and Muscadelle. Climate permitting, noble rot forms and the grapes are late harvested by painstakingly combing through the vineyard time after time. The grapes become shrivelled with extremely high sugar concentration. To comply with legislation, natural alcohol content in the finished wine must be between 15% and 12% actual alcohol. The difference between the two comes from the unfermented sugar. Residual sugar content must be at least 45g per litre.

Once the grapes have been harvested, they have to be handled with great care and must be pressed as gently as possible. The wines are fermented either in tanks or barrels and are usually matured under oak for anything between 18 to 36 months.

WINE STYLES: AC Sauternes yields sweet white wines displaying an old gold hue. They are rich, unctuous wines bolstered by a touch of acidity which allows them to age well. They exhibit fragrances of citrus fruit, acacia honey, apricot and hazelnut. Serve chilled as an appetiser, with foie gras, dishes cooked in a butter sauce, elaborate white meat dishes or desserts.

CLASSED GROWTHS:

Wines from Sauternes are classed either as AC Sauternes or AC Barsac, or occasionally both.

Superior First growth: *Château d'Yquem (Sauternes).*

First growths: *Château la Tour Blanche (Sauternes), Château Lafaurie-Peraguey (Sauternes), Château Rayne Vigneau (Sauternes), Château Suduiraut (Sauternes), Château Coutet (Sauternes and Barsac), Château Climens (Sauternes and Barsac), Château Guiraud (Sauternes), Château Rieussec (Sauternes), Château Rabaud-Promis (Sauternes), Château Sigalas Rabaud, Château Clos Haut-Peraguey (Sauternes).*

Second growths: *Château Doisy-Daëne (Sauternes and Barsac), Château Doisy Védrines (Sauternes and Barsac), Château d'Arche (Sauternes), Château Filhot (Sauternes), Château Broustet (Sauternes and Barsac), Château Nairac (Sauternes and Barsac), Château Caillou (Sauternes and Barsac), Château Suau (Sauternes and Barsac), Château de Malle (Sauternes), Château Romer du Hayot (Sauternes), Château Doisy Dubroca (Sauternes and Barsac), Château Lamothe Despujols (Sauternes), Château Lamothe (Sauternes), Château de Myrat (Sauternes and Barsac).*

BORDEAUX

Barsac

CHÂTEAU DOISY VÉDRINES +33 5 56 68 59 99
2e Cru Classé de Sauternes 1855

FUTURES ▼ Vintage 2012 Price: ❍ 92/100

CHÂTEAU MYRAT +33 5 56 27 15 06
2e Cru Classé de Sauternes 1855

FUTURES ▼ Vintage 2012 Price: ❍ 90/100

VIGNOBLES DUBOURDIEU +33 5 56 62 51 46
2e Cru Classé de Sauternes 1855

FUTURES ▼ Château Suau Vintage 2012 Price: ❍ 93/100

Blaye Côtes de Bordeaux

CHÂTEAU COUTRIL +33 5 57 64 61 86

▼ Corps et Ame 2009 Price: ❍ 86/100

CHÂTEAU LA HAIE +33 6 72 94 53 37

▼ Vintage 2010 Price: ❍ 90/100

CHÂTEAU LA MARTELLERIE +33 5 57 32 94 06

▼ Vintage 2009 Price: ❍ 78/100

▼ Elevé en Fûts de Chêne 2009 Price: ❍ 78/100

▼ Cuvée Maël 2009 Price: ❍❍ 85/100

CHÂTEAU POUYAU DE BOISSET +33 5 57 64 27 53

ORG ▼ Vintage 2011 Price: ❍ 86/100

CHÂTEAU SEGONZAC +33 5 57 42 18 16

CV ▼ Vintage 2011 Price: ❍ 85/100

CV ▼ Héritage Malbec 2011 Price: ❍❍ 88/100

CV ▼ Vieilles Vignes 2011 Price: ❍ 88/100

CHÂTEAUX EN BORDEAUX +33 5 57 43 43 82

▼ Château Le Virou Les Vieilles Vignes 2011 Price: ❍ 78/100

VIGNOBLE BERTINERIE +33 5 57 68 70 74

▼ Château Bertinerie Merlot - Cabernet 2009 Price: ❍ 86/100

▼ Château Bertinerie Cru Réserve 2009 Price: ❍❍ 89/100

VIGNOBLES JEAN CHÉTY ET FILS +33 5 57 42 10 28

▼ Château Haut-Colombier Vintage 2010 Price: ❍ 86/100

CV▼ Château Haut-Colombier Vintage 2012 Price: ❍ 86/100

Bordeaux

CASTENET +33 5 56 61 40 67

▼ Château Castenet Greffier Vintage 2012 Price: ❍ 85/100

CHÂTEAU DE PERRE +33 5 56 62 83 31

▼ Cuvée Excellence 2011 Price: ❍ 81/100

▼ Château Calebret Cuvée Premium 2012 Price: ❍ 84/100

▼ R 2012 Price: ❍ 84/100

CHÂTEAU GARRINEAU +33 5 56 61 07 64

▼ Garrineau Rosé Envie d'Eté 2012 Price: ❍ 85/100

CHÂTEAU LAMOTHE-VINCENT +33 5 56 23 96 55

▼ Vintage 2011 Price: ❍ 85/100

CHÂTEAU LARTIGUE LES CÈDRES +33 5 56 30 10 28

▼ Château Lartigue - Cèdres Vintage 2011 Price: ❍ 84/100

CHÂTEAU LAVERGNE DULONG +33 5 56 72 19 52

ORG▼ L 2012 Price: ❍ 88/100

CHÂTEAU LE TROS +33 5 57 24 26 85

▼ Cuvée Spéciale - élevé en fûts de chêne 2010 Price: ❍ 84/100

CHÂTEAU L'ESCART +33 5 56 77 53 19

ORG▼ Château le Bergey Vintage 2011 Price: ❍ 86/100

CHÂTEAU LOUDENNE +33 5 56 73 17 88

▼ Vintage 2011 Price: ❍❍ 87/100

CHÂTEAU MARJOSSE +33 5 57 55 57 80

▼ Vintage 2011 Price: ❍ 87/100

CHÂTEAU MAYNE PARGADE +33 5 56 23 91 23

▼ Château Jean de Bel Air Vintage 2012 Price: ❍ 83/100

CHÂTEAU TOUTIGEAC +33 5 56 23 90 10

▼ O toutigeac 2009 Price: ❍ 82/100

▼ Vintage 2011 Price: ❍ 82/100

▼ Château de Toutigeac X toutigeac 2010 Price: ❍ 83/100

▼ Vintage 2012 Price: ❍ 84/100

▼ Château Pradeau Mazeau
Grande Réserve 2011 Price: ❍ 85/100

▼ Château de Hartes Vintage 2011 Price: ❍ 85/100

CHÂTEAUX ET DOMAINES CASTEL +33 5 56 95 54 00

▼ Vintage 2011 Price: ❍ 87/100

COURREGES WINES +33 5 56 91 21 96

▼ Les Allées du Bonheur Vintage 2011 Price: ❍ 80/100

DOMAINE DE VALMENGAUX +33 5 57 74 48 92

CV▼ Vintage 2009 Price: ❍❍ 87/100

CV▼ Vintage 2010 Price: ❍❍ 87/100

DULON +33 5 56 23 69 16

▼ Château Julian Vintage 2011 Price: ❍ 80/100

▼ Château Grand Jean 2012 Price: ❍ 83/100

EARL NADAU +33 5 56 23 94 58

▼ Château Perron la Gourdine Vintage 2011 Price: ❍ 85/100

EARL ROCHET +33 5 56 61 02 42

▼ Château Malbat Vintage 2011 Price: ❍ 85/100

EARL VIGNOBLES TREJAUT +33 5 56 76 41 33

▼ Château la Grave Peynet Vintage 2012 Price: ❍ 83/100

▼ Château la Grave Peynet Vintage 2012 Price: ❍ 83/100

LES VIGNERONS RÉUNIS DE MONSÉGUR +33 5 56 61 61 85

▼ Château Grand Billard Vintage 2012 Price: ❍ 83/100

▼ Château Tuilerie Pagès Vintage 2012 Price: ❍ 83/100

▼ Château Peynaud Bagnac Vintage 2012 Price: ❍ 84/100

▼ M de Monségur 2012 Price: ❍ 85/100

SARL LADIMEX +33 5 57 40 39 79

▼ Château Donjon de Bruignac Vintage 2011 Price: ❍ 84/100

SCEA CHÂTEAU FOURREAU +33 5 57 40 50 08

▼ Château Fourreau Vintage 2011 Price: ❍ 82/100

Bordeaux - *Bordeaux*

SCEA VIGNOBLES LAURENT MAZEAU +33 5 56 76 40 58

▼ Château de Naujan Vintage 2011 Price: ❍ 79/100

▼ Château Vieil Orme Vintage 2011 Price: ❍ 83/100

UNION PRODIFFU +33 5 56 61 33 73

▼ Famille Excellor Vintage 2011 Price: ❍ 83/100

▼ Famille Excellor Sauvignon 2012 Price: ❍ 83/100

▼ Famille Excellor Vintage 2012 Price: ❍ 83/100

VIGNERONS DE TUTIAC +33 5 57 32 48 33

▼ Château Galochet Vintage 2010 Price: ❍ 82/100

▼ Château Les Vieilles Murailles Vintage 2012 Price: ❍ 82/100

▼ Château Belordre Vintage 2012 Price: ❍ 82/100

▼ Château Tertre de Bayard Vintage 2012 Price: ❍ 83/100

▼ Château Chapron Vintage 2011 Price: ❍ 84/100

VIGNOBLES CAMINADE +33 5 57 24 48 37

▼ Château Caminade Vintage 2011 Price: ❍ 84/100

VIGNOBLES CARTEYRON +33 5 57 24 46 98

▼ Château Penin Natur 2011 Price: ❍ 86/100

VIGNOBLES FRANCIS COURSELLE +33 5 56 23 00 01

▼ Château Thieuley Vintage 2011 Price: ❍ 85/100

▼ Château Thieuley Vintage 2011 Price: ❍ 86/100

VIGNOBLES GAGNE +33 5 56 23 98 50

CV▼ Château Bran de Compostelle Vintage 2011 Price: ❍ 82/100

VIGNOBLES JEAN-NOËL BOIDRON +33 5 57 51 64 88

▼ Mayne d'Olivet Vintage 2010 Price: ❍❍ 83/100

VIGNOBLES ROUX +33 5 56 61 98 93

▼ Château Laforêt Vintage 2012 Price: ❍ 79/100

▼ Château Roux de Beauces Vintage 2012 Price: ❍ 80/100

▼ Château Coustaut La Grangeotte Vintage 2012 Price: ❍ 82/100

▼ Château Le Faure Vintage 2012 Price: ❍ 82/100

▼ Château Le Faure Vintage 2012 Price: ❍ 82/100

▼ Château Gros Chêne Vintage 2012 Price: ❍ 82/100

▼ Château Sarcley Vintage 2012 Price: ❍ 82/100

▼ Château Haut Philippon Vintage 2012 Price: ❍ 82/100

- Château Roux de Beauces Vintage 2012 Price: ❍ 82/100
- Château La Peyrère Vintage 2012 Price: ❍ 83/100
- Château Les Tuileries Vintage 2012 Price: ❍ 83/100
- Château Palène Cuvée Valentine 2012 Price: ❍ 84/100
- Château Laforet Vintage 2012 Price: ❍ 84/100
- Château Haut Philippon Vintage 2012 Price: ❍ 84/100
- Château Les Tuileries Vintage 2012 Price: ❍ 85/100
- Château Haut Grand Champs Stéphanie 2012 Price: ❍ 85/100

Bordeaux Clairet

CHÂTEAU DE LISENNES +33 5 57 34 13 03

- Vintage 2012 Price: ❍ 85/100

VIGNOBLES FRANCIS COURSELLE +33 5 56 23 00 01

- Château Thieuley Vintage 2012 Price: ❍ 86/100

VIGNOBLES ROUX +33 5 56 61 98 93

- Château Haut Philippon Vintage 2012 Price: ❍ 84/100

Bordeaux rosé

CHÂTEAU BELLE ASSISE +33 5 57 24 61 62

- Rosé de Belle Assise 2012 Price: ❍ 84/100

Bordeaux sec

FOURNIER CASTEJA +33 5 56 62 68 16

- Château de Birot Blanc de Birot 2012 Price: ❍ 84/100

Detailed instructions are featured at the start of the book.

Bordeaux supérieur

BESTHEIM +33 3 89 49 09 29

▼ Château Fillon Cuvée Première 2010 Price: ❍ 85/100

▼ L'Apogée de Château de Fillon Vintage 2010 Price: ❍ 86/100

CHÂTEAU BOIS MALOT +33 5 56 38 94 18

▼ Tradition 2008 Price: ❍ 84/100

▼ Château des Valentons Canteloup Vintage 2010 Price: ❍ 85/100

▼ Château Bois-Malot Nobilis 2010 Price: ❍ 86/100

CHÂTEAU CANTELAUDETTE +33 5 57 24 84 71

▼ A du Château d'Arveyres Vintage 2010 Price: ❍ 86/100

CHÂTEAU D'ABZAC +33 5 57 49 32 82

▼ Oak-aged 2010 Price: ❍ 85/100

▼ Vintage 2010 Price: ❍ 85/100

CHÂTEAU DE LISENNES +33 5 57 34 13 03

▼ Cuvée Prestige - Elevé en Fûts de Chêne 2009 Price: ❍ 85/100

▼ Cuvée Tradition - Elevée en barrique 2009 Price: ❍ 85/100

▼ L'Esprit de Lisennes 2009 Price: ❍❍ 86/100

CHÂTEAU DES ARRAS +33 5 57 43 00 35

▼ Elevé en fût de chêne 2010 Price: ❍ 84/100

CHÂTEAU FONT-MERLET +33 5 56 32 73 18

▼ Vintage 2011 Price: ❍ 85/100

CHÂTEAU GRAND FRANÇAIS +33 5 57 69 50 23

ORG▼ Vintage 2010 Price: ❍ 85/100

ORG▼ Cuvée Spéciale
Elevée en fût de chêne 2010 Price: ❍ 88/100

CHÂTEAU HAUT CRUZEAU +33 5 56 21 11 11

▼ Vintage 2010 Price: ❍ 86/100

CHÂTEAU LA CADERIE +33 5 57 49 41 32

ORG▼ Authentique 2010 Price: ❍ 84/100

CHÂTEAU LA FRANCE +33 5 57 55 24 10

▼ Cuvée Gallus 2010 Price: ❍ 87/100

CHÂTEAU LAJARRE +33 5 57 40 50 59

▼ Eléonore 2011 Price: ❍ 83/100

CHÂTEAU LAMOTHE-VINCENT +33 5 56 23 96 55

▼ Héritage 2011 Price: ❍ 86/100

▼ Le Grand Rossignol 2010 Price: ❍❍ 87/100

CHÂTEAU L'ESCART +33 5 56 77 53 19

CV▼ Chateau L'Escart Cuvée Eden
Elevé en fûts de chêne 2011 Price: ❍ 87/100

CV▼ Omar Khayam 2011 Price: ❍❍ 88/100

CV▼ Chateau L'Escart Agape 2010 Price: ❍❍❍ 89/100

CHÂTEAU MAYNE PARGADE +33 5 56 23 91 23

▼ Château Maison Noble Saint Martin
Vintage 2011 Price: ❍ 86/100

CHÂTEAU PRIEURÉ MARQUET +33 6 17 19 41 45

▼ Vintage 2010 Price: ❍ 86/100

CHÂTEAU THURON +33 5 56 71 23 92

▼ Tradition 2009 Price: ❍❍ 85/100

CHÂTEAUX ET DOMAINES CASTEL +33 5 56 95 54 00

▼ Château de Techeney 2011 Price: ❍ 86/100

▼ Château de Mirefleurs Price: ❍ 86/100

▼ Château de Goëlane 2011 Price: ❍ 87/100

▼ Château de Lort 2011 Price: ❍ 88/100

DULON +33 5 56 23 69 16

▼ Château Julian Vintage 2010 Price: ❍ 82/100

EARL ROCHET +33 5 56 61 02 42

▼ Château Malbat L'Authentique 2011 Price: ❍ 84/100

GFA DES POMMIER +33 5 56 61 31 56

▼ Château Vrai Caillou Vintage 2010 Price: ❍ 82/100

MICHEL GONET ET FILS +33 5 57 24 51 23

ORG▼ Château Lesparre Vintage 2011 Price: ❍ 84/100

REGAUD +33 5 56 61 61 92

▼ Château La Tuilerie du Puy
Cuvée Grand Chêne 2011 Price: ❍ 83/100

▼ Château La Tuilerie du Puy
Le Vigneron Inconnu 2011 Price: ❍❍ 87/100

SARL LADIMEX +33 5 57 40 39 79

▼ Château Donjon de Bruignac Premium 2010 Price: ❍❍ 85/100

SCEA CHÂTEAU FOURREAU +33 5 57 40 50 08

▼ Château Fourreau
Elevé en Fûts de Chêne 2011 Price: ❍❍ 83/100

SCEA CHÂTEAU LA FAVIÈRE +33 5 57 49 72 08

▼ Château La Favière Vintage 2010 Price: ❍ 85/100

▼ Muse de La Favière Vintage 2010 Price: ❍ 85/100

▼ Muse de La Favière Vintage 2009 Price: ❍ 86/100

▼ Château La Favière Vintage 2009 Price: ❍ 88/100

SCEA VIGNOBLES AVRIL +33 5 57 84 32 11

▼ Château Pascaud Vintage 2009 Price: ❍ 83/100

▼ Château Pascaud Réserve 2009 Price: ❍ 85/100

VIGNERONS DE TUTIAC +33 5 57 32 48 33

▼ Château Sable Rouge Vintage 2012 Price: ❍ 82/100

VIGNOBLES BERNARD COUDERT +33 5 57 84 44 07

▼ Château Castagnac Vintage 2010 Price: ❍ 81/100

VIGNOBLES BORDERIE +33 5 57 69 83 01

▼ Château Les Gravières de la Brandille
Vintage 2010 Price: ❍ 85/100

▼ Château Les Gravières de la Brandille
Cuvée Prestige 2010 Price: ❍ 86/100

VIGNOBLES CARTEYRON +33 5 57 24 46 98

▼ Château Penin Les Cailloux 2010 Price: ❍❍ 88/100

VIGNOBLES GAGNE +33 5 56 23 98 50

CV▼ Château Bran de Compostelle
Cuvée Louisa2010 Price: ❍ 83/100

Cadillac

JEAN MÉDEVILLE ET FILS +33 5 57 98 08 08

▼ Château Fayau 2010 Price: ❍ 84/100

SCEA BONNEAU ET FILS +33 5 56 76 44 26

▼ Château Moulin de Corneil Vintage 2010 Price: ❍❍ 84/100

VIGNOBLES ARNAUD & MARCUZZI +33 5 56 62 60 91

▼ Domaine du Vic Vintage 2010 Price: ❍ 88/100

Cadillac Côtes de Bordeaux

CHÂTEAU CLOS CHAUMONT +33 5 56 23 37 23

▼ Vintage 2010 Price: ❍❍❍ 84/100

CHÂTEAUX ET DOMAINES CASTEL +33 5 56 95 54 00

▼ Vintage 2011 Price: ❍ 87/100

DOMAINE DE BAVOLIER +33 5 56 20 76 72

▼ Vintage 2010 Price: ❍ 85/100

FOURNIER CASTEJA +33 5 56 62 68 16

▼ Château de Birot Vintage 2011 Price: ❍ 80/100

▼ Château Le Thys Vintage 2011 Price: ❍ 82/100

SCEA BONNEAU ET FILS +33 5 56 76 44 26

▼ Château Moulin de Corneil Prestige - Elevé en Fût de Chêne 2010 Price: ❍ 85/100

Canon Fronsac

DE COURNUAUD +33 5 57 24 96 93

▼ Château Lafond Vintage 2010 Price: ❍ 87/100

▼ Château Lafond Vintage 2009 Price: ❍ 87/100

▼ Château Mazeris Vintage 2010 Price: ❍❍ 88/100

Castillon Côtes de Bordeaux

CHÂTEAU HAUT ROCHER +33 5 57 40 18 09

▼ Château Brehat Vintage 2010 Price: ❍ 83/100

FRANÇOISE ET PHILIPPE LANNOYE +33 5 57 55 23 28

▼ Château Moulin de Clotte Cuvée Dominique - élevé en fût de chêne 2010 Price: ❍❍ 87/100

Côtes de Bordeaux

BARON DE MONTFORT - CHÂTEAU DU ROCHER +33 5 57 40 18 20

CV▼ Château Lagrange-Monbadon Vintage 2010 Price: ❍ 85/100

CV▼ Château de Monbadon Vintage 2010 Price: ❍ 87/100

CHÂTEAU DE POTIRON +33 5 56 72 19 76

▼ Cuvée Privilège 2010 Price: ❍ 85/100

▼ Cuvée Excellence 2010 Price: ❍❍ 86/100

CHÂTEAU PENEAU +33 5 56 23 05 10

▼ Oak-aged 2010 Price: ❍ 79/100

CHÂTEAU RÉAUT +33 5 56 62 66 54

▼ Vintage 2010 Price: ❍❍ 85/100

CHÂTEAU SAINTE-CATHERINE +33 5 56 72 11 64

▼ Vintage 2009 Price: ❍ 88/100

DULON +33 5 56 23 69 16

▼ Château du Vallier Vintage 2008 Price: ❍ 83/100

VIGNOBLES ARNAUD & MARCUZZI +33 5 56 62 60 91

▼ Château du Payre Vintage 2011 Price: ❍ 86/100

Côtes de Bourg

BONNET ET FILS +33 5 57 64 91 39

▼ Château Haut-Guiraud Vintage 2011 Price: ❍ 84/100

CHÂTEAU DE BLISSA +33 5 57 64 84 24

▼ Vintage 2011 Price: ❍ 85/100

▼ Vintage 2010 Price: ❍❍ 86/100

▼ Vintage 2010 Price: ❍ 87/100

▼ Vintage 2011 Price: ❍ 87/100

CHÂTEAU GRAND-MAISON +33 6 08 88 10 69

▼ Vintage 2009 Price: ❍❍ 85/100

▼ Spéciale 2009 Price: ❍ 85/100

CHÂTEAU GROS MOULIN +33 5 57 68 41 56

▼ Elevé en fûts de chêne 2009 Price: ❍ 86/100

CHÂTEAU HAUT-MACÔ +33 5 57 68 81 26

▼ Vintage 2010 Price: ❍ 86/100

▼ Cuvée Jean Bernard 2009 Price: ❍ 88/100

CHÂTEAU LE CLOS DU NOTAIRE +33 5 57 68 44 36

▼ Vintage 2010 Price: ❍ 87/100

▼ Notaris Grande Réserve 2010 Price: ❍❍ 89/100

CHÂTEAU LE TERTRE DE LEYLE +33 5 57 64 23 81

▼ Vintage 2010 Price: ❍ 85/100

▼ Vieilli en fût de chêne 2010 Price: ❍ 86/100

CHÂTEAU MACAY +33 5 57 68 41 50

▼ Vintage 2010 Price: ❍ 87/100

▼ Vintage 2009 Price: ❍ 87/100

CHÂTEAU VIEUX PLANTIER +33 5 57 64 34 60

▼ Vintage 2010 Price: ❍ 85/100

▼ Cuvée Prestige - vieilli en fût de chêne 2010 Price: ❍ 86/100

CHÂTEAUX ET DOMAINES CASTEL +33 5 56 95 54 00

▼ Vintage 2011 Price: ❍ 88/100

VIGNERONS DE TUTIAC +33 5 57 32 48 33

▼ Château Le Puy Joubert
Elevé en fûts de chêne 2011 Price: ❍ 84/100

VIGNOBLES RODET +33 5 57 68 40 31

▼ Château Brulesecaille Vintage 2010 Price: ❍ 89/100

Detailed instructions are featured at the start of the book.

Crémant de Bordeaux

CHÂTEAU DE LISENNES +33 5 57 34 13 03

▼ Lisennes Brut Price: ❍ 84/100

Entre-Deux-Mers

CASTENET +33 5 56 61 40 67

▼ Château Castenet Greffier Vintage 2012 Price: ❍ 86/100

CHÂTEAU MARJOSSE +33 5 57 55 57 80

▼ Vintage 2011 Price: ❍ 87/100

CHÂTEAU MAYNE PARGADE +33 5 56 23 91 23

▼ Château Maison Noble Saint Martin 2012 Price: ❍ 86/100

DULON +33 5 56 23 69 16

▼ Château Grand Jean Vintage 2012 Price: ❍ 86/100

GFA DES POMMIER +33 5 56 61 31 56

▼ Château Vrai Caillou Entre-Deux-Mers 2012 Price: ❍ 82/100

REGAUD +33 5 56 61 61 92

▼ Château La Tuilerie du Puy
Cuvée Tradition 2012 Price: ❍ 83/100

VIGNOBLES ROUX +33 5 56 61 98 93

▼ Château Les Tuileries Vintage 2012 Price: ❍ 82/100

▼ Château Haut Philippon Vintage 2012 Price: ❍ 82/100

▼ Château Laforêt Vintage 2012 Price: ❍ 83/100

▼ Château Gros Chêne Vintage 2012 Price: ❍ 83/100

▼ Château Roux de Beauces Vintage 2012 Price: ❍ 83/100

▼ Château Sarcley Vintage 2012 Price: ❍ 85/100

Detailed instructions are featured at the start of the book.

Francs Côtes de Bordeaux

CHÂTEAU FRANC-CARDINAL +33 5 57 40 63 39

▼ Vintage 2010 Price: ❍ 84/100

Fronsac

CHARLES LEYMARIE ET FILS +33 5 57 51 07 83

▼ Château Tour Rozier Vintage 2009 Price: ❍ 84/100

▼ Château Les Tonnelles Prestige 2009 Price: ❍ 84/100

CHÂTEAU LES ROCHES DE FERRAND +33 5 57 24 95 16

▼ Vintage 2010 Price: ❍ 85/100

▼ Vintage 2010 Price: ❍❍ 85/100

EARL CHÂTEAU LES TROIS CROIX +33 5 57 84 32 09

▼ Château les Trois Croix Vintage 2010 Price: ❍❍ 84/100

PHILIPPE ET VÉRONIQUE JEAN +33 5 57 24 93 10

▼ CHATEAU CHADENNE Vintage 2009 Price: ❍❍❍ 92/100

VIGNOBLES BERNARD COUDERT +33 5 57 84 44 07

▼ Château Castagnac Vintage 2010 Price: ❍ 84/100

Graves

CHÂTEAU DE CHANTEGRIVE +33 5 56 27 17 38

▼ Vintage 2011 Price: ❍ 84/100

+33 5 56 27 17 38

▼ Vintage 2010 Price: ❍❍ 89/100

CHÂTEAU DU HAUT MARAY +33 5 56 76 83 33

▼ Vintage 2010 Price: ❍❍ 89/100

CHÂTEAU DU SEUIL — +33 5 56 27 11 56

▼ Château l'Avocat Vintage 2010 Price: ❍❍ — 87/100

▼ Vintage 2010 Price: ❍❍ — 88/100

CHÂTEAU MAGENCE — +33 5 56 63 07 05

▼ Château Brannens Vintage 2010 Price: ❍ — 85/100

▼ Vintage 2012 Price: ❍❍ — 86/100

▼ Elevé en fût de chêne 2012 Price: ❍❍ — 86/100

▼ Elevé en fût de chêne 2011 Price: ❍❍ — 87/100

CHÂTEAUX ET DOMAINES CASTEL — +33 5 56 95 54 00

▼ Vintage 2011 Price: ❍❍ — 89/100

▼ Vintage 2012 Price: ❍❍ — 89/100

COURBIN & FILS — +33 9 79 60 18 36

▼ Château l'Hermitage Vintage 2010 Price: ❍ — 84/100

JEAN MÉDEVILLE ET FILS — +33 5 57 98 08 08

▼ Château Boyrein Vintage 2010 Price: ❍ — 87/100

VIGNOBLES BONNET — +33 5 56 63 24 24

▼ Château de Respide Callipyge
Elevé en Fûts de Chêne 2010 Price: ❍❍ — 90/100

VIGNOBLES JEAN PERROMAT — +33 5 56 27 01 13

▼ Vintage 2011 Price: ❍ — 86/100

▼ Château de Cérons Vintage 2010 Price: ❍❍ — 87/100

Graves de Vayres

CHÂTEAU CANTELAUDETTE — +33 5 57 24 84 71

▼ Cuvée Prestige 2010 Price: ❍ — 82/100

▼ Vintage 2009 Price: ❍❍ — 84/100

MICHEL GONET ET FILS — +33 5 57 24 51 23

ORG▼ Château des Bordes Vintage 2011 Price: ❍ — 85/100

ORG▼ Château Lathibaude Vintage 2011 Price: ❍ — 85/100

CONV▼ Château Lathibaude Vintage 2010 Price: ❍ — 85/100

CV▼ Château des Bordes Vintage 2010 Price: ❍ — 86/100

▼ Edouard d'Eck Vintage 2011 Price: ❍ 86/100

ORG▼ Château Lesparre Vintage 2011 Price: ❍ 86/100

ORG▼ Edouard d'Eck Vintage 2010 Price: ❍ 87/100

CONV▼ Château Lesparre Vintage 2010 Price: ❍ 88/100

YVES ET ALAIN CAILLEY +33 5 56 30 85 47

▼ Château Toulouze Vintage 2010 Price: ❍ 85/100

▼ Château Toulouze Grande Cuvée 2010 Price: ❍❍ 86/100

Haut-Médoc

CAMBON LA PELOUSE +33 5 57 88 40 32

▼ Château Trois Moulins Vintage 2010 Price: ❍ 87/100

Cru bourgeois du Médoc

▼ Château Trois Moulins Vintage 2009 Price: ❍ 87/100

CHÂTEAU ANEY +33 5 56 58 94 89

Cru bourgeois du Médoc

▼ Vintage 2010 Price: ❍❍ 86/100

CHÂTEAU BELGRAVE +33 5 56 59 40 20

5e Cru Classé du Médoc 1855

FUTURES▼ Vintage 2012 Price: ❍ 89/100

CHÂTEAU BELLEGRAVE DU POUJEAU +33 6 07 14 09 47

Cru bourgeois du Médoc

▼ Vintage 2010 Price: ❍❍ 89/100

CHÂTEAU CAMENSAC +33 5 56 59 41 69

5e Cru Classé du Médoc 1855

FUTURES▼ Vintage 2012 Price: ❍ 91/100

CHÂTEAU CANTEMERLE +33 5 57 97 02 82

5e Cru Classé du Médoc 1855

FUTURES▼ Vintage 2012 Price: ❍ 88/100

CHÂTEAU CITRAN +33 5 56 58 21 01

▼ Vintage 2011 Price: ❍ 88/100

CHÂTEAU DE COUDOT +33 5 56 58 90 71

▼ Vintage 2010 Price: ❍❍ 89/100

CHÂTEAU DE MALLERET +33 5 56 35 05 36

▼ Vintage 2010 Price: ❍❍ 88/100

CHÂTEAU DE VILLAMBIS +33 5 56 73 90 90

Cru bourgeois du Médoc

▼ Vintage 2007 Price: ○ 87/100

CHÂTEAU D'ESTEAU +33 5 56 59 57 02

▼ Vintage 2009 Price: ○○ 84/100

▼ Vintage 2006 Price: ○○ 85/100

▼ 7 & + 2010 Price: ○ 85/100

▼ Vintage 2008 Price: ○○ 86/100

CHÂTEAU LA TOUR CARNET +33 5 56 73 30 90

4e Cru Classé du Médoc 1855

FUTURES▼ Château la Tour Carnet Vintage 2012 Price: ○ 88/100

CHÂTEAU LA LAGUNE +33 5 57 88 82 77

3e Cru Classé du Médoc 1855

FUTURES▼ Vintage 2012 Price: ○ 92/100

CHÂTEAU LE FOURNAS BERNADOTTE +33 5 56 59 57 04

▼ Château Bernadotte Vintage 2009 Price: ○○○ 88/100

▼ Château Bernadotte Vintage 2010 Price: ○○○ 90/100

CHÂTEAU PEYRABON +33 5 56 59 57 10

▼ Vintage 2010 Price: ○○ 89/100

CHÂTEAU PUY CASTÉRA +33 5 56 59 58 80

▼ Vintage 2009 Price: ○○ 87/100

CHÂTEAU TOUR MARCILLANET +33 5 56 59 92 94

▼ Vintage 2009 Price: ○○ 85/100

CHÂTEAUX ET DOMAINES CASTEL +33 5 56 95 54 00

Crus bourgeois du Médoc

▼ Château d'Arcins 2011 Price: ○ 85/100

▼ Château Barreyres 2011 Price: ○○ 87/100

DOMAINES LAPALU +33 5 56 41 50 18

▼ Château Lieujean Vintage 2011 Price: ○○ 85/100

▼ Château Liversan Vintage 2011 Price: ○○ 86/100

▼ Château Lagrave Vintage 2011 Price: ○○ 87/100

HAUT-BELLEVUE +33 5 56 58 91 64

Cru bourgeois du Médoc

▼ Vintage 2010 Price: ○○ 87/100

MONGRAVEY +33 5 56 58 84 51

▼ Vintage 2010 Price: ○○ 88/100

VIGNOBLES MARENGO PÈRE ET FILS +33 5 56 59 56 92
Cru bourgeois du Médoc

▼ Château Hourtin-Ducasse 2010 Price: ○○ 88/100

VIGNOBLES MARIE-LAURE LURTON +33 5 56 58 22 01

▼ Château de Villegeorge 2009 Price: ○○ 89/100

VIGNOBLES MEYRE +33 5 56 58 07 28
Cru bourgeois du Médoc

▼ Château Bibian 2010 Price: ○○ 87/100

Lalande de Pomerol

CHARLES LEYMARIE ET FILS +33 5 57 51 07 83

▼ Château Tour Grand Colombier Vintage 2007 Price: ○ 85/100

CHÂTEAU BELLES-GRAVES +33 5 57 51 09 61

▼ Vintage 2010 Price: ○○ 86/100

▼ Vintage 2008 Price: ○○ 88/100

▼ Vintage 2009 Price: ○○ 90/100

CHÂTEAU DE ROQUEBRUNE +33 5 57 51 44 54

▼ Cuvée Reine 2010 Price: ○○ 88/100

CHÂTEAU LES ROCHES DE FERRAND +33 5 57 24 95 16

▼ Vintage 2010 Price: ○○ 85/100

▼ Vintage 2010 Price: ○○ 86/100

CHÂTEAU VIEUX CHEVROL +33 5 57 51 09 80

▼ Vintage 2010 Price: ○○ 89/100

CHÂTEAU VOSELLE +33 5 57 51 61 77

▼ Vintage 2010 Price: ○ 86/100

DELBECK VIGNOBLES ET DÉVELOPPEMENTS +33 5 57 24 70 94

▼ Château Ame de Musset Vintage 2010 Price: ○○ 87/100

FOUCARD & FILS +33 5 57 51 11 40

▼ Château de Musset Cuvée Première 2009 Price: ○○ 87/100

▼ Château de Musset Cuvée Première 2010 Price: ○○ 88/100

VIGNOBLES G. ARPIN +33 9 71 58 23 49

▼ Vieux Château Gachet Vintage 2010 Price: ○○ 88/100

VIGNOBLES JB BRUNOT & FILS +33 5 57 55 09 99

- Château Le Gravillot Vintage 2010 Price: OO 88/100

Listrac-Médoc

CAVE GRAND LISTRAC +33 5 56 58 03 19

- Grand Listrac Vintage 2010 Price: O 85/100
- Château Saint-Martin Vintage 2010 Price: OO 86/100
- Château des Merles Vintage 2009 Price: OO 88/100

VIGNOBLES LARTIGUE +33 5 56 58 27 63

- Château Maine Lalande 2010 Price: OO 88/100

VIGNOBLES MEYRE +33 5 56 58 07 28

Cru bourgeois du Médoc

- Château Cap Léon Veyrin Vintage 2010 Price: OO 88/100

Loupiac

MARC DUCAU & DANIEL SANFOURCHE +33 5 56 62 99 88

- Château Loupiac-Gaudiet Vintage 2010 Price: OO 85/100

VIGNOBLES LACOSTE +33 5 56 62 10 50

- Château de Cranne Vintage 2011 Price: O 86/100

Lussac-Saint-Emilion

CHÂTEAU BEL-AIR +33 5 57 74 60 40

- Vintage 2010 Price: OO 86/100

CHÂTEAU CANTENAC +33 5 57 51 35 22

- Château Moulin de Grenet Vintage 2010 Price: O 89/100

CHÂTEAU LA CLAYMORE +33 5 57 74 67 48

- Vintage 2010 Price: OO 85/100

VIGNOBLES BORDERIE +33 5 57 69 83 01

▼ Château Les Combes Vintage 2010 Price: ❍ 85/100

▼ Château Les Combes Louis Gabriel 2010 Price: ❍❍ 87/100

VIGNOBLES DU CHÂTEAU DES LANDES +33 5 57 74 68 05

▼ Grand Héritage 2010 Price: ❍❍❍ 87/100

VIGNOBLES JB BRUNOT & FILS +33 5 57 55 09 99

▼ Château Tour de Grenet Vintage 2010 Price: ❍ 87/100

Margaux

CHÂTEAU CANTENAC-BROWN +33 5 57 88 81 81

3e Cru Classé du Médoc 1855

FUTURES▼ Vintage 2012 Price: ❍ 90/100

CHÂTEAU DAUZAC +33 5 57 88 32 10

5e Cru Classé du Médoc 1855

FUTURES▼ Vintage 2012 Price: ❍ 90/100

CHÂTEAU DESMIRAIL +33 5 57 88 34 33

3e Cru Classé du Médoc 1855

FUTURES▼ Vintage 2012 Price: ❍ 91/100

CHÂTEAU DU TERTRE +33 5 57 88 52 52

5e Cru Classé du Médoc 1855

FUTURES▼ Vintage 2012 Price: ❍ 89/100

CHÂTEAU GISCOURS +33 5 57 97 09 09

3e Cru Classé du Médoc 1855

FUTURES▼ Vintage 2012 Price: ❍ 91/100

CHÂTEAU KIRWAN +33 5 57 88 71 00

3e Cru Classé du Médoc 1855

FUTURES▼ Vintage 2012 Price: ❍ 92/100

CHÂTEAU LASCOMBES +33 5 57 88 70 66

▼ Chevalier de Lascombes Vintage 2008 Price: ❍❍❍ 90/100

CHÂTEAU MALESCOT SAINT-EXUPÉRY +33 5 57 88 97 20

3e Cru Classé du Médoc 1855

FUTURES▼ Vintage 2012 Price: ❍ 89/100

CHÂTEAU MARGAUX +33 5 57 88 83 83

1er Cru Classé du Médoc 1855

FUTURES▼ Vintage 2012 Price: ❍ 97/100

CHÂTEAU LASCOMBES

▼ Vintage 2008 **96/100**

Deep garnet-red. Racy nose of ripe red berry fruits with subtle oak undercurrents. Full-bodied palate showing a cheeky youthfulness. Fruit flows into liquorice tones. Power framed by stuffing. Already drinking well but with the capacity to age.

Price: OOOO

Wine and food pairing: Angus roast beef
Serving Temperature: 16-18°C
Ready to drink: 2014-2020

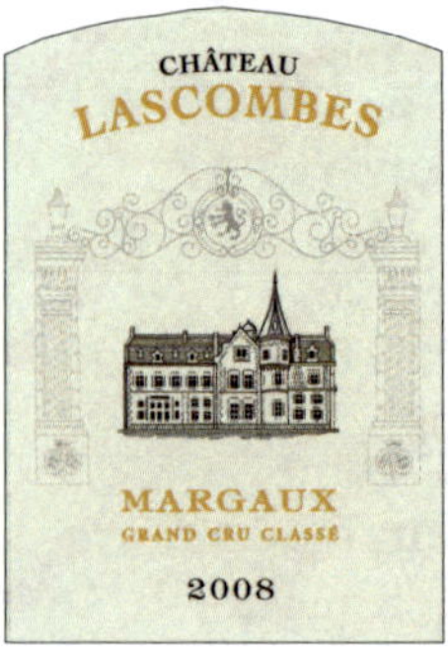

This estate is one of the oldest in Médoc, its first wines made by the Chevalier de Lascombes – who gave his name to the second of the estate's wines – as early as the first half of the 18th century. The estate covers 118 hectares in the Margaux appellation. The estate's new owners, the Health Professionals Mutual Fund (MACSF), have entrusted the existing team to continue producing a wine that is fully in keeping with its rank of second cru classé, as they have been over the last decade, most notably with the more recent vintages: 2006, 2008, 2009 and 2010 achieve a rare level of fullness. Seminars can be organised at the estate, benefiting from a superb setting and an outstanding welcome.

Château Lascombes
1 cours de Verdun - 33460 Margaux
Tel.: +33 (0)5 57 88 70 66 - Fax: +33 (0)5 57 88 72 17
E-mail: k.barbier@chateau-lascombes.fr
Website: http://www.chateau-lascombes.com

CHÂTEAU MARQUIS DE TERME
+33 5 57 88 30 01

4e Cru Classé du Médoc 1855

FUTURES ▼ Vintage 2012 Price: ❍ 91/100

CHÂTEAU PRIEURÉ-LICHINE
+33 5 57 88 36 28

4e Cru Classé du Médoc 1855

FUTURES ▼ Vintage 2012 Price: ❍ 91/100

CHÂTEAU RAUZAN-GASSIES
+33 5 57 88 71 88

2e Cru Classé du Médoc 1855

▼ Vintage 2012 Price: ❍ 92/100

CHÂTEAU RAUZAN-SÉGLA
+33 5 57 88 82 10

2e Cru Classé du Médoc 1855

FUTURES ▼ Vintage 2012 Price: ❍ 92/100

HAUT-BELLEVUE
+33 5 56 58 91 64

▼ 2010 Price: ❍❍❍ 89/100

MONGRAVEY
+33 5 56 58 84 51

Cru bourgeois du Médoc

▼ Vintage 2010 Price: ❍❍❍ 91/100

SOCIÉTÉ VITICOLE HENRI LURTON
+33 5 57 88 83 33

2e Cru Classé du Médoc 1855

FUTURES ▼ Château Brane-Cantenac Vintage 2012 Price: ❍ 93/100

VIGNOBLES MARIE-LAURE LURTON
+33 5 56 58 22 01

Cru bourgeois du Médoc

▼ Château La Tour de Bessan Vintage 2009 Price: ❍❍❍ 89/100

VIGNOBLES MIAILHE
+33 5 57 88 34 04

▼ S de Siran Vintage 2010 Price: ❍ 87/100

▼ Château Siran Vintage 2010 Price: ❍❍❍ 91/100

Médoc

CHÂTEAU CARMENÈRE
+33 6 52 70 63 28

▼ Petite Réserve 2011 Price: ❍ 83/100

CHÂTEAU DAVID
+33 5 56 09 44 62

Cru bourgeois du Médoc

▼ Vintage 2010 Price: ❍ 89/100

CHÂTEAU DE LUSSAN +33 5 56 09 03 30

▼ Cuvée Elégance 2011 Price: ❍ 85/100

▼ Vieilles Vignes 2011 Price: ❍❍ 86/100

CHÂTEAU FLEUR LA MOTHE +33 5 56 59 67 06

▼ Vintage 2010 Price: ❍❍ 87/100

CHATEAU FONTIS +33 5 56 09 06 06

Cru bourgeois du Médoc

▼ Vintage 2010 Price: ❍❍ 87/100

CHÂTEAU HOURBANON +33 5 56 41 02 88

▼ Vintage 2010 Price: ❍ 75/100

CHÂTEAU LA TOUR DE BY +33 5 56 41 50 03

▼ Vintage 2009 Price: ❍❍❍ 90/100

CHÂTEAU LE BOURDIEU +33 5 56 41 58 52

Cru bourgeois du Médoc

▼ Vintage 2010 Price: ❍❍ 88/100

CHÂTEAU LESTRUELLE +33 5 56 09 05 01

Crus bourgeois du Médoc

▼ Vintage 2010 Price: ❍ 86/100

CHÂTEAU LAULAN

▼ Vintage 2010 **86/100**

Deep garnet. Inviting nose of plum, refined spice and a touch of toast with an uplifting peony scent. Round attack, concentrated, dense and nervy palate exuding an impression of harmony. A hint of firmness mid-palate. A promising wine.

Price: ❍

Serving Temperature: 16-18°C - Ready to drink : 2014-2016

Château Laulan Ducos
4 route de Vertamont
33590 Jau Dignac et Loirac
Tel.: +33 05 56 09 42 37 - Fax: +33 05 56 09 48 40
E-mail: chateau@laulanducos.com
Website: www.laulanducos.com

▼ Château Maison Blanche Vintage 2010 Price: ❍ 87/100

CHÂTEAU LOUDENNE +33 5 56 73 17 88

Cru bourgeois du Médoc

▼ Vintage 2010 Price: ❍❍ 85/100

CHÂTEAU SIGOGNAC +33 5 56 09 05 04

▼ Vintage 2010 Price: ❍❍ 87/100

CHÂTEAUX EN BORDEAUX +33 5 57 43 43 82

Cru bourgeois du Médoc

▼ Château Vernous Vintage 2011 Price: ❍ 84/100

CHÂTEAUX ET DOMAINES CASTEL +33 5 56 95 54 00

▼ Château Tour Prignac 2011 Price: ❍ 85/100

▼ Château Tour Prignac Grande Réserve 2010 Price: ❍❍ 87/100

COURREGES WINES +33 5 56 91 21 96

▼ Château Cérestin La Lande Vintage 2012 Price: ❍ 87/100

DOMAINES LAPALU +33 5 56 41 50 18

▼ Château Lacombe Noaillac 2011 Price: ❍❍ 85/100

▼ Château les Traverses La Franque 2011 Price: ❍❍ 86/100

▼ Les Chevaux de Patache d'Aux 2011 Price: ❍❍ 86/100

▼ Château Leboscq Vintage 2011 Price: ❍❍ 87/100

▼ Château Patache d'Aux 2011 Price: ❍❍ 88/100

DWL FRANCE +33 5 56 41 37 00

▼ Château de Panigon Vintage 2011 Price: ❍ 83/100

▼ Château Amour Vintage 2011 Price: ❍ 86/100

GILLET CYRIL +33 5 56 41 50 42

Cru bourgeois du Médoc

▼ Vintage 2010 Price: ❍❍ 87/100

JEAN BOIVERT ET FILS +33 5 56 73 30 30

▼ Château de Conques Vintage 2010 Price: ❍❍ 85/100

Cru bourgeois du Médoc

▼ Château Les Ormes Sorbet Vintage 2009 Price: ❍❍ 89/100

Prices mentioned in this book are guideline and can vary depending on point of sale. The shops, wineries or publisher can in no way be held responsible for this.

LES VIGNERONS D'UNI-MÉDOC +33 5 56 41 03 12

▼ Château Moulin de Hontemieux Vintage 2011 Price: ❍ 84/100

ORG▼ Château Moulin De Riba Vintage 2011 Price: ❍ 85/100

UIJTTEWAAL A ET F +33 5 56 59 80 88

Cru bourgeois du Médoc

▼ Château Gemeillan Vintage 2010 Price: ❍ 83/100

Cru bourgeois du Médoc

▼ Château Saint-Hilaire Vintage 2010 Price: ❍ 84/100

VIGNOBLES BEUVIN +33 6 66 77 66 36

▼ Les Hauts de Tousquiron Vintage 2009 Price: ❍❍ 87/100

VIGNOBLES DUBOSCQ +33 5 56 59 30 54

▼ Château Layauga-Duboscq

Cuvée Renaissance 2009 Price: ❍❍ 89/100

Montagne-Saint-Emilion

VIGNOBLES CAPDEMOURLIN +33 5 57 74 62 06

▼ Vintage 2008 Price: ❍❍ 87/100

▼ Vintage 2009 Price: ❍❍ 88/100

VIGNOBLES G. ARPIN +33 9 71 58 23 49

▼ Château Gachon Vintage 2010 Price: ❍ 87/100

VIGNOBLES JEAN-NOËL BOIDRON +33 5 57 51 64 88

▼ Bonbec par Boidron Vintage 2005 Price: ❍❍ 85/100

▼ Château Calon Vintage 2010 Price: ❍❍ 85/100

Moulis

CHÂTEAU BISTON-BRILLETTE +33 5 56 58 22 86

▼ Château Biston Vintage 2010 Price: ❍❍ 88/100

Cru bourgeois du Médoc

▼ Vintage 2010 Price: ❍❍ 89/100

CHÂTEAU LAGORCE BERNADAS +33 5 53 24 77 98

▼ Vintage 2010 Price: ○○ 87/100

COUBRIS JLC +33 5 56 17 13 17

▼ Château La Mouline Vintage 2010 Price: ○○ 91/100

HAUT-BELLEVUE +33 5 56 58 91 64

▼ Vintage 2010 Price: ○○ 87/100

VIGNOBLES LARTIGUE +33 5 56 58 27 63

▼ Château Myon de l'Enclos Millésime 2010 Price: ○○ 89/100

VIGNOBLES MARIE-LAURE LURTON +33 5 56 58 22 01

Cru bourgeois du Médoc

▼ Château Duplessis Vintage 2009 Price: ○○ 88/100

Pauillac

BORIE MANOUX +33 5 56 00 00 70

5e Cru Classé du Médoc 1855

FUTURES▼ Château Batailley 2012 Price: ○ 92/100

5e Cru Classé du Médoc 1855

FUTURES▼ Château Lynch-Moussas 2012 Price: ○ 92/100

CHÂTEAU D'ARMAILHAC +33 5 56 73 20 20

5e Cru Classé du Médoc 1855

FUTURES▼ Vintage 2012 Price: ○ 93/100

CHÂTEAU BELLEGRAVE +33 5 56 59 05 53

▼ Vintage 2010 Price: ○○○ 88/100

CHÂTEAU CLERC MILON +33 5 56 73 20 20

5e Cru Classé du Médoc 1855

FUTURES▼ Vintage 2012 Price: ○ 91/100

CHÂTEAU DUHART-MILON +33 5 56 73 18 18

FUTURES▼ Vintage 2012 Price: ○ 90/100

CHÂTEAU GRAND-PUY DUCASSE +33 5 56 59 00 40

5e Cru Classé du Médoc 1855

FUTURES▼ Vintage 2012 Price: ○ 92/100

CHÂTEAU GRAND-PUY LACOSTE +33 5 56 59 06 66

5e Cru Classé du Médoc 1855

FUTURES▼ Vintage 2012 Price: ○ 92/100

CHÂTEAU HAUT-BAGES LIBÉRAL +33 5 56 58 02 37

5e Cru Classé du Médoc 1855

FUTURES▼ Vintage 2012 Price: ❍ 91/100

CHÂTEAU LAFITE ROTHSCHILD +33 5 56 73 18 18

FUTURES▼ Vintage 2012 Price: ❍ 95/100

CHÂTEAU MOUTON ROTHSCHILD

1er Cru Classé du Médoc 1855

FUTURES▼ Vintage 2012 Price: ❍ 96/100

CHÂTEAU PEYRABON +33 5 56 59 57 10

▼ Château La Fleur Peyrabon 2010 Price: ❍❍❍ 90/100

CHÂTEAU PICHON LONGUEVILLE BARON +33 5 56 73 17 17

2e Cru Classé du Médoc 1855

FUTURES▼ Vintage 2012 Price: ❍ 89/100

CHÂTEAU PICHON LONGUEVILLE COMTESSE DE LALANDE +33 5 56 59 19 40

2e Cru Classé du Médoc 1855

FUTURES▼ Vintage 2012 Price: ❍ 94/100

DOMAINES JEAN-MICHEL CAZES +33 5 56 73 24 00

5e Cru Classé du Médoc 1855

FUTURES▼ Château Lynch-Bages 2012 Price: ❍ 93/100

VIGNOBLES QUIÉ +33 5 56 59 66 69

5e Cru Classé du Médoc 1855

FUTURES▼ Château Croizet-Bages 2012 Price: ❍ 90/100

Pessac-Léognan

CHÂTEAU PAPE CLÉMENT +33 5 57 26 38 38

Grand Cru Classé de Graves (white)

FUTURES▼ Vintage 2012 Price: ❍ 93/100

Grand Cru Classé de Graves (red)

FUTURES▼ Vintage 2012 Price: ❍ 93/100

CHÂTEAU BOUSCAUT +33 5 57 83 12 20

Grand Cru Classé de Graves (white)

FUTURES▼ Vintage 2012 Price: ❍ 91/100

Grand Cru Classé de Graves (red)

FUTURES▼ Vintage 2012 Price: ❍ 92/100

Detailed instructions are featured at the start of the book.

CHÂTEAU DE FIEUZAL +33 5 56 64 77 86

Grand Cru Classé de Graves (white)

FUTURES ▼ Vintage 2012 Price: ❍ 88/100

Grand Cru Classé de Graves (red)

FUTURES ▼ Vintage 2012 Price: ❍ 92/100

CHÂTEAU DE LÉOGNAN +33 5 56 64 14 96

▼ Château Léognan Vintage 2009 Price: ❍❍❍ 88/100

CHÂTEAU FERRAN +33 9 77 64 23 11

▼ Vintage 2009 Price: ❍❍ 88/100

▼ Vintage 2011 Price: ❍❍ 90/100

CHÂTEAU HAUT-BAILLY +33 5 56 64 75 11

Grand Cru Classé de Graves (red)

FUTURES ▼ Vintage 2012 Price: ❍ 90/100

CHÂTEAU HAUT-LAGRANGE +33 5 56 64 09 93

▼ Château Haut Lagrange Vintage 2010 Price: ❍❍ 91/100

CHÂTEAU LE SARTRE +33 5 56 64 08 78

▼ Château Bois-Martin Vintage 2011 Price: ❍❍ 88/100

▼ Vintage 2010 Price: ❍❍ 90/100

▼ Château Bois-Martin Vintage 2010 Price: ❍❍ 90/100

▼ Vintage 2011 Price: ❍❍ 91/100

CHÂTEAU LES CARMES HAUT-BRION +33 5 56 93 23 40

FUTURES ▼ Vintage 2012 Price: ❍ 94/100

CHÂTEAU MALARTIC-LAGRAVIÈRE +33 5 56 64 75 08

▼ La Réserve de Malartic Vintage 2010 Price: ❍ 88/100

▼ Château Gazin Rocquencourt Vintage 2010 Price: ❍ 91/100

Grand Cru Classé de Graves (white)

▼ Château Malartic-Lagravière 2010 Price: ❍ 91/100

Grand Cru Classé de Graves (red)

FUTURES ▼ Château Malartic-Lagravière 2012 Price: ❍ 92/100

Grand Cru Classé de Graves (white)

FUTURES ▼ Château Malartic-Lagravière 2012 Price: ❍ 92/100

Grand Cru Classé de Graves (red)

▼ Château Malartic-Lagravière 2010 Price: ❍ 94/100

CHÂTEAU OLIVIER +33 5 56 64 73 31

Grand Cru Classé de Graves (red)

FUTURES ▼ Vintage 2012 Price: ❍ 91/100

Grand Cru Classé de Graves (white)

FUTURES ▼ Vintage 2012 Price: ❍ 92/100

Grand Cru Classé de Graves (red)

▼ Vintage 2010 Price: ❍❍❍ 92/100

CHÂTEAU SMITH HAUT-LAFITTE +33 5 57 83 11 22

Grand Cru Classé de Graves (red)

FUTURES ▼ Vintage 2012 Price: n/a 91/100

Grand Cru Classé de Graves (white)

FUTURES ▼ Vintage 2012 Price: n/a 91/100

CHÂTEAU LA MISSION HAUT-BRION +33 5 56 00 29 30

Grand Cru Classé de Graves (red)

FUTURES ▼ Vintage 2012 Price: n/a 96/100

CHÂTEAU HAUT-BRION

Grand Cru Classé de Graves (red)

FUTURES ▼ Vintage 2012 Price: n/a 96/100

DOMAINE DE CHEVALIER +33 5 56 64 16 16

Grand Cru Classé de Graves (white)

FUTURES ▼ Vintage 2012 Price: n/a 90/100

Grand Cru Classé de Graves (red)

FUTURES ▼ Vintage 2012 Price: n/a 93/100

MICHEL GONET ET FILS +33 5 57 24 51 23

▼ Château Saint Eugène Vintage 2011 Price: n/a 85/100

▼ Château Haut l'Evêque Vintage 2011 Price: n/a 85/100

▼ Château d'Eck Vintage 2011 Price: n/a 86/100

▼ Château Saint Eugène Vintage 2010 Price: n/a 88/100

▼ Château Haut l'Evêque Vintage 2010 Price: n/a 89/100

▼ Château d'Eck Vintage 2010 Price: n/a 90/100

VIGNOBLES JEAN KRESSMANN +33 5 57 97 71 11

Grand Cru Classé de Graves (white)

FUTURES ▼ Château Latour-Martillac 2012 Price: n/a 90/100

VIGNOBLES PERRIN +33 5 57 96 56 20

Grand Cru Classé de Graves (red)

FUTURES ▼ Château Carbonnieux 2012 Price: n/a 89/100

Grand Cru Classé de Graves (white)

FUTURES ▼ Château Carbonnieux 2012 Price: n/a 89/100

VIGNOBLES THOMASSIN +33 5 56 64 75 39

▼ Château de France 2008 Price: OOO 91/100

▼ Château de France 2011 Price: OOO 91/100

Detailed instructions are featured at the start of the book.

Pomerol

BERNARD MOUEIX +33 5 57 25 50 45

▼ Château Taillefer 2010 Price: ❍❍❍ 91/100

CHARLES LEYMARIE ET FILS +33 5 57 51 07 83

▼ Château La Bassonnerie 2007 Price: ❍❍ 87/100

▼ Château La Bassonnerie 2008 Price: ❍❍ 89/100

CHÂTEAU LA GANNE +33 5 57 51 18 24

▼ Vintage 2010 Price: ❍❍❍ 90/100

CHÂTEAU PLINCE +33 5 57 51 68 77

▼ Vintage 2006 Price: ❍❍❍ 89/100

VIGNOBLES G. ARPIN +33 9 71 58 23 49

▼ Château Franc-Maillet 2010 Price: ❍❍❍ 93/100

VIGNOBLES JEAN-NOËL BOIDRON +33 5 57 51 64 88

▼ Château Cantelauze 2010 Price: ❍❍❍ 88/100

VIGNOBLES PAGANELLI-ESTAGER +33 6 11 22 66 00

▼ Domaine du Rempart 2011 Price: ❍❍❍ 88/100

▼ Domaine du Rempart 2010 Price: ❍❍❍ 89/100

VIGNOBLES PÉRÉ-VERGÉ +33 3 20 64 20 56

▼ Château Montviel 2009 Price: ❍❍❍ 92/100

Puisseguin-Saint-Emilion

CHÂTEAUX EN BORDEAUX +33 5 57 43 43 82

▼ Château La Vaisinerie Merlot 2011 Price: ❍ 83/100

▼ Château La Vaisinerie Quercus 2010 Price: ❍ 83/100

FOUCARD & FILS +33 5 57 51 11 40

▼ Château Chêne-Vieux Cuvée Première 2010 Price: ❍ 88/100

▼ Château Chêne-Vieux Cuvée Première 2009 Price: ❍ 89/100

FRANÇOISE ET PHILIPPE LANNOYE +33 5 57 55 23 28

▼ Château Lanbersac
Cuvée Vieilles Vignes 2010 Price: ❍❍ 85/100

Sainte-Croix-du-Mont

CHÂTEAU DES ARROUCATS +33 5 56 62 07 37

▼ Vintage 2010 Price: ❍ — 88/100

Saint-Emilion

CHÂTEAU CLOS SAINT-EMILION PHILIPPE +33 5 57 51 05 93

▼ Cuvée du Père 2011 Price: ❍❍ — 87/100

VIGNOBLES OUZOULIAS +33 5 57 51 07 55

ORG▼ Clos Chante l'Alouette 2010 Price: ❍❍ — 88/100

VIGNOBLES PAGANELLI-ESTAGER +33 6 11 22 66 00

▼ Château La Pointe Chantecaille 2011 Price: ❍❍ — 88/100

VIGNOBLES PUYOL +33 5 57 24 73 31

▼ Joseph Daragon 2011 Price: ❍ — 87/100

+33 5 57 24 73 31

▼ Château Beaurang 2010 Price: ❍❍ — 88/100

Saint-Emilion Grand Cru

BARON DE MONTFORT - CHÂTEAU DU ROCHER +33 5 57 40 18 20

CV▼ Château du Rocher 2010 Price: ❍❍ — 86/100

BERNARD MOUEIX +33 5 57 25 50 45

▼ Château Tauzinat l'Hermitage 2010 Price: ❍❍❍ — 90/100

BORIE MANOUX +33 5 56 00 00 70

1er Grand Cru Classé de Saint-Emilion B

FUTURES▼ ChâteauTrottevieille 2012 Price: ❍ — 92/100

CLOS TRIMOULET

▼ Vintage 2010 **90/100**

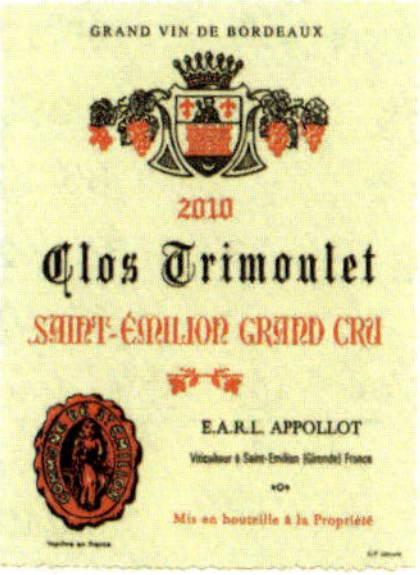

Beautiful deep red. After swirling, the nose deploys fruity tones with subtle mineral undercurrents. Wonderful full, expressive and crunchy attack. Substantial length on the finish driven by crunchy fruit and liquorice fragrances.

Price: ○○

Serving Temperature: 16-18°C
Ready to drink : 2014-2016

Appollot
Clos Trimoulet - 33330 Saint Emilion
Tel.: +33 05 57 24 71 96 - Fax: +33 05 57 74 45 88
E-mail: contact@clos-trimoulet.com
Website: http://www.clos-trimoulet.com

CHÂTEAU ANGÉLUS — +33 5 57 24 71 39

1er Grand Cru Classé de Saint-Emilion A

FUTURES▼ Vintage 2012 Price: ○ — 94/100

CHÂTEAU BEAUSÉJOUR DUFFAU — +33 5 57 24 71 61

1er Grand Cru Classé de Saint-Emilion B

FUTURES▼ Vintage 2012 Price: ○ — 93/100

CHÂTEAU BELLE ASSISE — +33 5 57 24 61 62

▼ Les Francs de Belle Assise 2010 Price: ○○○ — 87/100

▼ Château Orme Brun 2010 Price: ○○ — 89/100

▼ Les Grands Ormes 2010 Price: ○○ — 90/100

CHÂTEAU CADET-BON — +33 5 57 74 43 20

Grand Cru Classé de Saint-Emilion

▼ Vintage 2010 Price: ○○○ — 92/100

CHÂTEAU CANON — +33 5 57 55 23 48

1er Grand Cru Classé de Saint-Emilion B

FUTURES▼ Vintage 2012 Price: ○ — 94/100

Detailed instructions are featured at the start of the book.

CHÂTEAU CANTENAC +33 5 57 51 35 22

▼ Sélection Madame 2010 Price: ○○ 88/100

▼ Vintage 2010 Price: ○○○ 90/100

CHÂTEAU CHEVAL BLANC +33 5 57 55 55 55

1er Grand Cru Classé de Saint-Emilion A

FUTURES▼ Château Cheval-Blanc 2012 Price: ○ 96/100

CHÂTEAU CLOS SAINT-EMILION PHILIPPE +33 5 57 51 05 93

▼ Vintage 2011 Price: ○○ 86/100

CHÂTEAU COUTET +33 5 57 74 43 21

CV▼ Vintage 2010 Price: ○○ 89/100

CHÂTEAU CROQUE MICHOTTE +33 5 57 51 13 64

ORG▼ Vintage 2009 Price: ○○○ 89/100

ORG▼ Vintage 2010 Price: ○○○ 90/100

CHÂTEAU DE LA COUR +33 5 57 84 64 95

▼ Vintage 2010 Price: ○○ 91/100

CHÂTEAU FLEUR CARDINALE +33 5 57 40 14 05

Grand Cru Classé de Saint-Emilion

▼ Vintage 2010 Price: ○ 91/100

▼ Vintage 2009 Price: ○ 91/100

CHÂTEAU GODEAU +33 5 57 24 72 64

▼ Vintage 2008 Price: ○○ 87/100

CHÂTEAU GRAND CORBIN MANUEL +33 5 57 25 09 68

▼ Vintage 2009 Price: ○○ 89/100

CHÂTEAU GRAND-PONTET +33 5 57 74 46 88

▼ Vintage 2011 Price: ○ 89/100

CHÂTEAU HAUT ROCHER +33 5 57 40 18 09

▼ Vintage 2010 Price: ○○ 89/100

CHÂTEAU HAUTE NAUVE +33 5 57 24 73 21

▼ Son Altesse de Haute-Nauve 2010 Price: ○○ 87/100

CHÂTEAU LA ROSE-POURRET +33 5 57 24 71 13

▼ Vintage 2010 Price: ○○ 88/100

CHÂTEAU LANIOTE +33 5 57 24 70 80

Grand Cru Classé de Saint-Emilion

▼ Vintage 2010 Price: ○○○ 88/100

CHÂTEAU LARCIS DUCASSE +33 5 57 24 70 84

1er Grand Cru Classé de Saint-Emilion B

FUTURES▼ Vintage 2012 Price: ○ 87/100

CHÂTEAU MONLOT +33 5 57 74 49 47

▼ Vintage 2011 Price: ❍ 82/100

CHÂTEAU PAVIE MACQUIN +33 5 57 24 74 23

1er Grand Cru Classé de Saint-Emilion B

FUTURES▼ Vintage 2012 Price: ❍ 93/100

CHÂTEAU PETIT VAL +33 5 57 24 70 86

▼ Vintage 2010 Price: ❍❍ 86/100

CHÂTEAU SAINT-LÔ +33 5 33 20 01 44

▼ Vintage 2010 Price: ❍❍ 86/100

CHÂTEAU TOUR GRAND FAURIE +33 5 57 74 49 03

▼ Vintage 2007 Price: ❍❍ 87/100

▼ Vintage 2011 Price: ❍❍ 87/100

▼ Vintage 2010 Price: ❍❍ 89/100

▼ Vintage 2009 Price: ❍❍ 91/100

CHÂTEAU TOUR POURRET +33 5 57 55 23 28

▼ Château Ambe Tour Pourret Vintage 2010 Price: ❍❍❍ 88/100

CLOS FOURTET +33 5 57 24 70 90

1er Grand Cru Classé de Saint-Emilion B

FUTURES▼ Château Clos Fourtet Vintage 2012 Price: ❍ 92/100

DOMAINE DE VALMENGAUX +33 5 57 74 48 92

CV▼ La Dame de Onze Heures 2010 Price: ❍❍❍ 90/100

ETS THUVENIN +33 5 57 55 09 13

1er Grand Cru Classé de Saint-Emilion B

FUTURES▼ Château Valandraud 2012 Price: ❍ 95/100

FAMILLE MANONCOURT +33 5 57 24 77 26

▼ Château de Millery 2010 Price: ❍ 88/100

▼ Petit Figeac 2010 Price: ❍ 89/100

▼ Château La Fleur Pourret 2010 Price: ❍ 90/100

▼ La Grange Neuve de Figeac 2010 Price: ❍ 92/100

1er Grand Cru Classé de Saint-Emilion B

FUTURES▼ Château Figeac 2012 Price: ❍ 96/100

▼ Château Figeac 2010 Price: ❍ 98/100

FAURE BARRAUD +33 5 57 24 65 93

▼ Château Franc Patarabet Vintage 2010 Price: ❍❍ 88/100

▼ Château Franc Patarabet Cuvée Les Menuts
Vieilles Vignes 2009 Price: ❍❍ 90/100

JEAN-PIERRE MOUEIX SA +33 5 57 51 78 96
1er Grand Cru Classé de Saint-Emilion B

FUTURES▼ Château Belair-Monange 2012 Price: ❍ 89/100

MAISON MALET ROQUEFORT +33 5 57 56 40 80
1er Grand Cru Classé de Saint-Emilion B

FUTURES▼ Château La Gaffelière 2012 Price: ❍ 95/100

VIGNOBLES CAPDEMOURLIN +33 5 57 74 62 06
Grand Cru Classé de Saint-Emilion

▼ Château Petit Faurie de Soutard 2010 Price: ❍❍❍ 90/100

VIGNOBLES COMTES VON NEIPPERG +33 5 57 24 71 33
1er Grand Cru Classé de Saint-Emilion B

FUTURES▼ La Mondotte Vintage 2012 Price: ❍ 91/100

FUTURES▼ Château Canon La Gaffelière 2012 Price: ❍ 91/100

VIGNOBLES DOMINIQUE LAURET +33 5 57 24 72 95

▼ Château Pindefleurs Vintage 2010 Price: ❍❍❍ 88/100

VIGNOBLES JACQUES BERTRAND +33 5 57 24 73 94

▼ Château Franc Pipeau Vintage 2010 Price: ❍❍ 87/100

▼ Château Carteau Côtes Daugay 2010 Price: ❍❍ 89/100

VIGNOBLES JB BRUNOT & FILS +33 5 57 55 09 99

▼ Château Piganeau Vintage 2010 Price: ❍❍ 89/100

VIGNOBLES JEAN-NOËL BOIDRON +33 5 57 51 64 88
Grand Cru Classé de Saint-Emilion

▼ Château Corbin Michotte Vintage 2010 Price: ❍❍❍ 90/100

VIGNOBLES OUZOULIAS +33 5 57 51 07 55

ORG▼ Château Tourbadon 2010 Price: ❍ 86/100

ORG▼ Domaine du Haut Patarabet 2009 Price: ❍❍ 88/100

ORG▼ Château Franc-Pourret 2009 Price: ❍❍ 89/100

VIGNOBLES PERSE +33 5 57 55 43 43
1er Grand Cru Classé de Saint-Emilion A

FUTURES▼ Château Pavie 2012 Price: ❍ 94/100

VIGNOBLES QUENIN +33 5 57 40 18 02

▼ Château de Pressac 2010 Price: ❍❍❍ 89/100

Prices mentioned in this book are guideline and can vary depending on point of sale. The shops, wineries or publisher can in no way be held responsible for this.

Saint-Estèphe

ARNAUD SA +33 5 56 59 32 26

▼ Vintage 2010 Price: OO 88/100

▼ Vintage 2010 Price: OO 89/100

CHÂTEAU LA HAYE +33 5 56 59 32 18

▼ Vintage 2010 Price: OOO 89/100

CHÂTEAU LA PEYRE +33 5 56 59 32 51

▼ Vintage 2010 Price: OO 88/100

CHÂTEAU LAFON-ROCHET +33 5 56 59 32 06

4e Cru Classé du Médoc 1855

FUTURES▼ Vintage 2012 Price: O 92/100

4e Cru Classé du Médoc 1855

▼ Vintage 2009 Price: OOOO 92/100

CHÂTEAU TOUR SAINT-FORT +33 5 56 34 16 16

Cru bourgeois du Médoc

▼ Vintage 2010 Price: OO 88/100

CHÂTEAU TRONQUOY-LALANDE +33 5 56 59 30 12

▼ Vintage 2010 Price: OOO 88/100

VIGNOBLES JEAN ANNEY +33 5 56 59 32 89

▼ Château Tour des Termes Vintage 2010 Price: OOO 87/100

VIGNOBLES AUDOY +33 5 56 59 30 22

5e Cru Classé du Médoc 1855

FUTURES▼ Château Cos Labory Vintage 2012 Price: O 92/100

VIGNOBLES DUBOSCQ +33 5 56 59 30 54

▼ Château Haut-Marbuzet Vintage 2010 Price: OOO 92/100

▼ Château Haut-Marbuzet Vintage 2009 Price: OOO 94/100

Saint-Georges Saint-Emilion

CHÂTEAU SAINT-GEORGES +33 5 57 74 62 11

▼ Vintage 2011 Price: OOO 89/100

Bordeaux - *Saint-Georges Saint-Émilion*

CHÂTEAU TOUR GRAND FAURIE +33 5 57 74 49 03

▼ Château Feytit Divon Vintage 2010 Price: ❍❍ 87/100

DELBECK VIGNOBLES ET DÉVELOPPEMENTS +33 5 57 24 70 94

▼ Château Tour du Pas Saint-Georges 2010 Price: ❍❍ 88/100

VIGNOBLES JEAN-NOËL BOIDRON +33 5 57 51 64 88

▼ Château Calon Vintage 2010 Price: ❍❍ 83/100

Saint-Julien

CHÂTEAU BEYCHEVELLE +33 5 56 73 20 70

4e Cru Classé du Médoc 1855

FUTURES▼ Vintage 2012 Price: ❍ 92/100

CHÂTEAU BRANAIRE-DUCRU +33 5 56 59 25 86

4e Cru Classé du Médoc 1855

FUTURES▼ Vintage 2012 Price: ❍ 90/100

CHÂTEAU DU GLANA +33 5 56 59 06 47

▼ Vintage 2010 Price: ❍❍❍ 90/100

CHÂTEAU GRUAUD LAROSE +33 5 56 73 15 20

2e Cru Classé du Médoc 1855

FUTURES▼ Vintage 2012 Price: ❍ 92/100

CHÂTEAU LAGRANGE +33 5 56 73 38 38

3e Cru Classé du Médoc 1855

FUTURES▼ Vintage 2012 Price: ❍ 91/100

CHÂTEAU LÉOVILLE BARTON +33 5 56 59 06 05

3e Cru Classé du Médoc 1855

FUTURES▼ Château Langoa Barton 2012 Price: ❍ 89/100

2e Cru Classé du Médoc 1855

FUTURES▼ Vintage 2012 Price: ❍ 92/100

CHÂTEAU LÉOVILLE POYFERRÉ +33 5 56 59 08 30

2e Cru Classé du Médoc 1855

FUTURES▼ Vintage 2012 Price: ❍ 90/100

CHÂTEAU TALBOT +33 5 56 73 21 50

4e Cru Classé du Médoc 1855

FUTURES▼ Vintage 2012 Price: ❍ 92/100

DOMAINES HENRI MARTIN +33 5 56 59 08 18

4e Cru Classé du Médoc 1855

FUTURES▼ Château Saint-Pierre Vintage 2012 Price: ❍ 89/100

Sauternes

CHÂTEAU BROUSTET +33 5 56 27 16 87

2e Cru Classé de Sauternes 1855

FUTURES ▼ Vintage 2012 Price: ❍ 92/100

CHÂTEAU CAILLOU +33 5 56 27 16 38

2e Cru Classé de Sauternes 1855

▼ Vintage 2009 Price: ❍❍❍ 92/100

▼ Les Erables de Caillou Vintage 2009 Price: ❍❍❍ 89/100

CHÂTEAU COUTET +33 5 56 27 15 46

1er Cru Classé de Sauternes 1855

FUTURES ▼ Vintage 2012 Price: ❍ 94/100

CHÂTEAU DE MALLE +33 5 56 62 36 86

2e Cru Classé de Sauternes 1855

FUTURES ▼ Vintage 2012 Price: ❍ 92/100

CHÂTEAU HAUT-BERGERON +33 5 56 63 24 76

▼ Vintage 2010 Price: ❍❍❍ 91/100

CHÂTEAU LA TOUR BLANCHE +33 5 57 98 02 73

1er Cru Classé de Sauternes 1855

FUTURES ▼ Vintage 2012 Price: ❍ 92/100

CHÂTEAU LAMOTHE DESPUJOLS +33 5 56 76 67 89

2e Cru Classé de Sauternes 1855

▼ Vintage 2010 Price: ❍❍❍ 88/100

CHÂTEAU ROMER +33 5 56 63 24 04

2e Cru Classé de Sauternes 1855

FUTURES ▼ Vintage 2012 Price: ❍ 90/100

CORDIER MESTREZAT GRANDS CRUS +33 5 56 11 29 00

1er Cru Classé de Sauternes 1855

FUTURES ▼ Château de Rayne Vigneau 2012 Price: ❍ 90/100

1er Cru Classé de Sauternes 1855

FUTURES ▼ Château Sigalas-Rabaud 2012 Price: ❍ 90/100

PIERRE ET DENIS DUBOURDIEU +33 5 56 62 96 51

FUTURES ▼ Château Doisy-Daëne 2012 Price: ❍ 93/100

VIGNOBLES BON +33 5 56 63 28 29

▼ Château Les Rochers 2011 Price: ❍❍ 86/100

VIGNOBLES DU HAYOT +33 5 56 27 15 37

2e Cru Classé de Sauternes 1855

▼ Château Romer du Hayot 2010 Price: ❍❍❍ 88/100

VIGNOBLES PAULY +33 5 56 76 61 53

1er Cru Classé de Sauternes 1855

FUTURES▼ Château Haut Peyraguey 2012 Price: ❍ 90/100

VIGNOBLES PÉTROFFE +33 5 56 76 60 54

1er Cru Classé de Sauternes 1855

FUTURES▼ Château Lafaurie-Peyraguey 2012 Price: ❍ 89/100

WINE SCORES:

95-100/100: an outstanding wine, when a great 'terroir' meets exceptional winemaking expertise.

90-94/100: a superlative wine combining finesse, complexity and remarkable winemaking.

85-89/100:a wine of extremely high standard, which we enjoyed for its typicity and character.

80-84/100: a quality wine combining balance, structure and neatness for a pleasurable wine drinking experience.

75-79/100: a wine deemed acceptable.

70-74/100: a wine with defects, unacceptable.

65-69/100: a wine with major defects, inadmissible.

50-64/100: unacceptable wine, not worthy for sale.

Note: *wines scoring less than 75/100 are not included in our publications.*

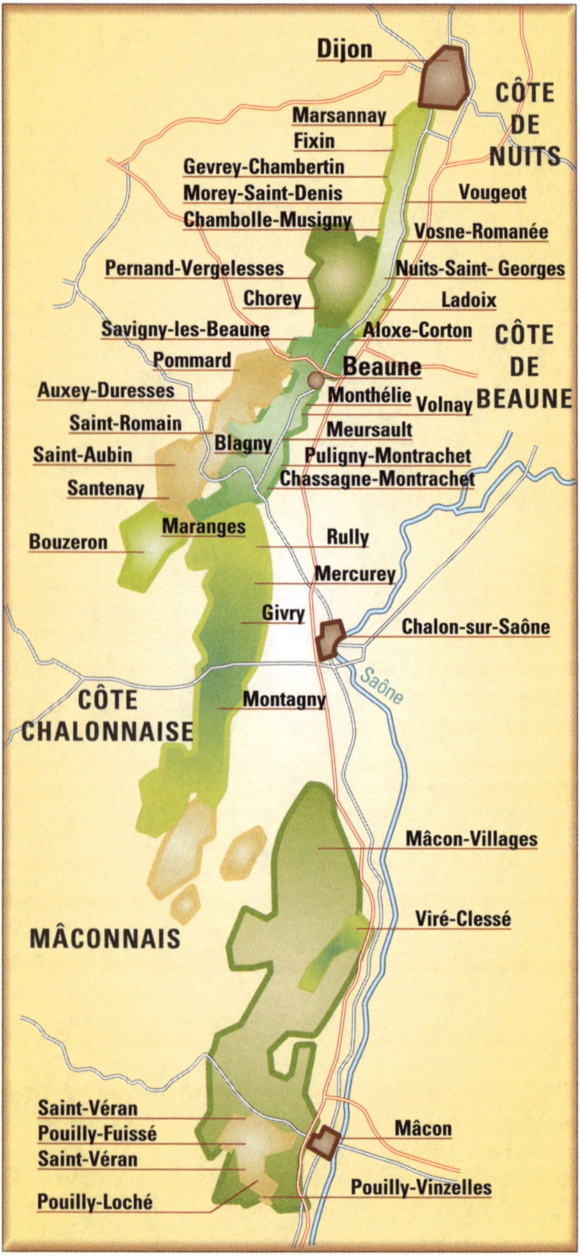
Dijon
CÔTE DE NUITS
Marsannay
Fixin
Gevrey-Chambertin
Morey-Saint-Denis
Chambolle-Musigny
Vougeot
Vosne-Romanée
Nuits-Saint- Georges
Pernand-Vergelesses
Chorey
Ladoix
Savigny-les-Beaune
Aloxe-Corton
CÔTE DE BEAUNE
Pommard
Beaune
Auxey-Duresses
Monthélie
Volnay
Saint-Romain
Meursault
Blagny
Saint-Aubin
Puligny-Montrachet
Chassagne-Montrachet
Santenay
Maranges
Bouzeron
Rully
Mercurey
Givry
Chalon-sur-Saône
Saône
CÔTE CHALONNAISE
Montagny
Mâcon-Villages
Viré-Clessé
MÂCONNAIS
Saint-Véran
Pouilly-Fuissé
Saint-Véran
Mâcon
Pouilly-Vinzelles
Pouilly-Loché

BURGUNDY

A MULTI-FACETED WINE REGION

The wine region of Burgundy is a jigsaw puzzle with myriad pieces; understanding its intricacies requires both time and patience. The aim of this wine guide is to provide the ways and means of finding one's way around the appellations, climate-specific sites, first growths and great growths; a map of the region also locates all the appellations... In this multi-faceted wine region, there are only a few large, clear-cut geographical entities. Before detailing them, here is an overall picture of the area.

The diversity of Burgundy is so great that it is impossible to generalise, either about its geography, the appellations, the different climates, aspects, soil permeability or structure...
The character of the wines covers such a broad spectrum that it would be a challenge to do so. There are two generalisations, however, that can be made, on the climatic influences and area under vine. Burgundy's climate is defined both by westerly maritime winds, which shed most of their rainfall over the Morvan mountain range, and continental influences which bring the predominantly cold, dry northerly winds that vines need to ward off disease. On-stream area under vine covers around 26,000 hectares, equivalent to roughly 6% of French vineyard acreage, spread over 3 departments: Yonne, 6,200 hectares, Côte-d'Or, 9,550 and Saône-et-Loire, 10,950 ha.
On the varietal front, three leading actors take centre stage, with a clutch of supporting roles. The vast majority of red wines are drawn from Pinot noir, Burgundy's quintessential noble varietal, and the whites from Chardonnay, though Bourgogne Aligoté is also made from the grape of the same name.
Although they are made on a more boutique scale, in Yonne, red wines around Auxerre are made entirely or partly from the Cesar grape variety, or occasionally from Tressot (virtually obsolete).

In the northern part of Côte-d'Or and Yonne, Sacy, Pinot blanc and Melon are blended into Crémant de Bourgogne. Sauvignon, far from its favoured sites here, is used in Saint-Bris-le Vineux (Yonne). The stage is now set, enter Burgundy's large geographical entities, from the northernmost reaches down to the northern boundaries of Beaujolais in Rhône-Alpes.

CHABLIS

Chablis wines belong to the elite circle of legendary French wines. They are often copied but remain peerless. Running the gamut from the Grands Crus (7 in number), the Premiers Crus (around 40), down through to the 'generic' or Petit Chablis, they all have one point in common: they are all drawn from the Chardonnay varietal, which thrives here on Kimmeridgian calcareous clay marl. The only cloud on this otherwise unspoilt horizon, is the harsh weather conditions which bring frequent bouts of frost in the winter and spring. Yet, this is precisely what gives Chablis its highly distinctive character. The same goes for its neighbours around Auxerre and Tonnerre.

The northern part of Burgundy is anything but uniform. The first area, around Auxerre, boasts Irancy (south of Auxerre), a red wine from Pinot noir and the native varietal Cesar, and Saint-Bris, a young AC (January 2003) drawn from Sauvignon and yielding fresh, fruity wines, as its flag bearers. In the second area, around Tonnerre, east of Chablis, this role is played by Epineuil, a fruity red wine made from Pinot noir. North and south of this area, Côte Saint-Jacques near Joigny (north of Auxerre) and Vézelay (south of Auxerre) also produce noteworthy wines.

CÔTE DE NUITS

Wines from the Côte de Nuits boast two great qualities: they are delicate and complex. From the gateway of Dijon in the north down to Corgoloin, the most southerly outpost, the Côtes de Nuits is a string of jewels, threading together twenty or more of France's greatest growths and its finest flagships: Chambertin, Clos-Saint-Denis, Bonnes Mares, Clos de Tart, Musigny, Grands-Echezeaux, Clos de Vougeot, Richebourg, Romanée-Conti...are just some of the more famous names. Pinot noir is by far the most ubiquitous grape variety here, covering at least 99% of the area under vine, on a mixture of soil types formed of encrinal limestone and Bajocian marl, strewn, sometimes profusely, with stony scree. The soil type is so unusual that no great white wine has ever been grown here.

CÔTE DE BEAUNE

This is where the white wines are avenged: Corton-Charlemagne, Chevalier-Montrachet, Bâtard-Montrachet, Montrachet... Seven of Côte de Beaune's eight great growths are white from Chardonnay, with just one embracing both red and white wines, the famous Corton. From Ladoix, the name of both an appellation and a hamlet in the parish of Ladoix-Serrigny north of Beaune, to Maranges, the northern gateway to Saône-et-Loire, Côte de Beaune unravels a string of great growths on marl or Middle or Upper Oxfordian limestone soils. These enable it to produce, particularly around Chassagne-Montrachet and Puligny-Montrachet, some of the greatest white wines in the world.

CÔTE CHALONNAISE

Once it passes Chagny, the Côte widens, branches out, grows in size... Basically, it breathes. Four main ACs share an area no less than 25 kilometres by seven : Rully, Mercurey, Givry and Montagny (the last one is whites only) which, along with Bourgogne Aligoté and Bouzeron (a village appellation also made from Aligoté), form the backbone of the Côte Chalonnaise range. The soil type here is predominantly Jurassic: calcareous clay along the Dheune valley, which provides some unexpected ground for Chardonnay to thrive on; or brown limestone for Pinot noir.
Interestingly, the Crémant de Bourgogne appellation, which is used widely throughout Burgundy, actually originated in Rully (in Saône-et-Loire).

MÂCONNAIS

Stretching from Saint-Gengoux-le-National down to the northern frontiers of Beaujolais, the Mâconnais can be divided into two distinct areas: in the north, the 'sub-regional' appellations of white (from Chardonnay) and red wines (from Gamay) : Mâcon, Mâcon Supérieur, Mâcon-Villages, intermingled with a clutch of village ACs like Mâcon-Loché, Mâcon-Prissé, Mâcon-Fuissé, Mâcon-Cruzille and Viré-Clessé. Moving south lies the second portion of the appellation, home to the other village appellations which yield some great white wines such as Saint-Véran, Pouilly-Fuissé, Pouilly-Loché and Pouilly-Vinzelles.
The Mâconnais is a frontier land, where the climate alternates between continental influences, and the occasional bout of frost they bring with them, and Mediterranean influences, and their characteristic sunshine and moderate rainfall. This creates just

the right balance for the primarily calcareous-clay-type soils to yield their finest qualities before they metamorphose into granite in northern Beaujolais.

WINE STYLES

Summing up the multifarious flavours encountered in Burgundy, home to both the greatest growths and basic wines, is a tall order. In a nutshell, though, Pinot noir delivers sterling quality red fruit aromas and boasts remarkably elegant expression. The whites alternate between great suppleness and a commensurate amount of complexity in the great growths (Chablis, Meursault...), and pleasantly graceful, simple freshness (Aligoté, Mâcon-villages, Bourgogne Chardonnay...). Chardonnay expresses varietal aromas of hazelnut and wild flowers. Crémants can prove remarkable, provided the vines grow on limestone soils.

REVIEW OF RECENT VINTAGES

• **2008** • The red wines are very successful, with a lovely aroma of fruit, good concentration, and rounded and silky tannins. They can be drunk when young, but the best show a promising potential for aging. The whites are powerful with a ripe nose and above all an acidity that guarantees freshness. A great year.

• **2009** • It seems that years ending in nine are lucky in Burgundy: think of 1959, 1989 and, more recently, 1999. The 2009 reds are full-bodied and very ripe, sometimes with a jammy nose. They can easily be enjoyed when young. The whites are also full-bodied and some give off exotic aromas.

• **2010** • Well-balanced, fresh, pure whites. The minerality evident on the palate is archetypal of Burgundy sites. The reds show fresh red fruit aromatics, great perfume and unfurl silky tannins and wonderful harmony between acidity and roundness.

• **2011** • very unusual weather patterns leading to one of the sixth-earliest vintages in 300 years! A vintage where the winegrower came into his own, as is often the case in Burgundy. Good reds with consistency between villages and growths. The whites can tend to suffer from a lack of acidity but will be perfect when young.

• **2012** • This region experienced every type of weather in 2012: a mild winter, a cool spring that brought frost, a hot May, a cool, rainy June, and an unstable summer that included a heat wave, hail and thunderstorms. The yield was rather low, but the wines have turned out quite well. The whites are expressive, with a very well-balanced palate. The reds are dense, with mature, silky tannins. This vintage is likely to be ready to drink soon.

THE BURGUNDY APPELLATIONS

AC ALOXE-CORTON

OVERVIEW: a village appellation in the Côte de Beaune, set in the village of the same name and the neighbouring village of Ladoix-Serrigny. The wines are virtually all reds from Pinot noir with a minute proportion of whites grown on 1.7 ha. The soils are formed of whitish marl and brown or yellowish Callovian or Upper Bathonian limestone.

Climate sites classed as first growths: Several climate-specific sites are classed as first growths (37.5 ha in total). In Aloxe-Corton: Les Valozières, Les Paulands, Les Maréchaudes, Clos des Maréchaudes, Les Chaillots, Les Fournières, Clos du Chapitre, Les Guérets, Les Vercots. In Ladoix-Serrigny : Clos des Maréchaudes, La Maréchaude, Les Petites Folières, Les Moutottes, La Coutière, La Toppe au Vert.

WINE STYLES: the red wines display a crimson hue. They conjure up aromas of red or black fruit (cherry), spices, toast; over time, they take on tones of truffles and leather. In the early years, the reds reveal a strong tannic character, they are firm, generous and elegant. They can be enjoyed with game, guinea fowl, cheeses… 115

AC AUXEY-DURESSES

OVERVIEW: a village appellation in the Côte de Beaune, set halfway between Meursault and Saint-Romain. In the past, the majority of the wines were sold under the Côte de Beaune-Villages label. The appellation area is surrounded by hills and there are two distinct soil types: those that are conducive to red wines (calcareous clay) and those more suitable for whites (limestone marl).

Climate sites classed as first growths: approximately 30 ha are classed as first growths: Climat du Val, Clos du Val, Les Bréterins, La Chapelle, Reugne, Les Duresses, Bas des Duresses, Les Grands Champs, Les Ecusseaux.

WINE STYLES: three-quarters of the wines are red from Pinot noir. They display a reasonably pale hue, aromas of blackcurrant, raspberry, blackberry, animal, musk and smoky notes. They are harmonious, lively, supple, slightly tannic wines which pair well with braised ham, grilled or roast meats. They are also well-balanced and deep. The whites, with their translucid hue, develop aromas of hazelnut, russet apple, fresh almonds. They combine creaminess with good acidity and can be served with oven-cooked fish or even poultry served in a cream sauce.

AC BÂTARD-MONTRACHET GRAND CRU

OVERVIEW: A great growth appellation in the Côte de Beaune, located in the villages of Puligny-Montrachet (6.02 ha) and Chassagne-Montrachet (5.85 ha), with a combined total of 11.24 ha. Chardonnay grows here on calcareous clay type soils with high stone and clay content. Bâtard-Montrachet wines are rich, heady, firm white wines with fragrances of almonds, hawthorn and honey. They can be paired with fish served in a sauce or shellfish.

AC BEAUNE

OVERVIEW: Beaune is Côte d'Or's most extensive village appellation. It is famed for its Hospices wine auction which is held at the end of November and is used as a gauge for the region's wine economy. The proceeds provide funding for the local hospital. The vines grow primarily on hillside sites where the soil is brown limestone interspersed with clay or sand.

Climate sites classed as first growths: the appellation boasts 42 first growths with a total 317.55 ha under vine (equating to ¾ of the area): Les Boucherottes, Les Vignes Franches, Clos des Ursules, Les Chouacheux, Les Epenotes, Le Clos des Mouches, Les Montrevenots, Les Aigrots, Les Sizies, Pertuisots, Clos Saint-Landry, Les Avaux, Les Tuvilains, Belissand, Les Seurey, Clos e la Mousse, Les Reversées, Les Sceaux, Les Teurons, Clos du Roi, Blanches Fleurs, A l'Ecu, Clos de l'Ecu, Les Fèves, Les Cent Vignes, Les Marconnets, En Genêt, En l'Orme, Les Perrières, Les Bressandes, Les Toussaints, Les Grèves, Sur les Grèves, Sur les Grèves-Clos-Sainte-Anne, Aux Cras, Le Bas des Teurons, Aux Coucheria, Clos de la Feguine, Montée Rouge, La Mignotte, Clos des Avaux, Champs Pimont.

WINE STYLES: 90% of output is red, made from Pinot noir. The wines boast a deep hue and fruity aromas (cherry, strawberry) with animal undertones developing down the years. Although they are invariably elegant, they vary in structure. The wines from the centre and south of the appellation tend to be powerful and tannic, whilst those from the north are more supple and delicate. The whites (10% of output), with their pale yellow colour, are fat, rich and unctuous. Their acidity enhances their structure and releases aromas of hazelnuts and occasionally tropical fruits (pineapple). The reds sit well alongside marinated meats, poultry and cheeses.

AC BIENVENUES-BÂTARD-MONTRACHET

OVERVIEW: A great growth in the Côte de Beaune located in the village of Puligny-Montrachet, yielding white wines only, from Chardonnay. The appellation covers just 3.53 ha. Its quality and characteristics make it highly reminiscent of Bâtard-Montrachet, which is quite logical since this area extends out eastwards from Bâtard-Montrachet. Bâtard-Montrachet, Bienvenues-Bâtard-Montrachet and Criots-Bâtard-Montrachet have only been classed as individual appellations since the 1937.

AC BLAGNY

OVERVIEW: the only village appellation in Burgundy which does not carry a village name. Blagny is in fact a hamlet which straddles both Meursault and Puligny-Montrachet. The appellation covers only red wines since the whites are labelled Meursault or Puligny-Montrachet.

Climate sites classed as first growths: Blagny boasts 4.08 ha of first growths. In Meursault: La Jeunelotte, La Pièce sous le Bois, Sous le Dos d'Ane, Sous Blagny. In Puligny-Montrachet: Sous le Puits, La Garenne or Sur La Garenne, Hameau de Blagny.

WINE STYLES: Blagny are firm, robust and reasonably well-constituted red wines. Difficult to approach when young, they cellar well. They display pleasant aromas of blackcurrant and strawberry and match well with Epoisses cheese.

AC BONNES-MARES GRAND CRU

OVERVIEW: Most of this 16.24-hectare vineyard is located in the village of Chambolle-Musigny in the Côte de Nuits though the most northerly plots are in Morey-Saint-Denis. The area is divided between more than forty wine growers. The soil comprises a thin layer of limestone on a bedrock of Jurassic limestone, lightened by stones and gravel. These red wines are robust, powerful, dense and elegant and are famed for their lengthy lifespan. With a crimson hue, they display aromas of spices, animal notes and a hint of undergrowth. Enjoy with fillet steak in sauce chasseur, duck with truffles, wild game.

AC BOURGOGNE

OVERVIEW: AC Bourgogne is the umbrella name given to appellation wines throughout Burgundy. Pinot noir is the only permitted varietal for the regional appellation though in Yonne, two old traditional varieties - Cesar and Tressot - which have become virtually obsolete, can also be used.

WINE STYLES: the range of wine styles is extremely diversified due to the possibilities afforded by blending wines from very different growing environments or 'terroirs'. As a rule, the red wines display a moderately intense hue with crimson tints. Down the years, the colour turns ruby then orangy-red. Predominant aromas are cherry, raspberry and occasionally floral notes. As the wines age, humus, venison, truffle, stewed fruit and mild spices enter the scene.

The wine structure is supple, with moderate tannins and occasionally quite distinct acidity. Early-drinking is rewarded and pairings include white meat, vol-au-vents, ham, kidneys, lamb...The whites display the tell-tale aromas of Chardonnay : white flowers, almonds and fresh hazelnuts, lemon, occasionally augmented by woody notes. The balance between fat and freshness is one of their strong points. Try with chicken, oven-cooked fish, scallops...

Some villages in Yonne are entitled to add their name to the Bourgogne appellation. Although this relatively new classification rewards growers geared to making quality wines, actual output remains quite low.

• **Bourgogne Chitry** • Located south-east of Auxerre, on the border with Chablis, in the village of Chitry. The soil is formed of Kimmeridgian limestone marl. The elegant, fruity wines pair with grilled or roast red meat, duck, sauteed veal or beef bourguignon. The generous, round whites are a perfect match for poultry or fish.

• **Bourgogne Côte d'Auxerre** • The area is set south-east of Auxerre in the villages of Augy, Quenne, Saint Bris le Vineux, Vincelottes, Champs-sur-Yonne, Vaux and Auxerre.

The reds are full with delicate tannins and fragrances of raspberry and morello cherry. The whites are fat and delicate with aromas of hazelnut and flowers.

• **Bourgogne Côte Saint-Jacques** • This area located north-west of Auxerre on south, south-east facing hillsides overlooking the Yonne, covers the village of Joigny in the Yonne department. This is Burgundy's most northerly wine region and fewer than 13 hectares are labelled under the appellation annually.

• **Bourgogne Coulanges-la-Vineuse** • The aptly named village of Coulanges, south of Auxerre, has lent its name to this area covering Charentenay, Coulanges La Vineuse, Escolives-Sainte Camille, Jussy, Migé, Mouffy and Val de Mercy in the Yonne department.

• **Bourgogne Epineuil** • The growing area is located north-east of Chablis, near Tonnerre in the village of Epineuil. Grown on calcareous clay soils, the reds are tannic, elegant wines suitable for laying down. Try with red meat, roast poultry or veal stew. The fruity, soft whites are well-suited to fish.

• **Bourgogne Tonnerre** • An area located north-east of Chablis, on plots set in the villages of Epineuil, Dannemoine, Junay, Molosmes, Tonnerre and Vézinnes in the Yonne department.

Bourgogne Vezelay: centring on the famous basilica where tourists flock, providing a ready-made clientele, this appellation covers around 50 hectares in the villages of Asquins, Saint Père, Tharoiseau and Vézelay in the Yonne department.

AC BOURGOGNE ALIGOTÉ

OVERVIEW: a regional appellation grown throughout Burgundy which takes its name from the eponymous varietal. Most Aligotés are made in the Côte Chalonnaise.

WINE STYLES: Bourgogne Aligoté are light, lively, vigorous wines that are supple, delicate, fresh and moderately well-constituted with acidulous overtones. They exhibit a white gold colour with greenish tints, and exude fragrances of grape, green apple, vanilla and lemon. Try with cooked cold pork meats, fried or grilled fish, snails, oven-baked pike-perch, goats cheeses.

AC BOURGOGNE CLAIRET

These rosé wines can be grown throughout Burgundy. They are fruity and supple and must comply with the same regulations as for AC Burgundy. Pinot noir is the sole grape variety, except in Yonne, where it can be augmented with Cesar and Trousseau. They pair well with barbecues or cooked cold pork meats.

AC BOURGOGNE CÔTE CHALONNAISE

OVERVIEW: 44 towns and villages in Saône-et-Loire are entitled to this appellation: canton of Buxy (18 villages), Chagny (11 villages), Givry (12 villages) and Mont Saint Vincent (3 villages). The area was awarded AC status in 1990 so that growers outside the boundaries of the other local appellations (Mercurey, Givry, Rully and Montagny) could enjoy their own appellation. Production conditions are identical to those for AC Bourgogne.

WINE STYLES: the red wines are light, supple, delicate and round with fragrances of red fruits (cherry, raspberry, strawberry), bay, and pleasant tannins and acidity. Try with veal stew. The whites are rich, with a pleasant bouquet, developing aromas of flowers and dried fruit.

AC BOURGOGNE HAUTES CÔTES DE BEAUNE

OVERVIEW: the steep gradient separating Burgundy's 'mountain' from the valley floor of the Saône, is not only the prerogative of the Côte de Beaune and its northerly neighbour, the Côte de Nuits. Tucked away at higher elevations are the Hautes Côtes, an extremely fragmented area where vines have been growing at altitudes of between 300 and 450 metres since time immemorial. 22 villages in the Côte d'Or department and 7 in Saône-et-Loire are entitled to use this appellation.

WINE STYLES: drawn from Pinot noir and Chardonnay, these wines are lighter than those of the Côte, their acidity greater. They reward earlier drinking too and are approachable, pleasant wines from an aromatic perspective. Enjoyable with barbecues (reds), fish or shellfish (whites).

AC BOURGOGNE HAUTES CÔTES DE NUITS

OVERVIEW: the Hautes Côtes de Nuits borders on the Hautes Côtes de Beaune in the north and covers 16 villages in Côte d'Or, dotted between Dijon and Maranges, as well as the upper reaches of 4 localities in the Côtes de Nuits area. The vineyards are home to Pinot noir and Chardonnay vines and, despite their high elevation, they enjoy excellent aspect and suitable soils.

WINE STYLES: the reds exhibit a relatively deep hue and sterling quality fruit. On the palate, they display a pleasant mellowness, fat and freshness. Although they are quite robust, they are still soft and fruity, thereby pairing well with poultry for example. The whites are of a good standard, quite generous and highly aromatic. Try with langoustine and other shellfish.

AC BOURGOGNE ORDINAIRE AND BOURGOGNE GRAND ORDINAIRE (COTEAUX BOURGUIGNONS)

These appellations are on the wane. The area shares the same boundaries as AC Bourgogne, stretching over Côte d'Or, the Rhone, Yonne and Saône-et-Loire and covering 385 towns and villages. Gamay is allowed to be blended into the reds, alongside Pinot noir. The red wines have lower alcohol content than AC Bourgogne. Try with ham, duck with green pepper... The whites come primarily from Chardonnay and Aligoté and partner with snails, and the rosés go with cooked cold pork meats, barbecues and crudités.

AC BOURGOGNE PASSE-TOUT-GRAINS

OVERVIEW: the name of this appellation is a give-away as to the type of wine made here, because contrary to the other Burgundy ACs, this appellation is a blend of several varietals: at least 1/3 Gamay and at most 2/3 Pinot noir. Bourgogne Passe-Tout-Grains is made throughout the region, thereby covering 91 towns and villages in Côte d'Or, 85 in the Rhone, 154 in Saône-et-Loire and 54 in Yonne. The best wines come from sites in Côte d'Or on the valley floor.

WINE STYLES: with a deep colour and aromas of violet, fruit and animal notes in the early years, this is a quaffing wine, fruity and rustic with a certain amount of acidity.

AC BOUZERON

OVERVIEW: this particular site embraces two villages, Bouzeron and Chassey Le Camp, in the Saône-et-Loire department. The reputation of its Aligoté wines is long-established, entitling it to add its name to the Bourgogne Aligoté appellation initially, then subsequently warranting it an outright village appellation in 1998. The best Bourgogne Aligoté hail from this site and from Chitry.

WINE STYLES: Bouzeron wines display a pale yellow hue with greenish tints. They exhibit aromas of vanilla, are soft and silky on the palate and are enjoyable with cooked cold pork meats, fried or grilled fish and snails.

AC CHABLIS

OVERVIEW: Chablis is located not far from Auxerre, midway between Dijon and Paris. It grows along the hills flanking the river Serein and boasts a south/south-east aspect. It is Burgundy's most northerly appellation and embraces more than 18 towns and villages. Soil types ranging from marl to Jurassic limestone (Kimmeridgian) littered with marine fossils provide a foothold for the vines. The climate in Chablis is continental, with harsh winters, potentially disastrous spring frosts and scorching summers. Booming sales have led to the constant expansion of the region since the 1960s.

WINE STYLES: Chablis are white wines drawn from Chardonnay. They display recognisable aromas of acacia, honeysuckle, fern, honey, toast, hazelnut and mushroom. They boast elegant, complex fruitiness, and characteristic liveliness and fat. Whilst basic Chablis, usually vinted in vats, rewards early drinking, the more structured first growths have a cellaring capacity ranging from 5 to 10 years. Try with seafood, fish and snails.

CHABLIS PREMIER CRU

OVERVIEW: Here the vineyard classification system really comes into its own. The core of the wine region is formed of seven climate-specific sites comprising the Grand Cru appellation (see

specific heading) and forty or so climate-specific sites classed as Chablis Premiers Crus, labelled under 17 denominations: Les Beauregards, Beauroy, Berdiot, Chaume de Talma, Côte de Jouan, Côte de Léchet, Côte de Vaubarousse, Fourchaume, Les Fourneaux, Monts de Milieu, Montée de Tonnerre, Montmains, Vaillons, Vau Ligneau, Vau de Vey, Vaucoupin, Vosgros. The rest of the appellation is entitled to use the basic AC Chablis appellation. The outlying area, with its Portlandian limestone soils, is home to the Petit Chablis appellation.
WINE STYLES: Chablis 1er Cru wines are more robust though also more delicate than basic Chablis. Their lifespan ranges from 5 to 10 years and many of them spend some time under oak. They are the perfect match for grilled crayfish, lobster, fish in a white sauce, snails, seafood, oysters, goats cheese and veal stew.

AC CHABLIS GRAND CRU

OVERVIEW: in the heart of the Chablis area, seven great growth climate-specific sites occupy a hillside overlooking the right bank of the Serein. These are Blanchot (12.2 ha), Bougros (14.35 ha), Les Clos (25.87 ha), Grenouilles (9.38 ha), Les Preuses (10.81 ha), Valmur (10.55 ha) and Vaudésir (15.43 ha). The climate-specific site of La Moutonne, belonging to the Long Depaquit estate, is not officially classed as such by AC law. However 95 % of La Moutonne's vineyards are located in the Vaudésir appellation and 5% in Les Preuses, hence the owner sells La Moutonne under the Chablis Grand Cru appellation. This particular hillside, with the characteristic calcareous marl of Chablis, provides remarkable drainage and aspect for Chardonnay (known locally as Beaunois), which explains the outstanding potential of the wines.
WINE STYLES: Chablis Grand Cru exhibit a greenish-yellow hue and exude fragrances of honey, hazelnut and mineral notes. They are concentrated wines, often firm when young, which develop fat and mellowness over time. Good vintages will age for between 10 to 15 years, developing intense aromas of dried fruit, toast, gingerbread, slightly oxidised notes and occasionally gun flint. Serving them with oysters in a cream sauce, fish in a sauce, poultry, veal stew... enhances their flavour.

AC CHAMBERTIN GRAND CRU

A 13-hectare great growth in the Côte de Nuits, in the village of Gevrey-Chambertin. The vines grow halfway up a gently sloping hill, to the south of the village of Chambertin on marl or calcareous marl soils scattered with tiny stones. Woodland to the west shelters the vines from the wind. The red wines exhibit a liquorice hue, they are full-bodied, vigorous, robust, racy, generous and full, with good cellaring capacity. Try with game, coq au Chambertin, flavoursome cheeses…

AC CHAMBERTIN CLOS DE BÈZE GRAND CRU

These wines can be sold as Chambertin Clos de Bèze or AC Chambertin. Conversely, Chambertin cannot be sold as Chambertin Clos de Bèze. Located between Chambertin and Mazis-Chambertin, this site of just under 15 hectares is set at a higher elevation than Chambertin and its soils are shallower. The wines are sensual, opulent, delicate, with a powerful structure. They pair with game.

AC CHAMBOLLE-MUSIGNY

OVERVIEW: Chambolle-Musigny grows in the heart of the Côte de Nuits. Half of the village boasts either first or great growth status. The soils are limestone with stones or gravel, imparting greater finesse to the wines.

WINE STYLES: this appellation has a reputation for producing the most delicate and most feminine of all the wines in Côte d'Or. With an intense hue displaying purple then garnet-red tints as it ages, this is a racy wine boasting elegant tannins and very little acidity. The first growths are firm, with greater concentration. Deep aromas of raspberry, stewed strawberry, violet, undergrowth, spices, morello cherry, liquorice… Try with young pigeon, veal Orloff, fatted chicken, young wild boar, duck with girolle mushrooms.

CLIMATE SITES CLASSED AS FIRST GROWTHS:
(just over 50 hectares): *Les Véroilles, Les Sentiers, Les Baudes, Les Noirots, Les Lavrottes, Les Fuées, Aux Beaux Bruns, Aux Echanges, Les Charmes, Les Plantes, Aux Combottes, Derrière la Grange, Les Gruenchers, Les Groseilles, Aux Combottes, Les Feusselottes, Les Chatelots, Les Cras, Les Carrières, Les Chabiots, Les Amoureuses, Les Borniques, Les Hauts Doix, La Combe d'Orveau.*

AC CHAPELLE-CHAMBERTIN GRAND CRU

This 5.5-hectare appellation is located in the northern part of the Côte de Nuits, in the village of Gevrey-Chambertin. The soils are slightly richer than in Griotte-Chambertin and the wines are some of the fruitiest of the Chambertin great growths. They are robust and virile like Gevrey, yet more delicate. Their aromas are comparable to those of Clos de Bèze although they lack their grand finish. They sit nicely alongside fish in a sauce, though also shellfish and roast white meats.

AC CHARMES CHAMBERTIN GRAND CRU

A 28.97-hectare site adjacent to Mazoyères-Chambertin, in fact the production areas for Charmes-Chambertin and Mazoyères-Chambertin are identical. The soils are calcareous marl in type with an extremely high proportion of limestone. Charmes are less tannic, rounder and lighter than the other Chambertin great growths. They develop aromas of violet, liquorice and vanilla and woody undertones. They pair with wild boar, venison or pheasant.

AC CHASSAGNE-MONTRACHET

OVERVIEW: located in the far south of the Côte de Beaune, in the villages of Chassagne-Montrachet (Côte d'Or) and Remigny (Saône-et-Loire), this appellation area covers just over 300 hectares, half of which is divided between 55 first growths and 3 great growths. Chardonnay grows on clayey white limestone in the north-east, Pinot noir on the limestone marl in the north-west and south-west.

WINE STYLES: the white wines are fat, opulent, robust and golden in colour. They are dry, firm and long on the palate. Aromas reminiscent of almonds, ripe apple, white flowers, honey, fern and hawthorn are present, along with mineral notes and a hint of hazelnut, though also tropical fruit such as pineapple and grapefruit. The red wines conjure up aromas of blackcurrant, raspberry and a comprehensive range of ripe fruit, and venison. The wines are clean and round, fleshy, well-constituted, supply and velvety with delicate tannins.

CLIMATE SITES CLASSED AS FIRST GROWTHS:
Clos Saint-Jean, Cailleret, Les Chaumées, Les Vergers, Les Chenevottes, Les Macherelles, En Remilly, Dent de Chien, Vide Bourse, Blanchot-Dessus, La Maltroie, Les Brussonnes, Morgeot, Abbaye de Morgeot, Bois de Chassagne, La Grande Montagne, La Boudriotte, Les Champs Gains, Tonton Marcel, Champs Jendreau, Chassagne, Chassagne du Clos Saint-Jean, Clos Chareau, Clos Pitois, En Cailleret, En Virondot, Ez Crets, Ez Crottes, Francemont, Guerchère, La Cardeuse, La Chapelle, La Grande Borne, La Romanée, La Roquemaure, Les Baudines, Les Boirettes, Les Bondues, Les Chaumes, Les Combards, Les Commes, Les Embazées, Les Fairendes, Les Grandes Ruchottes, Les Grands Clos, Les Murées, Les Pasquelles, Les Petites Fairendes, Les Petits Clos, Les Places, Les Rebichets, Petingeret, Tête du Clos, Vigne Blanche and Vigne Derrière.

AC CHEVALIER-MONTRACHET GRAND CRU

This 7.47-hectare site is set above Puligny-Montrachet in a horizontal strip. The vines are planted on thin, stony soil of clayey white limestone and face east and south-east. With their body, firmness, mellowness and intensity they make pleasant wines to drink, though their most recognisable characteristics are their great finesse and delicacy. Sporting a bright golden hue, aromas of hazelnut, honey, almond, amber and exotic fruits, they pair with turbot and fish in a sauce, lobster, white meats.

AC CHOREY-LÈS-BEAUNE

OVERVIEW: the village is located in the vicinity of Beaune, in the plain, level with Savigny on an imaginary line from Dijon to Beaune. The appellation boasts no first growths.

WINE STYLES: predominantly red wines with fragrances of raspberry, morello cherry and blackcurrant, leading into crystallised fruit. They are light, supple, fruity, with low acidity and tannins. Their elegance outweighs their tannin content. They are delicate and feminine and are usually at their peak within their first decade. Pair with poultry fricassee, barbecued meats, mildly flavoured game birds or roast guinea fowl...

AC CLOS DES LAMBRAYS GRAND CRU

Located in the village of Morey-Saint-Denis between Clos-Saint-Denis and Clos de Tart, this 7.04 ha growth is, like Clos de Tart, a monopoly (owned by a German industrialist). In actual fact, it is a virtual monopoly as a few ares belong to neighbouring growers. The growth is set in the heart of the village and occupies a marl hillside which turns into calcareous clay at the foot of the hill. The wines combine power with finesse. They display fragrances of truffle and humus though rarely fruit. A perfect match for game, red meat and vacherin cheese.

AC CLOS DE LA ROCHE GRAND CRU

Covering almost 13.41 hectares, this Morey-Saint-Denis great growth occupies a hillside site with a due east aspect overlooking the road from Gevrey to Morey. The marl-rich, limestone soils impart structure and depth to these red wines, which are duly deep, well-constituted wines exhibiting great structure and body, whilst at the same time remaining delicate and graceful with bundles of fruit. The cellaring capacity of the wines is one of the longest in Burgundy, reaching and indeed extending beyond 20 years. Try with game or roast meat.

AC CLOS DE TART GRAND CRU

This 7.5-hectare Clos, established in 1141, is today a monopoly, owned entirely by a single owner (Maison J. Mommessin). It sits north of Morey-Saint-Denis, between Bonnes Mares and Clos des Lambrays. The soils are formed of shallow scree, covering a limestone bedrock. These red wines exude fragrances of strawberry, violet, and subsequently spices and undergrowth as they mature. With an extensive cellaring capacity, they are powerful, robust, elegant, silky and down the years become graceful. Their strong tannic framework mellows with age. Try with venison, leg of lamb...

AC CLOS DE VOUGEOT GRAND CRU

With its 50 hectares under vine, this great growth is the largest in the Côte d'Or and is located in the village of Vougeot, north of Nuits-Saint-Georges. Created between the 11th and 14th centuries by the monks of Cîteaux who built a wall around it, the growth is currently divided between almost 80 different owners ! The soil types are extremely varied. The higher elevations adjacent to Bonnes-Mares and Grands-Echezeaux, are home to light, gravely chalk resting on a bedrock of oolitic limestone. Further down the slopes, the soil is softer limestone containing clay and gravel and at the very bottom, it is rich in alluvial clay.

Classic Clos de Vougeot displays a deep red colour and aromas of red and black fruit (cherries, blackcurrant, blackberries), undergrowth and violet. As it matures, it develops aromas of fur, truffle and musk. A robust, firm, lively wine in its youth, it exhibits delicate tannins and a discrete touch of acidity. As a rule, the better wines come from the plots in the upper reaches of the Clos, though with such a great vineyard and range of growers, the wines cover a broad spectrum. Try with pheasant with apples.

AC CLOS SAINT-DENIS GRAND CRU

Located in the village of Morey-Saint-Denis, between Clos de la Roche and Clos des Lambrays. The original area under vine was a diminutive 2 hectares but this has been extended to a current area of 5.99 ha. Clos Saint-Denis red wines are moderately full but their aromatic range covers a broad spectrum: red and black fruit, spices, tobacco, musk... Try with poultry and game, or why not Peking duck as some people suggest !

AC CORTON GRAND CRU

The Corton great growth occupies the southern slopes of the Corton hillside overlooking the village of Aloxe-Corton. The only red great growth in the Côte de Beaune, it extends over 160 ha with barely a hundred of those on-stream. Voltaire used to say that he would rather drink this wine in private than serve it to his guests. White wines are also grown on 4.53 hectares. Corton wines display a deep-coloured hue and fragrances of red fruit (blackcurrant, cherry), truffle, leather, a touch of humus and spices. They are powerful wines, blessed with good acidity. Laying-down wines, they can be slightly firm over the first few years. Try with small or large game.

SOME CLIMATE SITE NAMES CAN BE ADDED TO THAT OF THE APPELLATION:

In Aloxe-Corton: *Les Pougets, Les Languettes, Le Corton, Les Renardes, Les Grèves, Le Clos du Roi, Les Chaumes, Les Perrières, Les Bressandes, Les Paulands, Les Maréchaudes, Les Fiètres, Le Meix Lallemand, Clos des Meix, Les Combes, La Vigne au Saint.*

In Ladoix-Serrigny: *Le Rognet et Corton, Clos des Cortons, Les Moutottes, Les Carrières, Basses Mourottes, Hautes Mourottes, Les Vergennes, Les Grandes Lolières, La Toppe au vert.*

AC CORTON CHARLEMAGNE (AND CHARLEMAGNE) GRAND CRU

This fifty or so hectare great growth extends westwards from Corton on the hill of the same name. Its climate sites straddle the villages of Aloxe-Corton, Ladoix and Pernand-Vergelesses. Corton-Charlemagne is the only wine area bearing the name of two emperors: Curtis d'Othon, hence the name Corton, and of course Charlemagne, who donated his vines to Saint-Andoche abbey in Saulieu in 775. Chardonnay thrives here on the limestone-rich soils, steep inclines facing south-west and north-east and a microclimate which ensures cooler temperatures. The appellation also embraces that of Charlemagne, which is no longer used.

These white wines with their golden hue display complex fragrances of citrus peel, fresh almonds, cinnamon, walnut, exotic fruits, honey, dried fruit, spices (pepper). Corton-Charlemagne are lively, fresh, full, rich, unctuous wines with great length, intensity, body, complexity and elegance. They are slightly firm when young and require a few years to fully express their qualities. Try with lobster Americaine, fish in a cream sauce, some white meats and certain types of cheese (Munster and blue).

AC CÔTE-DE-BEAUNE-VILLAGES

OVERVIEW: with the exception of Aloxe-Corton, Beaune, Pommard and Volnay, all of the village ACs in the Côte de Beaune are entitled to use this appellation and can choose between their own appellation or Côte-de-Beaune-Villages. Growers can also state the name of their village after 'Côte de Beaune' on labels.

WINE STYLES: depending on whether they are harvested in the northern portion of the appellation or in the south, wine styles can vary immensely. Those from the north display a light hue with elegant, supple, delicate, round aromas and pleasant tannins. Those from the south boast a deeper hue and a more marked tannic structure, they are well-rounded with good acidity.

AC CÔTE DE BEAUNE

OVERVIEW: stretching over the outlying hills around the town of Beaune, this appellation covers around 25 ha. It should not be confused with 'Côte de Beaune', the geographical term used to described the southern half of Côte d'Or (as opposed to Côte de Nuits in the north).

WINE STYLES: the wines are highly reminiscent of those from Beaune, with a relatively dark hue and typical red fruit fragrances such as strawberry, blackcurrant and cherry. Try with marinated meats such as beef, poultry, game birds or cooked cold pork meats.

AC CÔTE DE NUITS-VILLAGES

OVERVIEW: the villages entitled to use this appellation are Fixin, Brochon, Premeaux-Prissey, south-west of Dijon and Comblanchien and Corgoloin south of Nuits-Saint-Georges. Soil types vary greatly, ranging from predominantly limestone with patches of marl in the north, to stonier soils with a touch of clay in the south.

WINE STYLES: the wines are aromatic (blackberry, cherry, raspberry, blackcurrant, leading into liquorice and venison as they age) and mature rapidly. Wines from the south are supple, fruity and more delicate, whilst those from the north display a good tannic framework and fat. Such diversity is not only down to the varying soil make-up, but also the aspect of the vineyards and the climate. Try with poached eggs in a red wine sauce, beef bourguignon, mildly-flavoured cheeses...

AC CRÉMANT DE BOURGOGNE

OVERVIEW: Crémant is made throughout virtually the whole of Burgundy, but primarily in Yonne and the Côte Chalonnaise. Permitted varietals are divided into two groups: Pinot noir, Pinot gris and Chardonnay(first group); Gamay, Aligoté, Melon and

Sacy (second group). In the final blend, varietals in the first group must account for at least 30%, whilst Gamay is restricted to a maximum 20%.

Rules governing production: a basic yield of 7,500 kg/ha, i.e. 50 hl/ha, hand harvesting, an extraction rate restricted to 100 litres of juice per 150 kg of grapes, horizontal storage for at least nine months... After disgorging, CO_2 in Crémant de Bourgogne must be under at least 3.5 atmospheres of pressure.

WINE STYLES: Crémant has a brilliant hue, it is ethereal, light, fresh, vigorous, fruity and round with good liveliness imparted by Pinot noir. The best Crémants hail from the Rully area (Saône-et-Loire) and from Saint-Bris in Yonne. They are equally delicious as an appetiser with cheese puffs ('gougères') or with a main course of seafood.

AC CRIOTS BÂTARD-MONTRACHET GRAND CRU

This 1.57 ha great growth is entirely located in the village of Chassagne-Montrachet, in a place called Les Criots, south-west of Beaune. These great (and rare) white wines bear the tell-tale characteristics of the Montrachet great growths. They are dry yet not harsh and reveal remarkable fruit. Try with lobster or crayfish.

AC ECHEZEAUX GRAND CRU

This 34.79 ha great growth is located in the village of Flagey-Echézeaux in the Côte de Nuits. It yields elegant, velvety, fleshy wines with power and concentration. They boast delicate tannins and a long-lasting finish. With a deep red hue, they display fragrances of red and black fruit, cocoa bean, exotic wood and musk. They pair well with game birds (woodcock, partridge), lamb and soft, creamy cheeses.

AC FIXIN

OVERVIEW: with around a hundred hectares under vine located a few kilometres south of Dijon, this is one of the more northerly Côte de Nuits village appellations. It is geared virtually entirely to producing red wines and a large proportion of them are actually labelled under the Côte de Nuits-Villages appellation.

Climate sites classed as first growths: in Fixin: Arvelets, Clos du Chapitre, Clos Napoléon, Le Meix Bas, Clos de la Perrière, Hervelets. In Brochon: Clos de la Perrière.

WINE STYLES: grown on Bajocian limestone type soils with patches of marl, the reds are well-constituted, generous, robust, relatively tannic and rich in alcohol. Firm and blessed with good acidity, they exhibit animal or even wild notes (fur, musk), as well as red and black fruit (blackcurrant, cherry, blackberry). Try with a leg of lamb, game, red meat in a sauce, mature cheeses.

AC GEVREY-CHAMBERTIN

OVERVIEW: the vineyards in this Côte de Nuits wine area embrace two villages: Gevrey-Chambertin and Brochon, about 10 km from Dijon. They cover almost 410 ha and are divided into two parts by 'Lavaux Coomb'. The soil is formed of Bajocian encrinal limestone and upper Lias clay marl.

WINE STYLES: their deep hue covers a broad spectrum ranging from cherry-red to garnet. They display distinctive fragrances of red or black fruit (blackcurrant), animal notes, musk, fur, liquorice, bilberry, prune, nutmeg, pepper, leather. Wines from the steeper slopes are solid, powerful and generous, whilst those from the flatter soils tend to be more elegant. In the early years, they are often tannic, and the first growths remain firm throughout. Try with poultry, beef tenderloin, small or large game.

THE AREA IS HOME TO 26 FIRST GROWTHS:

La Bossière, La Romanée, Poissenot, Estournelles-Saint-Jacques, Clos des Varoilles, Lavaut Saint-Jacques, Champeaux, Petits Cazetiers, Combe au Moine, Les Goulots, Aux Combottes, Bel Air, Cherbaudes, Petite Chapelle, En Ergot, Clos Prieur, La Perrière, Au Closeau, Issarts, Les Corbeaux, Craipillot, Fonteny, Clos du Chapitre, Clos Saint-Jacques, Les Cazetiers, Champonet.

AC GIVRY

OVERVIEW: this appellation sits west of Chalon-sur-Saône, and occupies a strip 6km long by 3km wide. Reputedly Henry IV's favourite wines, they are grown in the village of Givry and the immediate vicinity, forming a barrier against urban sprawl.

WINE STYLES: the reds display a deep ruby-red hue with aromas of wild fruit, redcurrant, a touch of spices and animal tones, liquorice, raspberry and undergrowth. They are round, warm, delicate, lively, moderately robust wines. Try with white meat in a sauce. The whites display a golden colour with floral aromas such as thyme, wild rose, mineral and citrus notes (lemon). Smooth on the palate, they are rich, subtle and delicate with good length and fresh flavours. Enjoy with fish or tarts.

CLIMATE SITES CLASSED AS FIRST GROWTHS:

Clos du Cras Long, Clos des Vernoy, Les Grandes Vignes, Clos Marceaux, Les Garnds Prétans, Clos de la Barraude, Petit Marole, Clos du Celiiers aux Moines, Clos Charlé, Servoisine, Les Bois

Chevaux, Clos Saint-Pierre, Clos Saint-Paul, Clos Salomon, A Vigne Rouge, Clos Jus, Crausot, Crémillons, En Choué, La Grande Berge, La Plante, Le Paradis, Le Petit Prétan, Le Vigron, les Bois Gautiers, Champ Nalot, En Veau, La Brûlée, La Matrosse, La Grande Berge, La Petite Berge, Le Champ Lalot, Le Médenchot, Le Pied du Clou, Le Vernoy, Les Combes, Les Galaffres, Pied de Chaume and Clos Marole.

AC GRANDS ECHEZEAUX GRAND CRU

Located in the village of Flagey-Echezeaux, this growth has a misleading name: it is in fact four times smaller than neighbouring Echezeaux (7.53 ha) with just one plot (as opposed to 11 for Echezeaux). It has a due east aspect, gentle inclines, and the soil is calcareous clay. Good drainage is provided by the myriad stones here. These combine to produce silky, full, deep red wines, which are more powerful and generous than the Echezeaux. Similarly, they are also longer on the palate. They display aromas of cherry, strawberry, blackcurant and raspberry, leading into a bouquet of musk, leather and undergrowth as they mature. They pair well with roast meals, meat served with a sauce, game (venison, wild boar) and mildly-flavoured cheeses.

AC GRIOTTE-CHAMBERTIN GRAND CRU

This 2.7 ha growth is located in the village of Gevrey-Chambertin. The soil is strewn with small stones over a Bajocian bedrock. The wines are red, fleshy, delicate and soft. Their framework is bolstered more by their tannins than their acidity and they develop aromas of jammy cherries as they age. A suitable partner for white meat and poultry.

AC IRANCY

OVERVIEW: the appellation is located 15 km south of Auxerre, in and around Irancy, Vincelottes and Cravant in the Yonne department. Site-specific names (Palotte, Les Cailles, Les Mazelots…) can be appended to that of Irancy though in actual fact few growers do.

WINE STYLES: Irancy display a deep hue and fragrances of cherry, blackcurrant, spices, violet and 'terroir'. They are solid, robust, tannic wines which are lively and long-lasting on the palate. Although they can be slightly bitter in the early years, they have a prolonged cellaring capacity. The hallmark characteristics of these wines are partly derived from frequent use of the Cesar varietal, which is blended with Pinot. Try with coq au vin, kidneys in a Madeira sauce, beef bourguignon and cheeses.

AC LADOIX

OVERVIEW: Ladoix is in fact not a village but a hamlet within the parish of Ladoix-Serrigny. With around 140.95 ha under vine, it is nevertheless considered as a village appellation and embraces 11 climate sites classed as first growths.

WINE STYLES: with their fragrances of raspberry, cherry and undergrowth, the red wines are relatively robust and fleshy, with body and character. The first growths display great structure and more predominant tannins. Try with veal liver, roasted red meats, game. With their aromas of ripe apple, fresh fig and walnut, the whites are firm when young, gradually mellowing as they age.

CLIMATE SITES CLASSED AS FIRST GROWTHS:
La Micaude, La Corvée, Le Clou d'Orge, Les Joyeuses, Bois Roussot, Basses Mourottes, En Naget, Le Rognet et Corton, les Buis, Les Grêchons et Foutrières and Hautes Mourottes.

AC LA GRANDE RUE GRAND CRU

This 1.65-ha growth is set within the boundaries of Vosne-Romanée, between Romanée-Conti and La Tâche. It is under the sole ownership of Domaine Lamarche and was classed as recently as 1992. The soil is limestone in type, rich in iron with a stony, rocky or clay-marl subsoil. The wines are subtle and delicate whilst at the same time robust, well-constituted and powerful, combining to produce harmony and distinction. They are chewy and boast similarities with the neighbouring growths. Their musky fragrances and violet and raspberry tones are a joy to the senses.

AC LA TÂCHE GRAND CRU

A 6 ha great growth located in the village of Vosne Romanée. The limestone soils are shallow and particularly poor here. The growth is a monopoly of Domaine de la Romanée-Conti. Red La Tâche wines are concentrated and powerful on the nose. Although they can be very discrete when young, they gradually acquire complexity and finesse as they mature. Try with poultry-based dishes.

AC LATRICIÈRES CHAMBERTIN GRAND CRU

This 7.35 ha growth is located in the village of Gevrey-Chambertin, on the other side of the road from Chambertin. A thin layer of silica modifies the soil type, making it harder. Pinot noir is the sole grape variety and the wines are vigorous, virile and racy with a pleasant bouquet. Their finesse sets them apart from the other growths. Less powerful than the Chambertins, they boast fragrances of moss, undergrowth and game.

AC MÂCON AND MÂCON SUPÉRIEUR

(followed by the name of a locality)

OVERVIEW: barely 100 towns and villages with a combined are under vine of 2,391 ha are entitled to this appellation, which more or less fits within the same area as the district of Mâcon.

WINE STYLES: their hue covers a broad spectrum ranging from cherry-red to deep ruby-red with purplish tints. These are quaffing wines, light, pleasant and round on the palate, with well-balanced tannins. The whites display a limpid hue with green gold tints. They are supple wines with fragrances of citronella, fern and musk, which reward early drinking.

AC MÂCON-VILLAGES

OVERVIEW: this white wine appellation embraces 26 groups of towns and villages in the Mâcon area, including Azé, Chaintré, Chasselas, Chardonnay, Cruzille, Davayé, Fuissé, Igé, Lugny, Milly-Lamartine, Péronne, Pierreclos, Solutré-Pouilly, La Roche-Vineuse, Vergisson and Verzé. Overall area under vine is slightly in excess of 1,300 ha. The Burgundy climate draws out good varietal expression from Chardonnay. Wood is a less prominent flavour component than in Côte de Beaune and the prices are a lot more affordable too.

WINE STYLES: with a brilliant hue sporting greenish tints, the wines display aromas of hazelnut, almond, white peach, fern, butter and white flowers (hawthorn, acacia and wild rose), with lemony undertones. They boast a clean, silky attack, are fat, noticeably rich in alcohol with well-balanced acidity. Try with monkfish steak in a green pepper sauce, trout, chitterlings sausage, seafood, fish served with a sauce, white meats.

AC MARANGES

OVERVIEW: this 163 ha appellation is divided between three villages located in the far southern tip of the Côte de Beaune in Saône-et-Loire : Dezize, Sampigny and Cheilly, each of which is entitled to add its name to that of the appellation. Seven climate sites are classed as first growths within the appellation.

WINE STYLES: Maranges wines have a deep colour and aromas of red fruit and undergrowth. When fully mature, they develop aromas of fur and game. They are solid, robust, rich, tannic, fleshy wines which are full and firm. Try with a leg of venison, ribsteak, rabbit with a mushroom sauce, jugged hare.

CLIMATE SITES CLASSED AS FIRST GROWTHS:
In Cheilly-les-Maranges: *Les clos Roussots, la Fussière, Clos de la Boutière.*
In Dezize: *La Fussière, Clos de la Fussière, La Croix aux Moines.*
In Sampigny: *Les Clos Roussots, Le Clos des Rois, Le Clos des Loyères.*

AC MARSANNAY

OVERVIEW: this is the most northerly appellation in the Côte de Nuits, embracing three villages: Marsannay-la-Côte, Couchey and Chenôve. It is unusual in that it produces all three colours of wine: red, white and rosé. The rosé wines are made from Pinot noir and the appellation has built up its entire reputation as a producer of rosé. Out of an overall area under vine of 210 ha, 35 ha are dedicated to its rosé wine which is considered to be the best in Burgundy.

WINE STYLES: the reds, with their fragrances of blackcurrant, dried prunes and wild blackberry are clean, light, supple and scented. Try with cooked cold pork meats, or grilled meats. The rosés with their aromas of peach, strawberry and raspberry, display a hue ranging from salmon-pink to pale ruby-red. They are powerful, soft and fruity with good acidity. The fleshy, fat, full, supple whites have a long-lasting flavour and pair well with grilled fish.

AC MAZIS-CHAMBERTIN GRAND CRU

This 8.79-ha growth is adjacent to Clos de Bèze, south of Gevrey-Chambertin. The soils are extremely shallow, particularly in the upper reaches of the Clos The vineyards are planted to Pinot noir, which yields lighter, less austere wines than Chambertin. They are delicate, smooth, opulent, powerful wines bolstered by a good tannic framework, hence their need to mature. They display fragrances of red fruit leading into leather. They pair well with large game.

AC MAZOYÈRES-CHAMBERTIN GRAND CRU

This is a 1.72-ha growth (area on-stream) in the village of Gevrey-Chambertin. The soil is strewn with stones and has a strong limestone bias. The red wines offer crystallised aromas of stone fruits and leathery notes. Production areas for Charmes-Chambertin and Mazoyères-Chambertin are identical but most of the wines are usually labelled as Charmes-Chambertin.

AC MERCUREY

OVERVIEW: set midway between Rully and Givry, the boundaries of this appellation are etched by Mount Morin and the Orbiset river. With 646 ha under vine, including 32 classed as first growths, the Mercurey appellation produces almost as much wine as the other ACs in the Côte Chalonnaise (Givry, Rully, Montagny). The wines are grown in the village of Mercurey and in the immediate vicinity.

WINE STYLES: the reds exhibit aromas of small red fruit (blackcurrant, raspberry, morello cherry, strawberry) with undertones of leather and undergrowth. They have body, are chewy, rich, robust and well-balanced. They pair nicely with pheasant and tenderloin steak with ceps. The whites, with their golden colour and aromas of cinnamon, exotic fruit, amber and walnut, are fat and elegant. They are the perfect partner for fish served with a sauce.

CLIMATE SITES CLASSED AS FIRST GROWTHS:
Clos Marcilly, Les Croichots, La Cailloute, Les Combins, Les Champs Martin, Clos des Barraults, Clos des Myglands, Le Clos l'Evêque, Clos Voyens, Grand Clos Fortoul, Clos des Grands Voyens, Les Naugues, Les Crêts, Clos Tonnerre, Les Vasées, Les Byots, Sazenay, La Bondue, La Levrière, La Mission, Le Clos du Roy, Griffères, Les Velley, Clos du Château de Montaigu, Les Montaigus, Clos des Montaigus, Les Fourneaux, La Chassière, Les Ruelles, Les Naugues, Les Puillets, Les Saumonts and Clos de Paradis.

AC MEURSAULT

OVERVIEW: the village of Meursault is situated 8 km south-west of Beaune in Côte d'Or. The southern part of the village boasts the greatest concentration of first growths, which number 20 or so in total, including the flagship Les Perrières and Clos des Perrières. Of the appellation's 394 ha expanse, 105 ha are classed as first growths. The soil is formed of white marl on a Jurassic limestone bedrock. The proportion of clay here is higher than in the other appellations.

WINE STYLES: 95% of the wines are white. They display a golden hue and develop aromas of russet apple, crusty bread, hazelnut, bitter or dried almonds, foliage. Rich in alcohol, they exhibit fat and opulence. Try with foie gras, fish in a sauce, fatted chicken in a cream sauce or shellfish. Very occasionally red wines are made. They boast aromas of raspberry and are delicate with good structure, requiring a few years' ageing before they fully reveal their character.

CLIMATE SITES CLASSED AS FIRST GROWTHS:
Les Cras, Les Caillerets, Les Santenots Blancs, Les Plures, Les Santenots du Milieu, Charmes, La Jeunellotte, La Jeune-Lotte, La Pièce sous le Bois, Sous le Dos d'Ane, Sous Blagny, Perrières, Clos des Perrières, Genevrières, Le Porusot, Les Bouchères, Les Gouttes d'Or, Blagny, Les Ravelles, Porusot.

AC MONTAGNY

OVERVIEW: this is the Côte Chalonnaise's most southerly appellation, embracing four villages and an area under vine slightly in excess of 310 ha. The vines grow on hillside sites facing east-south-east and enjoy good sunshine exposure. The appellation is for white wines only and the AC boasts 49 climate sites classed as first growths. The vast majority of the wines are produced by the co-operative winery in Buxy.

WINE STYLES: with their golden colour, they offer aromas of lemon and grapefruit with tones of hazelnut, almond, fern and mineral notes. These white wines are racy and attractive with a delicate bouquet. They are soft, well-balanced, fresh, refined and elegant, with good length. Try with seafood, langoustine, fish served with a sauce or goats cheese.

CLIMATE SITES CLASSED AS FIRST GROWTHS:

In Montagny: *Vignes Saint-Pierre, les Combes, Saint-Ytage, Les Chaumelottes, Champ Toizeau, Vignes sur le Cloux, Les Garchères, Vignes Couland, Les Bouchots, Les Burnins, Les Perrières, Les Treuffères, Montcuchot, Vigne du Soleil, Les Maroques, Les Beaux Champs, les Macles, Creux de Beaux Champs, L'Epaule, Les Platières, Les Jardins, les Coères, Saint-Morille, Les Vignes Derrière, Les Bordes, Les Las, Les Gouresses, Les Paquiers, Montorge, Les Resses, Le Cloux, Sous les Feilles.*

In Buxy: *La Grande Pièce, Le Cos Chaudron, Les Vignes des près, Le Vieux Château, La Condemine du Vieux Château, Le Clouzot, Les Pidances, Les Coudrettes, Les Vignes Longues, Cornevent, Mont Laurent, Les Bonneveaux, Les Bassets.*

In Saint-Vallerin: *Les Paquiers, Les Cradoulettes, Les Coères, La Moullière, Les Resses.*

In Jully-lès-Buxy: *Les Coères, Les Chaniots, Chazelle.*

AC MONTHÉLIE

OVERVIEW: the village of Monthélie is located south of Volnay, more or less in the heart of the Côte de Beaune. Formerly owned by the Dukes of Burgundy and Cluny abbey, the appellation actually fits within quite a snug area. It sits on both sides of a coomb which is narrow to the north then opens up in the south. The appellation's 110 ha are devoted primarily to red wines. Life focuses so intensely on wine growing here that according to a local saying, a chicken could die of starvation during the grape harvest.

WINE STYLES: the reds exhibit an intense hue with purplish tints. They display aromas of red or black berries (cherry, bilberry, blackcurrant, redcurrant), prune, undergrowth, fern, mushrooms, violet, with a liquorice finish. They are robust, elegant, fresh wines in the early years with the potential to mature well.

The first growths display more up-front tannins, imparting greater structure. Try with roast lamb, poultry served with a sauce, game birds, cheeses. A tiny proportion of the wines are white, which are relatively mellow with good acidity. Try them with quenelles or poached fish with melted butter.

CLIMATE SITES CLASSED AS FIRST GROWTHS:

Les Riottes, Sur la Velle, Le Meix Bataille, Le Clos Gauthey, Les Vignes Rondes, Le Cas Rougeot, La Taupine, Les Champs Fulliot, Le Village, Le Château Gaillard, Clos des Toisières, Le Clou des Chênes, Les Barbières, Les Clous and Les Duresses.

AC MONTRACHET GRAND CRU

This Côte de Beaune growth straddles Chassagne and Puligny-Montrachet. The soil is limestone and the vines face south-east, which is conducive to good sunshine exposure. The highest elevations are home to soils of steep Rauracien limestone, followed by Callovian limestone further down and ultimately Bathonian limestone at the foot of the hill. They are shallow and poor. The 8 or so hectares of this great growth are divided amongst 20 or so different owners, who grow a single variety: Chardonnay. The white wines are racy, elegant, opulent, deep and intense with lashings of body. With their bright golden hue, they display fragrances of hazelnut, dried fruit, fern, butter and honey, unfolding into more mineral notes as they age. They pair with shellfish, sole in a white butter sauce and poultry in a cream sauce.

AC MOREY-SAINT-DENIS

OVERVIEW: set in the heart of the Côte de Nuits, this appellation boasts five great growths (Clos de la Roche, Clos Saint-Denis, Clos de Tart, Clos des Lambrays and part of Bonnes-Mares) and 20 first growths. The D122 road acts as boundary between the great growths in the west and the first growths. The combined area of the growths accounts for two-thirds of the appellation.

WINE STYLES: the reds boast good structure, body, vigour, elegance and delicacy. Their well-balanced structure makes them suitable for laying down. They combine the mellowness and finesse of Chambolle with the power and structure of Gevrey Chambertin. With their relatively deep-coloured hue, their aromas of red fruits (cherry morello cherry, blackcurrant), and their woody, spicy or animal nuances, they pair well with game, red meat and very mature cheeses.

CLIMATE SITES CLASSED AS FIRST GROWTHS:

Les Genavrières, Monts Luisants, Les Chaffots, Clos Baulet, Les Blanchards, Les Gruenchers, La Riotte, Les Milandes, Les Faconnières,

Les Charrières, Clos des Ormes, Aux Charmes, Aux Cheseaux, Les Chenevery, Le Village, Les Sorbès, Clos Sorbè, La Bussière, Les Ruchots, Côte Rôtie.

AC MUSIGNY GRAND CRU

Musigny sits on a relatively steep incline, overlooking Clos de Vougeot. One property, Domaine de Vogüé, owns 7 of the growth's total 9.32 ha., which cover a limestone rock terrace. Patches of red clay are dotted here though there is less limestone than in other parts. In fact, the soils veer more towards clay than chalk and are covered with a shallow layer of loam. The red wines are made from Pinot noir and the whites from Chardonnay. Musigny are well-balanced, supple wines with body. They are refined with delicate tannins and great length on the palate. Their aromatic spectrum embraces fragrances of strawberry, raspberry, violet and undergrowth. They pair with duck, poached chicken with bite-sized vegetables, capon and lamb.

AC NUITS-SAINT-GEORGES

OVERVIEW: this appellation covers both Nuits-Saint-Georges and Premeaux-Prissey. Stretching over a 4 km strip, the area is split into two parts, one located north of the town, the other in the far south of Nuits-Saint-Georges. Middle Jurassic limestone and marl soils are home to the vines here. The red wines are made from Pinot noir whilst a clutch of whites are produced from Chardonnay.

WINE STYLES: Nuits-Saint-Georges is a generous, well-constituted, robust wine with a strong framework and a powerful, complex bouquet. On the nose, it is fruity with notes of blackcurrant, cherry, prune stones, truffle and leather with nuances of undergrowth. It conjures up earthy, even gamey notes. Nuits-Saint-Georges can be served with roast red meat, mutton, Brie or Pont l'Evêque cheese.

CLIMATE SITES CLASSED AS FIRST GROWTHS:

In Nuits-Saint-Georges: *Aux Champs Perdrix, En la Perrière Noblot, Les Damodes, Aux Boudots, Aux Cras, La Richemone, Aux Murgers, Aux Vignerondes, Aux Chaignots, Aux Thorey, Aux Argillas, Aux Bousselots, Les Perrières, Les Hauts Pruliers, Château gris, Les Crots, Rue de Chaux, Les Procès, Les Pruliers, Roncière, Les Saints-Georges, Les Cailles, Les Porrets Saint-Georges, Clos des Porrets Saint-Georges, Les Vallerots, Les Poulettes, Les Chabœufs, Les Vaucrains, Chaînes Carteaux.*

In Premeaux : *Clos des Grandes Vignes, Clos de la Maréchale, Clos Arlot, Les Terres Blanches, Les Didiers, Clos des Forêts Saint-Georges, Aux Perdrix, Clos des Corvées, Clos des Corvées Pagets, Clos Saint-Marc, Les Argilières, Clos des Argilières.*

AC PERNAND-VERGELESSES

OVERVIEW: the appellation is located 8 km north of Beaune. Clayey, iron-rich, limestone and marl soils (Bathonian and Oxfordian) provide a foothold for the vines on sloping terrain, predominantly facing west or even north-west. 65 percent of the village's wines are red (Pinot noir). The whites (Chardonnay) come from the mountain at Corton.

WINE STYLES: the reds are firm in their early years, aromatic, elegant, ample and tannic. They display aromas of small red fruit (blackcurrant, redcurrant), liquorice, undergrowth, musk and floral notes. Try with stuffed fatted chicken, lamb, cheeses. The whites are solid wines with body, character and good acidity. They display a brilliant hue, aromas of vanilla, strawberry, citrus fruit (lemon, apple), honey, amber and are slightly spicy. Enjoyable with fish, either grilled or served with a cream sauce.

CLIMATE SITES CLASSED AS FIRST GROWTHS:

Clos Berthet, Sous Frétille, Village de Pernand, Creux de la Net, En Caradeux, Ile des Vergelesses, Les Fichots, Vergelesses.

AC PETIT CHABLIS

OVERVIEW: Petit Chablis grow on the rim of the Chablis wine region on Portlandian limestone soils (secondary era) which form the foundations of the plateaux.

WINE STYLES: considered as early wines, Petit Chablis are lively, fresh, clean, soft, pleasant and light. They have less staying power than Chablis and are usually at their peak within their first year. They display mineral, fruity and floral (acacia) type fragrances, a style particularly well-suited to cooked cold pork meats, seafood, grilled fish, jellied ham with parsley, snails…

AC POMMARD

OVERVIEW: situated 3 km west of Beaune, the area faces east and south-east. Although the appellation does not boast any great growths, it is home to 28 first growths which cover 37% of the appellation area. The soils are formed of soft, reasonably clayey limestone and Pinot noir is the sole grape variety.

WINE STYLES: Pommard have an intense colour (red-black) and are robust, warm and full-bodied, with great cellaring capacity. The wines from the northern part of the appellation tend to be softer than those from the south. Acidity is in the foreground, coupled with a certain amount of astringency. Pommard are firm and feature among the most tannic wines Burgundy has to offer. They have an intense bouquet with blackcurrant, musk, game, raspberry, bilberry and gingerbread. On the palate, notes of vanilla and liquorice are present. They can be served with game and mature, distinctive cheeses.

CLIMATE SITES CLASSED AS FIRST GROWTHS:

La Chanière, Les Charmots, La Platière, Les Arvelets, Les Saussiles, Les Pezerolles, En Largillière, Les Grands Epenots, Clos des Epeneaux, Les Petits Epenots, Les Boucherottes, Le Clos Micot, Les Combes-Dessus, Clos de Verger, Clos de la Commaraine, La Refène, Clos Blanc, Le Village, Derrière Saint-Jean, Les Rugiens-Bas, Les Chaponnières, Les Croix Noires, Les Poutures, Les Bertins, Les Fremiers, Les Jarolières, Les Rugiens-Hauts, Les Chanlins-Bas.

AC POUILLY-FUISSÉ

OVERVIEW: the production area embraces four villages situated in the southern part of the Mâconnais. The vines grow over a series of natural amphitheatres facing east and south-east, forming sites where winds to the west are deflected by the rocky ridges of Solutré and Vergisson. Although the appellation area does not boast any first growths, it is home to fifty or so climate-specific sites which can be stated on the label provided the wine has an ABV of 12% instead of 11% and has been aged at least until the 1st April following the harvest. The limestone-marl soils reveal various stages of the Jurassic era (Bathonian, Bajocian, Oxfordian, Kimmeridgian), promoting a varied range of 'terroirs'.

WINE STYLES: these white wines are well-balanced, rich, harmonious, lively and fleshy with powerful aromas and a long-lasting finish. Wines drawn from soils referred to as deep (clay marl) are powerful, fat and full. Those which come from stonier soils with only a thin layer of vegetation, are more mineral and delicate. Solutré wines are rich whilst those of Vergisson are more elegant though also lighter.

With a greenish-yellow hue, they display aromas of dried fruit such as grilled almonds, hazelnut, floral notes including honeysuckle, hawthorn, lily, honey and linden, though also gun-flint, warm brioche, gingerbread and a taste reflecting its 'terroir'. They pair with sweetbread, veal steak in a cream sauce, scallops and fish served with a sauce.

CLIMATE-SPECIFIC SITES:

In Fuissé: *Vignes des Champs, Les Prâles, Les Brûlés, En Chatenet, Les Perrières, Les Vignes Blanches, Le Clos, Les Ménétrières, Au Bourg, Les Travers, Les Murgers, Les Châtaigniers, Bois Seguin, Plan de Bourdon, Aux Prats, Clos Gaillard, Sur les Moulins.*

In Solutré-Pouilly: *Lamure, Les Quarts, La Frairie, Aux Champ Roux, Le Clos, En Servy, Aux Gerbaux, Vigne du Riat, Aux Chailloux,*

Aux Bouthières, Aux Peloux, En Courtesse, En Bertilonne.
In Vergisson: *Aux Vignes Dessus, Aux Charmes, Ronchevrat, Martelet, En France, Sur la Roche, La Côte, Les Croux, Les Crays, En Caramentrant, La Maréchaude.*
In Chaintré: *Maison du Villard, Aux Murs, Les Chevrières, En Vallée, Le Clos de M. Noly, En Cenan, La Bergerie, Aux Quarts, Les Plessys, Les Châtaigneries, La Grande Chattière, Les Hauts de Savy, Les Plantes Vieilles, Le Clos Ressier, Les Fourneaux, Les Verchères.*

AC POUILLY-VINZELLES

OVERVIEW: Pouilly-Vinzelles and neighbouring Pouilly-Loché belong to the most southerly group of Burgundy appellations. The two appellations in fact dovetail. The wines are grown and vinted in exactly the same way as in Pouilly-Fuissé; what differentiates them is the local soil type (predominantly Jurassic calcareous clay with patches of clay).
WINE STYLES: these white wines are highly reminiscent of Pouilly-Fuissé wines, with less body. Pouilly-Vinzelles are dry, lively, vigorous and warm with well-balanced mellowness. Sporting a greenish-yellow hue, they display aromas of honey, peony, acacia, pear, hazelnut and occasionally game. Try with fresh-water fish such as pike perch and pike, shellfish, white meats such as veal or goats cheeses.

AC POUILLY-LOCHÉ

Pouilly-Loché display a straw-yellow hue with aromas of wild rose, honeysuckle, apricot jam, quince, grilled almond, vanilla notes rounded off with mineral tones. Try them with a seafood platter, oven-baked sea bream, fish terrine. Fact: Pouilly-Loché can revert to the lesser Pouilly-Vinzelles appellation, whereas Pouilly-Vinzelles cannot upgrade to Pouilly-Loché.

AC PULIGNY-MONTRACHET

OVERVIEW: the village of Puligny is situated roughly a dozen kilometres from Beaune. The vines grow over the rolling, east facing hills which unfold behind the village as far as Blagny hamlet. The soil is calcareous clay, strewn with stones and is home to a predominant proportion of white wines. The red wines grown within the appellation area are also entitled to use AC Blagny or Côte de Beaune Village. The village's reputation centres on its four world-famous great growths (Montrachet, Bâtard-Montrachet, Chevalier-Montrachet and Bienvenues-Bâtard-Montrachet).

WINE STYLES: the whites are a pale yellow colour. They are rich, with great length on the palate and subtle acidity. Their texture and body are firm, with aromas of freshly-cut grass, butter, fern, hazelnut, marzipan, white flowers, acacia honey, exotic fruits and occasionally amber and quince. These sterling wines are the perfect partners for shellfish, fish served in a sauce, turbot, fatted chicken, strong-smelling cheeses. The less common reds pair with roast red meat, game birds and mild cheeses.

CLIMATE SITES CLASSED AS FIRST GROWTHS:
Sous le Puits, La Garenne, Hameau de Blagny, La Truffière, Champ Gain, Les Chalumeaux, Champ Canet, Clos de la Garenne, Les Folatières, Le Cailleret, Les Demoiselles, Les Pucelles, Clavaillon, Les Perrières, Clos de la Mouchère, Les Combettes, Les Referts.

AC RICHEBOURG GRAND CRU

Vines here grow on the higher part of the slope north of Romanée and Romanée-Conti. 10 growers share the growth's 7.4 ha. The soils are limestone with high clay content and the wines are drawn from Pinot noir. With their ruby-red hue, the wines are robust, intense, warm and highly expressive. They develop fragrances of ripe fruit, musk and leather.

AC ROMANÉE GRAND CRU

Burgundy's most minute growth (0.84 ha) overlooks Romanée-Conti. The texture of the soil is less clayey than in Romanée-Conti and the gradient steeper. The shallow soil combination lays on a limestone foundation and is littered with stones. Only Pinot noir grapes are grown here. The wines are hard when young and are racy, powerful, velvety and mellow. They boast body, flesh and fat with fragrances of black fruit, cherry and undergrowth, and require a few years' patience before they reach their fullest expression. They pair with thrush, partridge, veal and cheeses.

AC ROMANÉE-CONTI GRAND CRU

This 1.63 ha great growth is a monopoly of Domaine de la Romanée-Conti. It is set within the Vosne-Romanée appellation area to the west of the village. This red wine is extremely rich, powerful, full, well-constituted, sturdy and suave, with great aromatic length. It boasts a rich, sometimes opulent texture. With its crimson hue, it displays fragrances of ripe or crystallised red and black fruit (black cherry, bilberry), violet, resin, humus, musk, leather and animal notes. They are the ideal partner for any sophisticated dish.

AC ROMANÉE-SAINT-VIVANT GRAND CRU

From a size perspective, this is Vosne-Romanée's leading growth (9.4 ha), taking its name from Saint-Vivant monastery which was founded in 900. It is currently divided between 6 growers. The soils are deeper than in the other growths, combining limestone and clay. The wines are velvety, graceful, well-constituted, feminine and delicate, they are intense though less powerful than the neighbouring growths. They display fragrances of ripe red (cherry) and black fruit or crystallised fruit though also spices and rose. Recommended with pheasant, venison and hare.

AC RUCHOTTES-CHAMBERTIN GRAND CRU

This 3.3 ha site is adjacent to Clos de Bèze and Mazis-Chambertin in the village of Gevrey-Chambertin. It is a hillside site, yielding magnificently well-balanced red wines which pair well with red meat, roast or sautéed poultry, large game and strong, refined cheeses.

AC RULLY

OVERVIEW: Rully sits south of Chagny, in the northern reaches of the Côte Chalonnaise. The appellation embraces Rully and Chagny, boasting 23 first growths in the foothills of Mount Folie, Mount Varot and Mount Montpalais. The soils are clayey with a predominant proportion of limestone and marl. The red wines are made from Pinot noir, the whites from Chardonnay. Interestingly, Rully specialises in sparkling wines which are now used to make Crémant de Bourgogne.

WINE STYLES: the whites are robust, lively, well-balanced, delicate and subtle. They display a pale golden hue, with aromas of apple, hazelnut, spices and occasionally violet. The reds are elegant, delicate, fleshy and lively and their staying power makes them reminiscent of Mercurey wines. They display a glistening ruby-red hue and aromas of lilac, freshly-cut grass, violet, raspberry, cherry and crushed strawberries. The reds make a suitable partner for free-range poultry and white meats, the whites for pike quenelles, snails, veal escalope with a cream sauce and all white meats in a sauce.

CLIMATE SITES CLASSED AS FIRST GROWTHS:

In Rully: *Le Meix Caillet, Marissou, La Fosse, Les Pierres, Pillot, Raclot, Cloux, Rabourcé, Chapitre, Préaux, Molesme, Agneux, La Bressande, Champs Cloux, Le Meix Cadot, Montpalais, Grésigny, Margotés, Le Rearde, Vauvry, la Pucelle.*

In Chagny: *Clos du Chaigne, Clos Saint-Jacques.*

AC SAINT-AUBIN

OVERVIEW: Saint-Aubin is a village appellation in Côte d'Or located between Chassagne and Puligny-Montrachet. The appellation produces red wine from Pinot noir and white from Chardonnay. Two-thirds of the vineyards boast first growth status and although the area is primarily geared to producing red wines, its reputation is based on its whites. The vines enjoy a south-west or south-south-east aspect.

WINE STYLES: the whites display a pale golden hue and fragrances of green almonds, beeswax, hazelnut, cinnamon, amber and a touch of pepper. They are rich, harmonious, delicate and elegant wines. The reds display a deep colour with fragrances of blackcurrant, black cherry and a touch of leather. The reds pair with game patés, stuffed duck and lamb with girolle mushrooms and the whites with trout in a cream sauce or salmon with basil.

CLIMATE SITES CLASSED AS FIRST GROWTHS:
Derrière la Tour, En Créot, Bas de Vermarain in the east, Les Champlots, In Gamay, La Chatenière, En Remilly, Les Murgers des Dents de Chien, Les Combes, Le Charmoix, Village, Les Castets, Derrière chez Edouard, Le Puits, Sur le Sentier du Clou, Echaille, En la Ranché, En Montceau, En Vollon à l'Est, Es Champs, Le Bas de Gamay à l'Est, Les Combes au Sud, Les Cortons, Les Perrières, Les Travers de Marinot, Marinot, Pitangeret, Sous Roche Dumay, Vignes Moingeon and Les Frionnes.

AC SAINT-BRIS

OVERVIEW: Saint-Bris is grown in 7 villages in Yonne, a dozen kilometres south-east of Auxerre. The vineyards extend over a plateau of stony, limestone soils and are entirely planted to Sauvignon, making them unique in Burgundy.

WINE STYLES: these are fresh, pleasant, delicate, long-lasting, generous wines which are lively when young. They display fragrances of blackcurrant leaves, exotic fruits, acidulous fruits, gun-flint... They are equally delicious as appetisers or with fish, shellfish, grilled chitterlings sausage and cheese.

AC SAINT-ROMAIN

OVERVIEW: this area is located not far from Auxey-Duresses, at high elevations, on extremely stony limestone hills. Two varietals are grown here: Pinot noir for the reds and Chardonnay for the

whites. There are no first growths within the appellation area.
WINE STYLES: the reds are lively and slightly austere in their early years. As they mature, they acquire elegance from their mellow tannins. They display fragrances of cherry, redcurrant and blackcurrant bud leading into smoky tones and macerated fruits as they age. The whites are vigorous, clean and fresh, acquiring mellowness with age. They display vegetal scents, linden and honeysuckle, white flowers, toast, ripe yellow fruit such as mirabelle plums and honey.

AC SAINT-VÉRAN

OVERVIEW: the appellation area is located between the Mâconnais and Beaujolais, with eight villages entitled to use the name. The vineyards enjoy a south-south-east aspect and grow on Jurassic calcareous clay and limestone soils. The terrain is rugged in places and Chardonnay is the sole varietal used here.
WINE STYLES: the wines are dry, round and soft. They display a pale greenish-gold hue and aromas of hazelnut, grilled almonds, honey, gun-flint, white flesh fruit such as pear and peach, though also acacia and honeysuckle. They can be served with oysters, chitterlings sausages, eel with parsley, grilled salmon in a hollandaise sauce, white meats…

AC SANTENAY

OVERVIEW: vineyards in Santenay stretch from east to west, running alongside the Dheune river, fifteen or so kilometres from Beaune. The soils are formed of hard limestone interspersed with marl. One of the oddities here is the way in which the vines are pruned: Guyot pruning is most commonly used in Burgundy, but in Santenay it is supplanted by Royat cordon pruning because of the depth and richness of the soils; this slows down the ageing process of the vines.
WINE STYLES: although they are only moderately concentrated, they can be firm when young, maturing towards greater depth… They display aromas of almond, strawberry, chestnut and prunes for the mature wines. They pair with grilled ribsteak, coq au vin, beef bourguignon…The whites, which are few and far between, are dry, robust and vigorous with an extremely well-developed fragrance.
CLIMATE SITES CLASSED AS FIRST GROWTHS:
La Comme, Les Gravières, Clos de Tavannes, Les Gravières-Clos de Tavannes, Beauregard, Clos Faubard, Clos des Mouches, Beaurepaire, Passetemps, La Maladière, Grand Clos Rousseau, Clos Rousseau.

AC SAVIGNY LES BEAUNE

OVERVIEW: situated north of Beaune, this area is encircled by Beaune mountain in the south and Noël and Chenôve forests in the north. The vineyards are divided into two parts: one west of the village, the other further south-east. One of Savigny's claims to fame is as the home of Dr Guyot who lent his name to a system of pruning. The first growths are planted on two different types of soil: the ones in the south occupy sandy, gravely soil whilst those in the north grow on richer soils formed of limestone and iron-rich clay. The varietals used for the appellation are Chardonnay and Pinot blanc for the whites and Pinot noir for the reds.

WINE STYLES: with their brilliant colour, the reds are pleasant wines with low tannin content and acidity. They are supple, light and graceful. The first growths hailing from the south are light and soft and reward early drinking. Wines from the north are more robust and reward patience. Predominant aromas in the red wines are morello cherry, blackcurrant, strawberry and undergrowth. The whites are lively in the early years then mellow with age. They are harmonious, delicate and sturdy with fragrances of hawthorn, hazelnut, apple and occasionally exotic fruits. They pair with white meat, poultry, scallops, fish…

CLIMATE SITES CLASSED AS FIRST GROWTHS:
Les Charnières, Les Talmettes, Les Vergelesses, Bataillière, Basses Vergelesses, Aux Fourneaux, Champ Chevrey, Les Lavières, Aux Gravains, Petits Godeaux, Aux Serpentières, Aux Clous, Aux Guettes, Les Rouvrettes, Les Narbantons, Les Peuillets, Les Marconnets, La Dominode, Les Jarrons, Les Hauts Jarrons, Redrescul, Les Hauts Marconnets.

AC VIRÉ-CLESSÉ

OVERVIEW: Viré-Clessé embraces four villages in the Mâconnais. It is farmed by 70 growers over a combined area under vine of 390 hectares. The only permitted grape variety is Chardonnay. The vines grow either halfway up hillsides or at the summit on calcareous clay soils. In Clessé, the limestone dates back to the Oxfordian period whilst in Viré, Bajocian bedrock prevails. The entire area enjoys an east/south-east aspect.

WINE STYLES: wines bearing the Viré-Clessé appellation display characteristic aromas of hawthorn, exotic fruit and rose. They are lively, fruity, supple, harmonious wines with great length on the palate. They are the perfect partner for fish, either grilled or served with a sauce, frogs legs or oysters.

AC VOLNAY

OVERVIEW: a Côte de Beaune appellation where over half of the vineyards are classed as first growths. The village of Volnay sits between Meursault, in the south, and Pommard, in the north. Interestingly, 29 hectares of vines within Meursault are entitled to the Volnay first growth appellation, in which case they become Volnay-Santenots. Whites are also grown here and, depending on the specific plots, they are entitled to use the Meursault, Meursault first growth or Meursault-Santenots appellations.

WINE STYLES: they are round, velvety, silky, soft and full. They are prime examples of the Côte de Beaune's most 'feminine' wines. They mature more rapidly than Pommard. Their hue runs the gamut from vermilion to deep ruby-red. They display aromas of raspberry, strawberry, cherry, blackberry, mushroom, violet, spices and vanilla. They pair with veal kidneys, partridges, thrushes, marinated meats and soft cheeses such as reblochon or brie.

CLIMATE SITES CLASSED AS FIRST GROWTHS:

In Volnay: *Chanlin, Pitures-Dessus, Lassolle, Clos des Ducs, Le Village, Clos de la Cave des Ducs, Clos de l'Audignac, Clos de la Chapelle, Clos du château des Ducs, Clos de la Rougeotte, Frémiets-Clos de la Rougeotte, Clos de la Barre, Clos de la Bousse d'Or, Les Brouillards, Les Mitans, En l'Ormeau, Les Angles, Pointes d'Angle, Frémiets, La Gigotte, Les Grands Champs, Les Lurets, Robardelle, Carelle sous la Chapelle, Carelles, Le Ronceret, Les Aussy, Champans, Les Caillerets, Les Caillerets-Clos des 60 Ouvrés, En Chevret, Taille Pieds, Clos du Verseuil, Clos des Chênes.*

In Meursault: *Santenots Blancs, Les Santenots du Milieu, Les Santenots-Dessous, Clos des Santenots, Les Plures, Les Vignes Blanches.*

AC VOSNE-ROMANÉE

OVERVIEW: the appellation embraces the villages of Vosne-Romanée and Flagey-Echezeaux. The soils are limestone with varying amounts of clay on reasonably steep inclines which provide for efficient drainage. Pinot noir is the only permitted varietal. Vosne-Romanée is the privileged home of some of the most prestigious wines in the world, boasting eight great growths: Romanée-Conti, Romanée-Saint-Vivant, Echezeaux, Grands Echezeaux, La Romanée, La Grande-Rue, La Tâche and Richebourg.

WINE STYLES: the most predominant character trait here is the silkiness of the wines with subtle tannins and acidity. The wines are fleshy with excellent length. On the palate, they are powerful yet epitomise delicacy, lacking any form of aggressiveness. They display fragrances of cherry, strawberry, undergrowth, blackcurrant, boxwood and spices with notes of mint and bitter almond. They pair with pheasant paté, roast hare, venison steak and roast beef.

CLIMATE SITES CLASSED AS FIRST GROWTHS:
Les Beaux Mont, Les Suchots, Aux Brûlées, La Croix Rameau, Clos des Réas, Les Gaudichots, Les Chaumes, Aux Malconsorts, Au-Dessus des Malconsorts, Cros Parentoux, Aux Reignots, En Orveaux, Les Rouges, Les Petits Monts.

AC VOUGEOT

OVERVIEW: 73% of the hamlet of Vougeot is given over to vineyards. Although it is renowned world-wide for Clos de Vougeot château (a great growth), it also produces wines under a village appellation and as first growths, to the south-east, on the border with Chambolle-Musigny. The soil types are varied: they are limestone combined with varying amounts of clay. The two permitted varietals are Pinot noir (reds) and Chardonnay (whites).

WINE STYLES: the reds are harmonious, elegant, racy and pleasantly round. With their sparkling crimson, dark ruby-red colour, they are powerful and complex with truffle, violet, animal nuances, blackcurrant, raspberry, blackberry and bilberry. As they age, they develop aromas of venison and havana cigars. Try with partridge or a leg of venison. The whites are fruity, supple, dry and relatively robust first growths. On the palate, they are round, fleshy and long-lasting with excellent balance. They partner well with foie gras or salmon in a sorrel sauce.

CLIMATE SITES CLASSED AS FIRST GROWTHS:
Les Cras, Le Clos Blanc, Les Petits Vougeots, Clos de la Perrière.

• • •

BURGUNDY

Aloxe Corton

CHÂTEAU DE SANTENAY +33 3 80 20 61 87

▼ Les Brunettes et Planchots 2011 Price: ○ 88/100

DOMAINE EDMOND CORNU & FILS +33 3 80 26 40 79

▼ Vintage 2010 Price: ○○○ 88/100

DOMAINE NUDANT JEAN-RENÉ +33 3 80 26 40 48

▼ Clos de la Boulette 2010 Price: ○○○ 91/100

Beaune

DOMAINE BRIGITTE BERTHELEMOT +33 3 80 21 68 61

▼ 1er Cru Grèves 2010 Price: ○○○ 92/100

CHÂTEAU DE SANTENAY +33 3 80 20 61 87

▼ 1er Cru - Clos du Roi 2011 Price: ○ 91/100

DOMAINE BRIGITTE BERTHELEMOT +33 3 80 21 68 61

▼ Longbois 2011 Price: ○○ 90/100

▼ 1er Cru Bélissand 2010 Price: ○○ 89/100

CHÂTEAU DE LA CHARRIÈRE +33 3 80 20 64 36

▼ 1er Cru Clos des Vignes Franches 2011 Price: ○○ 85/100

CHÂTEAU DE SANTENAY +33 3 80 20 61 87

▼ 1er Cru - Montée Rouge 2011 Price: ○ 93/100

CLAVELIER & FILS +33 3 80 62 94 11

▼ 1er Cru Les Perrières 2010 Price: ○○○ 89/100

DOMAINE BAROLET-PERNOT PÈRE ET FILS +33 3 80 21 20 88

▼ 1er Cru - Teurons 2006 Price: ○○○ 85/100

DOMAINE BRIGITTE BERTHELEMOT +33 3 80 21 68 61

▼ 1er Cru Clos des Mouches 2010 Price: ○○○ 93/100

Bonnes Mares Grand Cru

DOMAINE FOUGERAY DE BEAUCLAIR +33 3 80 52 21 12

▼ Vintage 2011 Price: ❍❍❍❍❍ 97/100

Bourgogne

JAFFELIN +33 3 80 22 12 49

▼ Chardonnay - Les Chapitres de Jaffelin 2011 Price: ❍ 83/100

CHAMPCREVIN +33 3 25 29 35 00

▼ Pierre Rousseau Cuvée Symphonie 2011 Price: ❍ 83/100

CHÂTEAU DE LA CHARRIÈRE +33 3 80 20 64 36

▼ Vintage 2011 Price: ❍ 86/100

DOMAINE DES CHENEVIÈRES +33 3 85 33 31 27

▼ La Baronne 2011 Price: ❍ 85/100

DOMAINE METGE-TOPPIN +33 9 63 63 84 86

▼ Château de L'Hestrange Vintage 2012 Price: ❍ 84/100

JAFFELIN +33 3 80 22 12 49

▼ Pinot noir 2011 Price: ❍ 84/100

Bourgogne Aligoté

DOMAINE GÉRARD BERGER-RIVE & FILS +33 3 85 91 13 81

▼ Les Sensiels de Berger-Rive Perle d'Ange 2011 Price: ❍ 85/100

DOMAINE GOISOT ANNE ET ARNAUD +33 3 86 53 32 15

▼ Vintage 2011 Price: ❍ 84/100

Bourgogne Côtes d'Auxerre

DOMAINE GOISOT ANNE ET ARNAUD +33 3 86 53 32 15

▼ Cuvée du Manoir 2010 Price: ❍ 86/100

DOMAINE GOISOT ANNE ET ARNAUD +33 3 86 53 32 15

▼ Pinot Noir 2011 Price: ❍ 84/100

Bourgogne Hautes Côtes de Beaune

DOMAINE GÉRARD BERGER-RIVE & FILS +33 3 85 91 13 81

▼ Manoir de Mercey Au Paradis 2011 Price: ❍❍ 86/100

CHÂTEAU DE SANTENAY +33 3 80 20 61 87

▼ Château de Santenay - Philippe le Hardi Clos de la Chaise Dieu - Monopole 2011 Price: ❍ 87/100

DOMAINE BRIGITTE BERTHELEMOT +33 3 80 21 68 61

▼ Domaine Berthelemot Vintage 2010 Price: ❍ 88/100

DOMAINE GÉRARD BERGER-RIVE & FILS +33 3 85 91 13 81

▼ Manoir de Mercey Clos des Dames 2011 Price: ❍❍ 86/100

Bourgogne Hautes Côtes de Nuits

DOMAINE MICHEL GROS +33 3 80 61 04 69

▼ Vintage 2009 Price: ❍❍ 88/100

DOMAINE YVES CHALEY ET FILLE +33 3 80 61 43 81

▼ Cuvée de la Tour Saint-Denis Les Cloupetits 2011 Price: ❍❍ 88/100

Detailed instructions are featured at the start of the book.

Bouzeron

DOMAINE CHANZY	+33 3 85 87 23 69
▼ Clos de la Fortune 2011 Price: ○○	87/100

DOMAINE MICHEL BRIDAY	+33 3 85 87 07 90
▼ Cuvée Axelle 2011 Price: ○	86/100

Chablis

DOMAINE ALAIN GEOFFROY	+33 3 86 42 43 76
▼ Vintage 2011 Price: ○○	86/100
▼ Domaine Le Verger Cuvée Vieilles Vignes Élevé en fûts de chêne 2011 Price: ○○	86/100

GARNIER ET FILS	+33 3 86 47 42 12
▼ Domaine Garnier & Fils Vintage 2011 Price: ○○	86/100

RAOUL GAUTHERIN & FILS	+33 3 86 42 11 86
▼ Vintage 2011 Price: ○	84/100

DOMAINE ALAIN GEOFFROY	+33 3 86 42 43 76
▼ Domaine Le Verger Vintage 2011 Price: ○○	87/100

DOMAINE DU CHARDONNAY	+33 3 86 42 48 03
▼ Vintage 2011 Price: ○	85/100

DOMAINE DU CHÂTEAU DE FLEYS	+33 3 86 42 47 70
▼ Vieilles Vignes 2011 Price: ○	88/100

DOMAINE GOISOT ANNE ET ARNAUD	+33 3 86 53 32 15
▼ Vintage 2011 Price: ○	85/100

DOMAINE HEIMBOURGER	+33 3 86 41 40 88
▼ Vintage 2010 Price: ○	87/100

DOMAINE JEAN COLLET & FILS	+33 3 86 42 11 93
▼ Vintage 2011 Price: ○	86/100

DOMAINE JOLLY ET FILS	+33 3 86 47 42 31
▼ Vintage 2011 Price: ○	86/100

DOMAINE SERVIN +33 3 86 18 90 00

▼ Vintage 2011 Price: ○ 85/100

GARNIER ET FILS +33 3 86 47 42 12

▼ Grains Dorés 2009 Price: ○○ 89/100

LES TEMPS PERDUS +33 3 86 41 46 05

CV▼ Vintage 2011 Price: ○○ 84/100

RAOUL GAUTHERIN & FILS +33 3 86 42 11 86

▼ Cuvée Vieille Vigne
Élevée en fût de chêne 2011 Price: ○ 87/100

Chablis Grand Cru

DOMAINE JEAN COLLET & FILS +33 3 86 42 11 93

▼ Valmur 2011 Price: ○○○ 91/100

DOMAINE NATHALIE & GILLES FÈVRE +33 3 86 18 94 47

▼ Les Preuses 2010 Price: ○○○ 95/100

DOMAINE SERVIN +33 3 86 18 90 00

▼ Blanchot 2010 Price: ○○○ 90/100

GARNIER ET FILS +33 3 86 47 42 12

▼ Vaudésir 2010 Price: ○○○○ 92/100

RAOUL GAUTHERIN & FILS +33 3 86 42 11 86

▼ Grenouilles 2011 Price: ○○○ 93/100

Chablis Premier Cru

DOMAINE DU CHÂTEAU DE FLEYS +33 3 86 42 47 70

▼ Mont de Milieu 2011 Price: ○○ 91/100

DOMAINE DU CHARDONNAY +33 3 86 42 48 03

▼ 2011 Price: ○○ 90/100

DOMAINE NATHALIE & GILLES FÈVRE +33 3 86 18 94 47

▼ Fourchaume 2011 Price: ○○○ 90/100

Burgundy - *Chablis Premier Cru*

DOMAINE JEAN COLLET & FILS	+33 3 86 42 11 93
▼ Vaillons 2010 Price: OO	89/100
RAOUL GAUTHERIN & FILS	+33 3 86 42 11 86
▼ Montmains 2011 Price: OO	89/100
DOMAINE ALAIN GEOFFROY	+33 3 86 42 43 76
▼ Beauroy 2011 Price: OO	88/100
DOMAINE DU CHARDONNAY	+33 3 86 42 48 03
▼ Vintage 2010 Price: OO	88/100
GARNIER ET FILS	+33 3 86 47 42 12
▼ Montmains 2011 Price: OO	88/100
RAOUL GAUTHERIN & FILS	+33 3 86 42 11 86
▼ Mont de Milieu 2011 Price: OO	88/100
DOMAINE JEAN COLLET & FILS	+33 3 86 42 11 93
▼ Montmains 2011 Price: OO	86/100
DOMAINE ALAIN GEOFFROY	+33 3 86 42 43 76
▼ Fourchaume 2011 Price: OO	90/100

DOMAINE DU CHÂTEAU DE FLEYS

▼ Mont de Milieu - Vieilles Vignes 2011 **92/100**

Pale gold. Expressive nose of butter, almond, hazelnut, a festival of white flowers and a touch of gunflint. Very fat and chewy yet aromatic expression is not obscured. Excellent hallmark Chablis Chardonnay traits. The best is yet to come.

Price: OO

Serving Temperature: 9-11°C
Ready to drink : 2014-2016

Domaine du Château de Fleys
2 rue des Fourneaux
89800 Fleys
Tel.: +33 03 86 42 47 70 - Fax: +33 03 86 42 81 09
E-mail: philippon.beatrice@orange.fr
Website: http://www.chablis-philippon.com

DOMAINE DU CHARDONNAY +33 3 86 42 48 03

▼ Vintage 2010 Price: ❍❍ 91/100

DOMAINE JEAN COLLET & FILS +33 3 86 42 11 93

▼ Montée de Tonnerre 2011 Price: ❍❍ 90/100

DOMAINE JOLLY ET FILS +33 3 86 47 42 31

▼ Fourchaume - L'Homme Mort 2011 Price: ❍❍ 88/100

DOMAINE NATHALIE & GILLES FÈVRE +33 3 86 18 94 47

▼ Vaulorent 2011 Price: ❍❍❍ 90/100

DOMAINE SERVIN +33 3 86 18 90 00

▼ Les Forêts 2011 Price: ❍❍ 86/100

GARNIER ET FILS +33 3 86 47 42 12

▼ Mont de Milieu 2011 Price: ❍❍ 90/100

LES TEMPS PERDUS +33 3 86 41 46 05

CV▼ Montmains 2011 Price: ❍❍ 89/100

RAOUL GAUTHERIN & FILS +33 3 86 42 11 86

▼ Vaillons 2011 Price: ❍❍ 90/100

Chassagne-Montrachet

CHÂTEAU DE LA CHARRIÈRE +33 3 80 20 64 36

▼ Les Champs de Morjot 2011 Price: ❍❍ 89/100

Clos de Vougeot Grand Cru

CHÂTEAU DE SANTENAY +33 3 80 20 61 87

▼ Vintage 2010 Price: ❍ 88/100

Detailed instructions are featured at the start of the book.

DOMAINE HENRI REBOURSEAU

▼ Vintage 2000 **95/100**

Deeply-coloured orange-brown. Very open nose intermixing black cherry, prune, undergrowth and humus. Sumptuous attack showing fat, fullness and presence flowing into a more mineral mid-palate (graphite) with wonderful persistency. Sterling effort.

Price: ○○○○○

Wine and food pairing: Roast duck
Serving Temperature: 16-18°C
Ready to drink: From now on

In 1919, General Henri Rebourseau turned his father's vines around their 18th-century home into a vineyard. His son Pierre later took over, helping the estate to prosper into the 1980s. Today, one of the general's great grandchildren, Jean de Surrel, manages the estate. It stretches over 13 hectares, forming a patchwork of extremely well-situated terroirs: from Gevrey-Chambertin to Premier Cru Le Fonteny, passing through Charmes-Chambertin, Mazis-Chambertin, Chambertin and Chambertin-Clos-De-Bèze. All the wealth and diversity of the terroirs of Gevrey-Chambertin are found here, not to mention the emblematic Clos de Vougeot, of which the estate owns 2.20 hectares located at the heart of the walled vineyard.

Domaine Henri Rebourseau
10 place du Monument
21220 Gevrey Chambertin
Tel.: +33 (0)3 80 51 88 94 - Fax: +33 (0)3 80 34 12 82
E-mail: domaine@rebourseau.com
Website: http://www.domaine-rebourseau.fr

Corton Charlemagne Grand cru

DOMAINE BERTAGNA +33 3 80 62 86 04

ORG ▼ Vintage 2011 Price: ○○○○○ 97/100

Côte de Nuits-Villages

DOMAINE FOUGERAY DE BEAUCLAIR +33 3 80 52 21 12

▼ Vintage 2011 Price: ○○○ 88/100

Crémant de Bourgogne

CHAMPCREVIN +33 3 25 29 35 00

▼ Brut Price: ○ 87/100

DOMAINE METGE-TOPPIN +33 9 63 63 84 86

▼ Château de L'Hestrange Vintage 2011 Price: ○ 85/100

Echezeaux Grand Cru

DOMAINE NUDANT JEAN-RENÉ +33 3 80 26 40 48

▼ Domaine Nudant Vintage 2010 Price: ○○○○ 96/100

Detailed instructions are featured at the start of the book.

Fixin

DOMAINE FOUGERAY DE BEAUCLAIR

▼ Clos Marion 2011 **90/100**

Limpid hue with ruby tints. Racy nose of morello cherry, plum and a whiff of toast. Suave attack, harmoniously defined, round palate showing elegant, precise fruit expression. Silky firmness and refined spices on the finish.

Price: ○○○

Serving Temperature: 16-18°C
Ready to drink : 2014-2015

Domaine Fougeray de Beauclair
44 rue de Mazy - 21160 Marsannay la Côte
Tel.: +33 03 80 52 21 12 - Fax: +33 03 80 58 73 83
E-mail: fougeraydebeauclair@wanadoo.fr
Website: http://www.fougeraydebeauclair.fr

DOMAINE FOUGERAY DE BEAUCLAIR +33 3 80 52 21 12

▼ Clos Marion 2011 Price: ○○○ 90/100

MAISON FOUGERAY DE BEAUCLAIR +33 3 80 52 21 12

▼ Terre des Anges Cuvée Romane 2011 Price: ○○○ 87/100

Gevrey-Chambertin

DOMAINE PHILIPPE LECLERC +33 3 80 34 30 72

▼ 1er Cru Les Champeaux 2010 Price: ○○○ 92/100

▼ En Champs 2010 Price: ○○○ 90/100

CHÂTEAU DE BEAUFORT +33 6 28 27 10 38

▼ Domaine Coudray-Bizot

1er Cru Les Cazetiers 2006 Price: ○ 87/100

DOMAINE HENRI REBOURSEAU +33 3 80 51 88 94

▼ Vintage 2001 Price: ○○○ 89/100

DOMAINE PHILIPPE LECLERC +33 3 80 34 30 72

▼ 1er Cru Les Cazetiers 2010 Price: ○○○ 93/100

Irancy

DOMAINE ERIC DARLES +33 3 86 42 57 31

▼ Eric Darles Vintage 2008 Price: ○ 85/100

DOMAINE HEIMBOURGER +33 3 86 41 40 88

▼ Cuvée Pierre 2010 Price: ○ 81/100

Ladoix

DOMAINE EDMOND CORNU & FILS +33 3 80 26 40 79

▼ Vintage 2010 Price: ○○ 87/100

▼ Vintage 2010 Price: ○○ 90/100

Mâcon-Chaintré

TERROIRS ORIGINELS +33 4 74 69 53 86

▼ Pascal Berthier Les Champs Bardes

Vieilles Vignes 2011 Price: ○○ 89/100

Detailed instructions are featured at the start of the book.

Mâcon-Chardonnay

CHÂTEAU DE MESSEY +33 3 85 51 33 83

▼ Château de Messeym Les Crêts 2011 Price: ○○ 85/100

Mâcon-Milly-Lamartine

LOUIS DORRY +33 6 32 60 05 01

▼ Les Collonges 2010 Price: ○○ 91/100

Mâcon-Villages

DOMAINE DES CHENEVIÈRES +33 3 85 33 31 27

▼ Vintage 2011 Price: ○ 83/100

DOMAINE ROGER LUQUET +33 3 85 35 60 91

▼ Vintage 2011 Price: ○ 85/100

Maranges

DOMAINE EDMOND MONNOT ET FILS +33 3 85 91 16 12

▼ 1er Cru La Fussière 2009 Price: ○○ 89/100

▼ 1er Cru La Fussière 2010 Price: ○○ 89/100

DOMAINE CLAUDE NOUVEAU +33 3 85 91 13 34

▼ 1er Cru La Fussière 2010 Price: ○○ 88/100

DOMAINE EDMOND MONNOT ET FILS +33 3 85 91 16 12

▼ 1er Cru Le Clos des Loyères 2009 Price: ○○ 90/100

Marsannay

DOMAINE FOUGERAY DE BEAUCLAIR +33 3 80 52 21 12

- ▼ Saint Jacques 2011 Price: ○○ 89/100
- ▼ Les Aiges Pruniers 2011 Price: ○○ 87/100
- ▼ Les Favières 2011 Price: ○○ 87/100
- ▼ Saint Jacques 2011 Price: ○○○ 89/100

MAISON FOUGERAY DE BEAUCLAIR +33 3 80 52 21 12

- ▼ Terre des Anges Les Angelots 2011 Price: ○○○ 89/100

Mazis-Chambertin Grand Cru

DOMAINE HENRI REBOURSEAU +33 3 80 51 88 94

- ▼ Vintage 2000 Price: ○○○○○ 93/100

Mercurey

CHÂTEAU DE SANTENAY +33 3 80 20 61 87

- ▼ Philippe le Hardi Vintage 2011 Price: ○ 85/100
- ▼ 1er Cru - Les Puillets 2011 Price: ○ 89/100

DOMAINE GÉRARD BERGER-RIVE & FILS +33 3 85 91 13 81

- ▼ Manoir de Mercey Châteaubeau 2011 Price: ○○ 88/100

DOMAINE MICHEL BRIDAY +33 3 85 87 07 90

- ▼ 1er Cru Clos Marcilly 2010 Price: ○○ 87/100

Meursault

DOMAINE GUY BOCARD +33 3 80 21 26 06

▼ Guy Bocard Les Narvaux 2010 Price: ○○○ 93/100

DOMAINE ALAIN PATRIARCHE +33 3 80 21 24 48

▼ Les Tillets 2011 Price: ○○○ 90/100

▼ Les Grands Charrons 2011 Price: ○○○ 92/100

DOMAINE BRIGITTE BERTHELEMOT +33 3 80 21 68 61

▼ Domaine Berthelemot Les Tillets 2011 Price: ○○○ 91/100

DOMAINE GUY BOCARD +33 3 80 21 26 06

CV▼ Guy Bocard 1er Cru Charmes 2010 Price: ○○○ 97/100

DOMAINE VINCENT BOUZEREAU +33 3 80 21 61 08

▼ Vintage 2011 Price: ○○○ 89/100

Nuits Saint Georges

CLAVELIER & FILS +33 3 80 62 94 11

▼ Clavelier Vintage 2010 Price: ○○○ 86/100

DOMAINE BERTAGNA +33 3 80 62 86 04

ORG▼ 1er Cru Les Murgers 2011 Price: ○○○○ 92/100

DOMAINE MICHEL GROS +33 3 80 61 04 69

▼ Vintage 2009 Price: ○○○ 90/100

DOMAINE NUDANT JEAN-RENÉ +33 3 80 26 40 48

▼ Domaine Nudant Vintage 2010 Price: ○○○ 92/100

Pernand-Vergelesses

DOMAINE DUBREUIL-FONTAINE PÈRE & FILS +33 3 80 21 55 43

▼ 1er Cru - Clos Berthet 2011 Price: ○○○ 90/100

▼ 1er Cru - Iles des Vergelesses 2011 Price: ○○○ 90/100

Petit Chablis

DOMAINE DU CHARDONNAY +33 3 86 42 48 03

▼ Vintage 2011 Price: ○ — 84/100

DOMAINE JOLLY ET FILS +33 3 86 47 42 31

▼ Vintage 2011 Price: ○ — 84/100

Pommard

CHÂTEAU DE LA CHARRIÈRE +33 3 80 20 64 36

▼ Cuvée Tradition 2011 Price: ○○ — 87/100

DOMAINE BRIGITTE BERTHELEMOT +33 3 80 21 68 61

▼ Domaine Berthelemot Noizons 2010 Price: ○○○ — 88/100

DOMAINE LOÏC DURAND +33 3 80 26 02 57

▼ Vieilles Vignes 2011 Price: ○○○ — 88/100

Pouilly-Fuissé

DOMAINE DENUZILLER +33 3 85 35 80 77

▼ La Frérie 2011 Price: ○○ — 88/100

▼ Prestige 2011 Price: ○○ — 88/100

CHÂTEAU DE POUILLY +33 3 85 35 83 65

▼ Vintage 2009 Price: ○○ — 90/100

DOMAINE AUVIGUE +33 3 85 34 17 36

▼ Cuvée Hors Classe 2011 Price: ○○ — 90/100

DOMAINE DENUZILLER +33 3 85 35 80 77

▼ Le Clos 2011 Price: ○○ — 91/100

DOMAINE ROGER LUQUET +33 3 85 35 60 91

▼ Vintage 2011 Price: ○○ — 89/100

Puligny-Montrachet

CHÂTEAU DE BEAUFORT +33 6 28 27 10 38

▼ Domaine Coudray-Bizot

1er Cru Les Combettes 2007 Price: O — 93/100

DOMAINE BAROLET-PERNOT PÈRE ET FILS +33 3 80 21 20 88

▼ La Brelance 2011 Price: OO — 90/100

DOMAINE CHANZY +33 3 85 87 23 69

▼ Les Reuchaux 2010 Price: OOO — 87/100

Rully

DOMAINE GÉRARD BERGER-RIVE & FILS +33 3 85 91 13 81

▼ Manoir de Mercey En Rosey 2011 Price: OO — 88/100

DOMAINE MICHEL BRIDAY +33 3 85 87 07 90

▼ Les 4 Vignes 2011 Price: OO — 84/100

DOMAINE BELLEVILLE +33 3 85 91 06 00

▼ La Crée 2011 Price: OO — 88/100

DOMAINE CHANZY +33 3 85 87 23 69

▼ Vintage 2010 Price: OO — 89/100

DOMAINE GÉRARD BERGER-RIVE & FILS +33 3 85 91 13 81

▼ Manoir de Mercey Cuvée Louise 2011 Price: OO — 88/100

DOMAINE MICHEL BRIDAY +33 3 85 87 07 90

▼ Vintage 2011 Price: OO — 85/100

Saint-Aubin

CHÂTEAU DE SANTENAY +33 3 80 20 61 87

▼ Philippe le Hardi En Vesvau 2011 Price: O — 89/100

Saint-Bris

LES TEMPS PERDUS		+33 3 86 41 46 05
CV ▼	Sauvignon 2011 Price: ○	86/100
DOMAINE GOISOT ANNE ET ARNAUD		+33 3 86 53 32 15
▼	Vintage 2011 Price: ○	82/100
LES TEMPS PERDUS		+33 3 86 41 46 05
CV ▼	Sauvignon - Vieilles Vignes 2011 Price: ○○	86/100

Saint-Romain

DOMAINE BAROLET-PERNOT PÈRE ET FILS		+33 3 80 21 20 88
▼	Poillange 2011 Price: ○○	89/100

Saint-Véran

DOMAINE AUVIGUE		+33 3 85 34 17 36
▼	Les Chênes 2011 Price: ○	90/100
DOMAINE ROGER LUQUET		+33 3 85 35 60 91
▼	Vintage 2010 Price: ○	89/100

Santenay

CHÂTEAU DE LA CHARRIÈRE		+33 3 80 20 64 36
▼	1er Cru Clos Rousseau 2010 Price: ○○	86/100
▼	Sous La Roche 2011 Price: ○○	88/100

Burgundy - *Santenay*

DOMAINE CLAUDE NOUVEAU +33 3 85 91 13 34

▼ 1er Cru Grand Clos Rousseau 2010 Price: OO 91/100

▼ Le Chainey 2011 Price: OO 85/100

Savigny les Beaune

DOMAINE FOUGERAY DE BEAUCLAIR +33 3 80 52 21 12

▼ Les Golardes 2011 Price: OOO 90/100

▼ Les Golardes 2010 Price: OOO 88/100

DOMAINE DUBREUIL-FONTAINE PÈRE & FILS +33 3 80 21 55 43

▼ 1er Cru - Les Vergelesses 2010 Price: OO 88/100

MAISON FOUGERAY DE BEAUCLAIR +33 3 80 52 21 12

▼ Terre des Anges Vintage 2011 Price: OOO 86/100

Vosne Romanée

CHÂTEAU DE BEAUFORT +33 6 28 27 10 38

▼ Domaine Coudray-Bizot

1er Cru La Croix Rameau 2006 Price: O 90/100

DOMAINE MICHEL GROS +33 3 80 61 04 69

▼ 1er Cru Clos des Réas

Monopole 2009 Price: OOOO 95/100

Vougeot

DOMAINE BERTAGNA +33 3 80 62 86 04

ORG▼ 1er Cru Clos de La Perrière 2011 Price: OOOO 89/100

Aisne
Reims
Châlon-sur-Marne
Montagne de Reims
Epernay
Châlon-sur-Marne
Vallée de la Marne
Côtes des Blancs
Côtes de Sézanne
Marne
Aube
Seine
Troyes
Côtes des Bar

CHAMPAGNE

STILL SCALING THE HEIGHTS

Champagne can only be produced in the French region of the same name. Although its preparation may be linked to a specific set of skills and expertise, it is also associated with a terroir which is as influential as it is diverse. In other words, we should talk not of champagne, but instead of champagnes - each of which have their own individual characteristics and styles, making it possible for any champagne-lover to find a wine to astonish and delight, depending on individual taste and circumstances. To help you to know what to look for when choosing and tasting a champagne, we present a 'behind-the-scenes' look at this subtle brew.

The vineyards of Champagne mainly cover three départements: Marne, Aube and Aisne. Three grape varieties are used predominantly in this area: Chardonnay, Pinot Noir and Pinot Meunier, which are grown across highly diverse terroirs. These fluctuations are due to various combinations of climate, subsoil and relief.

Three princes, one great terroir: There are a total of 313 crus produced in as many communes. The latter themselves are subdivided into parcels of land and lieux-dits, each of which impart extremely specific qualities and characteristics upon the grapes. There is a hierarchical scale for categorising the crus, identifying 17 Grands Crus and 41 Premiers Crus from among their ranks. Generally speaking, the three major grape varieties have their favourite areas. The Montagne de Reims and the Côte des Bar are favoured by Pinot Noir, the Marne Valley is the preferred home of Pinot Meunier, and Chardonnay's soil of choice is in the Côte des Blancs. Champagne harvesting is performed exclusively by hand. The grapes must be vinified whole, a requirement which necessitates their transportation in small containers such as baskets and crates. The pressing stage follows immediately afterwards, with three successive pressings taking place. The first pressing, which is known locally as cuvée, is considered to be of the highest quality, and is generally reserved for the production of the finest wines. Once the juices have passed through the settling vat, where the impurities separate off and sink to the bottom, they are transferred into vats or barrels and begin the fermentation phase. Champagne houses vinify the grapes separately by variety and - wherever possible - by individual cru, taking the particular structure into consideration.

WHERE TIME AND SKILL COMBINE: Having separated the resting wine from its lees by means of racking, a wine referred to as clair (signifying 'non-effervescent') is obtained. The cellar-master then blends his various vins clairs together to produce one or more cuvées of a particular style. The aim at this stage is to produce the best possible combinations in the pursuit of harmony. There is universal agreement that blending lends a cuvée complexity. The artist's palette contains a wide variety of nuances: each vin clair exhibits the individual characteristics of its original grape, which will vary depending on cru, or - at a more basic level - on grape variety. Chardonnay's boast is that it lends refinement and ageing potential. Pinot Noir gives power and red fruit aromas. Pinot Meunier bestows fruitiness, and develops more quickly over time. The wine producer therefore makes a choice from among the grape varieties and crus from which the wines have been produced, but also - if the end product is not a vintage champagne - from among several different years. Of course, the blends depend on the various grapes at the producer's disposal, yet they must also conform to the "house style", not only as a means of differentiation from other champagnes, but also to satisfy the requirements of consumers whose loyalty depends on the year-to-year consistency of the wine. Creating a range of different types of wines also provides the producer with a wide range of styles and prices. Once blending has taken place, the wine is bottled along with a small quantity of sugar liqueur and a few yeasts, an addition which encourages the second fermentation. The law specifies a minimum of fifteen months' cellaring for non-vintage bruts and a full three years for vintage champagnes. During bottle fermentation, a deposit forms in the bottle. The process by which it is removed is known as remuage (riddling): the bottles are placed in a partially inverted position on slanted racks known as pupîtres and, over a period of several weeks, they are turned one quarter-turn per day while being gradually lifted further towards the vertical. The bottle ultimately ends up sur pointe (completely inverted) with the deposit settled in the neck. The old method of removing this deposit involved unstoppering the bottle and turning it over quickly; the pressure in the bottle would cause the deposit to be expelled. The preferred modern method is a simpler mechanical technique consisting of immersing the end of the bottle in a freezing 'bath' and then turning the bottle over, causing the plug of ice containing the deposit to be expelled by pressure. The bottle then receives its final cork, topped with a cap in the house colours; both of these are held in place by a muzzle. The package is completed by the addition of neck and body labels, and the champagne is ready to be sent out.

CHOOSING A CHAMPAGNE

Below is a presentation of the various types of champagne. Information on the following characteristics can be found on the bottle label, allowing you to make an informed choice.

• **GRAPE VARIETY** • Grape variety: the wine may have been blended from one or more varieties. Champagne produced solely from Chardonnay (a white grape with white juice) is known as blanc de blancs. Likewise, a champagne produced only from Pinot Noir and/or Pinot Meunier (black grapes with white juice) is known as a blanc de noirs. The liqueur d'expédition (the sweetening "dosage" - a mixture of sugar and wine added at the bottling stage in some cases) lends further nuances to the wine. Depending on the quantity of the dosage added, the wine will assume a more or less sweet character, classified as follows. 0-6g of sugar per litre: extra-brut; under 15 g: brut; 12-20g: extra-dry; 17-35g: sec; 33-50g: demi-sec; over 50g: doux.

• **NON-VINTAGE BRUT CHAMPAGNES** • These are the most common types of champagne, combining wines from a number of different years, and usually from a range of varieties and crus too. They include a proportion of reserve wine, preserving a degree of constant style.

• **VINTAGES** • These are produced from grapes from just one year (which determines the vintage); they may, however, come from a variety of crus. Vintages are not produced as a matter of course every year, but rather in years with particularly high-quality harvests.

• **PREMIERS AND GRANDS CRUS** • To be a Grand Cru, a wine must be produced exclusively from Grand Cru-classified terroirs; there are a total of 17 of these. Premiers Crus are produced using grapes taken from Premier Cru-classified communes, to which a proportion of Grand Cru may in some cases be added. Rosé champagnes: Champagne is the only French region where rosé wines may be produced from a combination of red and white wine. Rosé champagnes are therefore obtained in part by adding still red wine, but they can also be produced using the saignée (bleeding) technique; in other words, by macerating the juice of black grapes along with their skins to extract colour and aromas. Rosés may be vintage champagnes, or indeed be rated Grand Cru or Premier Cru.

RECENT VINTAGE

• **2009** • The beginning of the growing season was difficult, with frost followed by hailstorms, and a mildew problem in July. But there was a happy ending as the month of August was hot and dry, saving the harvest. With a good alcohol potential and level of acidity, this vintage should produce excellent blends.

• • •

CHAMPAGNE

Champagne

ALEXANDRE PENET +33 3 51 00 28 80

- Extra Brut Blanc de Blancs Grand Cru Price:OOO 87/100

CAVE COOPÉRATIVE U.P.R. CHAMPAGNE LE MESNIL +33 3 26 57 53 23

- Brut blanc de blancs grand cru Price:OOO 88/100

CAVE DES SIX COTEAUX CHAMPAGNE CHARLES HESTON +33 3 26 03 08 78

- Brut blanc de noirs l'Agat Price:OO 86/100
- Brut Sélection Chardonnay Price:OO 84/100
- Brut L'Ambassadrice Price:OO 84/100
- Brut Sélection Nature Price:OO 83/100
- Brut La Charles Heston Price:OO 83/100
- Brut Cuvée Tradition Price:OO 81/100
- Brut L'Eveil Price:OO 79/100
- Brut Sélection Price:OO 78/100

CHAMPAGNE A. MARGAINE +33 3 26 97 92 13

- Brut blanc de blancs 1er cru Spécial Club 2008 Price:OOO 90/100
- Brut 1er cru Le Brut Price:OO 86/100

CHAMPAGNE ADAM-GARNOTEL +33 3 26 03 40 22

- Brut Millénium Price:OO 86/100
- Brut rosé Price:OO 84/100
- Brut tradition Price:OO 83/100

CHAMPAGNE ALAIN BAILLY +33 3 26 97 41 58

- Brut Cuvée Prestige Price:OO 84/100

CHAMPAGNE ALBERT DE MILLY +33 3 26 52 33 44

- Brut Tradition Price:OO 77/100

CHAMPAGNE ALEXANDRE LE BRUN +33 3 26 59 73 51

- Extra brut Révélation Blanc de Meunier 2009 Price:OOO 86/100
- Brut Rosé Dilection 2008 Price:OOO 85/100
- Brut Tradition Price:OO 83/100
- Champagne Jean Claude Le Brun Brut Cuvée de Réserve Price:OOO 82/100

Detailed instructions are featured at the start of the book.

CHAMPAGNE ALEXANDRE LE BRUN

▼ Extra brut grand cru Fascination 2007 87/100

Yellow-gold. Open, expressive nose intermixing ripe fruits (apple, candied lemon) with patisserie notes. Ample, vinous and full-bodied palate. Melted and framed by freshness. A full, persistent style that works best with food.

Price: OOO

Wine and food pairing: Roasted duck
Serving Temperature: 9-11°C
Ready to drink: From now on

After travelling around the world twice (New Zealand, Australia, Sweden, Germany, England and Spain) 28-year-old Alexandre Le Brun chose to return to Monthelon where his ancestors had lived since 1750. He farms 3 hectares in 8 districts (Sézanne, Grauves, Chouilly, Monthelon, Mancy, Morangis, Epernay and Chavot-Courcourt). Alexandre is totally independent, boasting his own press, tanks and cellar. He vinifies each parcel separately and designed his winery accordingly. He also uses integrated pest management and experiments with a variety of soil management techniques. In the winery, alcoholic fermentation occurs at extremely low temperatures (10°) and native yeast is used. This is the first time this talented, self-taught wine grower has been selected by the guide. Watch this space!

Champagne Alexandre Le Brun
9 rue Saint Vincent
51530 Monthelon
Tel.: +33 (0)3 26 59 73 51 - Mobile: +33 (0)6 81 59 23 76
E-mail: contact@champagne-lebrun.fr
Website: http://www.champagne-lebrun.fr

CHAMPAGNE BEAUMONT DES CRAYÈRES	+33 3 26 55 29 40
▼ Brut Nostalgie 2002 Price:○○○○	89/100
▼ Brut Fleur de Prestige 2004 Price:○○○	85/100
▼ Brut Grande Réserve Price:○○○	83/100
▼ Brut Grand Rosé Price:○○○	83/100
▼ Brut Grand Prestige Price:○○○	83/100

CHAMPAGNE BERNARD BIJOTAT	+33 3 23 70 12 51
▼ Brut blanc de blancs Price:○○	87/100
▼ Brut Price:○○	85/100
▼ Brut rosé Price:○○	83/100

CHAMPAGNE BERNARD LONCLAS	+33 3 26 73 98 20
▼ Brut blanc de blancs Price:○○	86/100
▼ Brut Sélection Price:○○	84/100

CHAMPAGNE BONNET GILMERT	+33 3 26 59 49 47
▼ Brut blanc de blancs grand cru Précieuse d'Ambroise Price:○○○	90/100
▼ Brut blanc de blancs grand cru Cuvée de Réserve 2007 Price:○○○	89/100
▼ Brut blanc de blancs grand cru Cuvée de Réserve Price:○○	86/100

CHAMPAGNE BOUCHÉ PÈRE & FILS	+33 3 26 54 12 44
▼ Brut Cuvée Saphir Price:○○○	88/100

CHAMPAGNE BOULACHIN-CHAPUT	+33 3 25 27 27 13
▼ Brut Rosé de Saignée Price:○○	84/100
▼ Brut Carte Noire Price:○○	81/100

CHAMPAGNE BRUNOT	+33 3 26 55 23 24
▼ Brut 1er cru Grande Réserve Price:○○	83/100
▼ Brut rosé 1er cru Price:○○	80/100

CHAMPAGNE CHARLES COLLIN	+33 3 25 38 31 00
▼ Brut La Belle Gabrielle Price:○○○	87/100
▼ Brut Cuvée Charles Price:○○	86/100
▼ Brut rosé Cuvée Charles Price:○○○	86/100
▼ Brut Sélection Price:○○	81/100

CHAMPAGNE CHARLES ELLNER	+33 3 26 55 60 25
▼ Extra brut Intégral Price:○○	88/100
▼ Brut rosé Price:○○	86/100
▼ Brut 1er cru Price:○○	86/100

Detailed instructions are featured at the start of the book.

CHAMPAGNE CHARLES ELLNER

▼ Brut Prestige 2004 — 90/100

Beautiful light gold. Open nose intermixing brioche, mineral and fruit notes. Wonderful creamy, well-integrated attack flowing into a sensation of lingering freshness. Closely-integrated and complex. A very successful 2004 for a sophisticated aperitif.

Price: ○○○

Serving Temperature: 9-11°C
Ready to drink : From now on

Champagne Charles Ellner
6 rue Côte Legris - 51200 Epernay
Tel.: +33 03 26 55 60 25 - Fax: +33 03 26 51 54 00
E-mail: info@champagne-ellner.com
Website: http://www.champagne-ellner.com

CHAMPAGNE CHARLES MIGNON +33 3 26 58 33 33

- ▼ Brut grand cru Cuvée Comte de Marne 2008 Price:○○○○ — 91/100
- ▼ Brut Grand Cru - Cuvée Comte de Marne Price:○○○ — 90/100
- ▼ Rosé Grand Cru Comte de Marne Price:○○○○ — 89/100
- ▼ Champagne Louis Tollet Brut Rosé 1er cru Price:○○○ — 88/100
- ▼ Champagne Léon Launois Brut Rosé Cuvée Réservée Price:○○○ — 87/100
- ▼ Brut Rosé 1er Cru Premium Réserve Price:○○○ — 86/100
- ▼ Brut 1er Cru Premium Réserve Price:○○○ — 86/100
- ▼ Brut Premium Réserve Price:○○○ — 85/100
- ▼ Champagne Louis Tollet Brut 1er cru Price:○○○ — 84/100

CHAMPAGNE CHARPENTIER +33 3 23 82 10 72

- ▼ Brut blanc de blancs Terre d'Emotion Price:○○○ — 90/100
- ▼ Brut Rosé Terre d'Emotion Price:○○○ — 90/100
- ▼ Brut blanc de noirs Terre d'Emotion Price:○○○ — 88/100
- ▼ Brut Verité Terre d'Emotion Price:○○○ — 88/100

CHAMPAGNE CHASSENAY D'ARCE +33 3 25 38 34 75

- ▼ Brut Confidences Price:○○○ — 89/100
- ▼ Extra Brut Pinot blanc 2005 Price:○○○ — 88/100

▼ Brut rosé Price:OOO 86/100
▼ Brut Cuvée Première Price:OO 84/100

CHAMPAGNE CHÂTEAU DE BOURSAULT +33 3 26 58 42 21

▼ Brut rosé de saignée Price:OOO 86/100
▼ Brut Tradition Price:OO 85/100

CHAMPAGNE CHEURLIN-DANGIN +33 3 25 38 50 26

▼ Brut Cuvée Spéciale Price:OO 79/100

CHAMPAGNE CLAUDE CAZALS +33 3 26 57 52 26

▼ Extra brut blanc de blancs grand cru Clos Cazals 2002 Price:OOOO 95/100

CHAMPAGNE CLAUDE RIGOLLOT +33 3 25 27 43 18

▼ Brut 2000 Price:OO 87/100
▼ Brut Rosé Price:OO 86/100
▼ Champagne Claude Rigollot & Fils Brut Blanc de Blancs Price:OO 85/100

CHAMPAGNE COLLARD-PICARD +33 3 26 52 36 93

▼ Brut Cuvée des Archives 2002 Price:OOOO 91/100
▼ Brut blanc de blancs grand cru Cuvée Dom.Picard Price:OOO 87/100
▼ Extra brut Essentiel 2006 Price:OOO 87/100
▼ Brut Rosé Price:OOO 87/100
▼ Champagne Collard -Picard Brut Cuvée Sélection Price:OO 84/100
▼ Brut Cuvée Prestige Price:OOO 83/100

CHAMPAGNE CUPERLY +33 3 26 05 44 60

▼ Brut blanc de noirs Prestige Price:OOO 88/100
▼ Brut blanc de blancs Prestige Price:OOO 85/100
▼ Brut grand cru Cuvée Prestige Price:OO 85/100

CHAMPAGNE D. MASSIN +33 3 25 38 74 97

▼ Brut Cuvée Prestige Price:OO 87/100
▼ Brut Cuvée Réserve Price:OO 84/100

CHAMPAGNE DAVID BILLIARD +33 6 85 61 47 41

▼ Brut 1er cru Cuvée Prestige Élevée en fût de chêne Price:OOO 87/100
▼ Brut 1er cru Tradition Price:OO 86/100
▼ Brut Sélection Price:OO 81/100

Prices mentioned in this book are guideline and can vary depending on point of sale. The shops, wineries or publisher can in no way be held responsible for this.

Champagne

CHAMPAGNE DE CASTELLANE +33 3 26 51 19 19

- Brut rosé Price:OOO 86/100
- Brut Price:OOO 85/100

CHAMPAGNE DE CASTELNAU +33 3 26 77 89 00

- Brut 2002 Price:OOO 88/100
- Brut 2004 Price:OOO 88/100
- Brut blanc de blancs 2000 Price:OOO 88/100
- Brut blanc de blancs 2002 Price:OOO 87/100
- Brut Réserve Price:OO 85/100
- Brut rosé Price:OOO 83/100

CHAMPAGNE DE SAINT GALL +33 3 26 57 94 22

- Brut blanc de blancs 1er cru Price:OOO 87/100
- Brut 1er cru Tradition Price:OOO 84/100

CHAMPAGNE DEUTZ +33 3 26 56 94 00

- Brut Cuvée William Deutz 2000 Price:OOOOO 97/100
- Champagne Amour de Deutz Brut 2005 Price:OOOOO 96/100
- Brut rosé Price:OOO 90/100
- Brut Classic Price:OOO 90/100

CHAMPAGNE DHONDT-GRELLET +33 3 26 57 97 09

- Brut blanc de blancs grand cru Price:OO 89/100
- Brut blanc de blancs 1er cru 2008 Price:OOO 87/100

CHAMPAGNE DIDIER DOUÉ +33 3 25 79 44 33

- Brut blanc de blancs 2005 Price:OO 90/100
- Extra brut Nature Price:OO 87/100
- Brut Prestige Price:OO 87/100
- Brut Sélection Price:OO 83/100

CHAMPAGNE DOM CAUDRON +33 3 26 52 45 17

- Brut 2006 Price:OOO 86/100
- Brut Cuvée Carnolyne Price:OOO 86/100
- Brut Vieilles Vignes Price:OO 85/100
- Brut Camille Philippe Price:OO 83/100
- Brut rosé Camille Philippe Price:OOO 79/100

CHAMPAGNE DOYARD-MAHÉ +33 3 26 52 23 85

- Champagne Doyard Mahé Brut blanc de blancs 1er cru 2006 Price:OOO 87/100
- Champagne Doyard Mahé Brut blanc de blancs 1er cru Carte d'Or Price:OO 85/100

CHAMPAGNE DRAPPIER +33 3 25 27 40 15

- Brut Cuvée Charles de Gaulle 2006 Price:OOO 88/100
- Brut Carte d'Or - Magnum 1995 Price:OOOO 87/100

CHAMPAGNE DRAPPIER

Brut Millésime Exception 2005 **92/100**

Golden yellow. The nose opens up to white-fleshed fruits, patisserie notes and a smoky, mineral dimension. The palate shows astonishing opulence. Melted attack leading into a firmer mid-palate. Still austere yet very compelling.

Price: OOO

Wine and food pairing: Sweetbreads
Serving Temperature: 9-11°C
Ready to drink: From now on

The 53-hectare vineyard is located in the heart of the Côte des Bar along the hillside of Urville. Planted by the Gallo-Romans in the first years AD, it was one of the first to be farmed by the Cistercian monks from Clairvaux Abbey. More recently, the Drappier Champagne house prided itself on being a purveyor to Charles de Gaulle. The vineyard is planted to a predominant proportion of Pinot Noir, which covers 70 percent of the area under vine, alongside Chardonnay (15 percent) and Pinot Meunier (15 percent). It produces highly idiosyncratic Champagnes of extremely consistent quality which are housed in splendid vaulted cellars dating back to the 12th century.

Champagne Drappier
14 rue des Vignes
10200 Urville
Tel.: +33 (0)3 25 27 40 15 - Fax: +33 (0)3 25 27 41 19
E-mail: info@champagne-drappier.com
Website: http://www.champagne-drappier.com

Champagne

CHAMPAGNE DUCHÊNE +33 3 26 55 56 19

▼ Champagne Duchêne Florence Brut Tradition Price:OO 85/100

CHAMPAGNE DUVAL-LEROY +33 3 26 52 10 75

▼ Brut Femme de Champagne 2000 Price:OOOO 93/100

▼ Brut Rosé 1er Cru Prestige Price:OOO 92/100

▼ Brut 1er Cru Fleur de Champagne Price:OOO 87/100

CHAMPAGNE ETIENNE CALSAC +33 6 11 83 69 49

▼ Brut blanc de blancs 1er cru Infiniment Blanc Price:OO 86/100

▼ Brut L'Echappée Belle Price:OO 85/100

CHAMPAGNE EUGÈNE RALLE +33 3 26 49 40 12

▼ Brut grand cru Cuvée ER Price:OO 85/100

CHAMPAGNE FLEURY PÈRE & FILS +33 3 25 38 20 28

ORG▼ Extra brut Boléro 2004 Price:OOO 91/100

ORG▼ Extra brut Robert Fleury 2004 Price:OOO 91/100

ORG▼ Brut rosé de saignée Price:OOO 89/100

ORG▼ Brut blanc de noirs Price:OOO 87/100

CHAMPAGNE FOREST-MARIÉ +33 3 26 03 13 23

▼ Brut 1er Cru Cuvée St-Crespin Price:OO 83/100

CHAMPAGNE FRANCIS COSSY +33 3 26 49 75 56

▼ Brut 2006 Price:OO 87/100

▼ Brut 1er cru Réserve Price:OO 86/100

▼ Extra brut 1er cru 2006 Price:OO 86/100

CHAMPAGNE FRANCK BONVILLE +33 3 26 57 52 30

▼ Brut blanc de blancs grand cru
Les Belles Voyes Price:OOO 92/100

▼ Brut blanc de blancs grand cru Prestige Price:OO 90/100

CHAMPAGNE FRANÇOIS SECONDÉ +33 3 26 49 16 67

▼ Brut blanc de blancs 2007 Price:OOO 87/100

▼ Brut rosé Price:OO 86/100

▼ Brut Clavier Price:OO 83/100

CHAMPAGNE FREDESTEL +33 3 26 57 06 19

▼ Brut blanc de blancs 1er cru Nature
Les Petits Pieds d'Emma 2008 Price:OOO 85/100

CHAMPAGNE GABRIEL FRESNE +33 3 26 59 98 09

▼ Brut Diapason Price:OO 79/100

CHAMPAGNE GARDET +33 3 26 03 42 03

▼ Brut Réserve Price:OOO 88/100

▼ Brut Tradition Price:OOO 85/100

CHAMPAGNE GATINOIS +33 3 26 55 14 26

▼ Brut Grand Cru Rosé Price:OOO 88/100

▼ Brut Grand Cru Réserve Price:OOO 86/100

CHAMPAGNE GONET SULCOVA

▼ Brut grand cru 2006 **90/100**

Light yellow. Open, refined nose blending white-fleshed fruits and brioche. Lovely full, mellow and fresh mouthfeel. Fleshy, very honest and persistent across the palate. Enjoyable sensation of firmness on the finish imparting elegance.

Price: OOO

Serving Temperature: 9-11°C
Ready to drink : From now on

Champagne Gonet Sulcova
13 rue Henri Martin - 51200 Epernay
Tel.: +33 03 26 54 37 63 - Fax: +33 03 26 54 87 73
E-mail: gonet-sulcova@wanadoo.fr
Website: http://www.champagne-gonet-sulcova.fr

CHAMPAGNE GERMAR BRETON +33 3 25 27 73 03

- ▼ Brut blanc de blancs Price:OO — 84/100
- ▼ Brut Price:OO — 82/100
- ▼ Brut rosé Price:OO — 80/100

CHAMPAGNE GONET SULCOVA +33 3 26 54 37 63

- ▼ Brut blanc de blancs Price:OO — 88/100
- ▼ Champagne Vincent Gonet Brut Price:OO — 86/100

CHAMPAGNE GOSSET +33 3 26 56 99 56

- ▼ Brut Grand Millésime 2004 Price:OOOO — 96/100
- ▼ Brut Grand Blanc de Blancs Price:OOOO — 95/100
- ▼ Brut Grand Rosé Price:OOO — 92/100
- ▼ Brut Grande Réserve Price:OOO — 90/100

CHAMPAGNE GRATIOT GÉRARD +33 3 23 82 06 89

- ▼ Brut rosé Price:OOO — 83/100
- ▼ Brut Prélude Price:OOO — 83/100
- ▼ Brut Maison Price:OOO — 80/100
- ▼ Brut Désiré 2005 Price:OOO — 77/100

Detailed instructions are featured at the start of the book.

CHAMPAGNE GOSSET

▼ Extra brut Celebris Vintage 2002 **97/100**
Beautiful light gold, amber tints. Delightful, refined nose opening up to notes of fresh croissant then dried fruit, gingerbread... The palate shows seductive balance of fullness and freshness, fine bubbles, persistency and complexity. A superlative 2002.

Price: OOOOO

Wine and food pairing: Fillets of turbôt
Serving Temperature: 9-11°C
Ready to drink: From now on

The oldest xine House in Champagne was founded in 1584 by Pierre Gosset, Mayor of Aÿ, who was producing a still wine 100 years before the méthode champenoise for producing sparkling wines was discovered. The House's grapes are today harvested among others in the districts of Aÿ, Bouzy, Mareuil and Rilly-la-Montagne. Gosset remains attached to its history and its traditions: for example, magnums and jeroboams are still riddled by hand. In addition, the elegant bottles of the Grandes Cuvées are the exact replicas of the 18th-century versions. The house produces a range of Champagnes of exceptionally high quality that are fruity, complex and endowed with remarkable personality; this year, in addition to the Celebris 2002, unbeatable since its launch, the House offers a premium Brut Grand Blanc de Blancs.

Champagne Gosset
12, rue Godart Roger - 51200 Epernay
Tel.: +33 (0)3 26 56 99 56 - Fax: +33 (0)3 26 51 55 88
E-mail: info@champagne-gosset.com
Website: http://www.champagne-gosset.com

CHAMPAGNE GOSSET

▼ **Extra brut rosé Celebris 2007** **97/100**

Salmon-pink and light copper. Open nose recalling orange flesh and red berry fruits backed by subtle gingerbread. Wonderful full structure, volume and freshness leading into an elegantly austere finish. A consummate rosé Champagne.

Price: ○○○○○

Wine and food pairing: Seared sea scallops
Serving Temperature: 9-11°C
Ready to drink: From now on

Venere black rice risotto with seared sea scallops

8 large sea scallops, 200 g Venere black rice, 1 white onion, 3 knobs of white butter, 50 cl water, Fish stock, 5 cl white wine, 10 cl cream, Vanilla powder, Salt

Prepare the risotto: *Peel and dice the white onion. In a saucepan, gently soften the onion in a knob of white butter. Add 200 g of Venere black rice and stir well. Pour 5 cl of white wine into the rice, bring to a boil and allow to reduce. Then add the water and fish stock. Leave this to cook for 40–45 minutes, stirring from time to time and checking for overcooking. Season to taste. Add the cream and a large knob of butter to retain a creamy consistency.*

Prepare the sea scallops: *Rinse off the scallops and dry them with a paper towel. Melt a large knob of butter in a pan. Sear the scallops for 2–3 minutes on each side, sprinkling each side with vanilla powder.*

Serve: *Use a mould to shape the risotto on the plate. Place the scallops on the side.*

Champagne Gosset
12, rue Godart Roger - 51200 Epernay
Tel.: +33 (0)3 26 56 99 56 - Fax: +33 (0)3 26 51 55 88
E-mail: info@champagne-gosset.com
Website: http://www.champagne-gosset.com

Champagne

CHAMPAGNE GREMILLET +33 3 25 29 37 91

- ▼ Brut Cuvée Evidence Price:○○○ 86/100
- ▼ Brut Chardonnay Cuvée des Dames Price:○○○ 85/100
- ▼ Brut Sélection Price:○○ 85/100

CHAMPAGNE GUY CHARBAUT +33 3 26 52 60 59

- ▼ Brut 1er cru Memory 1998 Price:○○○ 92/100
- ▼ Brut rosé 1er cru Price:○○ 86/100
- ▼ Brut 1er cru 2005 Price:○○ 85/100
- ▼ Brut Sélection Price:○○ 84/100
- ▼ Brut 1er Cru Blanc de blancs Price:○○ 83/100

CHAMPAGNE GUY DE CHASSEY +33 3 26 57 04 45

- ▼ Brut grand cru Lucien Beaufort Price:○○ 83/100

CHAMPAGNE HENRI GOUTORBE +33 3 26 55 21 70

- ▼ Brut 1er Cru Cuvée Prestige Price:○○ 87/100

CHAMPAGNE HENRIOT +33 3 26 89 53 00

- ▼ Brut Cuvée des Enchanteleurs 1998 Price:○○○○○ 99/100
- ▼ Brut 2006 Price:○○○ 93/100
- ▼ Brut rosé Price:○○○ 92/100
- ▼ Brut blanc de blancs Price:○○○ 92/100
- ▼ Brut Souverain Price:○○○ 90/100

CHAMPAGNE HEUCQ PÈRE & FILS +33 3 26 58 10 08

- ▼ Brut Prestige Price:○○ 86/100

CHAMPAGNE J. DE TELMONT +33 3 26 58 40 33

- ▼ Brut Blanc de Blancs
Grand Couronnement 2000 Price:○○○○ 92/100
- ▼ Brut O.R 1735 2002 Price:○○○○ 92/100
- ▼ Brut Grand Vintage 2004 Price:○○○ 90/100
- ▼ Brut blanc de blancs 2006 Price:○○○ 88/100
- ▼ Brut Grand rosé Price:○○○ 87/100
- ▼ Brut Grande Réserve Price:○○○ 87/100

CHAMPAGNE J. DUMANGIN FILS +33 3 26 03 46 34

- ▼ Brut blanc de blancs Premium Price:○○○ 91/100
- ▼ Brut 1er cru rosé Price:○○○ 89/100
- ▼ Brut 17 Price:○○ 88/100

CHAMPAGNE J. M. GOBILLARD & FILS +33 3 26 51 00 24

- ▼ Brut rosé Cuvée Prestige 2008 Price:○○○ 90/100
- ▼ Brut Cuvée Prestige 2008 Price:○○○ 90/100
- ▼ Brut Privilège des Moines
Élevé en fûts de chêne Price:○○○ 89/100
- ▼ Brut blanc de blancs Price:○○ 88/100

▼ Brut blanc de noirs Price:❍❍ 87/100
▼ Brut rosé Price:❍❍ 87/100
▼ Brut 1er cru Grande Réserve Price:❍❍ 85/100
▼ Brut Tradition Price:❍❍ 83/100

CHAMPAGNE JACQUART +33 3 26 07 88 40

▼ Brut Cuvée Alpha 2005 Price:❍❍❍❍❍ 90/100
▼ Brut blanc de blancs 2006 Price:❍ 88/100
▼ Brut Mosaïque Price:❍ 86/100
▼ Brut rosé Price:❍ 85/100

CHAMPAGNE JACQUES CHAPUT +33 3 25 27 00 14

▼ Brut blanc de noirs Price:❍❍ 88/100
▼ Brut L'Authentic Price:❍❍❍ 87/100
▼ Brut Nature Le Mythic Price:❍❍ 87/100

CHAMPAGNE JACQUES COPINET +33 3 26 80 49 14

▼ Brut Blanc de Blancs Sélection Price:❍❍ 86/100
▼ Brut Blanc de Blancs Chardonnay Price:❍❍ 85/100
▼ Brut Blanc de Blancs - Marie Etienne Price:❍❍❍ 84/100
▼ Brut Extra Quality Price:❍❍ 83/100
▼ Brut rosé Price:❍❍❍ 83/100

CHAMPAGNE JEAN CÉDRIC DEGUY +33 3 26 86 16 12

▼ Brut Cuvée Miss Emma Price:❍❍❍ 87/100
▼ Brut rosé Cuvée Miss Clémence Price:❍❍❍ 85/100
▼ Brut Cuvée Sélectionnée Price:❍❍ 85/100

CHAMPAGNE JEAN MARNIQUET +33 3 26 52 32 36

▼ Brut blanc de blancs 1er cru Price:❍❍ 86/100
▼ Brut 1er cru 2008 Price:❍❍ 86/100
▼ Brut 1er cru Grande Réserve Price:❍❍ 82/100

CHAMPAGNE JEAN VALENTIN & FILS +33 3 26 49 21 91

▼ Brut 2008 Price:❍❍ 87/100
▼ Brut blanc de blancs 1er cru Saint Avertin Price:❍❍ 85/100
▼ Brut Sélection Price:❍❍ 84/100
▼ Brut Rosé 1er cru Price:❍❍ 84/100
▼ Brut 1er cru Tradition Price:❍❍ 82/100

CHAMPAGNE JEAN VELUT +33 3 25 74 83 31

▼ Brut rosé Price:❍❍ 86/100
▼ Brut blanc de blancs Price:❍❍ 86/100
▼ Brut Price:❍❍ 82/100

Detailed instructions are featured
at the start of the book.

Champagne

CHAMPAGNE JEAN VESSELLE
+33 3 26 57 01 55

- ▼ Brut grand cru Cuvée Le Petit Clos 1999 Price:OOOO — 94/100
- ▼ Demi-sec rosé Cuvée Friandise Price:OO — 90/100
- ▼ Brut Réserve Price:OO — 89/100
- ▼ Brut Oeil de Perdrix Price:OO — 89/100

CHAMPAGNE JEAN-MICHEL PELLETIER
+33 3 26 52 65 86

- ▼ Brut Cuvée Anaelle 2004 Price:OO — 84/100
- ▼ Brut Séléction Price:OO — 83/100
- ▼ Brut rosé Price:OO — 82/100
- ▼ Demi-sec Tradition Price:OO — 79/100

CHAMPAGNE JEAN-PAUL DEVILLE
+33 9 61 05 54 65

- ▼ Brut 2004 Price:OOO — 87/100
- ▼ Brut rosé Price:OO — 85/100
- ▼ Brut Carte d'Or Price:OO — 83/100

CHAMPAGNE JOËL GOBANCÉ
+33 3 26 97 42 39

- ▼ Brut cuvée Anne-Elizabeth Price:OO — 87/100
- ▼ Brut rosé Price:OO — 83/100
- ▼ Brut Réserve Price:OO — 82/100
- ▼ Brut Carte Blanche Price:OO — 81/100

CHAMPAGNE L & S CHEURLIN
+33 3 25 38 55 04

- ▼ Brut Coccinelle & Papillon Price:OOO — 83/100
- ▼ Brut Lucie Cheurlin Price:OO — 82/100

CHAMPAGNE LACOURTE GODBILLON
+33 3 26 49 74 75

- ▼ Brut 1er Cru 2006 Price:OOO — 87/100
- ▼ Extra Brut 1er Cru Price:OOO — 87/100
- ▼ Brut 1er Cru Price:OOO — 85/100
- ▼ Brut Blanc de Blancs 1er Cru Price:OOO — 84/100

CHAMPAGNE LAMBLOT
+33 3 26 03 80 00

- ▼ Brut 2005 Price:OOO — 87/100
- ▼ Brut Sélection Price:OO — 83/100
- ▼ Brut Tradition Price:OO — 81/100

CHAMPAGNE LAURENT-PERRIER
+33 3 26 58 91 22

- ▼ Brut Grand Siècle Price:O — 96/100
- ▼ Brut 2004 Price:OOOO — 92/100
- ▼ Brut Cuvée Rosé Price:OOOO — 90/100
- ▼ Brut Price:OOO — 89/100

CHAMPAGNE LE GALLAIS
+33 3 26 58 94 55

- ▼ Brut Cuvée Millésimée 2004 Price:OOO — 87/100
- ▼ Brut Cuvée du Manoir Price:OO — 86/100

Detailed instructions are featured at the start of the book.

CHAMPAGNE MAURICE PHILIPPART

▼ Brut rosé 1er cru — 88/100

Deep orangy pink. Fruity nose suggestive of cherries in brandy. Full, generous attack nicely balanced by a sensation of lingering freshness. Focused, long-lasting cherry aromas. An expressive, characterful pink Champagne.

Price: ○○

Serving Temperature: 9-11°C
Ready to drink : From now on

Champagne Maurice Philippart
3 rue des Vignes - 51500 Chigny Les Roses
Tel.: +33 03 26 03 42 44 - Fax: +33 03 26 03 46 05
E-mail: contact@champagne-mphilippart.com
Website: http://www.champagne-mphilippart.com

CHAMPAGNE MAURICE VESSELLE

▼ Brut grand cru 2000 — 91/100

Yellow-gold. Profound, open and complex nose opening up to dried fruit (citrus, fig) and patisserie notes with mineral touches. Full-bodied, fleshy attack framed by freshness. Superb aromatic expression of candied orange. A successful Champagne.

Price: n/a

Serving Temperature: 9-11°C
Ready to drink : From now on

Champagne Maurice Vesselle
2 rue Yvonnet - 51150 Bouzy
Tel.: +33 03 26 57 00 81 - Fax: +33 03 26 57 83 08
E-mail: champagne.vesselle@wanadoo.fr
Website: www.champagnevesselle.com

Champagne

CHAMPAGNE LECLERC BRIANT — +33 3 26 54 45 33

ORG ▼ Brut 1er Cru Cumières Les Crayères Price:❍❍❍ — 90/100

ORG ▼ Brut 1er Cru Cumières Les Chèvres Pierreuses Price:❍❍❍ — 88/100

ORG ▼ Brut rosé Rubis de Noirs 2004 Price:❍❍❍ — 85/100

ORG ▼ Brut Cuvée Extra Price:❍❍❍ — 85/100

CHAMPAGNE LOUIS DE SACY — +33 3 26 97 91 13

▼ Brut blanc de blancs Cuvée Inédite Price:❍❍❍❍ — 90/100

▼ Brut Grand Cru Price:❍❍❍ — 89/100

▼ Brut Originel Price:❍❍❍ — 87/100

CHAMPAGNE LOUIS ROEDERER — +33 3 26 40 42 11

CV ▼ Brut Cristal 2005 Price:❍❍❍❍❍ — 99/100

CV ▼ Brut rosé 2008 Price:❍❍❍❍ — 96/100

CV ▼ Brut Vintage 2006 Price:❍❍❍❍ — 94/100

CV ▼ Brut Premier Price:❍❍❍ — 91/100

CHAMPAGNE MALARD — +33 3 26 32 40 11

▼ Extra brut Ladystyle Price:❍❍❍❍ — 89/100

▼ Brut blanc de blancs grand cru Excellence Price:❍❍❍ — 88/100

▼ Brut 1er cru Excellence Price:❍❍❍ — 85/100

CHAMPAGNE MALETREZ FRÉDÉRIC — +33 3 26 97 63 92

▼ Brut 1er Cru Vieille Réserve 2000 Price:❍❍❍ — 87/100

▼ Brut rosé 1er Cru Price:❍❍ — 86/100

▼ Brut 1er Cru Réserve Price:❍❍ — 82/100

CHAMPAGNE MAURICE PHILIPPART — +33 3 26 03 42 44

▼ Brut blanc de blancs 1er cru Price:❍❍ — 85/100

▼ Brut 1er cru Carte d'Or Price:❍❍ — 82/100

CHAMPAGNE MAURICE VESSELLE — +33 3 26 57 00 81

▼ Brut grand cru Collection 1985 Price:❍ — 93/100

▼ Brut grand cru 2004 Price:❍ — 92/100

▼ Brut grand cru Collection 1988 Price:❍ — 91/100

▼ Brut grand cru Collection 1998 Price:❍ — 90/100

▼ Brut grand cru Cuvée Réservée Price:❍ — 89/100

▼ Brut Grand Cru rosé Price:❍ — 88/100

CHAMPAGNE MICHEL ARNOULD & FILS — +33 3 26 49 40 06

▼ Brut grand cru Réserve Price:❍❍ — 86/100

CHAMPAGNE MICHEL GONET — +33 3 26 57 50 56

▼ Extra brut grand cru Blanc de blancs Prestige 2004 Price:❍❍❍ — 92/100

▼ Brut blanc de blancs grand cru 2005 Price:❍❍❍ — 90/100

CHAMPAGNE MICHEL GONET

Brut blanc de blancs grand cru 2004 **94/100**

Golden hue. Profound, complex nose marrying gingerbread, spice and delicate toast and rancio notes. Wonderful presence on the attack, full, fresh and melted, naturally flowing into a finish of elegant austerity. A superlative Champagne for gourmet food.

Price: OOO

Wine and food pairing: Foie gras
Serving Temperature: 9-11°C
Ready to drink: From now on

The Michel Gonet house has 40 hectares of vineyards distributed over 4 districts, includingOger, Mesnil sur Oger, Vindey and Montgueux planted with chardonnay grapes variety. External growth was started in the 1970 by Michel Gonet, constantly seeking new challenges after buying Château de Vindey (wine of gods!) in Champagne. A string of acquisitions then ensued in Bordeaux area, starting with Château Lesparre in PDO Gravs de Vayres, then Château Haut Bacalan, Eck and St Eugène in Pessac Léognan, and recently an house in the Champagne Avenue n°37 in Epernay thereby demonstrating its ability to diversify.

Champagne Michel Gonet
196 avenue Jean Jaurès
51190 Avize
Tel.: +33 (0)3 26 57 50 56 - Fax: +33 (0)3 26 57 91 98
E-mail: info@champagnegonet.com
Website: www.gonet.fr

CHAMPAGNE MICHEL TURGY +33 3 26 57 53 43

▼ Brut blanc de blancs grand cru 2005 Price:○○○ 90/100
▼ Brut blanc de blancs grand cru Réserve Sélection Price:○○ 87/100

CHAMPAGNE NICOLAS FEUILLATTE +33 3 26 59 55 50

▼ Brut Rosé - Cuvée 225 Vintage 2006 Price:○○○○ 91/100
▼ Brut Cuvée Spéciale 2005 Price:○○○ 91/100
▼ Brut Grand Cru 2005 Price:○○○ 90/100
▼ Brut Chardonnay 2005 Price:○○○ 88/100
▼ Cuvée Spéciale Magnum 1998 Price:○○○○ 86/100
▼ Brut Rosé - Palmes d'Or 2005 Price:○○○○○ 85/100
▼ Brut Rosé Price:○○○ 85/100

CHAMPAGNE NOËL LEBLOND-LENOIR +33 3 25 38 53 33

▼ Brut Cuvée Prestige Price:○○ 87/100
▼ Brut Sublime de Frion Price:○○ 86/100
▼ Brut Rosé Price:○○ 86/100
▼ Brut Perle de Dizet Price:○○ 86/100
▼ Brut Réserve Price:○○ 84/100
▼ Brut Tradition Price:○○ 84/100

CHAMPAGNE P. LANCELOT-ROYER +33 3 26 57 51 41

▼ Brut blanc de blancs grand cru
Cuvée des Chevaliers Price:○○ 90/100
▼ Brut blanc de blancs Cuvée de Réserve R.R. Price:○○ 88/100

CHAMPAGNE PALMER & CO +33 3 26 07 35 07

▼ Champagne Amazone de Palmer Brut Price:○○○ 93/100
▼ Extra brut Price:○○○ 90/100
▼ Brut 2004 Price:○○○ 89/100
▼ Brut rosé Price:○○○ 85/100

CHAMPAGNE PANNIER +33 3 23 69 51 30

▼ Extra brut 2002 Price:○○○ 91/100
▼ Brut rosé Price:○○○ 89/100
▼ Extra brut Exact Price:○○○ 88/100
▼ Brut Sélection Price:○○○ 86/100

CHAMPAGNE PATRICE MARC +33 3 26 58 46 88

▼ Brut 2008 Price:○○○ 87/100
▼ Brut Grande Cuvée Price:○○○ 86/100
▼ Brut Initiale Noir & Blanc Price:○○ 79/100

CHAMPAGNE PAUL BERTHELOT +33 3 26 55 23 83

▼ Brut 1er cru Eminence Price:○○ 87/100
▼ Brut 1er cru La Marquise Price:○○○ 87/100
▼ Brut rosé Price:○○ 87/100
▼ Brut Blason d'Or Price:○○ 85/100

CHAMPAGNE PALMER & CO

▼ Blanc de blancs 2007 — 89/100

Light yellow. The nose marries biscuity, fruity and lemony notes. Fullness and a silky, melted texture are key components on the palate. Although the attack is fairly supple, the mid-palate and finish are dominated by freshness. Refined and persistent.

Price: ○○○

Serving Temperature: 9-11°C
Ready to drink : From now on

Champagne Palmer & Co
67 rue Jacquart
51100 Reims
Tel.: +33 03 26 07 35 07 - Fax: +33 03 26 07 45 24
E-mail: contact@champagne-palmer.fr
Website: www.champagne-palmer.fr

CHAMPAGNE PALMER & CO

▼ Brut Réserve — 86/100

Light gold. Enticing nose with white-fleshed fruit and citrus in a lead role. Well-balanced palate marked by a measure of vinosity. Supple, generous attack. Freshness recurs on the finish with more floral aromatics.

Price: ○○○

Serving Temperature: 9-11°C
Ready to drink : From now on

Champagne Palmer & Co
67 rue Jacquart
51100 Reims
Tel.: +33 03 26 07 35 07 - Fax: +33 03 26 07 45 24
E-mail: contact@champagne-palmer.fr
Website: www.champagne-palmer.fr

CHAMPAGNE PAUL DÉTHUNE	+33 3 26 57 01 88
▼ Brut grand cru Cuvée Prestige Princesse des Thunes Price:OOO	95/100
▼ Brut rosé grand cru Price:OOO	90/100
▼ Brut grand cru Price:OOO	89/100

CHAMPAGNE PAUL LAURENT	+33 3 26 81 91 11
▼ Brut rosé Cuvée du Fondateur Price:OO	85/100
▼ Brut Réserve Cuvée du Fondateur Price:OO	85/100

CHAMPAGNE PENET-CHARDONNET	+33 3 26 97 94 73
▼ Extra Brut Grand Cru Réserve Price:OOOO	88/100

CHAMPAGNE PERTOIS-LEBRUN	+33 3 26 57 54 25
▼ Brut blanc de blancs grand cru 2006 Price:OOO	90/100
▼ Brut blanc de blancs grand cru Price:OO	87/100

CHAMPAGNE PETITJEAN-PIENNE	+33 3 26 57 58 26
▼ Brut blanc de blancs grand cru Coeur de Chardonnay Price:OO	87/100
▼ Brut blanc de blancs grand cru 2006 Price:OO	86/100

CHAMPAGNE PAUL LAURENT

▼ Brut Cuvée Prestige L'Essentiel **86/100**

Light gold. Open nose marrying vegetal and dried fruit notes. Vinous, powerful and idiosyncratic palate revealing more of the nose aromatics. Would work well with food such as white meats.

Price: OOO

Serving Temperature: 9-11°C
Ready to drink : From now on

Champagne Paul Laurent
4 rue des Pressoirs
51260 Bethon
Tel.: +33 03 26 81 91 11 - Fax: +33 03 26 81 91 22
E-mail: champagne.paul.laurent@wanadoo.fr
Website: http://www.champagnepaullaurent.com

CHAMPAGNE PHILIPPE GAMET +33 3 26 51 87 54

▼ Brut 2008 Price:○○ 86/100

▼ Brut Cuvée Caractères Price:○○○ 85/100

▼ Brut Cuvée 5000 Price:○○ 80/100

CHAMPAGNE PHILIPPONNAT +33 3 26 56 93 00

▼ Brut Clos des Goisses 2003 Price:○○○○○ 98/100

▼ Brut rosé 1er cru Cuvée 1522 2006 Price:○○○○ 96/100

▼ Brut grand cru 1522 2004 Price:○○○○ 93/100

▼ Brut Grand Blanc 2005 Price:○○○ 91/100

▼ Brut Royale Réserve Price:○○○ 90/100

▼ Extra Brut Royale Réserve Non Dosé Price:○○○ 89/100

CHAMPAGNE PIERRE ARNOULD +33 3 26 49 40 12

▼ Brut grand cru Effrontée Price:○○○ 89/100

CHAMPAGNE PIERRE GIMONNET & FILS +33 3 26 59 78 70

▼ Brut Special Club
Grands Terroirs de Chardonnay 2005 Price:○○○ 90/100

▼ Brut blanc de blancs 1er cru Cuvée Cuis Price:○○○ 89/100

▼ Pierre Gimonnet & Fils Brut rosé 1er cru Price:○○○ 87/100

CHAMPAGNE PIERRE MIGNON +33 3 26 59 22 03

▼ Brut Prestige Rosé de Saignée Price:○○ 87/100

▼ Brut Prestige Price:○○ 85/100

CHAMPAGNE PIERREL +33 3 26 51 00 90

▼ Brut Cuvée Les Oressences Price:○○○ 86/100

▼ Champagne Marquis de La Fayette Brut Price:○○ 83/100

CHAMPAGNE PLOYEZ-JACQUEMART +33 3 26 61 11 87

▼ Brut Liesse d'Harbonville 1998 Price:○ 90/100

▼ Extra brut Vintage 2005 Price:○ 86/100

CHAMPAGNE POINTILLART & FILS +33 3 26 49 74 95

▼ Extra brut 1er cru Blanc de Blancs en barrique Price:○○ 87/100

▼ Brut 1er cru Sélection Price:○○ 86/100

▼ brut Cuvée R de Rosé Price:○○ 86/100

▼ Brut 1er cru Price:○○ 85/100

▼ Brut 1er cru 2004 Price:○○ 84/100

▼ Brut 1er cru Rencontre Price:○○ 84/100

CHAMPAGNE POISSINET-ASCAS +33 3 26 58 12 93

CV▼ Brut Prestige Price:○○ 80/100

CHAMPAGNE PRAT +33 3 26 52 12 16

▼ Champagne Georges de La Chapelle
Brut Cuvée Nostalgie Price:○○○ 86/100

▼ Champagne Georges de La Chapelle Brut Price:○○ 85/100

CHAMPAGNE PIERRE GIMONNET & FILS

▼ Brut blanc de blancs 1er cru 2006 **92/100**

Light yellow-gold. Open, elegant nose offering up chalky notes then flowing into riper aromatics of candied lemon and pastry cream. The palate is full and generous yet fresh. Focused, lingering finish. A Champagne for white-tablecloth dining.

Price: ○○○

Wine and food pairing: Sushis
Serving Temperature: 9-11°C
Ready to drink: From now on

The Gimonnet family was already cultivating grapes in the district of Cuis before 1750, but it was only after the crisis of the 1930s that Pierre Gimonnet truly began to produce wine. Specialising in Blanc de Blancs (made from 100% Chardonnay), Olivier and Didier Gimonnet, Pierre's grandsons, tend a 28-hectare vineyard planted solely with Chardonnay in the terroirs of Cramant, Chouilly and Oger (Grands Crus), as well as in the districts of Cuis and Vertus (Premier Cru). The result is a very nice range of Blancs de Blancs with seductive freshness and balance, whose scores this year fall between 87 and 92/100. A House with Champagnes that merit a detour!

Champagne Pierre Gimonnet & fils
1 rue de la République
51530 Cuis
Tel.: +33 (0)3 26 59 78 70 - Fax: +33 (0)3 26 59 79 84
E-mail: info@champagne-gimonnet.com
Website: http://www.champagne-gimonnet.com

CHAMPAGNE PIERRE MIGNON

Brut Cuvée de Madame 2005 **88/100**

Beautiful gold with a hint of amber. Open nose with emphasis on creamy and brioche notes. Wonderful silky, supple attack leading into a fresh, persistent mid-palate. Melted and creamy throughout. A deftly-crafted Champagne.

Price: ○○○

Serving Temperature: 9-11°C
Ready to drink : From now on

Champagne Pierre Mignon
5 rue des Grappes d'Or - 51210 Le Breuil
Tel.: +33 03 26 59 22 03 - Fax: +33 03 26 59 26 74
E-mail: info@pierre-mignon.com
Website: www.pierre-mignon.com

CHAMPAGNE R. RENAUDIN +33 3 26 54 03 41

- Brut Réserve Price:○○ — 88/100

CHAMPAGNE RAINETEAU-GRIMET +33 3 26 83 90 32

- Brut rosé Price:○○ — 84/100
- Brut Cuvée Noir Tentation Price:○○ — 83/100
- Brut Tradition Price:○○ — 79/100

CHAMPAGNE RÉMY MASSIN & FILS +33 3 25 38 74 09

- Extra brut Intégrale Price:○○ — 87/100
- Brut 2004 Price:○○ — 87/100
- Brut Cuvée Louis-Aristide Price:○○○ — 86/100

CHAMPAGNE RENÉ JOLLY +33 3 25 38 50 91

- Brut Blanc de noirs Price:○○ — 83/100

CHAMPAGNE RICHARD CHEURLIN +33 3 25 38 55 04

- Brut Cuvée Jeanne 2007 Price:○○○ — 79/100

Prices mentioned in this book are guideline and can vary depending on point of sale. The shops, wineries or publisher can in no way be held responsible for this.

CHAMPAGNE ROYER PÈRE & FILS

Brut Prestige **86/100**

Light yellow. Delicate nose with notes of fresh fruit and a subtle pastry touch in the background. Full, fleshy palate with body nicely counterbalanced by a sensation of freshness. Focused, persistent fruity aromas. Save for the aperitif

Price: n/a

Serving Temperature: 9-11°C - Ready to drink : From now on

Champagne Royer père & fils
120 Grande Rue
10110 Landreville
Tel.: +33 03 25 38 52 16 - Fax: +33 03 25 38 37 17
E-mail: infos@champagne-royer.com

CHAMPAGNE ROYER PÈRE & FILS	+33 3 25 38 52 16
Brut blanc de blancs Price:○	86/100
Brut Vintage 2007 Price:○	86/100
Brut Réserve Price:○	85/100
Brut rosé Price:○	84/100
CHAMPAGNE SADI MALOT	+33 3 26 97 90 48
Brut blanc de blancs 1er cru Vieille Réserve Price:○○○	89/100
Brut blanc de blancs 1er cru Cuvée de Réserve Price:○○	87/100
Brut blanc de blancs 1er cru 2007 Price:○○○	87/100
CHAMPAGNE SALMON	+33 3 26 61 82 36
Brut rosé Price:○	83/100
Brut AS Price:○	79/100
Brut Sélection Price:○	78/100
CHAMPAGNE SOUTIRAN	+33 3 26 57 07 87
Brut grand cru Collection Privée Price:○○○	91/100
Brut grand cru Perle Noire Price:○○○	87/100
Brut grand cru Signature Price:○○○	86/100

Detailed instructions are featured at the start of the book.

CHAMPAGNE TAITTINGER +33 3 26 85 45 35

▼ Brut blanc de blancs
Comtes de Champagne 2004 Price:❍❍❍❍❍ 95/100

▼ Brut Comtes de Champagne rosé 2005 Price:❍❍❍❍❍ 91/100

▼ Brut grands crus Prélude Price:❍❍❍ 91/100

▼ Brut 2006 Price:❍❍❍ 86/100

▼ Brut Réserve Price:❍❍❍ 85/100

CHAMPAGNE TROUILLARD +33 3 26 55 37 55

▼ Brut Cuvée du Fondateur 2006 Price:❍❍❍ 90/100

▼ Extra brut blanc de noirs Price:❍❍ 88/100

▼ Brut Cuvée Elexium Price:❍❍ 87/100

▼ Brut Extra Sélection Price:❍❍ 86/100

CHAMPAGNE VEUVE A. DEVAUX +33 3 25 38 30 65

▼ Brut Ultra D de Devaux Price:❍❍❍ 92/100

▼ Brut D de Devaux 2002 Price:❍❍❍ 91/100

▼ Brut D de Devaux rosé Price:❍❍❍ 91/100

▼ Brut D de Devaux Price:❍❍❍ 90/100

CHAMPAGNE VEUVE CLICQUOT PONSARDIN +33 3 26 89 54 40

▼ Brut Vintage 2004 Price:❍❍❍❍ 92/100

CHAMPAGNE VEUVE DOUSSOT +33 3 25 29 60 61

CV▼ Brut L by VD Price:❍❍❍ 91/100

▼ Brut Cuvée Ernestine 2008 Price:❍❍ 86/100

▼ Brut rosé Tendresse Price:❍ 82/100

▼ Brut Tradition Price:❍❍ 82/100

CHAMPAGNE VIGNON PÈRE & FILS +33 3 26 49 80 39

▼ Brut grand cru Les Marquises Réserve Price:❍❍❍ 87/100

▼ Brut rosé grand cru Les Marquises Price:❍❍ 86/100

▼ Brut blanc de blancs grand cru
Les Marquises Cuvée Prestige Price:❍❍ 86/100

CHAMPAGNE VINCENT D'ASTRÉE +33 3 26 54 03 23

▼ Brut 1er Cru Empreinte du Temps 2005 Price:❍❍❍ 87/100

▼ Brut rosé 1er Cru Rêve d'Eté Price:❍❍ 85/100

▼ Brut 1er Cru Réserve - Esprit Terroir Price:❍❍ 83/100

THE COLOUR OF THE WINES :

- ■ Red wine
- ■ Dry white wine
- ■ Rose wine
- ● Sweet white wine
- ▲ Sparkling brut
- ▲ Sparkling brut rose
- ◆ Brandy
- ● Liqueur wine

CIE CHAMPENOISE PH-CH. PIPER HEIDSIECK +33 3 26 84 43 00

Champagne Charles Heidsieck

▼ Champagne Charles Heidsieck Brut blanc de blancs Blanc des Millénaires 1995 Price:OOOOO 97/100

▼ Champagne Charles Heidsieck Brut rosé 1999 Price:OOOO 92/100

▼ Champagne Charles Heidsieck Brut 2000 Price:OOOO 92/100

▼ Champagne Charles Heidsieck Brut rosé Réserve Price:OOOO 89/100

Champagne Piper-Heidsieck

▼ Champagne Piper Heidsieck Demi-sec Cuvée Sublime Price:OOO 90/100

▼ Champagne Piper-Heidsieck Brut 2006 Price:OOO 89/100

▼ Champagne Piper-Heidsieck Brut rosé Sauvage Price:OOO 89/100

▼ Champagne Piper Heidsieck Brut Price:OOO 87/100

DIFFUSION GEORGES VESSELLE +33 3 26 57 00 15

▼ Champagne Georges Vesselle Brut grand cru Juline Price:OOO 91/100

▼ Champagne Georges Vesselle Brut rosé grand cru Price:OOO 90/100

▼ Champagne Georges Vesselle Brut grand cru Price:OO 90/100

EARL CHAMPAGNE LEBLOND LENOIR PASCAL +33 3 25 38 54 04

▼ Brut Prestige Price:OO 85/100

▼ Brut 2009 Price:OO 85/100

▼ Brut - Esprit de Blancs 2008 Price:OO 84/100

▼ Brut - Grande Réserve Price:OO 83/100

▼ Brut - Désir de Matthieu Price:OO 83/100

▼ Brut Tradition Price:OO 82/100

▼ Brut rosé Price:OO 80/100

EARL PIOT SEVILLANO +33 3 26 58 23 88

▼ Brut rosé Price:OO 83/100

▼ Brut Florilège 2007 Price:OO 83/100

▼ Champagne Piot Sévillano Brut Tradition Price:OO 80/100

MARKS & SPENCER FRANCE +33 6 46 11 55 62

▼ Champagne Oudinot Brut Vintage 2005 Price:OOO 89/100

▼ Champagne Oudinot Cuvée Brut Price:OOO 87/100

Detailed instructions are featured at the start of the book.

CHAMPAGNE PIPER-HEIDSIECK

▼ Brut Rare 2002 — 97/100

Light gold. Delicate nose with notes of lemon, candied citrus backed by butter, brioche, patisserie and dried fruit. Wonderful framework on the palate combining fullness, finesse and exuberance enhancing complex, lingering aromas. A superlative Champagne.

Price: ○○○○○

Serving Temperature: 9-11°C - Ready to drink : From now on

Cie Champenoise PH-CH. Piper Heidsieck
12, allée du Vignoble - 51100 Reims
Tel.: +33 03 26 84 43 00 - Fax: +33 03 26 84 43 49
E-mail: alexandra.rendall@champagnes-ph-ch.com
Website: www.piper-heidsieck.com

CHAMPAGNE CHARLES HEIDSIECK

▼ Brut Réserve — 90/100

Beautiful light gold. Endearing nose intermixing fruity, brioche and biscuit notes. Fleshy, full and melted palate showing lovely refined bubbles and freshness. Closely-integrated and harmonious. A nicely crafted dry Champagne.

Price: ○○○

Serving Temperature: 9-11°C
Ready to drink : From now on

Cie Champenoise PH-CH. Piper Heidsieck
12, allée du Vignoble - 51100 Reims
Tel.: +33 03 26 84 43 00 - Fax: +33 03 26 84 43 49
E-mail: alexandra.rendall@champagnes-ph-ch.com
Website: www.piper-heidsieck.com

Champagne

NOIZET CAROLE +33 3 26 97 77 45

- ▼ Cuvée Perle Noir Price:○○ — 86/100
- ▼ Brut rosé Cuvée Roseraie Price:○○ — 84/100
- ▼ Brut Fleur de Vigne Price:○○ — 83/100
- ▼ Champagne Carole Noizet Brut Réserve Price:○○ — 83/100

SCEV CHAMPAGNE MANCEAUX ROGER +33 3 26 03 42 57

- ▼ Brut blanc de blancs 1er cru Price:○○○ — 85/100
- ▼ Brut 1er Cru Grande Réserve Price:○○ — 83/100
- ▼ Brut 1er Cru Cuvée de Réserve Price:○○ — 81/100

UNION VINICOLE DES CÔTEAUX DE BÉTHON +33 3 26 80 48 19

- ▼ Champagne G. Gruet et Fils Brut blanc de blancs Price:○○ — 87/100
- ▼ Champagne G. Gruet et Fils Brut rosé Price:○○ — 86/100
- ▼ Champagne G. Gruet et Fils Brut Grande Réserve Price:○○ — 85/100

VADIN PLATEAU +33 3 26 55 23 36

- ▼ Brut rosé Price:○○ — 88/100
- ▼ Brut Or Noir 2007 Price:○○○ — 86/100
- ▼ Brut Grande Réserve Price:○○ — 85/100

Coteaux Champenois

CHAMPAGNE MAURICE VESSELLE +33 3 26 57 00 81

- ▼ Maurice Vesselle Bouzy Rouge 2006 Price:○ — 84/100

DIFFUSION GEORGES VESSELLE +33 3 26 57 00 15

- ▼ Georges Vesselle Bouzy rouge Grand Cru Cuvée Véronique-Sylvie Price:○○○ — 89/100

VADIN PLATEAU +33 3 26 55 23 36

- ▼ Vadin-Plateau Cumières Rouge Price:○○ — 86/100

Ratafia

CAVE DES SIX COTEAUX +33 3 26 03 08 78

- ▼ Charles Heston Meunier Price:○ — 86/100
- ▼ Charles Heston Chardonnay Price:○ — 86/100
- ▼ Charles Heston Pinot noir Price:○○ — 85/100

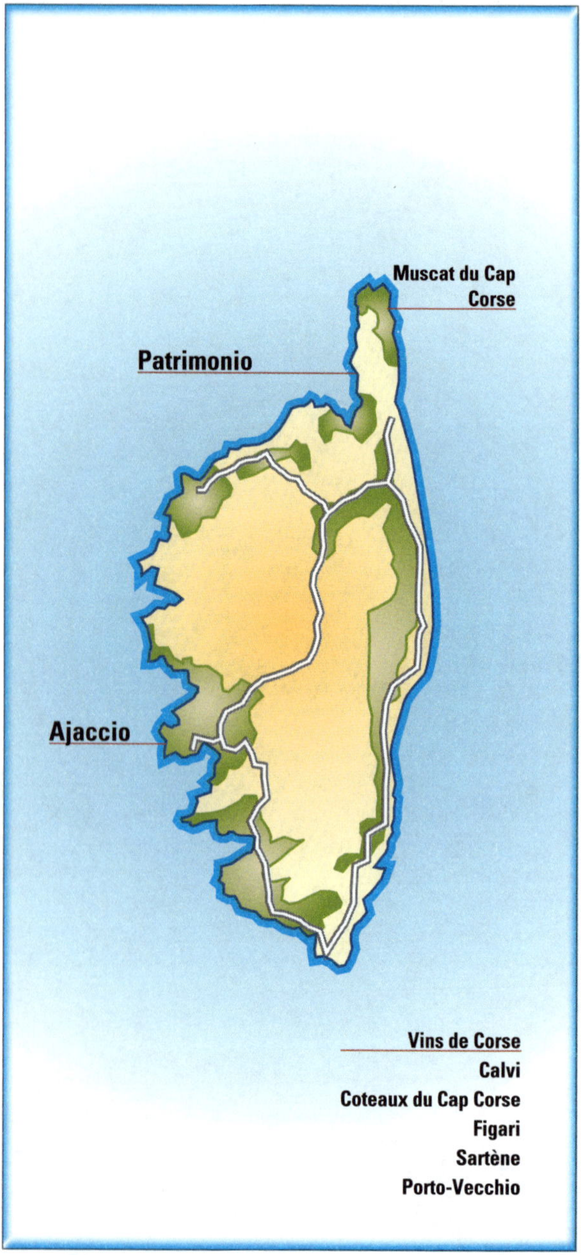
Muscat du Cap
Corse
Patrimonio
Ajaccio
Vins de Corse
Calvi
Coteaux du Cap Corse
Figari
Sartène
Porto-Vecchio

CORSICA

A VINEYARD WITH A DIFFERENCE

Although wine growing was introduced to Corsica, as it was to Provence, by the Greeks in Antiquity, making it one of France's oldest wine regions, centuries were to elapse before it prospered. After two world wars had left it on the wane, it enjoyed a new lease of life in the 1960s. Quality was initially poor, though gradually, promising wine regions emerged. Nowadays they form a ring around the island, like a crown studded with jewels, each one refined and expressive.

The north-south aligned mountain range stretching from one side of the island to the other harbours countless, highly idiosyncratic 'terroirs' embodied by myriad distinctive wines. Despite this diversity, soil formations can be divided into two major types - the upper western slopes are predominantly crystalline and granite, lacking in loam which makes them slightly prone to erosion. The eastern basin has a high proportion of shale and alpine type soils with large and sometimes recent deposits of sediment...

The island's idiosyncrasies also apply to its astonishing range of grape varieties,. Sciacarello and Niellucio are major varieties for the reds and rosés, along with Barbarossa, Grenache, Cinsault and Carignan. For the whites, Vermentino, otherwise known as Corsican Malvoisie, has become a household name and is the most prevalent white varietal. Other grape varieties play a minor role - such as Ugni Blanc - and some are even scarce, such as Rossola and Codivarta, both of which are only blended to make AC Vin de Corse-Coteaux du Cap Corse.

In terms of character, such a comprehensive range of grape varieties is reflected in a broad selection of wines. These can vary from light wines (like some Sciaccarello...) to more dense wines, like those made from Niellucio, which are described as well-balanced, round wines, suitable for lengthy cellaring. Conversely, the rosés and whites should be drunk young (two to three years old), the whites extracting finesse, freshness and exotic aromas from the Vermentino varietal. INAO has granted appellation status to some of the island's regions, in recognition of their quality. Depending on their character and quality standards, the wines follow a three-tier hierarchy. On the first rung are wines labelled under the regional appellation 'Vins de Corse', followed by five 'Villages' appellations, and at the very top, two growths, 'Ajaccio' and 'Patrimonio'...

For wine lovers yet to discover wines from the 'Isle of Beauty', time is of the essence. There are still many gems, with price tags making them very affordable.

REVIEW OF RECENT VINTAGE

• **2012** • This was a good year for winegrowing on the island. The winter was mild, with a bit more rain than in Provence (more than 125 mm of precipitation). The spring benefited from hot, sunny days interspersed with relatively steady rains. The summer was very sunny, hot and dry, especially in July and August.

THE CORSICAN APPELLATIONS

A.C. AJACCIO

OVERVIEW: until 1984, this appellation was known as Coteaux d'Ajaccio. It stretches from the Gulf of Porto to the Sartène area, over 36 towns and villages. This highly-fragmented wine region is centred chiefly on the granite hillsides of the Gulf of Ajaccio and Sagone. Some vineyards are the highest in Corsica.

WINE STYLES: the majority of the wines are red, made from at least 40% Sciacarello. They are nervy, vigorous, fragrant wines (pepper, vanilla, dry leaf, roasted coffee, raspberry), with a solid framework. Firm when young, they have the potential to mature well. Try with red meat served with a sauce, game, or ewe milk cheese. The salmon-pink colour rosés display aromas of quince and grapefruit. They pair well with cured ham. The whites are drawn from at least 80% Vermentino and smell pleasantly of linden and freshly-cut hay. Try with shallow-fried red mullet or sauteed squid.

A.C. PATRIMONIO

OVERVIEW: situated in the southern part of Cap Corse between Bastia and the citadel of Saint-Florent, Patrimonio was the first area to be granted AC status in Corsica. Seven villages are entitled to the appellation. Patrimonio is made from 95% Niellucio for the red wines and Vermentino only for the whites. The wines are 50% red and 30% rosé. The vineyards are planted on hillside sites formed of limestone and clay scree. The soils are consistent, which is unusual for Corsica. The mountains form a buffer against the wind. Fog is prevalent both in the autumn and the winter.

WINE STYLES: the reds with their deep hue (ruby-red) exhibit balsamic fragrances (pine trees), dried fig, raspberry, violet and toasted aromas. They are powerful, dense, fleshy, warm and robust – more so than wines from Ajaccio - with a full mouthfeel. Try with game or goats cheese. The pleasant, fruity rosés are full-bodied with a slight acidulous note and pair with Corsican cooked cold pork meats. The pale yellow colour whites display floral and apple aromas. They are supple, fruity and well-structured. They are suitable for fish and shellfish.

A.C. VIN DE CORSE

OVERVIEW: these wines can be grown throughout the AC Corse production area (except for the Patrimonio region). Most Corsican wines (Vin de Corse) come from the hills overlooking the eastern plains and the middle Golo valley in the Corte area. A local appellation name (Sartène, Calvi, Cap-Corse, Figari, Porto-Vecchio) can be appended to AC Vin de Corse.

Native grapes are the most prevalent though Mediterranean varietals from the mainland are also grown. For red and rosé wines, the range comprises Nieluccio, Sciacarello and Grenache noir augmented with a maximum 50% of Cinsault, Mourvedre, Barbarossa, Syrah, Carignan and Vermentino (20% maximum for the latter two). For the whites, the range is simpler: Vermentino (75% minimum) and Ugni blanc (25% maximum).

WINE STYLES: the reds have a pleasant bouquet, are well-constituted, warm and supple. Aromas of fresh fruit and undergrowth are present, with gamey, spicy notes. Try with barbecues, roast meats (beef, goat), patés. The rosés have a deep colour, good vinosity and are clean. The whites are fat and supple with a slight bitterness. They pair with fish, sea urchins, goats or ewe milk cheese, and cooked cold pork meats.

VINS DE CORSE-CALVI: the appellation comes from Balagne, in the north-western part of the island. Vines grow mainly on the plains or Figarella and Regino valleys and along the coast. The reds are supple, concentrated and fragrant, the rosés are delicate, round and fruity. The whites are particularly complex and display great aromatic power. They should be drunk young.

VINS DE CORSE-CAP-CORSE: this is the island's most northerly wine area, set in the Regliano region. A broad selection of wines are made on a boutique scale. They range from particularly complex dry white wines with great aromatic power made from Malvoisie and Codivarta to red wines with good cellaring capacity and dessert wines known as 'rappus'... The region also boasts its own appellation - Muscat du Cap Corse - made from small-berry Muscat.

VINS DE CORSE-FIGARI: this is the Isle of Beauty's most southerly wine area. The gulf of Figari is dry and hot, making it highly conducive for growing red vines. The vines are planted on gently sloping hills, all facing south. The resultant wines are well-constituted and distinctive. They are considered to be amongst the island's best.

VINS DE CORSE-SARTÈNE: Sartène is situated in southern-western Corsica, near the Rizzanese river. It was the first wine growing region in Corsica to introduce modern techniques in the 19th century. 16 villages are entitled to the appellation. The reds, particularly those from the Montanaccio varietal, a local variation of Sciacarello, are round, distinctive and long on the palate. The rosés are robust with a pleasant bouquet. The whites are full and fragrant.

VINS DE CORSE-PORTO-VECCHIO: this appellation occupies the far south-eastern tip of Corsica, along the coast. Local farming focuses on wine, which is grown around Porto-Vecchio and Bonifacio. The reds are round, fruity, well-balanced and elegant. The rosés are delicate and aromatic. The whites are dry and fruity.

• • •

CORSICA

Ile de Beauté

CAVE COOPÉRATIVE AGHIONE +33 4 95 56 60 20

▼ U San Muletto - Irrésistible 2012 Price: ❍ DG1 83/100

Vin de Corse

▼ Génération Price: ❍ 83/100

COSTE CASERONE +33 7 60 02 08 88

▼ Duo 2012 Price: ❍❍ 85/100

▼ Coste Caserone by Suleone Trio Price: ❍❍ 86/100

Vin de Corse Calvi

DOMAINE A RONCA +33 4 95 61 06 69

CV▼ A Ronca Vintage 2012 Price: ❍ 85/100

CV▼ A Ronca Vintage 2012 Price: ❍ 84/100

CV▼ A Ronca Vintage 2011 Price: ❍ 87/100

Prices mentioned in this book are guideline and can vary depending on point of sale. The shops, wineries or publisher can in no way be held responsible for this.

Vin de Corse Porto-Vecchio

DOMAINE DE TORRACCIA +33 4 95 71 50 03

ORG▼ Vintage 2012 Price: ❍ 86/100

ORG▼ Vintage 2012 Price: ❍ 85/100

WINE SCORES:

95-100/100: an outstanding wine, when a great 'terroir' meets exceptional winemaking expertise.

90-94/100: a superlative wine combining finesse, complexity and remarkable winemaking.

85-89/100:a wine of extremely high standard, which we enjoyed for its typicity and character.

80-84/100: a quality wine combining balance, structure and neatness for a pleasurable wine drinking experience.

75-79/100: a wine deemed acceptable.

70-74/100: a wine with defects, unacceptable.

65-69/100: a wine with major defects, inadmissible.

50-64/100: unacceptable wine, not worthy for sale.

***Note:** wines scoring less than 75/100 are not included in our publications.*

DOMAINE DE TORRACCIA

▼ Vintage 2010 **86/100**

ORG Limpid garnet with faint bricking. Appealing floral, spicy and toasted nose with morello cherry and plum in the background. The palate focuses on lightness, tension and finesse with lovely precise aromas. Hint of firmness. A successful effort.

Price: ❍

Wine and food pairing: Meat kebabs
Serving Temperature: 16-18°C
Ready to drink: 2013-2015

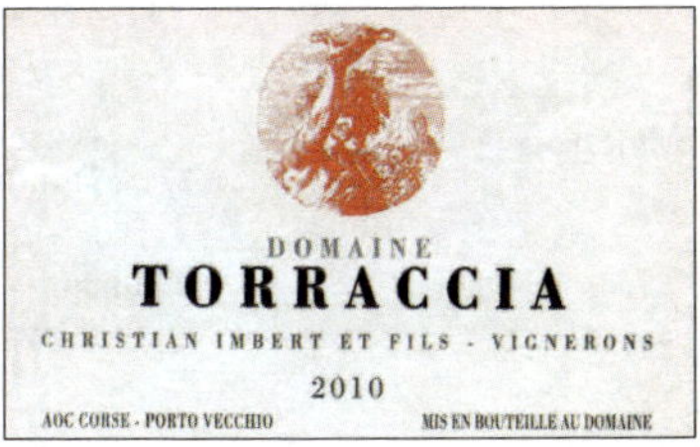

Christian Imbert discovered Corsica on his return from Africa in the 1960s. He quickly realised that it is a region that lends itself to winegrowing. Yet rather than planting productive, lucrative grapes, he decided to concentrate on typical Corsican varieties: Sciaccarellu, Niellucciu, Grenache, a little Syrah (reds and rosés) and Malvasia for the whites. The Domaine de Torraccia thus found its roots among the Mediterranean scrub and granite, and its wines embody the generosity of the winemaker that created them. This vineyard is truly representative of the heart and soul of Corsican wine and is a perfect illustration of the potential of the island's wine production.

Domaine de Torraccia
Torraccia
20137 Porto Vecchio
Tel.: +33 (0)4 95 71 43 50 - Fax: +33 (0)4 95 71 50 03
E-mail: torracciaoriu@wanadoo.fr

Muscat de Lunel
Clairette du Languedoc
Hérault
Faugères
Montpellier
St-Chinian
Languedoc
Muscat de St-Jean-de-Minervois
Muscat de Mireval
Cabardès
Minervois
Muscat de Frontignan
Languedoc
Malepère
Narbonne
Corbières
Blanquette de Limoux
Fitou
Maury
Côtes du Roussillon-Villages
Aude
Perpignan
Rivesaltes et Muscat de Rivesaltes
Têt
Côtes du Roussillon
Collioure
Banyuls

LANGUEDOC-ROUSSILLON

STILL PUSHING THE BOUNDARIES OF QUALITY

Languedoc-Roussillon is France's leading wine region in terms of acreage. It is now an integral part of the country's wine scene, after ridding itself of its jug wines in the 1980s. It is a constant source of intrigue to wine lovers and has made such a quantum leap in quality that it is now a fully-fledged member of France's elite circle of premium wine regions. This has nurtured new talent, not only amongst the younger wine categories (including Vins de Pays d'Oc) but also the more traditional ones (Fitou, Corbières, Minervois, Saint-Chinian, Côtes du Roussillon-Villages...).

Languedoc spans three departments (Gard, Hérault and Aude), and Roussillon just one: Pyrénées-Orientales. The region caters for the most catholic tastes: sparkling wines and crémants, dry whites, rosés, light or full-bodied reds, all three colours of regional wines and delicious dessert wines, amongst the region's great hallmarks.

To present a clear picture of these, we have decided to subdivide them into three categories:

APPELLATION WINES

Grown on hillside sites, they are blended from a typically Mediterranean varietal range and boast distinctive characteristics. The region plays host to the following appellations: Languedoc (sometimes followed by a site-specific name), Faugères, Saint-Chinian, Minervois, Corbières, Fitou, Côtes du Roussillon and Côtes du Roussillon-villages (some stating the village name), Collioure...

REGIONAL WINES

Generally single varietals, produced from 'imported' plants (Cabernet-Sauvignon for reds or Chardonnay for whites, for example). The regional denomination, Vin de Pays d'Oc, can be grown throughout this vast province.

DESSERT WINES

These are in a league of their own, if only because of the way they are made. The basic principle is simple: fermentation of the nascent wine is arrested by adding a neutral spirit. This fortification process is known as 'mutage' because it literally silences the characteristic sound of fermentation ('muter' in old French means 'to become mute'). These delicate wines with a pleasant bouquet subsequently undergo lengthy stabilisation and ageing before being released. The Languedoc appellations only produce Muscat wines in this way: Lunel, Mireval, Frontignan and Saint-Jean-de-Minervois, whereas Roussillon offers: Muscat de Rivesaltes, Rivesaltes, Maury and Banyuls (as well as Banyuls Grand Cru predominantly from Grenache noir).

RED VARIETALS

The most ubiquitous varietals are: Carignan, Cinsault, Grenache noir, Mourvedre and Syrah. Two noteworthy exceptions are Cabardès (a young AC set north of Carcassonne) and Malepère (an AC located south-west of Carcassonne) which supplement this range with 'Bordeaux' varietals including Cabernet Franc, Cabernet-Sauvignon, Cot noir and Merlot noir.

WHITE VARIETALS

Bourboulenc, Clairette, Grenache blanc, Macabeu, Marsanne, Picpoul, Roussanne, Terret blanc and Vermentino. There are a clutch of significant exceptions. Muscats: in Languedoc, they are entirely drawn from the small berry Muscat; the Muscat de Rivesaltes appellation (Pyrénées-Orientales) also permits Muscat of Alexandria. Then there is Limoux where still white wines are made from Chardonnay, Chenin and Mauzac.

WINE STYLES

amongst the red wines, the elegance of Faugères, complexity of Corbières, tannic structure of Saint-Chinian, inimitable taste of 'terroir' in Fitou deserve a special mention. Of the whites, the most remarkable are without a doubt the fresh, aromatic

Languedoc Picpoul de Pinet, Limoux and Vins de Pays d'Oc, though also the extremely distinctive character of the Muscats. Rounding off this selection are the Maury, Rivesaltes and Banyuls, the richest and most complex of our dessert wines.

REVIEW OF RECENT VINTAGES

• **2011** • At the risk of sounding repetitive, once again a dry, hot spring was followed by a very average summer saved by a delightful September. These southerly vineyards easily turned this to good account by producing plentiful volumes and aromatic, well-balanced wines. 2011 is definitely a year for wines from the South!

• **2012** • This region received a lot of sun and 20% less precipitation than usual in 2012. This resulted in healthy grapes apart from a bit of coulure (dropping of flowers) and powdery mildew. This vintage is still young, but is promising, with a good balance of sugar and acid.

THE LANGUEDOC-ROUSSILLON APPELLATIONS

BANYULS AND BANYULS GRAND CRU

OVERVIEW: Of all the Grand Roussillon dessert wine appellations, AC Banyuls is the best known. The area sits within the same boundaries as AC Collioure and embraces four towns and villages (Banyuls sur Mer, Collioure, Port Vendres, Cerbère). It climbs the abrupt hillsides on terraces propped up with dry stone walls. The skeletal soils lay on Cambrian shale. Banyuls is divided into a basic AC Banyuls and a Banyuls Grand Cru.

WINE-MAKING TECHNIQUES: Banyuls is a dessert wine made by the fortification process, whereby the wine grower adds 96% proof neutral spirit to grapes during alcoholic fermentation in a ratio of 5 to 10% of must volume. By using this process, yeast activity is arrested before all the sugar has been turned into alcohol and aroma compounds can be fully extracted from young wines. The ageing phase begins two to four weeks after maceration. Banyuls Grand Cru must spend at least 30 months in oak whilst basic Banyuls is aged either in glass demi-johns or carefully sealed barrels kept in a cool, damp environment. They can also be stored outside to develop slightly oxidised aromas. Grenache noir, the appellation's primary varietal, must account for at least 50% of the blend for Banyuls and 75% for Banyuls Grand Cru. Some single vintage wines bottled prior to oxidation are labelled 'Rimage'.

WINE STYLES: AC Banyuls yields red, rosé and white dessert wines from the same varietal range. The red wines boast a ruby-red hue with mahogany tints in the early years, evolving into brick-red with copper tints over time. On the palate, they are supple, powerful, well-constituted, tannic wines with intense aromas of dried and crystallised fruits, morello cherries in brandy, vanilla, coffee.... Try as an appetiser or with desserts like chocolate cake. White Banyuls, with their elegant straw-yellow hue, are highly unusual. They can be made either as sweet, dry aged in new oak or medium sweet wines. Their character stems from the Grenache blanc varietal and they reveal delicate floral, citrus fruit and honeyed notes. Enjoy with foie gras, blue cheeses or desserts with honey.

AC BLANQUETTE DE LIMOUX

OVERVIEW: Blanquette de Limoux is one of Languedoc-Roussillon's oldest controlled appellations. The area is located 25 kilometres south of Carcassonne in the Aude department and covers 41 towns and villages. The vines grow on light, stony calcareous clay soils and the climate is unusual in that it alternates between Ocean and Mediterranean. The area specialises in sparkling wines made from the local varietal Mauzac, which can be blended with Chardonnay and Chenin blanc.

WINE-MAKING TECHNIQUES: there are two types of Blanquette: ancestral method Blanquette de Limoux is a single varietal made from Mauzac. It undergoes secondary (natural) fermentation in the bottle. Blanquette de Limoux itself is a blended wine: Mauzac (at least 90%), Chardonnay and Chenin. Like Crémant de Limoux it undergoes secondary fermentation in the bottle induced by adding a blend of yeast and sugar. This is when the bubbles form. The wines age for at least 9 months on the lees, following which they are disgorged (the sediment is removed by refrigeration) and the dosage is then added. This will determine whether a wine is dry or medium dry. Crémant de Limoux is made in the same way though it matures for longer than Blanquette, spending at least 15 months in the cellar.

WINE STYLES: Blanquette and Crémant de Limoux are sparkling wines with a pale hue highlighted with golden tints. Aromas of apricot, acacia, hawthorn, peach blossom or apple, citrus fruit and toast are present. They can be enjoyed as appetisers, with savoury or smoked canapés, red mullet, anchovies, squid, patés or white meat.

AC CABARDÈS

OVERVIEW: the Cabardès wine region is located a dozen kilometres north-west of Carcassonne. It extends outwards from the Minervois appellation and covers 18 towns and villages in the Aude department. Like its neighbour, it occupies the southern slopes of Mount Noire, with Carcassonne below in the plain. This is Languedoc-Roussillon's most westerly wine region and it plays host to a broad range of soil types: limestone stones on the valley floor followed by primary rocks (granite then shale and gneiss) at higher elevations. The most unusual feature of this region, however, is its climate: it is caught between Mediterranean and Ocean influences, augmented by the altitude factor. Cabardès is one of the few appellations combining varietals of Atlantic or Continental origin and Mediterranean grape varieties. Here, Cabernet-Sauvignon, Merlot, Cabernet Franc, Fer Servadou grow alongside Grenache, Syrah and Cinsault.

WINE STYLES: Cabardès appellation wines can be either red or rosé. The red wines are supple, full and complex, boasting a host of aromas (red and black fruit, prunes, crystallised fruit, spices, liquorice, undergrowth...). They pair well with cooked cold pork meats, poultry, mutton chops, cassoulet and goats cheese. The rosé wines are dry, lively, delicate and fruity. Try them with cooked cold pork meats, mutton kebabs, chicken with almonds or tagine.

AC CLAIRETTE DE BELLEGARDE

OVERVIEW: the Clairette de Bellegarde appellation area is set between Nîmes and Arles, in the Gard department. It covers a single town, Bellegarde, verging on the Costières de Nîmes appellation. Soil make-up is primarily formed of pebbles and sandstone and the Mediterranean-type climate is hot and dry, with plenty of sunshine and a favourable aspect. Wine styles: Clairette de Bellegarde is made from a single varietal, Clairette, and can be aged either in tanks or barrels. With its attractive pale gold hue, this dry white wine displays tell-tale aromas of walnuts, spices, fennel and a hint of grapefruit. It is soft and unctuous with relatively low acidity. The locals tend to pair it with grilled fish or shellfish.

AC COLLIOURE

OVERVIEW: the Collioure appellation area is set in the Pyrénées-Orientales department. The vines are planted on sheer hillsides sharing the same 'terroir' as Banyuls. Covering 727 hectares and four villages, the appellation stretches over poor, shale soils and basks in a hot, dry Mediterranean climate. The vines enjoy abundant sunshine, allowing the grapes - Grenache noir, Mourvedre, Carignan, Cinsault and Syrah - to achieve full ripeness (the proportion of Grenache noir, Mourvèdre and Syrah, either together or individually, must be at least 60% of the total blend with the highest single varietal accounting for anything up to 90%).
Collioure wines are vinted traditionally at controlled temperatures, after destemming and a prolonged two-week vatting period. The rosés are made from red varietals though also a maximum 30% of Grenache gris. The whites are blended from Grenache blanc, Grenache gris, Macabeu, Marsanne, Tourbat and Vermentino.
WINE STYLES: Collioure wines are either red or rosé. The red wines display a superb cherry-red hue. They are powerful, warm wines. In the early years, they exude fragrances of small black fruit (cherry, blackberry) and red fruit. As they age, they acquire their hallmark finesse and bouquet making them a perfect match for meat, stews and game. The rosé wines display a beautiful deep pink colour. They are harmonious, delicate, powerful and extremely aromatic (ripe red fruit). Try them with barbecued meat, fish, paella, mixed salads, cooked cold pork meats or Collioure anchovies. The white wines are rich, intense and driven by floral, exotic and mineral notes.

AC CORBIÈRES

OVERVIEW: the Corbières wine region spans from Narbonne to Perpignan and from Carcassonne to the Mediterranean. It embraces 105 towns and villages in the Aude department. The predominant soil type is calcareous clay interspersed with : shale, red sandstone, marl and stony terraces. Although the climate is strongly defined by the influence of the Mediterranean, the most westerly sites experience an Ocean climate.
The multifaceted nature of the region has led to the implementation of sub-zones. There are currently 11 such zones: Boutenac (recently promoted to 'growth' status), Durban, Fontfroide, Lagrasse, Lézignan, Montagne d'Alaric, Quéribus, Saint-Victor, Serviès, Sigean and Termenès. These converge into four major areas:

• The maritime Corbières form the western rim of the appellation and their defining characteristics are low elevation, predominantly limestone soils and a definite Mediterranean climate.
• The upper Corbières occupy the south-western portion of the area and its most mountainous section, home to the highest peaks in the Corbières. The climate therefore defines a threshold, restricting the development of vineyards. Vines do grow here however on predominantly shale-type soils conducive to producing top-flight wines.
• Alaric Corbières: located in the north-western part of the appellation, this area takes its name from Mount Alaric, a 600-metre-high summit overlooking the Aude valley. A multiplicity of soil types can be found here but the Mediterranean climate, strongly influenced by the Ocean, provides consistency throughout.
• The central Corbières: situated squarely in the middle of the Corbières, hence its name, this area boasts marl and sandstone soils as well as an extremely arid, hot climate.

WINE STYLES: AC Corbières wines come in all three colours. The reds (over 90% of total output) are blended from a classic selection of Mediterranean varieties: Carignan (less widespread in some areas), Grenache, Lladoner Pelut, Mouvedre, Syrah, Cinsault...The wines are fragrant, moderately tannic and warm though often need to mature for a few years. Aromatically, they cover a comprehensive range, evolving over time: red fruit fragrances (blackcurrant, blackberry), initially moving on to spices (pepper, liquorice, moorland, thyme, rosemary) then, a few years later, to worn leather, coffee, cocoa, undergrowth, game... This makes them suitable for a wide variety of food pairings: duck with orange, mutton stew, roast pigeon...

The rosés are blended from the same varietal range, augmented with Grenache gris, and are vinted using the 'bleeding' or direct to press method. Their hue embraces a broad spectrum, ranging from pale pink with salmon coloured tints to darker shades. They are aromatic wines (raspberry, violet, exotic fruits) and are fresh and round on the palate, often with a long finish. The white wines are drawn from Bourboulenc, Grenache blanc and Maccabeo (at least 50%), though also Clairette, Picpoul, Muscat, Terret, Marsanne, Roussanne and Vermentino. Direct press wines, they are robust and fat though remain fresh and well-balanced. Aromas of citrus fruit, pepper, cinnamon and floral notes are present. Some spend time in oak. They marry well with grilled fish, seafood, shellfish and chicken sauteed with mushrooms.

AC CORBIÈRES BOUTENAC

OVERVIEW: the Corbières Boutenac area is considered to be one of the appellation's finest terroirs and embraces 10 towns and villages between Lézignan and Thézan. The soils derive from the secondary (limestone and sandstone dolomitic outcrops) and tertiary eras (various types of molasse). Old vines plunge their roots deep into the ground in search of water, thereby ensuring the wines express optimum sense of place. The appellation was officially recognised in 2005 and only red wines are entitled to use it. Basic yields are lower than for Corbières (45 hl/ha instead of 50hl/ha) and wine making and ageing criteria are stricter.

AC CÔTES DU ROUSSILLON

OVERVIEW: AC Côtes du Roussillon covers an area stretching south of the Corbières down to the Albères on the Spanish border. 118 towns and villages in Pyrénées-Orientales qualify for the appellation which lines the Roussillon plain and climbs the surrounding hillsides. Several distinct sub-zones have been identified: the Agly, Têt and Tech valleys, the Aspres (a site-specific area embracing 37 towns and villages which can feature on labels. Only red wines are entitled to use it), the Albères and a coastal strip skirting the Mediterranean. The soils are generally littered with stones and run the gamut from red clay, granite, shale and gneiss to calcareous clay. The terrain is rugged, formed of rolling hills and poor, arid terraces (the Aspres, Fenouillèdes, Corbières and Albères hills). Summers are hot and rainfall occurs mainly in the autumn. The ripening process is enhanced by plentiful sunshine.

WINE STYLES: the ubiquitous red wines are required by law to come from a blend of at least three of the following varieties: Carignan (50% maximum), Grenache noir, Syrah, Mourvedre (these four varietals must account for at least 80% of the blend with the highest single varietal not exceeding 70%. The two latter varietals account for 25% of the blend, together or individually), Cinsault, Lladoner Pelut. The reds are full-bodied, fat, round, warm, well-constituted wines with good concentration and aromas (ripe red fruit, cherry, prune, wild berries, spices, liquorice). They boast great texture and depth. Try them with stews, grilled meats (lamb), beef stew with peppers, game and cheeses. Wines made by the whole grape fermentation process are sold shortly after the harvest and come primarily from the Carignan grape which is best suited to this process.

The rosés display an intense hue. They are slightly spicy, with aromas of red fruits (cherry), plum and liquorice. They are forward, fruity, full and powerful wines, relatively robust with well-balanced mellowness. The whites are blended from Grenache blanc, Macabeo, Tourbat (also known as Malvoisie in Roussillon), and can be supplemented with Marsanne, Grenache gris, Roussanne and Vermentino (50% maximum). They are delicate, fresh, vigorous, aromatic wines where the predominant aromas are floral. Enjoyable with fish (sardines), shellfish and snails.

AC CÔTES DU ROUSSILLON-VILLAGES

OVERVIEW: this region covers 32 towns and villages in Pyrénées-Orientales, dotted either side of the Agly valley. Soil types are varied but are frequently shale, gneiss and granite. Although Carignan is the mainstay of the varietal range, its share of the blend must not exceed 60%. Complementary varietals are Cinsault, Grenache, Lladoner Pelut, Syrah and Mourvedre (at least 30%). Four villages are entitled to add their name to the appellation and have now been promoted to 'growth' status: Latour-de-France, Lesquerde, Tautavel and Caramany, which must be blended from at least three varietals:

- Latour-de-France: 176 hectares in Latour-de-France and neighbouring villages. Soils are shale, calcareous clay and granite.

Lesquerde (granted in 1995): located in the far eastern part of the Agly valley, this village also covers plots in Lansac and Rasiguères.

- Tautavel: was created in 1997 on calcareous clay soils in the villages of Tautavel and Vingrau; growers use less Carignan here, tending to prefer Grenache and Lladoner Pelut. The wines must mature for at least a year.
- Caramany: gneiss soils along the Agly valley in Caramany, with a few outlying plots in Belesta and Cassagnes.

WINE STYLES: Côtes du Roussillon Villages are not only more robust than Côtes du Roussillon, they are also more harmonious, fleshy, powerful and complex. They are round, full, robust and long on the palate framed by firm tannins. A large proportion are oak-aged (three years). They display fragrances of small red fruits and stewed fruit (blackcurrant), spices (pepper), liquorice, bay and vanilla, gradually developing into scents of game, brandy and truffle. Try them with roasted red meats or meat in a sauce (rib steak), lamb, game and cheeses.

AC CRÉMANT DE LIMOUX

OVERVIEW: Crémant de Limoux was granted controlled appellation status in 1990. It bolsters the range of sparkling wines grown around Limoux: ancestral method Blanquette de Limoux and Blanquette de Limoux. It is grown within the same boundaries (41 towns and villages in Aude south of Carcassonne) though complies with different varietal and growing standards: an upper limit of 20% is applied to the traditional varietal Mauzac at the expense of Chardonnay and Chenin (20% minimum but less than 40%), the two main varieties (that can account for up to 90%). Secondary fermentation must occur in the bottle with 15 months bottle fermentation (versus 9 for Blanquette).

WINE STYLES: Crémant de Limoux is a sparkling wine with a pale hue highlighted with golden tints. It generally has a stronger structure than Blanquette though its fragrances can be more elusive: apricot, acacia, hawthorn, apple, toast... Excellent as an appetiser.

AC FAUGÈRES

OVERVIEW: Faugères is a small area covering 7 villages nestled amongst the lower slopes of Mount Noire which towers over the plain around Béziers. Soil types are reasonably consistent, with a predominant proportion of shale. Large chunks of scrubland have been cleared, particularly in the north, to make way for vineyards. The climate is Mediterranean, dry and hot, and the due south aspect of the vineyards promotes the ripening process. Great strides have been made in terms of varietal selection and the once ubiquitous Carignan grape has been joined by a host of other varieties over the last 25 years. Carignan and Cinsault (40% and 20% at most), Grenache and Lledoner Pelut (20% minimum) Syrah and Mourvedre (at least 5% for the latter one). The tiny proportion of white wines are labelled as Coteaux du Languedoc.

WINE STYLES: Faugères wines are red, rosé and white. The reds are heady, captivating, warm wines. Tannins are present but mellow and they frame a broad aromatic spectrum (cherry, raspberry, blackcurrant, crushed strawberries, liquorice, leather). All of this combines to produce silky wines with finesse. Try them with grilled beef tenderloin, partridge or wild boar fillet steak. The rosé wines are made using the 'bleeding' or direct to press method, and are round and harmonious. Aromas of red fruit, white flowers and smoky notes are present. A good match for cooked cold pork meats, starters and mixed salads. The whites are made from Roussane, Grenache blanc, Marsanne and Vermentino (Rolle) and draw impeccable minerality from the local schist soils.

AC FITOU

OVERVIEW: the Fitou appellation is located in southern Languedoc, between Perpignan and Narbonne. It embraces 9 villages divided into two wine growing regions in Aude: one following the coastline on calcareous clay soils, the other on higher elevations, where the soil is shallow shale. The climate is Mediterranean, humid on the coastline and more arid inland. Carignan forms the backbone of the varietal range (at least 30%), augmented with Grenache noir, Lladoner Pelut (these varietals must account for at least 70% of the blend), Syrah and Mourvedre, and a balance (10% at most) of Cinsault.

WINE STYLES: Fitou uses two different wine making techniques: traditional vinification methods (grapes crushed and destemmed) at controlled temperatures; and the whole grape fermentation process (grapes left uncrushed), primarily for Carignan. The resultant wines are often blended. They must age for at least 9 months. Blessed with a brilliant ruby-red hue, the wines are well-constituted, full, fat and generous with rich, complex aromas (wild flowers, moorland, red fruit (blackcurrant, cherry), spices, grilled almonds and leather layered onto venison and prune). Enjoy with game (wild boar, deer), roast beef with mushrooms or duck breast.

AC LANGUEDOC

OVERVIEW: the Languedoc appellation area (until recently Coteaux du Languedoc) follows the Mediterranean coastline from Nîmes to Narbonne. It covers 168 towns and villages spread over 3 departments (Aude, Hérault, Gard). To reflect the numerous 'terroirs' within this vast area (hard limestone in the scrublands, shale, gravel…) growers can add site-specific names to the appellation. There are 14 such sites for red and rosé wines and 2 for white wines. For reds and rosés, these are: La Clape, Quatourze, Cabrières, Montpeyroux, Saint-Saturnin, Pic-Saint-Loup, Saint-Georges-d'Orques, Les Coteaux de la Méjanelle, Saint-Drézéry, Saint-Christol and Les Coteaux de Vérargues, Grès de Montpellier, Terrasses du Larzac and Pézénas. For white wines: La Clape and Picpoul de Pinet. Five of these sites (growths) - La

Clape, Grès de Montpellier, Terrasses du Larzac, Pézénas and Pic Saint Loup - are classed as geographical denominations within the appellation area. They have been officially recognised by AC law and comply with more restrictive production criteria. The same law allows the others to use their denomination as a village appellation.

The varietal range is Mediterranean: for reds and rosés: Carignan (40% maximum), Cinsault (40% maximum), Grenache, Lladoner Pelut, Syrah and Mourvedre. For whites: Grenache blanc, Clairette, Bourboulenc, Picpoul blanc (50% minimum), which can be augmented with Ugni blanc, Terret, Carignan, Maccabeo, Marsanne, Roussanne and Rolle.

WINE STYLES: AC Languedoc produces red, rosé and white wines. The reds are vinted either traditionally or using the whole grape fermentation process. They are generous, powerful, velvety, elegant wines with aromas of raspberry, blackcurrant and spices (pepper). Wines for cellaring have characteristic aromas of leather, bay and moorland fragrances (thyme, rosemary, juniper). Try them with grilled meats or meats served in a sauce. The rosés are made by the 'bleeding' process and are fruity and warm. They combine fullness, suppleness and finesse (redcurrant, raspberry, cherry, floral notes) and are well suited to hors d'œuvre, cooked cold pork meats, fish and shellfish. The white wines are increasingly fermented in oak. Full, round and displaying characteristic acidity, they conjure up aromas of apricot, peach, honey and floral and toasted notes. They are enjoyable with shellfish and grilled fish.

AC LANGUEDOC CABRIÈRES

OVERVIEW: this site-specific area fits within the broader Languedoc appellation and is located around the village of the same name, near Clermont-l'Hérault and Salagou lake. Primary shale is the predominant soil type playing host to vineyards here, imparting highly distinctive characteristics to the wines.

WINE STYLES: Cabrières produces both red and rosé wines. White wines grown in the same area are labelled Clairette du Languedoc. The red wines display a hallmark personality, and are generally very concentrated and well-balanced with aromas of red fruits (raspberry, strawberry, blackcurrant) and peony. Over time, these evolve and take on spicy, smoky undertones and toasted aromas of roasted coffee. They can be served with game, grilled meats or meats served with a sauce. The rosés, known as 'ruby-reds' are made chiefly from Cinsault and are pleasant, light wines with delicate aromas (floral, fruity notes). They are well suited to cooked cold pork meats and hors d'œuvre.

AC LANGUEDOC COTEAUX DE VÉRARGUES

OVERVIEW: the Vérargues wine area is set between Sommières (in the Gard department) and Lunel (in Hérault), in and around the towns and villages of Beaulieu, Boisseron, Lunel, Lunel-Viel, Restinclières, Saint Geniès Les Mourgues, Saint-Seriès, Saturargues and Vérargues. Vines grow on terrace sites and calcareous clay scree, pebbles and sand, where the climate is Mediterranean and dry.

WINE STYLES: the red wines of Vérargues are relatively supple and display great aromatic finesse (red and black fruit, vanilla). They marry well with duck with prunes, game and grilled meats. The rosés are delicate and elegant (red fruit, spices, aniseed) and pair with barbecued meats and cooked cold pork meats.

AC LANGUEDOC GRÈS DE MONTPELLIER

OVERVIEW: 46 towns and villages set on the outskirts of Montpellier in the Hérault department qualify for this appellation. The dry climate and damp warm air rising from the sea promote early ripening and good balance throughout the growing cycle. Grenache, Mourvedre and Syrah (at least 70% for all three varietals combined and at least 20% Grenache) rub shoulders with a few old Carignan vines (30% maximum).

WINE STYLES: robust red wines to enjoy with red meat, meat in a sauce and game.

AC LANGUEDOC LA CLAPE

OVERVIEW: La Clape is a site-specific wine area (growth) within AC Languedoc. It is located east of Narbonne, in the Aude department, and embraces 5 villages: Armissan, Fleury, Salles-d'Aude, Vinassan and parts of Narbonne. La Clape boasts a variety of soil types: limestone plateaux clad in scrubland overlooking coombs which open up onto marl; Miocene molasse soils skirting the La Clape mountain range in the north, interspersed with limestone debris chiselled from the peaks as well as alluvial gravel. Frequent winds provide suitable ripening conditions for the grapes by curbing outbreaks of disease. The region is also blessed with low rainfall and plenty of sunshine.

WINE STYLES: La Clape produces primarily red wines but also yields some outstanding whites from Bourboulenc (also known locally as Malvoisie) and Grenache blanc, not to mention some extremely pleasant rosés. The red wines, drawn mainly from Grenache and Syrah, are fleshy, round and powerful. They display character and the tell-tale characteristics of their growing environment, exuding scents of the surrounding moorland and pine forests. Try with wild boar served with a sauce and red meats either grilled or served with a sauce. The rosé wines are light and well-balanced. Often described as a wine for immediate pleasure, they display floral (acacia, rose), peach, apricot and citrus notes. An ideal partner for barbecues, cooked cold pork meats or crudités. The white wines are powerful and complex, exhibiting a distinctive acidulous freshness. Fragrances of citrus fruit (grapefruit), exotic fruit, sweet almonds, peach and jasmine are present. Enjoy with fish soup or shellfish.

AC LANGUEDOC LA MÉJANELLE

OVERVIEW: La Méjanelle is a wine growing area located in four villages on the outskirts of Montpellier. The soil is scattered with pebbles of Alpine origin also known as 'grès'. The climate is Mediterranean with a maritime influence.

WINE STYLES: red wines from La Méjanelle are fleshy, fat and concentrated with aromas of ripe or crystallised red or black fruit, smoky notes, spices. Try with spit-roasted lamb or duck with olives. The rosés, drawn primarily from Grenache, are delicate and exhibit a host of aromas. The perfect match for barbecues and cooked cold pork meats.

AC LANGUEDOC MONTPEYROUX

OVERVIEW: Montpeyroux, which means 'Stony Mountain', is a wine growing area occupying the southern slopes of the Larzac, sandwiched between the plateau and the upper Hérault valley. The vines grow on sun-drenched soils littered with stones.

WINE STYLES: Montpeyroux red wines are on the whole warm and well-constituted. They are generous wines with mellow tannins and aromas bearing the tell-tale characteristics of their growing environment: the surrounding moorland (spices, stewed fruit, thyme, woody notes). Try with red meat or game.

AC LANGUEDOC PEZENAS

OVERVIEW: a newcomer to the Languedoc appellation system covering fifteen towns and villages around Pezenas in Hérault.

Grenache, Mourvedre and Syrah must form at least 70% of the blend though the maximum percentage for a single varietal is 75%. Mourvedre and Syrah, either together or individually, must form at least 20% of the blend and if Carignan is included in the varietal range, at least 20% of Grenache must be used.

WINE STYLES: this particular area produces some sterling red wines due to a long-standing tradition of quality wine making by a handful of independent estates and co-operative wineries. Try with barbecues or meat served with a sauce.

AC LANGUEDOC PICPOUL DE PINET

OVERVIEW: the Picpoul de Pinet appellation area embraces six villages bordering Thau lake in the department of Hérault. With the exception of La Clape, it is the only area where white wines qualify for the Coteaux du Languedoc appellation. The soil make-up is characteristically formed of limestone gravel resulting from the decomposition of limestone marl dating from several different periods (from the Cretaceous to the Pliocene epoch). Picpoul de Pinet wines are vinted using the direct to press method and ferment at low temperatures. They often mature on the lees which imparts more fat and roundness.

WINE STYLES: Picpoul de Pinet is a dry white wine made from a single varietal, Piquepoul. Boasting a pale yellow hue with greenish tints, it is fresh and extremely aromatic (lemon, mango, white flesh fruits (banana), grapefruit, peach and vanilla)... On the palate, it displays a distinctive lemony flavour with undertones of dried fruit and freshly-cut hay. Try as an appetiser or with shellfish from the nearby Thau lake (Bouzigues oysters, clams) and grilled fish.

AC LANGUEDOC PIC SAINT LOUP

OVERVIEW: the Pic Saint Loup wine growing area takes its name from the local mountain which is located twenty kilometres or so north of Montpellier and reaches a peak of 658 metres. Of all the site-specific areas of Languedoc, this is the most northerly. Vines are grown in 13 villages amongst the lower foothills, on soils of limestone scree and Oligocene conglomerate where they thrive. At this elevation (vines are grown at an altitude of around 200 metres) springtime temperatures are cooler than in other parts and rainfall is higher.

WINE STYLES: the Pic Saint Loup appellation produces both red and rosé wines. The reds are powerful, concentrated and boast a distinctive silky texture. They exhibit aromas of ripe fruit, bay, spices, mint, cinnamon, liquorice and vanilla. They pair well with red meat, game and cheeses. The rosés are rich, full and fruity (raspberry, redcurrant, strawberry), providing the ideal match for barbecues, mixed salads and patés.

AC LANGUEDOC QUATOURZE

OVERVIEW: the Quatourze wine region occupies a stony plateau in the southern part of Narbonne in Aude. It enjoys a dry, hot climate, allowing the grapes to fully ripen.

WINE STYLES: the reds are warm, powerful wines which does not undermine their finesse (red fruits, spices, pepper). Of all the wines grown around Narbonne, they display the deepest colour and greatest structure and pair well with grilled meats, roast poultry and game (marcassin stew). The rosé wines are pleasant with a distinctive bouquet. Try them with cooked cold pork meats, barbecues or vegetable terrine.

AC LANGUEDOC SAINT-CHRISTOL

OVERVIEW: this area covers a single village, Saint-Christol in the department of Hérault. Villafranchian gravel and pebbles form the predominant soil type and the climate is dry and hot, allowing the grapes to fully ripen. Mourvedre, in particular, thrives here.

WINE STYLES: Saint-Christol produces wines with character, often displaying distinctive spice aromas. They are rich, velvety and extremely fragrant, providing the perfect match for a leg of lamb, game and grilled red meat. The appellation also produces rosé wines.

AC LANGUEDOC SAINT-DRÉZÉRY

OVERVIEW: the Saint-Drézéry wine region is located north of Montpellier, in and around the village of the same name. It is AC Languedoc's most diminutive geographical denomination. Villafranchian gravel forms the predominant soil type and the climate is dry and hot, allowing the grapes to fully ripen.

WINE STYLES: Saint-Drézéry wines are powerful, elegant and aromatic (red fruit) with spices. Pair with red meat, either grilled or served with a sauce.

AC LANGUEDOC SAINT-GEORGES D'ORQUES

OVERVIEW: the Saint-Georges d'Orques appellation area is located 8 kilometres west of Montpellier and covers five villages.

Soil types are varied, alternating between calcareous clay and stones. Interspersed amongst these, is a good deal of flint mingled with decalcified clay, covering a significant portion of the area. The nearby sea has a moderating influence on the hot, dry Mediterranean climate.

WINE STYLES: Saint-Georges d'Orques boast a long-standing reputation for its wines. Prior to the advent of mass-produced wines, they were most certainly Languedoc-Roussillon's best known and loved red wines. They vary in style from rich, powerful wines with a great capacity for cellaring, to tender, flavoursome wines which reward early drinking. Either way, they are blessed with extremely delicate fruity characteristics (blackberry, cherry, morello cherry, vanilla, spices) and mild tannins. Try with red meat, game and cheeses.

AC LANGUEDOC SAINT-SATURNIN

OVERVIEW: the Saint-Saturnin wine region is nestled in the foothills of the Larzac. It covers the villages of Arboras, Jonquières, Saint-Guiraud and Saint Saturnin de Lucian. It occupies stony ground set on a subsoil of calcareous clay and enjoys a hot climate, sheltered from the wind. This particular site only produces classic red wines and 'overnight' wines which are vinted for just one night. The resultant wines are supple, easy-drinking and fruity.

WINE STYLES: the wines are supple, round and pleasant with a reasonably pale hue. They exhibit crunchy fruit flavours, freshness and good overall balance. Try with white meat, cooked cold pork meats, barbecues or jugged hare. The rosés, primarily drawn from Syrah, are fat, generous and fragrant wines (carnation, red fruit, pepper). They pair well with barbecues, cooked cold pork meats and hors d'œuvres.

AC LANGUEDOC TERRASSES DU LARZAC

OVERVIEW: The Terrases du Larzac area is one of the five specific AC Languedoc sites (growths). 32 towns and villages in the department of Hérault qualify for this appellation. The region covers an extensive, fragmented area. Grenache, Mourvedre and Syrah must form at least 60% of the blend, though the maximum percentage for a single varietal is 75%. Mourvedre and Syrah, either together or individually, must form at least 20% of the blend and if Carignan is included in the varietal range, at least 20% of Grenache must be used. The wines must be blended from grapes or wines drawn from at least two of the aforementioned grape varieties.

WINE STYLES: red wines only. Enjoy with barbecues or meat served with a sauce.

AC LIMOUX

OVERVIEW: although AC Limoux has a long history, it is still relatively unknown, mainly because for a long time it was in direct competition with local sparkling wines, Blanquette and Crémant de Limoux. It shares the same boundaries as its sparkling counterparts, covering 41 towns and villages in Aude, located south of Carcassonne. Its predominantly calcareous clay soils and especially its Ocean-cooled Mediterranean climate, are, however, particularly well-suited to growing top-flight still white wines. The reds (recognised in 2004) must be blended from at least three varietals: the primary varietals are Merlot (at least 50%), Cot, Syrah, Grenache and Carignan. The secondary varietals (at least 20%) are Cabernet Franc and Cabernet-Sauvignon.

WINE STYLES: The varietal range here comprises Mauzac (at least 15%), though also Chardonnay and Chenin which impart power, fat and aromatic complexity to the blend. Limoux is made on a boutique scale, with just over 1,000 hl made annually, though this is on an upward trend as demand for still white wines increases apace. The wines are fat and opulent and pair well with fish dishes and shellfish.

AC MALEPÈRE

OVERVIEW: AC Malpère is the most westerly of the Languedoc appellations. It sits squarely in the middle of a triangle formed by Carcassonne, Limoux and Castelnaudary, embracing 31 towns and villages in Aude. Vines grow on rolling hillsides of calcareous clay and gravely terraces, caught between Mediterranean and Ocean influences. The varietal range mirrors this unusual situation: Merlot, (40 % minimum), Cabernet Franc, Cot, Cabernet-Sauvignon, Grenache, Lledoner Pelut, Cinsaut for the reds, Cabernet Franc (40 % minimum), Cabernet-Sauvignon, Cinsaut, Cot, Grenache and Merlot for the rosés. The red wines are vinted traditionally at controlled temperatures. Some are aged in oak. The rosés are made using the 'bleeding' method and ferment at low temperatures.

WINE STYLES: Malepère produces both red and rosé wines. The red wines display a crimson hue with purple-blue tints.

They are robust, well-structured, fruity and round on the palate. Initial aromas of very ripe red fruit take on spicy, gamey, undergrowth tones as they age. Try with cassoulet, Languedoc stew or beef bourguignon. The rosés are full and lively on the palate, frequently offering good balance and a long-lasting finish (blackcurrant, strawberry, raspberry). Enjoy with stuffed vine leaves, fricassee of monkfish, cooked cold pork meats.

AC MAURY

OVERVIEW: this region covers four villages in Pyrénées-Orientales. Although the climate is Mediterranean, the vines also enjoy occasional Atlantic influences. Soil type is predominantly black shale which retains heat during the day and releases it by night. The fruit is destemmed and whole berries are macerated to make Maury. Traditionally, neutral spirit is added with the pomace still in the tanks. Skin contact then lasts for two weeks or more, extracting greater aromas, colour and tannins. A quarter of the wines are aged traditionally in oak and the remaining three quarters in concrete tanks. They remain in the cellar until the first September of the second year after the harvest. The Maury appellation, which until now was restricted to dessert wines, can now be used for dry wines grown on the same site. The new appellation came into force for wines made from the 2011 vintage onwards.

WINE STYLES: Maury is a fruity, complex red dessert wine. It is drawn primarily from Grenache and Macabeu. On the palate, it shows concentrated aromas of red or black fruit, vanilla, spices, dried figs, beeswax, cocoa and mocha. It is a robust, fleshy wine with a mellow softness derived from its sweetness. It makes an ideal appetiser, or can be served with foie gras or a chocolate dessert.

AC MINERVOIS

OVERVIEW: the Minervois appellation area stretches across the departments of Aude and Hérault, east and south of Carcassonne, covering 61 towns and villages. The region is subdivided into four distinct zones, each with its own characteristic climate and soil types: the extremely arid central zone with terraces formed of pebbles, sandstone, shale or limestone; a zone with identical soil types but a damper climate due to Ocean influences; an area of higher elevations where the soils are shale or karst; and an area defined by a Mediterranean climate buffeted by strong winds and formed of stony terraces. Six different sites have also been defined: Canal du Midi, Les Causses, La Circulade et ses Mourels, Coteaux et Contreforts, Trois Vallées and Les Terrasses.

The varietal range comprises Grenache, Lladoner Pelut, Syrah and Mourvedre (at least 60% combined), with a secondary range of Carignan, Cinsault, Piquepoul, Terret and Riveirenc. The main white varietals are: Grenache blanc, Bourboulenc, Maccabeo, Marsanne, Roussanne and Vermentino; these can be supplemented with Clairette, Picpoul, Terret and small-berry Muscat, to within an upper limit of 20%.

WINE STYLES: Minervois wines come in all three colours though reds account for 95% of production. The red wines are expressive, robust, full and generous with aromas of blackcurrant, violet, cinnamon and vanilla, ageing into notes of leather, crystallised fruit and prune. Try with mountain hams and sausages, small wild game, cassoulet or lamb stew. The rosés are drawn primarily from Syrah and are made using the 'bleeding' method. Try them with pissaladière, stuffed veal rolls, chicken with tarragon or stuffed vine leaves. The white wines are made using the direct to press method and often ferment in oak. They are delicate and elegant (peach, pear, blossom…). Try with mussels or salmon steak either grilled or served with a sauce.

AC MINERVOIS LA LIVINIÈRE

OVERVIEW: 6 villages in the Minervois region (Azille, Azillanet, Cesseras, Siran, La Livinière and Felines-Minervois), covering around 200 hectares, qualify for the site-specific Minervois-la-Livinière appellation. Only red wines are grown here, with Grenache, Syrah and Mourvedre forming the compulsory backbone of the varietal range (at least 60%). Yields are lower and the wines are made and aged to stricter standards than basic Minervois.

WINE STYLES: Minervois-la-Livinière is a red wine only appellation: at least 60% of the blend is Grenache, Mourvedre and Syrah, and at least 40% Mourvedre and Syrah. Several prime movers provide the drive behind the appellation, going to great lengths (and sometimes concentration) to continually elevate the quality of the wines. Watch this space…

AC MUSCAT DE FONTIGNAN

OVERVIEW: Muscat de Frontignan is France's oldest Muscat appellation (recognised in 1936). The appellation sits northeast of Sète in the department of Hérault, embracing just two small towns: Frontignan and Vic-la-Gardiole. The local soil is red clay littered with limestone gravel and is home to a single grape variety: small berry Muscat, also known as Muscat de Frontignan. The wine of the same name is a dessert wine made by adding spirit - anywhere from 5 to 10% of total volume - to the fermenting must. This technique, known as 'mutage', arrests fermentation and retains some of the wine's natural sugars, called residual sugar (at least 110g per litre). The wines must be fortified in this way before December 31st and have a minimum alcohol content of 15%. Prior to their release, they must spend a minimum amount of time ageing. Fact: Muscat de Frontignan bottles have a unique cable type design.

WINE STYLES: these are archetypal Muscat wines at the far end of the sweetness scale, containing more residual sugar than other wines, with 125g per litre compared with 115g for Beaumes-de-Venise and 100g for Rivesaltes. This makes them extremely rich, very syrupy with good vinosity. They are powerful, generous, elegant, delicate and full, displaying a pale yellow hue with topaz tints and fragrances of honey, linden, fresh grapes, ripe fruit and citrus fruit. They can be enjoyed as an appetiser or served with melon, foie gras, Peking duck, Roquefort cheese or desserts. Fact: the appellation also produces a liqueur wine whereby spirit is added to the must prior to fermentation. The resultant nectar boasts 185g of residual sugar.

AC MUSCAT DE LUNEL

OVERVIEW: Muscat de Lunel is grown in Lunel, Lunel-Vieil, Vérargues and Saturargues, in the department of Hérault. The soils are red clay scattered with gravel and are home to small-berry Muscat. The wines are made by adding spirit to the fermenting must, a technique known as 'mutage'.

WINE STYLES: Muscat de Lunel are slightly different to Muscat de Frontignan. They are rich, delicate, elegant, unctuous, powerful wines, which are racy, well-balanced, harmonious and fresh. They boast a golden hue and their fragrances are floral (linden), though also grape, dried fruit (quince, fig, orange or tangerine peel, dried apricot), exotic fruit (lychee, mango) and citrus fruit. Try with chocolate gateau, fruit-based desserts, pear mousse, melon, foie gras, blue cheeses, asparagus and, of course, as an appetiser.

AC MUSCAT DE MIREVAL

OVERVIEW: the Muscat de Mireval area is adjacent to Frontignan, south-west of Montpellier. The small-berry Muscat grapes grow on stony ground with a subsoil of red clay, where the soils are arid and poor and Mount Gardiole acts as a natural barrier to the northerly winds. The wines are made by adding spirit to the fermenting must, a technique known as 'mutage'.

WINE STYLES: Muscat de Mireval bear many similarities with Muscat de Frontignan. They are extremely syrupy, powerful, fruity, elegant, delicate wines which are fresh, racy and harmonious with fragrances of honey, ripe grapes, rose and dried fruit. They can be enjoyed as appetisers or with a dessert (apricot charlotte and all fruit-based gateaux), but also throughout the meal: melon, foie gras or blue cheeses like Roquefort.

AC MUSCAT DE RIVESALTES

OVERVIEW: do not confuse AC Muscat de Rivesaltes, which is dedicated to white wines, with AC Rivesaltes. Covering 89 towns and villages in Pyrénées-Orientales and 9 in Aude, the Muscat de Rivesaltes region is the largest Muscat appellation in the world, with 5,342 hectares under vine. Soil types are therefore extremely varied, ranging from sandy or stony soil to loam, which soak up the dry, hot Mediterranean weather. Muscat de Rivesaltes are dessert wines made by arresting fermentation with spirit. Early bottling is a prerequisite to retain primary aromas and prevent oxidation.

WINE STYLES: Muscat de Rivesaltes are dessert wines that can only be made from small-berry Muscat and/or Muscat of Alexandria. They are powerful, fragrant white wines, though also suave and fresh with a long-lasting finish. They show pleasant notes of exotic fruits, pineapple, papaya and white peach, leading into vanilla, spicy, buttery, smoky overtones with grilled hazelnuts as they age. Enjoy as an appetiser, with foie gras or asparagus. The more mature wines pair well with cheeses (mature Cantal, Maroilles, Bleu d'Auvergne, goats cheese), marinated Collioure anchovies or desserts (chocolate mousse, lemon tart, sorbets).

AC MUSCAT DE SAINT-JEAN-DE-MINERVOIS

OVERVIEW: located in the heart of the Minervois wine region, forty or so kilometres north-west of Béziers in Hérault, this appellation area has the highest elevation of all of the Languedoc Muscats, reaching 300 metres in places. The vines grow on the limestone plateaux of the upper Minervois region, overlooking the river Cesse. The stony nature of the soil imparts the wines their hallmark characteristics. The wines are made from small-berry Muscat by adding spirit to the fermenting must, a technique known as 'mutage'.

WINE STYLES: Saint-Jean Muscats have a tell-tale touch of acidity which makes them different from the other Muscats. They are vigorous, generous, delicate wines with fragrances of flowers, honey, apricot, lemon and other citrus fruits. They can be enjoyed as appetisers or with a dessert (fruit-based gateaux, peach salad…).

AC RIVESALTES

OVERVIEW: AC Roussillon is located in the Roussillon basin and straddles two departments: Aude and Pyrénées-Orientales. Soil types are therefore extremely varied, ranging from limestone and calcareous clay to loam though also primary soils: Silurian shale, gneiss and granite. The climate is Mediterranean, hot and dry. High temperatures are in fact a prerequisite if the grapes are to achieve sufficient sugar concentration to be transformed into dessert wine. Like Banyuls, the red blends are fermented on the skins in an oxidised atmosphere, and the wines can age for no more than a year. There is no skin contact for the whites which are made using the direct to press method.

WINE STYLES: the Rivesaltes appellation is used for red, rosé and white dessert wines, drawn from Grenache noir, gris and blanc, Maccabeu, Muscat and Malvoisie, a varietal range which differentiates them from wines under the Muscat de Rivesaltes appellation. The "Grenats" are obtained by macerating the must for all or part of the red wine fermentation process (75% Grenache noir) and ageing them in a reducing atmosphere for at least months in the bottle. They display an attractive, extremely bright red hue which develops brick-red tints as they age. They are tannic, powerful, well-balanced wines with a long finish, boasting complex aromas (blackberry, raspberry, blackcurrant and cherry, leading into notes of cocoa, gingerbread, orange peel and crystallised fruit after spending time in oak). Try with strongly-flavoured food: game or duck. The red wines (50% Grenache noir) aged in an oxidative atmosphere until at least March 1st following the harvest are known as "tuilés" (or "bricked"). They are intense wines with notes of toast, cocoa, coffee, tobacco and candied fruits. The white wines are blessed with a pale yellow hue which turns amber after the same ageing duration in an oxidative atmosphere as the "tuilés". On the palate, they are round and supple, with hints of fennel and mint, leading into honeyed tones with dried fruit, vanilla, resin and cocoa. As they mature, they often develop slightly oxidised tones. Serve with fish marinated in ginger, lemon or mint. Mature Rivesaltes, both red and white, pair extremely well with desserts and a selection of cheeses.

AC SAINT-CHINIAN

OVERVIEW: the Saint-Chinian appellation area is located north of Béziers in the Hérault department. The area covers 20 towns and villages and its soil types are subdivided into two highly distinct zones: calcareous clay in the south, shale in the north. The climate is typically Mediterranean, hot and dry, and the varietal range, once dominated by Carignan, has changed considerably over the past 25 years : Carignan (40% maximum), Cinsault (30% maximum), Grenache, Lladoner Pelut, Syrah and Mourvedre. The latter four varietals must account for at least 60% of the blend including at least 10% for Syrah and Mourvèdre together and 20% for Grenache and Lladoner combined. Interestingly, the two village sites Roquebrun and Berlou, both on the appellation's shale soils, have recently been allowed to state their names on the label, alongside that of Saint-Chinian. However, only red wines are entitled to use these additional geographic denominations. The white wines (officially recognised in 2005) are primarily made from Grenache blanc, Marsanne, Roussanne, Vermentino, augmented with Bourboulenc, Clairette, Macabeu and Carignan blanc. They were previously labelled Coteaux du Languedoc.

WINE STYLES: the red wines display a 'cockerel blood' red hue. On the palate, they are rich, full and velvety, with aromas of red fruit (raspberry, blackcurrant), spices (pepper) and bay, leading into notes of cocoa, roasted coffee, fruit in brandy and jammy red fruit in time. The red wines grown on shale soils are more aromatic and supple, whilst those hailing from the calcareous clay soils are harder and more austere though with greater ageing capacity. Enjoy with game, duck salad or cassoulet. The rosés are fat, harmonious and boast distinctive freshness. Serve with marinated chicken kebabs, paella or a red fruit dessert.

• • •

LANGUEDOC-ROUSSILLON

Banyuls

DOMAINE BERTA-MAILLOL — +33 4 68 88 00 54

▼ 2011 Price:○○ — 86/100

Blanquette de Limoux

AIMERY SIEUR D'ARQUES — +33 4 68 74 63 00

▼ Première Bulle Brut 2011 Price:○○ — 86/100

DOMAINE ROSIER — +33 4 68 31 48 38

▼ Brut - Jean Philippe 2011 Price:○ — 86/100

Cévennes

DOMAINE DE BERGUEROLLES — +33 4 66 24 01 84

▼ Le Clos 2011 Price:○ — 88/100

▼ Le Clos 2012 Price:○○ — 88/100

▼ Magnifica Preda 2012 Price:○○ — 88/100

DOMAINE DE GOURNIER — +33 4 66 83 30 91

▼ Cuvée Templière 2010 Price:○ — 88/100

▼ Don du Roy 2011 Price:○ — 85/100

▼ Les Hauts Calcaires 2010 Price:○ — 85/100

▼ G de G 2012 Price:○ — 84/100

▼ Cuvée Templière 2011 Price:○ — 89/100

Cité de Carcassonne

CHÂTEAU DE SERRES +33 4 68 25 03 94

▼ Vintage 2011 Price:❍ 80/100

DOMAINE SAINT MARTIN +33 4 68 79 82 77

▼ Merci ! 2010 Price:❍ 85/100

VIGNOBLES SARRAIL +33 4 68 78 01 42

▼ Domaine Sarrail Magdalena 2010 Price:❍ 88/100

▼ Domaine Sarrail Vintage 2012 Price:❍ 87/100

▼ Domaine Sarrail Vintage 2012 Price:❍ 86/100

▼ Domaine Sarrail Vintage 2012 Price:❍ 86/100

Clairette du Languedoc

CAVE LA CLAIRETTE D'ADISSAN +33 4 67 25 01 07

▼ Château d'Adissan Vintage 2012 Price:❍ 85/100

▼ La Clairette d'Adissan L'Eglantier 2012 Price:❍ 85/100

▼ Château d'Adissan Vintage 2012 Price:❍ 84/100

▼ La Clairette d'Adissan L'Eglantier 2012 Price:❍ 83/100

THE COLOUR OF THE WINES :

- ■ Red wine
- ■ Dry white wine
- ■ Rose wine
- ● Sweet white wine
- ▲ Sparkling brut
- ▲ Sparkling brut rose
- ◆ Brandy
- ● Liqueur wine

Collioure

DOMAINE BERTA-MAILLOL +33 4 68 88 00 54

▼ 2011 Price:○○ 83/100

Corbières

TERRE PATRIMOINES +33 4 68 75 25 25

▼ Château le Bouïs R 2011 Price:○ 89/100

▼ La Grange du Bouis Cuvée Roméo 2010 Price:○○○ 89/100

▼ Château le Bouïs La Cigale 2011 Price:○ 87/100

CHÂTEAU BEAUREGARD MIROUZE +33 4 68 45 19 35

▼ Fiaire 2009 Price:○○○ 89/100

CONV▼ Lauzina 2011 Price:○○ 88/100

CONV▼ Lauzina 2011 Price:○○ 86/100

CV▼ Le Grangeot de Beauregard Mirouze Vintage 2011 Price:○ 85/100

CHÂTEAU DE CABRIAC +33 4 68 79 19 15

▼ Cuvée Marquise de Puivert 2010 Price:○ 88/100

▼ Prieuré St Martin 2008 Price:○○ 88/100

▼ Tradition 2010 Price:○ 87/100

CHÂTEAU DU VIEUX PARC +33 4 68 27 47 44

▼ La séléction 2011 Price:○○ 88/100

▼ Vintage 2011 Price:○ 87/100

DOMAINE DE LA BAQUIÈRE +33 4 68 78 98 49

▼ Les Romarines 2012 Price:○ 83/100

CHANTOVENT SA +33 1 30 98 59 79

▼ Château Montrabech Pitt Vintage 2011 Price:○ 83/100

CHÂTEAU DU GRAND CAUMONT +33 4 68 27 10 82

▼ Cuvée Tradition 2011 Price:○ 86/100

CHÂTEAU GRAND MOULIN +33 4 68 27 40 80

▼ Terres Rouges 2010 Price:○ 85/100

DOMAINE DE LA BAQUIÈRE +33 4 68 78 98 49

▼ Grand Caprice 2011 Price:❍ 87/100

TERRE PATRIMOINES +33 4 68 75 25 25

▼ Château le Bouïs K 2009 Price:❍❍❍ 91/100

Coteaux de Peyriac

CHÂTEAU DU DONJON +33 4 68 77 18 33

▼ Le Merlot du Donjon Vintage 2009 Price:❍ 85/100

Coteaux du Libron

DOMAINE DE LA BARTHE +33 4 67 28 60 29

▼ Vintage 2012 Price:❍ 83/100

▼ Symphonie des Cinq Sens 2010 Price:❍❍ 86/100

DOMAINE DE LA BARTHE

▼ Métamorphose 2010 **86/100**

Deeply-coloured garnet. Distinctive nose with accents of jammy blackcurrant backed by pepper. Supple, soft palate showing seductive refined stuffing, freshness and fruit performance. A seductive Syrah. Pair with quail with grapes.

Price: ❍

Serving Temperature: 15-17°C - Ready to drink : 2014-2015

Domaine de La Barthe
14 route de Capestang - 34500 Beziers
Tel.: +33 04 67 28 60 29 - Fax: +33 04 67 28 60 29
E-mail: eychenne.yves@club-internet.fr
Website: http://www.domainedelabarthe.fr

Côtes Catalanes

EARL DOMAINE DES ENFANTS	+33 9 62 32 35 58
CV▼ Suis l'Etoile 2008 Price:OOO	93/100
CV▼ L'Enfant Perdu 2010 Price:OOO	91/100
CV▼ Tabula Rasa 2011 Price:OOO	89/100

CHÂTEAU DE LACROIX	+33 4 68 50 48 39
▼ Les Petits Grains 2011 Price:O	86/100

Côtes de Thongue

DOMAINE MONTROSE	+33 4 67 98 63 33
▼ Salamandre 2011 Price:OO	89/100
▼ Viognier 2012 Price:O	88/100
▼ La Balade des Lézards 2011 Price:O	87/100
▼ Vintage 2012 Price:O	87/100
▼ La Balade des Lézards 2012 Price:O	86/100

Côtes du Roussillon

CHÂTEAU DE LACROIX	+33 4 68 50 48 39
▼ Réserve 2009 Price:OO	89/100
▼ Réserve 2009 Price:OO	89/100
▼ Cuvée Louise 2011 Price:OO	88/100
▼ Serment de vigne 2011 Price:OO	84/100

DOMAINE DE VÉNUS	+33 4 68 59 18 81
▼ L'Effrontée 2009 Price:OO	91/100

Crémant de Limoux

DOMAINE ROSIER +33 4 68 31 48 38

▼ L 2011 Price:○ — 86/100

▼ Cuvée Ma Maison 2011 Price:○ — 86/100

AIMERY SIEUR D'ARQUES +33 4 68 74 63 00

▼ Toques et Clochers 2007 Price:○○ — 89/100

DOMAINES PAUL MAS +33 4 67 90 16 10

▼ Brut Rosé Prima Perla Price:○○ — 83/100

MAISON GUINOT +33 4 68 31 01 33

▼ Brut Tendre - Impérial Price:○ — 88/100

Faugères

DOMAINE LA TOUR PENEDESSES +33 4 67 95 17 21

ORG▼ La Montagne Noire 2011 Price:○○ — 88/100

Fitou

DOMAINE GRAND GUILHEM +33 4 68 45 86 67

▼ Angels 2011 Price:○○○ — 91/100

Gard

CHÂTEAU GUIOT +33 4 66 73 30 86

▼ Mas de Guiot Vintage 2010 Price:○ — 83/100

Detailed instructions are featured at the start of the book.

Languedoc

CHÂTEAU SAINT MARTIN DE LA GARRIGUE — +33 4 67 24 00 40

▼ Bronzinelle 2010 Price:○ — 88/100

DOMAINE LES GRANDES COSTES — +33 4 67 59 27 42

▼ La Sarabande 2008 Price:○○ — 90/100

▼ La Sarabande 2009 Price:○○ — 88/100

▼ Musardises 2011 Price:○ — 87/100

DOMAINES PAUL MAS — +33 4 67 90 16 10

▼ Château Paul Mas Belluguette 2012 Price:○○ — 89/100

▼ Château Paul Mas Clos des Mûres
Elevé en Fût de Chêne 2011 Price:○○ — 88/100

LA GRANGE — +33 4 67 24 69 81

▼ Icone Castalides 2011 Price:○○○ — 90/100

▼ Edition Castalides 2011 Price:○○ — 88/100

▼ Réserve Castalides 2011 Price:○ — 87/100

CAVE LA CLAIRETTE D'ADISSAN — +33 4 67 25 01 07

▼ La Clairette d'Adissan L'Eglantier 2012 Price:○ — 86/100

▼ Château d'Adissan Vintage 2012 Price:○ — 85/100

▼ Château d'Adissan Vintage 2012 Price:○ — 85/100

▼ La Clairette d'Adissan L'Eglantier 2011 Price:○ — 83/100

CAVE DE L'ORMARINE — +33 4 67 77 03 10

▼ Préambule 2012 Price:○ — 86/100

▼ Château Cazalis de Fondouce Vintage 2012 Price:○ — 84/100

▼ Préambule 2012 Price:○ — 83/100

CAVE DE ROQUEBRUN — +33 4 67 89 64 35

▼ Chemin des Olivettes 2012 Price:○ — 83/100

CHANTOVENT SA — +33 1 30 98 59 79

▼ Jean d'Alibert Vintage 2012 Price:○ — 84/100

CHÂTEAU DE LA BAUME — +33 4 67 38 16 22

▼ Vintage 2012 Price:○○ — 88/100

CHÂTEAU SAINT MARTIN DE LA GARRIGUE — +33 4 67 24 00 40

▼ Vintage 2010 Price:○○ — 91/100

▼ Bronzinelle 2011 Price:○ — 88/100

CHÂTEAU DE LA BAUME

▼ Vintage 2012 **88/100**

Deeply-coloured orange-brown. Very open nose intermixing black cherry, prune, undergrowth and humus. Sumptuous attack showing fat, fullness and presence flowing into a more mineral mid-palate (graphite) with wonderful persistency. Sterling effort.

Price: OO

Wine and food pairing: braised beef
Serving Temperature: 15-17°C
Ready to drink: From now on

Located in Puisserguier, around twenty kilometres from Béziers, and set amongst garrigue land in a Natura 2000 protected area, La Baume is a wine estate currently undergoing complete revitalisation. It already boasts 6 hectares under vine which will gradually increase to 18 hectares by 2015. The local soils, alternately limestone gravel and sandstone from the Eocene epoch, are outstanding. Syrah, Grenache and Mourvèdre vines averaging 20 years' old produce naturally healthy, concentrated grapes. During the wine making process, the overriding ambition is to bring out the maximum amount of fruit, freshness and minerality whilst avoiding excessive power and extraction. The result is convincing. An estate worth following.

Château de la Baume
34620 Puisserguier
Tel.: +33 4 67 38 16 22
E-mail: masdelabaume@gmail.fr

LES AMIS DE LA BAUME

▼ Vintage 2011 **86/100**

Deep garnet-red. Focused nose opening up to red and black fruits, spices and mineral undercurrents. The palate is melted and fresh, extremely supple and unveils savoury, crunchy fruit that lingers. A wine for instant pleasure that is remarkably drinkable.

Price: ❍

Wine and food pairing: barbecue foods
Serving Temperature: 15-17°C
Ready to drink:2013-2014

Les Amis de la Baume is Château de la Baume's second wine. Its name is a nod the estate's past when for decades it was a meeting place for a group of friends who are now scattered across the world. The convivial, festive spirit of those countless gourmet encounters remains and the estate's new owners (original members of this fun-loving group) have sought to capture that spirit in the wine. Made from Syrah and Grenache, 'Les Amis de la Baume' is a delightful, vibrant and perfumed wine showing instant accessibility so that others too can enjoy those fleeting moments.

Château de la Baume
34620 Puisserguier
Tel.: +33 4 67 38 16 22
E-mail: masdelabaume@gmail.fr

DOMAINE D'AIGUES BELLES +33 6 07 48 74 65

▼ Le Classique 2010 Price:○○ 86/100

DOMAINE D'ANGLAS +33 4 67 73 70 18

ORG▼ Vintage 2011 Price:○○ 88/100

DOMAINE LA TOUR PENEDESSES +33 4 67 95 17 21

ORG▼ Cuvée Antique 2010 Price:○ 86/100

DOMAINE LE NOUVEAU MONDE +33 4 67 37 33 68

▼ L'Estanquier 2008 Price:○○ 88/100

DOMAINE LES ANGES DE BACCHUS +33 6 17 31 57 18

▼ Vintage 2010 Price:○ 87/100

Languedoc Grès de Montpellier

DOMAINE SAINT-JEAN DU NOVICIAT +33 4 67 24 07 32

▼ N de Novi Millésime 2009 Price:○○○ 94/100

▼ Mas du Novi Prestigi 2009 Price:○○ 91/100

▼ Novi Vintage 2007 Price:○○ 91/100

DOMAINE DE VALMAGNE +33 4 67 78 47 32

▼ Abbaye de Valmagne Cardinal de Bonzi 2007 Price:○○ 90/100

DOMAINE HENRY +33 4 67 45 57 74

CV▼ Domaine Henry Paradines 2011 Price:○ 86/100

DOMAINE LES ANGES DE BACCHUS +33 6 17 31 57 18

▼ Vintage 2010 Price:○○ 91/100

DOMAINES PAUL MAS +33 4 67 90 16 10

▼ Château Paul Mas Clos de Savignac 2011 Price:○○ 87/100

Languedoc La Clape

DOMAINE DES KARANTES +33 4 68 43 61 70

▼ Château des Karantes Vintage 2011 Price:○○ 90/100

▼ Château des Karantes Bergerie 2012 Price:○ 87/100

▼ Château des Karantes Bergerie 2012 Price:○ 87/100

▼ Château des Karantes Vintage 2012 Price:○○ 85/100

Languedoc Montpeyroux

DOMAINE D'AUPILHAC +33 4 67 96 61 19

▼ Aupilhac Le Clos 2009 Price:○○○ 92/100

▼ Vintage 2010 Price:○○ 87/100

VILLA DONDONA +33 4 67 96 68 34

ORG▼ Oppidum 2010 Price:○○ 88/100

ORG▼ Vintage 2011 Price:○○ 88/100

ORG▼ Espérel 2011 Price:○○ 83/100

Languedoc Pézenas

LES CAVES MOLIÈRE +33 4 67 98 10 05

▼ Dom Juan 2010 Price:○ 86/100

▼ Marquise du Parc 2011 Price:○ 84/100

DOMAINE LA TOUR PENEDESSES +33 4 67 95 17 21

ORG▼ Les Volcans 2011 Price:○ 89/100

DOMAINES PAUL MAS +33 4 67 90 16 10

▼ Château Paul Mas Clos du Moulinas 2011 Price:○ 88/100

Languedoc Pic Saint-Loup

BERGERIE DU CAPUCIN +33 4 67 59 01 00

▼ Larmanela 2010 Price:○○ 93/100

▼ Dame Jeanne 2011 Price:○○ 90/100

▼ Dame Jeanne 2012 Price:○ 86/100

DOMAINE DE LAVABRE +33 4 67 59 02 25

▼ Château Lavabre Vintage 2006 Price:○○ 89/100

▼ Les Demoiselles de Lavabre Vintage 2008 Price:○○ 88/100

▼ Château Lavabre Vintage 2005 Price:○○○ 87/100

▼ Lavabre Tradition 2011 Price:○ 86/100

DOMAINE LES GRANDES COSTES +33 4 67 59 27 42

▼ Vintage 2010 Price:○○ 91/100

DOMAINE MAS DE L'ONCLE +33 4 67 67 26 16

CV▼ Louis 2011 Price:○○ 89/100

DOMAINE ZUMBAUM TOMASI +33 4 67 55 78 77

▼ Vintage 2010 Price:○○ 88/100

Languedoc Picpoul de Pinet

CAVE DE L'ORMARINE +33 4 67 77 03 10

▼ Carte Noire 2012 Price:○ 85/100

▼ Duc de Morny 2012 Price:○ 85/100

CHÂTEAU SAINT MARTIN DE LA GARRIGUE +33 4 67 24 00 40

▼ Picpoul du Pinet 2012 Price:○ 86/100

Languedoc Saint-Georges d'Orques

DOMAINE HENRY +33 4 67 45 57 74

CV▼ St-Georges d'Orques 2010 Price:○○ 87/100

CV▼ Vin Vermeil 2012 Price:○○ 83/100

Languedoc Terrasses du Larzac

CALMEL JOSEPH +33 4 68 72 09 88

▼ Les Crus 2011 Price:○○ 86/100

DOMAINES PAUL MAS +33 4 67 90 16 10

- ▼ Château Martinolles Vieilles Vignes 2011 Price:OO 89/100
- ▼ III B & Auromon Chardonnay 2011 Price:O 88/100
- ▼ Château des Crès Ricards Stécia 2011 Price:O 87/100

Limoux

DENOIS +33 4 68 31 39 12

- ▼ Vintage 2009 Price:OO 90/100
- CV▼ Vintage 2011 Price:OO 89/100
- CV▼ Jean-Louis Denois Grande Cuvée 2011 Price:OO 88/100
- CV▼ Vintage 2010 Price:OO 86/100

AIMERY SIEUR D'ARQUES +33 4 68 74 63 00

- ▼ Terroir Toques et Clochers Haute Vallée 2011 Price:OO 88/100

Malepère

CHÂTEAU DE SERRES +33 4 68 25 29 82

- ▼ Vintage 2010 Price:OO 86/100

Minervois

AGNEL PÈRE ET FILS +33 4 68 78 39 94

- ▼ Château Agnel Les Carmes 2010 Price:O 88/100

CHANTOVENT SA +33 1 30 98 59 79

- ▼ Michel et Philiippe Agnel Les Carmes 2008 Price:O 88/100

CHÂTEAU D'AGEL +33 4 68 91 37 74

- ▼ In Extremis 2010 Price:OOO 93/100
- ▼ Vintage 2010 Price:OOO 91/100
- ▼ Maestria 2011 Price:OO 88/100
- ▼ Les Bonnes - Maccabeu - Roussanne - Grenache 2012 Price:O 84/100

Languedoc-Roussillon - *Minervois*

CHÂTEAU CABEZAC +33 4 68 46 23 05

- ▼ Les Capitelles 2011 Price:○ — 92/100
- ▼ Cuvée Arthur 2009 Price:○○ — 90/100
- ▼ Le Petit Arthur 2008 Price:○ — 88/100
- ▼ La Garrigue 2011 Price:○ — 86/100

CHÂTEAU DU DONJON +33 4 68 77 18 33

- ▼ Vintage 2012 Price:○ — 88/100
- ▼ Prestige 2009 Price:○ — 87/100
- ▼ Grande Tradition 2011 Price:○ — 86/100

CHÂTEAU SAINTE-EULALIE +33 4 68 91 42 72

- ▼ Vintage 2011 Price:○ — 84/100

DOMAINE AIMÉ +33 4 68 91 14 10

- CV▼ Vintage 2011 Price:○ — 86/100

DOMAINE BORIE DE MAUREL +33 4 68 91 68 58

- CV▼ Cuvée Sylla 2010 Price:○○○ — 89/100
- CV▼ Borie de Maurel Belle de Nuit 2010 Price:○○ — 87/100
- CV▼ Esprit d'Automne 2011 Price:○ — 85/100

DOMAINE DE LA PRADE MARI +33 4 68 91 22 45

- ▼ Trésor des Anges 2009 Price:○○○ — 92/100
- ▼ Gourmandise des Bois 2009 Price:○○ — 91/100
- ▼ Conte des Guarrigues 2009 Price:○○ — 88/100

SAINT-JACQUES D'ALBAS +33 4 68 78 24 82

- ▼ Saint Jacques d'Albas La Chapelle 2008 Price:○○ — 90/100
- ▼ Château Saint-Jacques d'Albas Vintage 2010 Price:○ — 87/100
- ▼ Saint Jacques d'Albas Vintage 2011 Price:○ — 84/100

Minervois La Livinière

CHANTOVENT SA +33 1 30 98 59 79

- ▼ Jean d'Alibert Vintage 2008 Price:○ — 86/100

CHÂTEAU SAINTE-EULALIE +33 4 68 91 42 72

▼ Vintage 2010 Price:OO 90/100

DOMAINE AIMÉ +33 4 68 91 14 10

CV▼ Au Gré du Vent 2009 Price:OO 88/100

DOMAINE BORIE DE MAUREL +33 4 68 91 68 58

CV▼ La Féline 2010 Price:OO 90/100

Muscat de Frontignan

DOMAINE DU MAS DE MADAME +33 4 67 18 40 71

▼ Mas de Madame Vintage 2011 Price:OO 88/100

Muscat de Rivesaltes

CHÂTEAU DE LACROIX +33 4 68 50 48 39

▼ Vintage 2011 Price:OO 90/100

Pays d'Hérault - Collines de la Moure

DOMAINE DU MAS DE MADAME +33 4 67 18 40 71

▼ Mas de Madame Vintage 2012 Price:O 87/100

DOMAINE HENRY +33 4 67 45 57 74

CV▼ Domaine Henry Vintage 2012 Price:OO 84/100

Pays d'Hérault - Coteaux de Bessilles

DOMAINES PAUL MAS +33 4 67 90 16 10

ORG▼ Mas des Tannes Réserve 2011 Price:OO 90/100

Pays d'Hérault - Côtes du Céressou

CAVE LA CLAIRETTE D'ADISSAN +33 4 67 25 01 07

▼ La Clairette d'Adissan Douce Rosée 2012 Price:❍ 84/100

Pays d'Hérault - Pays de Caux

LES CAVES MOLIÈRE +33 4 67 98 10 05

▼ Rosé de Caux 2012 Price:❍ 85/100

Pays d'Oc

CAVE DE L'ORMARINE +33 4 67 77 03 10

▼ Haut de Senaux - Merlot 2012 Price:❍ 85/100

▼ Haut de Senaux - Viognier 2012 Price:❍ 85/100

▼ Haut de Senaux - Syrah 2012 Price:❍ 83/100

CHÂTEAU GUIOT +33 4 66 73 30 86

▼ L'Enclos de la Chance Les Jumeaux 2011 Price:❍❍ 88/100

▼ L'Enclos de la Chance Les Aiguillettes... 2012 Price:❍ 84/100

▼ L'Enclos de la Chance Les Aiguillettes... 2012 Price:❍ 79/100

DOMAINES ROBERT VIC +33 4 67 21 67 82

▼ Domaine Preignes le vieux Prestige Syrah 2010 Price:❍ 84/100

CHÂTEAU SAINT MARTIN DES CHAMPS +33 4 67 32 92 58

▼ Domaine Saint Martin des Champs Méli-Mélo 2012 Price:❍ 83/100

▼ Domaine Saint Martin des Champs Meli-Mélo 2012 Price:❍ 83/100

▼ Domaine Saint Martin des Champs Méli-Mélo 2011 Price:❍ 83/100

CHÂTEAUX ET DOMAINES CASTEL +33 5 56 95 54 00

▼ Vintage 2012 Price:❍ 85/100

DOMAINE AIMÉ +33 4 68 91 14 10

CV▼ Cabernet Franc 2011 Price:❍ 85/100

DOMAINE D'AIGUES BELLES	+33 6 07 48 74 65
▼ Le Blanc 2012 Price:❍❍	90/100
▼ Cuvée Nicole 2010 Price:❍❍	90/100
▼ L'Autre Blanc 2012 Price:❍❍	88/100
▼ Cuvée Lombarde 2010 Price:❍	86/100

DOMAINES PAUL MAS	+33 4 67 90 16 10
▼ La Forge Estate Cabernet Sauvignon 2012 Price:❍	88/100
▼ La Forge Estate Chardonnay 2012 Price:❍	87/100
▼ Arrogant Frog Chardonnay - Viognier 2012 Price:❍	87/100
ORG ▼ Mas des Tannes - Réserve 2012 Price:❍	86/100
▼ La Forge Estate Pinot Noir Réserve 2012 Price:❍	86/100
▼ Arrogant Frog Cabernet sauvignon - Merlot 2012 Price:❍	86/100
▼ Vignes de Nicole - Elevé en Fût de Chêne 2011 Price:❍	85/100

DOMAINE DE VILLARZENS	+33 4 68 76 29 86
▼ Villarzens Eburomagus 2009 Price:❍	87/100

DOMAINE DES CARABINIERS	+33 4 66 82 62 94
ORG ▼ Syrah 2012 Price:❍	83/100

DOMAINE DU MAS DE MADAME	+33 4 67 18 40 71
▼ Elégance Cuvée RéservéeRobert-Georges Sourinx 2009 Price:❍❍	87/100
▼ Mas de Madame Muscat Sec 2012 Price:❍	85/100
▼ Mas de Madame Muscat Moëlleux 2012 Price:❍	82/100

DOMAINE DU MAS DES BROUSSES	+33 4 67 57 33 75
▼ Le Chasseur des Brousses 2011 Price:❍	82/100

DOMAINES ROBERT VIC	+33 4 67 21 67 82
▼ Preignes Collection 2009 Price:❍❍	87/100
▼ Le Petit Pont Réserve 2010 Price:❍	82/100

DOMAINE SAINT-JEAN DU NOVICIAT	+33 4 67 24 07 32
▼ Mas du Novi Chardonnay 2011 Price:❍❍	87/100

JB VINS	+33 6 31 20 09 18
▼ Viognier 2011 Price:❍	88/100

Detailed instructions are featured at the start of the book.

DOMAINE CHAMPS BLANCS

▼ Spes Unica - Réserve - fûts de Chêne 2009 92/100

Superb deep and concentrated hue. Delicate nose marrying smoky vanilla oak and fragrances of spice and macerated stone fruits. Velvety, majestic palate. Racy oak enhancing the fruit, sappy stuffing... A real tribute to wine.

Price: ❍❍

Serving Temperature: 15-17°C
Ready to drink : 2014-2016

Domaine Champs Blancs
RD 612 - 34620 Puisserguier
Tel.: +33 04 67 93 31 41 - Fax: +33 04 67 32 29 72
E-mail: contact@champsblancs.com

LA GRANGE +33 4 67 24 69 81

▼ Terroir 2011 Price:❍ 85/100

▼ Terroir 2012 Price:❍ 84/100

MAS PELLIER +33 6 82 61 73 51

▼ Chardonnay 2011 Price:❍ 85/100

▼ Campalazard - élevé en fût de chêne 2010 Price:❍❍ 84/100

▼ Merlot 2010 Price:❍ 84/100

OPPIDUM +33 3 89 76 03 72

▼ Terres de Combecal 2007 Price:❍ 87/100

▼ Terres de Combecal 2007 Price:❍ 86/100

▼ Terres de Combecal 2006 Price:❍ 85/100

TERRE PATRIMOINES +33 4 68 75 25 25

▼ La Grange du Bouis Cuvée Juliette 2009 Price:❍❍❍ 92/100

Detailed instructions are featured at the start of the book.

Pays de l'Hérault - Monts de la Grage

CHÂTEAU DE CASTIGNO +33 4 67 38 05 50

CV▼ Terra Casta 2009 Price:❍ 86/100

Saint-Chinian

CALMEL JOSEPH +33 4 68 72 09 88

▼ Calmel + JJoseph Vintage 2011 Price:❍ 86/100

CAVE DE ROQUEBRUN +33 4 67 89 64 35

▼ Golden Vines 2011 Price:❍❍ 92/100

▼ Col de la Serre 2012 Price:❍ 84/100

▼ Col de la Serre 2012 Price:❍ 83/100

CAVE DES VIGNERONS DE ST CHINIAN +33 4 67 38 28 48

▼ Le Secret des Capitelles 2012 Price:❍ 88/100

▼ Le Chant des Guarrigues 2010 Price:❍ 88/100

▼ Esprit de Renaud de Valon 2009 Price:❍❍ 88/100

▼ Le Secret des Capitelles 2011 Price:❍ 87/100

▼ Renaud de Valon 2009 Price:❍ 87/100

▼ L'Excellence de Saint-Laurent 2011 Price:❍ 83/100

▼ L'Excellence de Saint-Laurent 2012 Price:❍ 82/100

CHÂTEAU DE CASTIGNO +33 4 67 38 05 50

CV▼ Secret des Dieux 2009 Price:❍❍ 92/100

CV▼ Vintage 2009 Price:❍❍❍ 90/100

CHÂTEAU MILHAU-LACUGUE +33 4 67 93 64 79

▼ Les Curées 2008 Price:❍❍ 90/100

▼ Les Truffières 2010 Price:❍❍ 88/100

▼ Cuvée des Chevaliers 2008 Price:❍ 85/100

▼ Cuvée Magali 2010 Price:❍ 84/100

CHÂTEAU MILHAU-LACUGUE

▼ Les Curées 2008 90/100

Intense colour. Profound, open nose showing delightful aromas of red fruits, stone fruits and garrigue with mineral undercurrents bordering on undergrowth. Full, lush, warm and melted palate. Lovely volume, power and persistency. A sterling wine.

Price: OO

Food pairing: leg of venison
Serving temperature: 15-17°C
Drinkability: from now on

A former Knights Hospitaller estate, Château Milhau-Lacugue farms vineyards facing South-South-East on clay-limestone soils from the Secondary and Tertiary periods formed by the whims of countless geological forces. Its 'Les Curées' blend mirrors all the qualities of a great growth with its idiosyncratic personality shaped by its boutique vineyard, a selection of Syrah and Grenache noir grapes and lengthy wine making process. As the air flows through the garrigue and along the valley floor, it imbues the grapes with myriad scents of wild plants that will later form part of the wine's unique personality.
Power combines with elegance and the wine gradually matures after years of cellaring.
Authentic, rich and distinguished, 'Les Curées' is a perfect match for the finest French cuisine.

Château Milhau-Lacugue
Route de Cazedarnes
34620 Puisserguier
Tel.: +33 4 67 93 64 79 - Fax: +33 4 67 93 64 79
E-mail : lacuguejean@yahoo.fr
Website : http://milhau-lacugue.com/

CHÂTEAU MILHAU-LACUGUE

▼ Les Truffières 2010 **88/100**

Beautiful intense hue. Concentrated nose of red and black fruits, notes of liquorice and spice. Wonderful attack with a melted, fine-grained mouthfeel. Good length and freshness is displayed across the palate with the liquoricy, mineral character recurring on the finish.

Price: OO

Food pairing: grilled pork ribs
Serving temperature: 15-17°C
Drinkability: from now on

'Les Truffières' by Château Milhau-Lacugue is a dense, elegant wine that takes its name from the truffle-bearing oak trees that grow wild here. The soils are clay-limestone with a South-South-East aspect exposed to a gentle daily breeze. In this unique location, Syrah and Grenache noir show outstanding expression, blending flowery and fruity elegance with dense, concentrated tannins.
A wine displaying archetypal Mediterranean traits, it is rich and complex and will gradually reveal itself after a few years' cellaring.
At a serving temperature of 17°C, 'Les Truffières' pairs well with all meat and game-based dishes, particularly slow-cooked meats.

Château Milhau-Lacugue
Route de Cazedarnes
34620 Puisserguier
Tel.: +33 4 67 93 64 79 - Fax: +33 4 67 93 64 79
E-mail : lacuguejean@yahoo.fr
Website : http://milhau-lacugue.com/

CHÂTEAU SAINT MARTIN DES CHAMPS	+33 4 67 32 92 58
▼ Sélection 2009 Price:❍	86/100
▼ Sélection 2012 Price:❍	85/100
DOMAINE BELLES COURBES	+33 4 67 36 32 24
▼ Vintage 2011 Price:❍	78/100
DOMAINE CARRIÈRE AUDIER	+33 4 67 97 77 71
▼ Château Vieussan Vintage 2010 Price:❍	87/100
▼ Le Souleilladou 2010 Price:❍	86/100
▼ Cuvée Aurélie 2011 Price:❍	86/100
▼ La Font du Drag 2010 Price:❍	85/100
▼ Château Vieussan Vintage 2012 Price:❍	83/100
DOMAINE GALTIER	+33 4 67 37 85 14
▼ Chateau Galtier Kermès 2010 Price:❍	87/100
▼ Chateau Galtier L'Obstinée 2010 Price:❍	86/100
DOMAINE LA CROIX STE EULALIE	+33 4 67 38 08 51
▼ Cuvée Clémence 2011 Price:❍❍	92/100
▼ Cuvée Baptiste 2010 Price:❍❍	91/100
▼ Cuvée Armandelis 2011 Price:❍	88/100
▼ Vintage 2012 Price:❍	87/100
DOMAINE LA MADURA	+33 4 67 38 17 85
▼ Grand Vin 2009 Price:❍❍	90/100
▼ Classic 2009 Price:❍	88/100
MAS CHAMPART	+33 4 67 38 20 09
▼ Clos de La Simonette 2010 Price:❍❍	88/100
MAS DE CYNANQUE	+33 4 67 25 01 34
CV▼ Althea 2011 Price:❍❍	89/100
CV▼ Acutum 2009 Price:❍❍	83/100
CV▼ Plein Grès 2010 Price:❍	81/100

THE COLOUR OF THE WINES :

■ Red wine	▲ Sparkling brut
■ Dry white wine	▲ Sparkling brut rose
■ Rose wine	◆ Brandy
● Sweet white wine	● Liqueur wine

Saint-Chinian Roquebrun

CAVE DE ROQUEBRUN +33 4 67 89 64 35

▼ Fiefs d'Aupenac 2011 Price:○○ 90/100

▼ Roches Noires 2012 Price:○ 86/100

▼ Seigneur d'Aupenac 2009 Price:○○ 91/100

DOMAINE CARRIÈRE AUDIER +33 4 67 97 77 71

▼ Saint Martin de Vieussan 2010 Price:○ 87/100

St Guilhem le Désert

MAS DE DAUMAS GASSAC +33 4 67 57 71 28

▼ Vintage 2012 Price:○○○ 88/100

▼ Vintage 2012 Price:○○○ 89/100

St-Guilhem-Le-Désert - Val de Montferrand

DOMAINE DE LA VIEILLE +33 4 67 55 35 17

▼ C. léon 2010 Price:○○ 88/100

Coteaux d'Ancenis
Muscadet Coteaux de la Loire
Angers
Sarthe
Coteaux de l'Aubance
Savennières
Quarts de Chaume
St-Nicolas de Bourgueil
Chaume
Saumur-Champigny
Nantes
Muscadet Sèvre et Maine
Coteaux du Layon
Muscadet Côtes de Grandlieu
Saumur
Anjou
Anjou-Villages
Gros Plant
Muscadet
Vins du Thouarsais
Bonnezeaux
Fiefs Vendéens-Brem
Fiefs Vendéens-Mareuil
Haut-Poitou
Poitiers
Fiefs Vendéens-Pissotte
Fiefs Vendéens-Vix
Coteaux du Vendômois
Orléans
Jasnières
Vins de l'Orléanais
Cheverny
Coteaux du Loir
Cour-Cheverny
Tours
Bourgueil
Vouvray
Touraine
Touraine Mesland
Montlouis
Chinon
Touraine Azay-le-Rideau
Valençay
Touraine Noble-Joué
Haut-Poitou
Vienne
Indre
Creuse
Poitiers
St-Pourçain
Côte Roannaise
Côtes d'Auvergne
Clermont-Ferrand
Côtes du Forez
Châteaumeillant
Montluçon
Coteaux du Giennois
Sancerre
Menetou-Salon
Quincy
Bourges
Pouilly Fumé et Pouilly-sur-Loire
Reuilly

LOIRE VALLEY

BRINGING FRESHNESS INTO THE EQUATION

Stretching 1,012 kilometres from start to finish, the Loire is France's longest river. It rises in the Massif Central and cuts through myriad landscapes before flowing into the Atlantic. Its catchment area covers an astounding 120,000 km2, giving some idea of the variety of wine styles the Loire can produce: dry, medium dry or sweet whites, sparkling wines, light rosés, smooth or robust reds suitable for ageing... providing an endless choice for discerning wine lovers.

For the sake of simplicity, several different zones can be identified, starting upstream:

THE AUVERGNE, BOURBONNAIS AND FOREZ REGIONS

Vines grow here in and around mountain valleys. This is Gamay and Pinot noir territory for the red wines. The climate is continental or semi-continental and the winters are harsh. The wines are light and fruity red and rosé, though Chardonnay, Sauvignon and a clutch of local varieties such as Tressalier or Saint-Pierre Doré are also grown here. The area is divided between four appellations: Côtes d'Auvergne, Côtes du Forez, Côte Roannaise and Saint-Pourçain, with a balance of regional wines including Vin de Pays d'Urfé.

THE BERRY, NIVERNAIS AND ORLÉANAIS REGIONS

Heading north from the Bourbonnais (Allier), you enter the Nivernais where the Allier river flows into the Loire. Between Nevers and Orléans (AC Sancerre, Pouilly-Fumé, Coteaux du Giennois) the winters are still cold and spring is fickle for wine growing. Berry is also home to vineyards starting with Menetou-

Salon, which extends out from Sancerre in the east, then Quincy and Reuilly lining the banks of the Cher river and its tributary the Arnon, south of Vierzon. The area is famed for its white wines, made primarily from the Sauvignon grape, though the reds and rosés made from Pinot noir can be appealing and in some instances, highly distinguished wines.

THE TOURAINE REGION AND SURROUNDING AREAS

The vineyards of Touraine start in Blois and stretch all the way to the outskirts of Saumur (which is actually part of the Anjou wine region). The climate is milder here than in the Nivernais, as the warm ocean breezes sweep this far up the valley, though it is still partly defined by continental influences. Perhaps this subtle combination explains why Touraine (just like neighbouring Anjou) is renowned for its relaxed lifestyle. The kings of France certainly fell under its charm and chose the area to build their architectural jewels, the Châteaux of the Loire. Vines flourish here too. In Chinon and Bourgueil, Cabernet Franc, known locally as Breton, yields sterling red wines which in good vintages will keep for twenty years. In Montlouis and Vouvray, Chenin produces splendid still and sparkling white wines. Although these majestic wines rule the roost in terms of notoriety, some of the lesser-known wines also harbour some great surprises.

THERE ARE NINE TRUE TOURAINE APPELLATIONS

Touraine, Touraine-Amboise, Touraine-Azay-le-Rideau, Touraine-Mesland, Bourgueil, Saint-Nicolas de Bourgueil, Chinon, Vouvray and Montlouis. In addition to these are six peripheral appellations: Cheverny (which links Touraine to the Orléanais), Valençay (the south-eastern extension of Touraine), Coteaux du Vendômois, Jasnières, Coteaux du Loir (in the north) and Haut-Poitou (heading south-west).

THE ANJOU AND SAUMUR REGIONS

Anjou is reached by crossing the border of Maine et Loire in the west. Initially, around Saumur, the landscape undergoes only minor changes. Its predominant feature is the chalky soil ('tuffeau') - hence the name 'white' Anjou - from which thousands of kilometres of caves have been carved out. The area is home to red wines, made primarily from Cabernet Franc, and renowned sparkling wines. Heading west, the dividing line between the Paris and Armorican basins marks the starting point of 'black' Anjou where the soil type is predominantly shale (slate). The resultant red wines are more robust and Chenin flourishes in some parts (the Layon valley) to produce superlative sweet wines. The rosés also deserve a mention. They can be dry though are more often medium sweet, making Anjou France's leading producer of this style, ahead of Provence.

All of this provides the context for a wide variety of appellations and wine styles.

THERE ARE MORE THAN TWENTY APPELLATIONS IN ALL

REDS: *Anjou, Anjou-Villages, Anjou-Gamay, Saumur, Saumur-Champigny.*

ROSÉS: *Rosé d'Anjou, Cabernet d'Anjou, Rosé de Loire, Cabernet de Saumur, Coteaux de Saumur.*

SWEET WHITES: *Coteaux de l'Aubance, Anjou-Coteaux de la Loire, Coteaux du Layon, Chaume, Quarts de Chaume, Bonnezeaux.*

DRY WHITES: *Savennières (occasionally medium dry), Anjou*

SPARKLING: *Anjou Mousseux, Saumur Mousseux, Crémant de Loire.*

PAYS NANTAIS

The Pays Nantais region stretches west from Anjou, on the other side of Ingrandes. With around 20,000 hectares under vine, it is the most extensive area in the entire Loire valley. The Ocean type climate and cool soils (this is the Armorican mountain range) make production of dry white wines the natural choice. The summers are not hot enough to grow sweet wines and too changeable to make reds. Some red wine is grown on the border with Anjou (Coteaux d'Ancenis) and in Fiefs Vendéens around Les Sables d'Olonne, but only in diminutive quantities. The vast majority of the wines are white, made from Folle Blanche (known as Gros Plant) though chiefly Melon de Bourgogne (Muscadet). They yield dry, fragrant white wines (particularly the Muscadet) which form the perfect partners for the fruits of the sea, both shellfish and fish.

Pays Nantais boasts seven appellations: Coteaux d'Ancenis, Muscadet, Muscadet Sèvre et Maine, Muscadet des Coteaux de la Loire, Muscadet des Côtes de Grand-Lieu, Gros Plant du Pays Nantais and Fiefs Vendéens.

REVIEW OF LATEST VINTAGES

• **2010** • This northerly wine region experienced a harsh winter with low rainfall promoting a disease-free crop. The wines are generally well-balanced, expressive and crunchy. The light and supple wines and sparkling wines (Saumur-Touraine) should be of a high standard. Good whites from Central France.

• **2011** • like everywhere else, the vintage was challenging due to nature with a dry summer, almost too dry, then heavy rainfall, again slightly too heavy and too late in the season. However, the wines performed extremely well despite lower acidity than in 2010. Due to its acreage and wide array of grape varieties and sites, this favoured region always has something to offer.

• **2012** • The volume is low, but the wines are mature thanks to a sunny August and September. The Muscadets should be worthy of lying down, as well as the late-harvest whites, which have good acidity. The reds are clean and mature, with a nice fruity crunch. A vintage to enjoy!

THE LOIRE VALLEY APPELLATIONS

A.C. ANJOU

OVERVIEW: the appellation covers 188 towns and villages (southern half of the Maine-et-Loire department, some of Vienne and Deux-Sèvres). This vast area can be roughly divided into two different soil series: the first type, in the Armorican mountain range, is clayey shale or Silurian slate, and the second, in the Paris basin, is limestone and sandy clay. The various areas are referred to as 'black', 'blue' and 'white' Anjou.

WINE STYLES: the reds are made from Cabernet Franc, Cabernet Sauvignon and Pineau d'Aunis. They can vary from supple wines that are fresh, aromatic and easy-drinking to wines with a pronounced tannic framework imparted by prolonged maceration. Fragrances of raspberry, blackcurrant, green pepper and spices are present. Drink when young with cooked cold pork meats, white or red meat.

The whites are blended from at least 80% Chenin (augmented with Chardonnay and Sauvignon) and are dry, elegant, distinctive and fragrant. The best examples hail from the shale soils. They proffer aromas of citrus fruit such as grapefruit as well as apple, peach stone and vegetal tones. Try with hors d'ouvre or fish. A small proportion of whites can be made as medium sweet or sweet. The rosés, which are constantly on the wane, are supple and soft.

A.C. ANJOU MOUSSEUX

Nine villages in the department of Vienne (subsumed into the Anjou appellation) are entitled to produce sparkling wines, including Pouancay, Berrie, Saint-Léger-de-Montbrillais, Ternay and Ranton. The minimum percentage of Chenin in the blend is 80%. Bottle fermentation takes place during a secondary fermentation in the bottle. These wines are recommended as appetisers or with desserts.

A.C. ANJOU COTEAUX DE LA LOIRE

OVERVIEW: this sweet wine appellation area covers 11 villages in Maine-et-Loire set on hillsides overlooking the Loire valley west of Angers. Production is centred primarily on the villages of Pommeraye and Montjean. All the grapes are handpicked and sorted in batches. The soil is shale and limestone. The grape variety used is Chenin.

WINE STYLES: initially, they are drier than Coteaux du Layon though subsequently become round and silky as they mature. The wines display a brilliant hue with golden shades and greenish tints. They conjure up fragrances of ripe fruit such as vine peach though also honey, linden and freshly-cut hay. The shale soil promotes animal notes whilst the limestone imparts more mineral tones. Try as an appetiser or with trout, pear tart or cheeses (Bresse, Fourme).

A.C. ANJOU-GAMAY

OVERVIEW: only Gamay is permitted for this appellation, hence the name. The area covers the entire Anjou region, excluding the Saumur area.

WINE STYLES: these are round, supple, light and fruity wines. They are designed to be drunk young and develop fragrances of red fruit such as red currant. Wines released soon after the harvest (primeur) display exotic fruit aromas as well. Recommended food pairings are poultry, grilled red meat, white meat and soft cheeses.

A.C. ANJOU-VILLAGES

OVERVIEW: 46 towns and villages within the Anjou appellation area are entitled to this red wine only appellation. Anjou-Villages differ from red Anjou both for their varietal range and wine making practices: there is no Pineau d'Aunis and vatting and ageing last longer. Another point of difference is that 'Villages' wines cannot be released until September 15th a year after the harvest. The best sites are located south of Angers, around Brissac, Thouarcé and Martigné-Briand...

WINE STYLES: made from Cabernet Franc and Cabernet Sauvignon, these wines are fruity and well-structured, and improve with age. Their hue ranges from crimson to garnet-red and they display fragrances of red fruit (blackberry, strawberry, blackcurrant, cherry), undergrowth and spices, leading into leather and fruit stone over time. Try with game, fish in a red wine sauce, roast or grilled red meat or cheeses.

A.C. BONNEZEAUX

OVERVIEW: Bonnezeaux is one of two Coteaux du Layon great growths in Anjou. the vineyards are located south of the Loire, twenty or so kilometres from Angers in the village of Thouarcé. Three south-south-west facing hillsides overlooking the Layon - La Montagne, Beauregard and Fesles - are home to the vines. The overripe grapes are harvested by hand and painstakingly sorted as they ripen. Minimum alcohol content is 13.5%. The appellation is shared by around fifty different growers. The vines are planted on decomposed shale rich in sandstone, quartz and phtanite. The topsoil is shallow and littered with stones. Chenin is the only white varietal grown.

WINE STYLES: Bonnezeaux are fresh, well-balanced, delicate sweet wines that are complex and elegant. Bursting with fruit, they are opulent, fat and robust with a well-balanced mellowness. As they mature, they become full, unctuous and ample. Sporting a golden hue with greenish tints, they display fragrances of stewed apricot, orange, quince, pineapple, verbena, vanilla, honey, acacia, hawthorn and linden. Try with foie gras and grapes, fish in a sauce such as turbot, blue cheeses...

A.C. BOURGUEIL

OVERVIEW: the Bourgueil area is spread over a 15 kilometre strip of land running perpendicular to the Loire, in Touraine.

Eight villages are entitled to the appellation (Bourgueil, Saint-Nicolas de Bourgueil, Benais, Chouzé-sur-Loire, Ingrandes de Touraine, La Chapelle sur Loire, Restigné and Saint-Patrice). Historically, the wines were highly regarded by Louis XI, Rabelais and Ronsard.

The area can be divided into three zones: the banks of the Loire, where stony patches provide suitable plots for vines, then a terrace which provides the focal point for the area, and finally the chalk plateau ('tuffeau') through which a tributary of the Loire - the Changeon - meanders.

WINE STYLES: Bourgueil produces mainly red wines from Cabernet Franc (Cabernet Sauvignon content is restricted to a maximum 10%). The different 'terroirs' are reflected in the wine styles. Gravely soils produce elegant, vigorous, delicate, supple, fruity wines. Conversely, chalk type soils yield well-structured, robust, tannic wines, which can be hard or firm when young. Bourgueil smells sweetly of violet, bell pepper, spices, raspberry and red currant and often exhibits gamey, earthy tones. Recommended food pairings include beef with morel mushrooms, stew, jugged hare, roast red meats...

A.C. CABERNET D'ANJOU

OVERVIEW: this rosé wine can be made in 188 towns and villages within the same boundaries as the Anjou appellation area. Soil types are varied, ranging from shale, to clay and limestone, very often covered in sand and gravel. The best sites are located along the hillsides of the upper and middle Layon valley. The area enjoys an ocean climate with mild winters, hot summers and low temperature variations between daytime and nightime.

WINE STYLES: most of the wines are medium sweet made from Cabernet Franc supported by a little Cabernet Sauvignon. They are fresh, light, soft and delicate with good length and are intended to be drunk young. Their orange or grenadine hue turns brick-red as they age. They display fragrances of raspberry, red currant, strawberry, fruit in brandy, vanilla and menthol notes though also exhibit floral nuances of iris, violet and rose. This charming wine can be served with mushroom pie, quiche, cooked cold pork meats, poultry, exotic dishes or fruit-based desserts (fruit mousse).

A.C. CABERNET DE SAUMUR

OVERVIEW: these rosé wines, made from Cabernet Franc and Cabernet Sau-vignon, are grown in the same appellation area as Saumur, hence the name, on limestone soils.

Wine styles: these rosés are not only drier than Cabernet d'Anjou, they are also more elegant. They are soft, fresh and round. Try with cooked cold pork meats, poultry…

AC CHÂTEAUMEILLANT

OVERVIEW: the appellation is situated south-west of Saint-Amand-Montrond, 60 km from Bourges, in Berry. It is spread over two departments (Indre and Cher). The soils are silica with a predominant proportion of sand and sandy clay on a meta-morphosed subsoil. Gamay thrives here on stony sandstone soils in a pre-mountain Limousin-type climate, though the area also grows Pinot noir and Pinot gris.

WINE STYLES: the reds are fruity, light quaffing wines which are lively and intended to be drunk young. Supple-menting them with a dash of Pinot noir and Pinot gris bolsters their framework though at the same time mellows them. Châteaumeillant exhi-bits a light hue and fragrances of wild strawberry and pepper. The rosés, known as 'vin gris', are fresh. Try with mixed salads or fresh goats cheese flavoured with herbs. Recom-mended pai-rings for the rosés are exotic cuisine from China, the Caribbean or Thailand.

A.C. CHEVERNY

OVERVIEW: this appellation is situated in north-eastern Touraine, between the Loire and the Sologne, near Blois. It embraces 24 towns and villages. The soils are sandy clay, sandy silica and calcareous clay. The area is home to stone quarries and the varietal range is comprised of Gamay, Cabernet, Pinot noir, Cot, Pineau d'Aunis, Pinot gris (reds), though also Chenin, Menu Pineau, Chardonnay, Romorantin and Sauvignon (whites).

WINE STYLES: the reds are lively, clean, fruity, light quaffing wines. Red and black fruit, blackcurrant and liquorice aromas are present. The whites, with their pale hue, are dry, lively and fresh with fragrances of hazelnut and honey. The rosés are supple and fresh. They display a salmon-pink colour and exude spicy, occa-sionally toasted notes. Cheverny wines are well suited to grilled veal, roast poultry, cheeses (reds), fish and shellfish (whites). The rosés are equally suitable as appetisers or with barbecues.

A.C. CHINON

OVERVIEW: the Chinon area sits at the point where Anjou, Saumur and Touraine meet. The appellation embraces 19 towns and villages (Beaumont-en-Véron, Avoine, Chinon, Cravant, Tavant, Avon les Roches...) set either side of the Vienne. There are three different soil types: gravel and sand along the banks of the Vienne, Senonian calcareous clay or silica clay hills and plateaux. Cabernet Franc and Cabernet Sauvignon (restricted to a maximum 10%) flourish on the south facing sites.

WINE STYLES: each 'terroir' produces a different style of wine. The reds grown on the gravely soils are light, fruity and extremely aromatic. They reward early drinking. Wines from the silica clay plateaux and hillside sites are well-constituted, robust, tannic and elegant. They display rich, dense aromas and are wines to keep which become full and deep down the years. With a ruby-red hue, Chinon exhibits aromas of blackcurrant, violet, mineral and vegetal notes. Humus and truffle, empyreumatic fragrances and animal notes occur as they mature.

Up until a few years ago, the character of Chinon wines was a result of blending wines from various sites. Nowadays, however, growers tend to separate site-specific wines and prefer old vines. Try with white and red meats (light Chinon), meats served in a sauce, game and cheeses (robust Chinon). Chinon also makes rosés with delicate, subtle aromas and limited edition whites from Chenin, which are dry and fruity.

AC CÔTES D'AUVERGNE

OVERVIEW: the Côtes d'Auvergne appellation is covering 54 towns and villages in Puy de Dôme (Auvergne). It boasts five growths which are entitled to add their name to the appellation: Corent, Boudes, Chanturgues, Châ-teaugay and Madargues, underscoring the diversity of the wines, despite the fact that the varietal range is restricted to Gamay for the reds and rosés and Chardonnay for the whites (a tiny minority).

WINE STYLES: Corent, for instance, which surrounds the plateau of the same name, boasts calcareous clay soils and produces mainly rosés ('vin gris'). These are pleasant, fruity wines which develop fragrances of apricot, yellow fruit, candied fruit and peppery notes. Boudes, which also has a strong focus on rosé wines, covers soils where the limestone content is higher and fragments of basalt occur. The hillock at Châteaugay, north-west of Clermont-Ferrand, has soils with lower clay content and more sand with a higher proportion of volcanic debris. This particular 'terroir' yields firm, rustic wines with medium cellaring capacity that pair with barbecues.

In Chanturgues, the hillside is protected from erosion by Miocene basalt flows and calcareous clay soils show through on the slopes. This growth produces wines which are both well-structured and supple with smoky, spicy aromas, black cherry and violet. They show at their best after a few years' ageing.

A.C. CÔTE ROANNAISE

OVERVIEW: the Côte Roannaise appellation stretches over 14 villages along the left bank of the Loire. Gamay, known locally as Saint-Romain, is the only grape variety grown here. The soils are predominantly granite and basalt covered with sand and alluvium at the foot of the hills.

WINE STYLES: the red and rosé wines are made by the semi-carbonic maceration process, hence their fresh, clean, lively, fresh and harmonious style and capacity to be drunk young. With their ruby-red hue, they exhibit fragrances of red fruit such as black-currant, raspberry, strawberry, red currant and bilberry. They pair with chitterlings sausage, slicing sausage, tripe and white meat.

A.C. COTEAUX D'ANCENIS

OVERVIEW: the appellation is situated east of Nantes, either side of the Loire. It embraces 27 towns and villages straddling Maine-et-Loire and Loire-Atlantique. There are two different types of soil: micaschist and crimson schist north of the Loire and gneiss and green schist south of the Loire. The wines often mention the grape variety on the label: Chenin and Pinot gris for the whites and Cabernet Sauvignon, Cabernet Franc and Gamay for the reds.

WINE STYLES: the reds and rosés are fruity, light, lively quaffing wines. They display a brilliant colour and fragrances of red fruit. They are the perfect partner for hors d'ouvre, cooked cold pork meats, duck with cherries, barbecues and cheeses. The whites with their pale green hue and aromas of fruit and honey are soft, round and rich and will cellar well. They pair with fish and white meat in a sauce.

A.C. COTEAUX DE L'AUBANCE

OVERVIEW: this appellation is located west of the river Aubance, east of Brissac and north of the Loire in an area often described as 'black' Anjou because of the dark colour of the shale or sandstone soils of the Armorican mountain range. Ten villages are allowed to use the appellation. The region enjoys a particularly dry late autumn, allowing the Chenin grapes to become overripe. Vines growing on the hills overlooking the Aubance bask in plentiful sunshine.

WINE STYLES: although the Coteaux de l'Aubance appellation produces sweet wines, its major focus is on medium sweet wines. They are rich, soft, delicate, distinguished wines which are fruity, round, full and vigorous. They exhibit a limpid hue with green gold and straw-yellow gold tints and fragrances of quince paste, candied fruits, fig, lemon, honey, white flowers and mineral notes. They make marvellous appetisers served with refined canapes though also accompany fruit tarts, vol-au-vents...

A.C. COTEAUX DE SAUMUR

OVERVIEW: thirteen towns and villages in Maine-et-Loire and Vienne located north of the Saumur appellation are entitled to this appellation which covers sweet wines made from Chenin. The wines can only be made when the weather conditions are suitable. The grapes are handpicked and painstakingly sorted as they ripen. The soil type is 'tuffeau' chalk.

WINE STYLES: they are fruity, delicate, fat, lively and soft displaying a straw-yellow gold hue with greenish tints. They develop fragrances of roasted grapes, toasted almonds, honey, honeysuckle and hazelnut. They can be married with a whole array of foods: mushroom pie, foie gras, fish in a creamy sauce, cheeses (blue), sweetbreads in a cream sauce, oven-baked chitterlings sausage...

A.C. COTEAUX DU LAYON

OVERVIEW: this appellation is shared by 27 towns and villages on either side of the Layon river, a left bank tributary of the Loire. Seven of these are entitled to append their name to the Coteaux du Layon appellation (Beaulieu-sur-Layon, Faye d'Anjou, Rablay-sur-Layon, Rochefort-sur-Loire, Saint-Aubin-sur-Luigné, Saint-Lambert-du-Lattay and Chaume. The soils are stony with a predominant proportion of shale, clay shale and silica, interspersed with gravely sand and volcanic sediment. Chenin is the only grape variety grown here.

WINE STYLES: Coteaux du Layon are sweet white wines which are rich, intense, round, unctuous and fat rounded off with a superb fruity freshness. They display a green gold hue and develop fragrances of linden, acacia, honey, apricot and citrus fruit, evolving into aromas of wax, quince and candied fruit as they mature. They are delicious as appetisers or with foie gras, Roquefort, poultry in a cream sauce, gizzards, goats cheeses or blue cheeses, fish such as pike-perch and salmon, and of course desserts: apple pie and all nougatine-based gateaux.

A.C. CHAUME

OVERVIEW: this minute appellation area (70 hectares) within the Coteaux du Layon is situated in the village of Rochefort-sur-Loire, north of the hamlet of Chaume itself. The vast majority of the soils are carboniferous puddingstone though there are occasional shale formations (spilite and phanite). The vines enjoy a south-east aspect and are sheltered both from northerly winds and ocean influences. Chenin is the sole varietal.

WINE STYLES: they are fat, rich, delicate, well-structured and full wines that are fleshy, unctuous and elegant. They display a brilliant hue tinted with green and fragrances of candied fruits (apricots), white flowers, white peaches and a delicate bitterness. They are served with foie gras, fish in a hollandaise sauce, cheeses (blue), melon...

A.C. COTEAUX DU LOIR

OVERVIEW: this 80-hectare area, which is home to a varietal range comprised of Gamay, Pinot noir, Chenin and Pineau d'Aunis, is set on the left bank of the Loir (22 towns and villages in Sarthe and Indre-et-Loire). It is the most northerly of the Loire appellations. Most of the wines are grown in and around Lhomme, Ruillé-sur-Loir, Chahaines and Marçon. The soils are clay silica on a bedrock of chalk ('tuffeau') with occurrences of limestone marl. The region enjoys a mild climate defined by the Atlantic.

WINE STYLES: the reds are light, lively, fresh quaffing wines with a pleasant bouquet. They are highly reminiscent of Touraine wines. They display a pale hue and fragrances of morello cherry, cinnamon and spices (pepper). They can be served with cooked cold pork meats (potted meat, Vire andouille), white meats, grilled red meats, meat pie, black pudding with apples, poultry. The whites (Pineau de la Loire) are dry, vigorous wines for cellaring. They develop vegetal aromas. A good match for fish and seafood, cooked cold pork meats and white meat served in a sauce.

A.C. COTEAUX DU VENDÔMOIS

OVERVIEW: with its 150 hectares under vine, this area is situated in the Loir valley in Loir-et-Cher, between Vendôme and Montoire. The soils are formed of flint clay on a bedrock of limestone. The red varietals used are Pineau d'Aunis, the main grape which must account for at least 30% of the blend, Gamay (30% maximum), Pinot noir and Cabernet. For the white wines, Chenin and Chardonnay (no more than 20% of the blend).

WINE STYLES: the reds are intended to be drunk young and fresh, when they develop aromas of red fruit, banana and vanilla. The rosés are pale in shade with peppery notes. They are recommended with fried smelt.

A.C. COTEAUX DU GIENNOIS

OVERVIEW: this 150-hectare area occupies undulating land between Gien and Cosne-sur-Loire (16 villages in all). In the Nevers region, Aligny-Cosne, La Celle-sur-Loire, Cosne-sur-Loire, Cours-lès-Cosnes, Myennes, Pougny-Saint-Loup and Saint-Père are entitled to add the name Cosne-sur-Loire to the AC Côtes de Gien appellation. The soils are limestone, gravel and silica along ancient terraces of the Loire.

WINE STYLES: the Pinot noir reds exhibit a ruby-red hue and are lively, supple, fresh and fragrant. They pair with ham in puff pastry, grilled or roast meats, veal, ox tongue with gherkins and grilled black pudding. The whites with tell-tale Sauvignon scents, should be tried with freshwater fish (perch).

A.C. CÔTES DU FOREZ

OVERVIEW: this appellation verges on the Massif Central, north of Saint-Etienne. It embraces 21 towns and villages and roughly 200 hectares of vines. The soils contain less limestone than in Auvergne, though when they are derived from decomposed granite rocks they are 80% clay silica and 20% volcanic in origin. A large share of the wines are vinted and sold by the co-operative winery. The wines are made using the carbonic maceration or semi-carbonic maceration process.

WINE STYLES: the Gamay varietal reds are clean, aromatic, lively, supple and harmonious, and designed to be drunk young.

The wines grown on basalt hillside sites are, however, more robust and richer in tannins and will keep for a few years. Try with cooked cold pork meats, grilled meats or poultry.

A.C. COUR CHEVERNY

OVERVIEW: Cour Cheverny wines are grown in Touraine, south-east of Blois (Loir-et-Cher department). The area covers a total 60 hectares spread over 11 villages in Sologne. Set north of the Cheverny area, this AC only produces white wines from a single grape variety -Romorantin - occasionally known as Donnery.

Three rivers meander through the Cour Cheverny area: the Beuvron, the Cosson and the Bièvre. The vines are planted on clay silica, with occasional occurrences of calcareous clay.

WINE STYLES: with their straw-yellow hue, Cour Cheverny wines concentrate aromas of apple, pear, acacia flower, honey and mineral notes. Delicate on the palate, their attack conjures up empyreumatic fragrances. With a lively, long mouthfeel, some of the wines can even prove to be elegant and age for a few years. They can be served with cooked cold pork meats, freshwater fish, salmon, seafood or grilled young cockerel.

AC CRÉMANT DE LOIRE

OVERVIEW: Crémant is a sparkling wine made in the traditional way (secondary fermentation in the bottle). The appellation covers the Saumur, Anjou and Touraine areas though most Crémants are made in the departments of Maine-et-Loire and Indre-et-Loire. Crémant de Loire must be stored for at least a year in growers' cellars before it can be released.

WINE MAKING PROCESS: all of the Loire grape varieties can be used, except for Sauvignon. Chenin forms the backbone of the blend, which differentiates it from Crémants from other regions which are often drawn from Chardonnay and Pinots. The grapes are not only harvested by hand, they are also crushed in a chainless press. Bottle fermentation takes place during a secondary fermentation in the bottle after a blend of yeast and sugar has been added. The wines are aromatic, lively, intense and clean with delicate, long-lasting bubbles. Try as appetisers, or with shellfish, fish and goats cheese.

AC FIEFS VENDÉENS

OVERVIEW: the appellation stretches north of Les Sables d'Olonne between La Roche-sur-Yon and Luçon and around

Fontenay-le-Comte. Back in 1955, growers began to replace hybrid varieties with noble grapes such as Pinot noir or Gamay. The current area under vine is around 500 hectares and most of the wines are red. Soil types are varied, ranging from clay silica, calcareous clay or gravel to sand. Four site-specific areas have been identified and are entitled to state the name of their main village on the label: Brem, Mareuil, Pissote and Vix.

WINE STYLES: they are light, pleasant and fruity. The reds display a deep garnet-red hue with fragrances of red fruits such as raspberry. Try pairing them with red or white meats or soft cheeses. They whites are a pale yellow colour with floral aromas and are the perfect partner for shellfish and fish.

AC GROS PLANT DU PAYS NANTAIS

OVERVIEW: in the 17th century, the Charentes varietal Folle blanche was introduced, courtesy of the Dutch. Local farmers dubbed it 'gros plant' because of the thickness of the vine's trunk. The area shares the same boundaries as Muscadet, though also spills over into the Retz area, bringing the total number of towns and villages up to around a hundred. Soil types are extremely varied, ranging from shale, micaschist and gneiss to Armorican mountain granite and a few pockets of Quaternary sand deposits.

The better quality wines come from Grand-Lieu lake where the soil is formed of sand and gravel. The climate is ocean, with mild winters and hot summers. A good deal of Gros Plant is vinted on the lees.

WINE STYLES: they are dry, light, vigorous, lively and fresh. They display a pale hue with greenish tints and develop fragrances of dried fruit, a slightly salty touch and mineral notes. Recommended food pairings include shellfish such as mussels, cockles, prawns, oysters or freshwater fish.

AC HAUT-POITOU

OVERVIEW: 47 towns and villages in Vienne and Deux-Sèvres are entitled to use this appellation. Virtually all the wines (95%) are made by the Neuville-de-Poitou co-operative winery and they grow on around 750 hectares of Jurassic calcareous clay and silica clay type soils.

WINE STYLES: the Gamay or Cabernet reds are aromatic, fresh, soft and lively. They sport a ruby-red hue and exude fragrances of cherry, morello cherry and blackcurrant and are well-suited to dishes such as sauteed veal or duck. The whites (Sauvignon, Chardonnay) are fresh, harmonious and expressive. Try with fish (turbot).

A.C. JASNIÈRES

OVERVIEW: the Jasnières appellation, which sits within the boundaries of AC Coteaux du Loir, covers just two villages in Sarthe: Lhomme and Ruillé-sur-Loir, over a total 65 hectares. The villages provide an ideal setting for vines with a strip of land four kilometres long by just a few hundred metres wide with a due south aspect. 'Le Perche' hill acts as a buffer against the northerly winds. The soils are littered with stones and calcareous clay on a bedrock of 'tuffeau'. Frequent occurrences of flint are a feature of this area.

WINE STYLES: these white wines, made from Chenin, are extremely dry and vigorous when young but are capable of maturing. As they age, they become more full and silky, developing a pleasant bouquet. The wines display a deep straw-yellow hue and exude fragrances of linden, hawthorn, honey, acacia, broom, exotic fruits (pineapple) and peach. They boast a characteristic mineral aspect (gunflint). Try them with white meat or fish.

A.C. MENETOU-SALON

OVERVIEW: this appellation is set in the upper reaches of the Loire, south of Pouilly-sur-Loire and west of Sancerre, in Cher. It extends over 350 hectares divided between 10 villages - Aubinges, Humbligny, Menetou-Salon, Morogues, Parassy, Pigny, Quantilly, Saint Céols, Soulangis and Vignoux sous les Aix. The soils are extremely consistent covering a single geological formation of the Secondary era (Upper Cretaceous): light Saint-Doulchard marl (Kimmeridgian), highly conducive to growing Sauvignon blanc.

WINE STYLES: 65% of the wines are fresh, vigorous, lively whites which are light, full and aromatic with great length on the palate. They boast a yellow hue with greenish tints and exude floral and balsamic aromas, citrus (lemon, grapefruit), white peach, gunflint, pepper and mint. They are the perfect match for shellfish, fish served on its own or in puff pastry, goats cheese or snails. The Pinot noir-based reds and rosés are delicate, supple, pleasant, round, light and fruity. They are intended to be drunk soon after release. Their relatively pale hue exhibits ruby-red tints. On the nose, they reveal fragrances of cherry, raspberry and red currant. Recommended food pairings include grilled meat, cheeses (Beaufort) or rabbit terrine.

A.C. MONTLOUIS

OVERVIEW: situated between Tours and Amboise, AC Montlouis produces still and sparkling wines. Three villages feature within the appellation area (Montlouis, Saint Martin le Beau and Lussault), between the Cher and the Loire, and total area under vine is around 400 hectares. When the weather conditions are right, Montlouis also produces some superlative sweet wines from Chenin grapes harvested in batches as they ripen. The soils are sandy clay or clayey sand on limestone plateaux and hillsides, on a bedrock of 'tuffeau'. A south-facing aspect provides maximum sunshine for hillside sites. The soils are lighter and sandier than in Vouvray.

WINE STYLES: Montlouis sparkling wines, which account for 40% of the entire AC, are light and pleasant. They undergo secondary fermentation in the bottle and are aged on laths for at least nine months. Dry Montlouis is quite similar in style to Vouvray. Less lively and perhaps more supple, it displays a more marked mineral character and is also more enjoyable in its early years. The calling card of sweet Montlouis is its aromatic complexity: verbena, bergamot, bitter almond, leading into dried honey, wax, quince jelly and candied angelica down the years. Try as an accompaniment to cooked cold pork meats, poultry, goats cheese, fish, shellfish or as an appetiser.

A.C. MUSCADET

OVERVIEW: the area stretches along the mouth of the Loire, from Anjou to the Retz region. Despite the local ocean climate, Muscadet is one of the first regions in France to start harvesting. A longer hang-time would jeopardise the wine's unique taste profile. Soils are extremely varied although two principal types can be identified: granite and eruptive rock, shale and micaschist. Within this vast area, three zones enjoy their own specific appellation: Muscadet de Sèvre-et-Maine (the largest), Muscadet des Coteaux de la Loire and Muscadet des Côtes de Grand-Lieu (see separate entries). The area covers a total 13,000 hectares under vine though only 2,000 are devoted to AC Muscadet.

WINE STYLES: made from the Melon de Bourgogne grape variety, Muscadet is a light, fresh white wine with well-balanced acidity, which requires early drinking. Often the wine is left on the lees for four to five months before bottling. This leaves a tiny remnant of carbonic gas, imparting a slight fizz which bolsters the wine's freshness (Muscadet sur Lie). Muscadet displays a pale yellow hue with greenish tints and develops floral (acacia, white flowers) and fruity fragrances (apple) and mineral notes. Try with oysters, shellfish (moules marinières), pike or crayfish fricassee.

A.C. MUSCADET COTEAUX DE LA LOIRE

OVERVIEW: this area extends over both banks of the Loire, in the localities of Ancenis, Carquefou, Champtoceaux, Ligné, Saint-Florent-le-Vieil and Varades. On the right bank of the Loire, the area overlaps Ancenis, whilst on the left bank it spills over into Anjou. Coteaux de Loire grow over some 300 hectares.

WINE STYLES: they are dry, fresh, elegant, supple, harmonious and fruity. They are more robust and well-constituted than Muscadet de Sèvre-et-Maine and can be cellared. Their hue is pale yellow with greenish tints and they develop mineral and gunflint notes due to the granite in the soil, though also fruity and floral aromas. Pair with oysters and seafood, grilled fish or fish served in a sauce (pike).

A.C. MUSCADET SÈVRE-ET-MAINE

OVERVIEW: two-thirds of Muscadet are grown in this area. The appellation is named after the Nantes branch of the Sèvre river and its tributary, the Petite Maine. 23 towns and villages with a combined area under vine of 10,000 hectares are entitled to the appellation. The soil, underpinned by an Armorican base, is varied: granite, shale, gabbro (dark brown soils) and gneiss, which promotes a certain diversity in wine styles within the appellation.

WINE STYLES: they are racy, elegant, fresh, supple, zippy and delicate, often with a slight sparkle. Muscadet sur Lie denotes a wine that has spent the winter in tanks on its lees allowing it to gain in complexity, finesse and bouquet. Muscadet de Sèvre-et-Maine displays a pale golden hue and reveals floral (acacia), fruity (unripe fruit, citronella, fresh grapes) and mineral fragrances. It is the perfect match for oysters, scallops, pike in a hot butter sauce, sole or crayfish fricassee.

A.C. MUSCADET CÔTES DE GRAND-LIEU

OVERVIEW: this appellation is located not far from Grand-Lieu lake, south-west of Nantes. It covers 250 hectares under vine, spread over 19 villages extending down to the tip of Vendée. Soil types are varied: micaschist, gneiss, sand with pebbles and even clayey sand south of the lake. The area enjoys a sunny, mild climate with plentiful rainfall which offsets the drying effect of the wind over the stony terrain.

WINE STYLES: they are delicate and relatively powerful. With their pale yellow hue, they exhibit a slightly salty taste, floral (acacia, white flowers), fruity (apple) and mineral fragrances. Recommended food pairings include oysters, seafood, grilled fish or fish served in a sauce.

A.C. POUILLY-FUMÉ

OVERVIEW: the appellation is named after the village of Pouilly-sur-Loire which sits on the right bank of the Loire. Although vines have grown here since at least the 7th century, in the 19th century the area chose to specialise in dessert grapes with a particular focus on the traditional varietal, Chasselas. Things have definitely moved on since then because nowadays Sauvignon (also know as Fumé) rules the roost here. Seven villages are entitled to the appellation including Pouilly, Saint-Andelain and Tracy. Soil types are varied: Kimmeridgian marl (white earth), hard limestone, flint interspersed with clay, and sandy or gravely terraces. The climate is temperate with a strong continental influence.

WINE STYLES: Pouilly-Fumé are fresh, lively fruity white wines which are powerful and elegant with a full mouthfeel. Their style does vary however depending on individual 'terroirs'. When they grow on limestone soils, blackcurrant bud and boxwood rise to the fore, whilst on flint, gunflint is the principal aroma. Marl soils coax floral fragrances out of the wines (tuberous, daffodils...). Try with shellfish, fish (pike, pike-perch, salmon) or white meat. An outstanding match for goats cheese.

A.C. POUILLY-SUR-LOIRE

OVERVIEW: the appellation area is the same as Pouilly-Fumé, on the right bank of the Loire in Nièvre, down-river from Nevers. Chasselas has been grown here since the 19th century and was shipped off to supply the Parisian market. The soils are clay silica and calcareous clay.

WINE STYLES: now in extremely short supply, these wines have low acidity, are dry, light supple, smooth, delicate and easy to drink. They are intended to be drunk young. The wines display a light golden hue and smoky, peppery fragrances with raisins and dried fruit, hazelnut, fresh almond, walnut and linden. They pair with trout mariniere, fried fish and goats cheeses.

A.C. QUARTS DE CHAUME

OVERVIEW: this area is located in Rochefort sur Loire and in Chaume, around the Layon river. The name of the appellation is a throwback to Mediaeval times when a lord would rent his land to an abbey in exchange for a quarter of the harvest. The noble-rotted grapes are picked in batches as they ripen. The vines are planted on shale soils covering 50 hectares on a south-facing hillside.

WINE STYLES: the wines are sweet, racy, firm, silky, delicate and rich. They have a full mouthfeel and are long on the palate, with a great propensity for ageing. Their well-defined structure and a certain austerity in their early years sets them apart from other Layons. They display a golden hue and reveal fragrances of wax, linden, candied fruits, honey, verbena and quince. Try with Roquefort in puff pastry, fish served with a sauce, poached poultry or turbot in a hollandaise sauce.

A.C. QUINCY

OVERVIEW: the appellation is situated in the villages of Quincy and Brinay (the left bank of the Cher). Sauvignon is the only permitted varietal. The vines occupy a plateau which is home to three different soil types: sandy gravel, sand, and sandy loam with sand and gravel. Silica and poor soils promote the ripening process. The area enjoys a hot, dry microclimate.

WINE STYLES: the wines are delicate, fruity, light, fresh and dry. These are elegant, distinguished wines that are also firm and vigorous. They can be drunk young though will also keep. They display a pale golden hue with the occasional greenish tint. On the nose, fragrances of almond, grapefruit, verbena, mushroom, fennel and thyme are present, and they can occasionally exude slightly smoky notes. Try them with fish, shellfish, cooked cold pork meats, goats cheeses, oysters, frogs legs…

A.C. REUILLY

OVERVIEW: the area occupies the banks of the Armon, in the villages of Reuilly, Dion, Cerbois, Chéry, Lazenay, Lury-sur-Armon and Preuilly. The soils are formed of limestone marl on the hillside sites, clayey sand and gravel on the upper terraces. In short, they form a bridge between soils in Sancerre and Quincy. Grape varieties used are Sauvignon (whites, the major variety) and Pinot noir (reds).

WINE STYLES: the reds are supple and light with fragrances of red fruit (cherry, raspberry) and flowers (violet). They are suitable partners for grilled meats, roast poultry or lentil soup. The soft, full rosés are delicate, flavoursome, easy-drinking wines which sport a magnificent coral pink hue and fruit tones. Perfect with paté roll, sauteed veal, mussel fritters. The whites are fresh, fruity and light with floral (acacia) and vegetal aromas (fern, mint). Serve with carp matelote or rabbit fricassee in wine.

A.C. ROSÉ D'ANJOU

OVERVIEW: these particular rosés are grown throughout Anjou, including the Saumur area. The Grolleau varietal forms the backbone of the blend but Cabernets, Gamay, Pineau d'Aunis and Cot can also be added, with no restriction on quantity.

WINE STYLES: they are fruity, light, thirst-quenching wines which are lively, round, soft, delicate, velvety and mild with a slightly sweet taste. Sugar content is offset by alcohol and acidity. They display a pale pink hue (onion peel) and predominantly fruity fragrances (raspberry, red currant, strawberry and pear drop). Recommended food pairings: cooked cold pork meats, white meat, grilled red meat and pork with grapefruit.

A.C. ROSÉ DE LOIRE

OVERVIEW: the catchment area for this appellation covers Anjou, Saumur and Touraine. Rosé de Loire must be made from at least 30% Cabernet Franc and/or Cabernet Sauvignon.

WINE STYLES: as a rule, they are clean, fresh, delicate, vigorous, fruity and light although diversity prevails in such a vast area. A statement that holds true for all of them though is that they are drier than Cabernet d'Anjou. Their hue covers a broad spectrum, from pale pink to grenadine red. Their fragrance is redolent of red fruit (strawberry, raspberry, red currant, pear drop) and apple. The perfect partner for hors d'ouvre (mixed salads, cold cuts), barbecues and white meat.

A.C. SAINT-NICOLAS DE BOURGUEIL

OVERVIEW: only plots set in the village of Saint-Nicolas de Bourgueil (Touraine) can apply for this appellation (slightly over 1,000 hectares). The vines grow mainly on gravel terraces where the soils are clayey gravel, though, like in Bourgueil, there are occurrences of sloping vineyards on calcareous clay. The red varietals Cabernet Franc and Cabernet Franc coax the best out of these soils.

WINE STYLES: usually lighter than Bourgueil, they are supple, soft, well-balanced, mellow and approachable wines. Even when they evolve quickly, they should not be drunk too soon. The dividing line between wines grown on 'tuffeau' and on gravel is becoming increasingly sharper. 'Tuffeau' imparts greater body and structure, yielding wines with a crimson hue and fragrances of red fruits like raspberry, blackberry, red currant, violet, liquorice and spices. Conversely, gravel produces lighter wines that can be drunk chilled. Pair them with white meats (pork fillet, veal cutlet), cooked cold pork meats or cheeses.

AC SAINT-POURÇAIN

OVERVIEW: the appellation is located in the department of Allier, along the river of the same name and its tributary, the Sioule. It embraces twenty villages spread over a strip five to seven kilometres wide covering south-east facing hillsides. Nowadays, most of the wine is made by the local co-operative winery. The red wines are macerated for varying lengths of time, depending on the varietal: three to six days for Gamay, ten to fourteen days for Pinot noir. The white wines must be blended from at least 90% Chardonnay and Tressallier.

WINE STYLES: the reds and rosés are light, supple and fruity with a brilliant hue. Fragrances of red fruit (cherry), plum and liquorice are present. Try with roast chicken, poultry and fish such as pike, carp, eel or tench. The whites are supple, fresh, full, lively, vigorous and pleasing to the palate with a limpid, brilliant colour. They boast a pale golden hue and smell sweetly of apple, lemon, acacia and dried fruit (hazelnut, almond). Serve them with fried freshwater fish (bleak, roach), trout, frogs legs and of course, Auvergne cheeses.

A.C. SANCERRE

OVERVIEW: Sancerre's aptitude for vine growing has been known since Roman times. Until the early 20th century, Sancerre wines were made from Chasselas, until consumer demand led growers to switch over Sauvignon. The varietal thrives in ideal conditions here and enabled the area to forge a reputation for quality. The vines grow on a hillock overlooking the Loire in a setting combining rolling hills and the valley floor.

The appellation area embraces ten villages: Baunay, Bué, Crézancy, Menetou-Râtel, Ménétreol, Montigny, Thanvenay, Veaugne, Vigny and Vinon. Three different soil types can be identified: calcareous clay-based 'white earth' in the west ('terres blanches'), stony, flint-rich soils in the east ('silex') and a series of predominantly limestone hillocks and hills littered with stones known aptly as 'Caillotes'. The climate is continental though the river to the east and the forest to the west have a moderating influence. There are 3,000 hectares under vine altogether.

WINE STYLES: white Sancerre is fruity, generous, fresh and elegant with a clean attack and round mouthfeel, though its character varies according to the different vineyard sites. Sancerre from the 'terres blanches' site is full, robust and well-constituted. 'Caillotes' produces extremely elegant wines, whilst the 'silex' area yields firmer, more structured wines. Aromas of grapefruit, mint, fern, boxwood, broom, acacia, quince, apple, honey, blackcurrant bud and gunflint (on flint soils) are present. A handful of growers produce oak-aged wines. Try with shellfish, fish, Parma ham, goats cheese, crottin de Chavignol (produced locally) and cooked cold pork meats.

Sancerre also produces red and rosé wines from Pinot noir. They are light, fruity, pleasant wines with supple tannins and fragrances of morello cherry, strawberry or red currant jam, venison, violet.... Enjoy with poultry or grilled meats.

A.C. SAUMUR

OVERVIEW: 38 towns and villages stretching from the hills around Saumur (Montsoreau) as far as Vienne (Montreuil-

Bellay) form this appellation area. 28 of them are located in Maine-et-Loire, nine in Vienne and one in Deux-Sèvres. Vines are established on hillsides and terraces overlooking the Loire and the Thouet. Soil types are varied although limestone prevails ('tuffeau') and the climate is characterised by low rainfall. A broad-ranging selection of grapes are grown here: Cabernet Franc, Cabernet Sauvignon and Pineau d'Aunis for the reds, Chenin, Chardonnay and Sauvignon (no more than 20%) for the whites.

WINE STYLES: Saumur reds are supple, clean, approachable wines with delicate tannins. Some of them gain in complexity and become more fleshy as they age. Fragrances of red fruits such as blackcurrant and raspberry are present and occasionally fresh mushroom notes can be detected, as a reminder of the local 'tuffeau' caves. Puy-Notre-Dame is one of the appellation's most dynamic and highly-regarded villages. The wines pair with an extensive array of food including barbecued meats, stuffed pork belly, roast meat and poultry (chicken) and veal kidneys.

The whites are elegant, fresh and light. They also display the tell-tale characteristics of the local 'tuffeau' which in Turquant and Brézé imparts aromas of gunflint. Fragrances of lime are present and there is even a slightly bitter touch. Try with eel matelote or pike in a hot butter sauce. The rosés, which are in short supply, make good partners for grilled chitterlings sausage and cooked cold pork meats.

A.C. SAUMUR-CHAMPIGNY

OVERVIEW: the appellation embraces nine villages, centred on the Loire, the Thouet and the Vienne. The soils are calcareous clay and the vines enjoy plentiful sunshine (in Latin, Champigny means 'fields of fire') on the characteristic white earth formed of 'tuffeau' limestone (Turonian chalk). The area is home to three red varietals: Cabernet Franc, Cabernet Sauvignon and Pineau d'Aunis.

WINE STYLES: Saumur-Champigny produces well-balanced, velvety wines which are relatively robust and full. With their elegant tannins though they can be drunk young. They have a deep ruby-red hue and exude fragrances of red and black fruit such as raspberry, red currant, blackberry and blackcurrant, soot and humus. As they mature, they take on spicy tones (pepper), tobacco and liquorice. The younger wines pair with red meat (beef fillet), grilled fish and soft cheeses, whilst the older examples match with poultry, rabbit, lamb and game.

A.C. SAUMUR MOUSSEUX

Within the boundaries of the Saumur appellation, 1,300 hectares are dedicated to producing sparkling wines from Chenin, using the traditional method. A clutch of large companies make most of the wines and have ensured their commercial success. Saumur Mousseux is equally delicious as an appetiser or with a meal.

AC SAUMUR PUY-NOTRE-DAME

The district of Puy-Notre-Dame is one of the most renowned and dynamic in the region, both in terms of tourism and winemaking. The vineyards grow on a Turonian limestone butte south of Saumur and were granted their own appellation in 2008.

WINE STYLES: The red wines are structured, made from Cabernet Franc grapes that attain depth and complexity in this terroir. These wines can be laid down and pair well with red meat and game.

A.C. SAVENNIÈRES

OVERVIEW: the appellation covers three villages north of the Loire and south-west of Angers, namely Savennières, Bouchemaine and Possonière, with a total area under vine of 150 hectares. It has been said that the vines here are real sun traps. Louis 11th used to compare Savennières to a drop of gold. Several hillside sites unquestionably boast ideal facings, including the highest site at Epiré, home to Coulée-de-Serrant (a 7-hectare walled vineyard) and La Roche-aux-Moines (25 ha). Such is the quality of these two site-specific vineyards that they enjoy their own appellations: Savennières Coulée de Serrant and Savennières Roche aux Moines. Just like Burgundy, Savennières has walled vineyards: Clos du Papillon, des Perrières, de la Bergerie, de Coulaine, Clos de la Goutte d'Or...

The soils are formed of shale and purple sandstone of volcanic origin from the St George series with countless variations. Only Chenin is grown here.

WINE STYLES: Savennières is either a dry or medium dry white wine. It is full, delicate, elegant, rich and robust, which can be austere in the early years though is blessed with a fantastic potential for maturing. The wines display a golden straw-yellow hue and a complex bouquet with floral (acacia) and mineral fragrances, ripe white fruit, honey, flesh, sap, peach, and citrus fruit (apple). As they age, these lead into quince, candied fruit, peat, smoky and above all mineral shades. These sterling wines pair with fish in a sauce (pike, pike-perch, monkfish, salmon) and shellfish, roast white meats, goats cheeses and asparagus.

A.C. TOURAINE

OVERVIEW: the appellation covers an area stretching from Blois to Candes-Saint-Martin on the banks of the Loire and its tributaries (Cher, Indre and Vienne). A total 171 towns and villages are entitled to use the appellation, including 127 in Indre-et-Loire.

Soil types are extremely varied, ranging from calcareous clay ('aubuis'), clay and flint ('perruches'), to sand and light gravel, sand on shell sand and 'tuffeau'. The climate is temperate with an ocean influence to the west and continental influence to the east. Of all the red varietals grown here (Cabernet Franc, Cabernet Sauvignon, Gamay, Cot, Pinot Meunier, Pinot gris and Pineau d'Aunis), the dominant grape is Gamay. For whites, Chenin, Sauvignon, Menu Pineau and Chardonnay are grown. Sauvignon does particularly well in the Cher valley.

WINE STYLES: the reds and rosés are light, fruity, early-drinking wines when they are vinted as new or primeur wines. The reds blended from Gamay, Cabernet and Cot are well-structured and robust, with medium ageing potential. Recommended pairings are meat (kid goat) and cheeses. The whites are lively with floral fragrances leading into mineral notes as they age. Wines made from Sauvignon display shades of broom whilst Chenin wines are redolent of quince. Try them with fish, shellfish, seafood and potted meat. The rosés are fresh, fruity (red fruit) and refined. The perfect match for starters and cooked cold pork meats.

A.C. TOURAINE-AMBOISE

OVERVIEW: these wines grow either side of the Loire, upriver from Tours. The focal point of the appellation is the village of

Cangey. The soils, which are stony or sandy on a limestone subsoil, are well-suited to the local grape varieties: Gamay, Cot, Cabernet Franc, Cabernet Sauvignon (reds) and Chenin (whites).

WINE STYLES: the reds are supple, easy-drinking wines when made from Gamay and stronger, fuller wines when blended. They are rich, delicate and fragrant. The duration of maceration makes Touraine-Amboise early-drinking wines or wines to be kept. They display a cherry-red hue and aromas of red fruit (cherry, blackcurrant) and slightly spicy notes. The rosés are delicate, fruity, approachable wines. The whites display a hue with pale yellow tints and fragrances of gunflint, acacia, apple, peach, apricot, dried fruit, liquorice and quince. Food pairings for the reds: grilled beef, leg of venison and cheese. For the whites: fish in a sauce. For the rosés: crudités, assortment of cold cuts, smoked salmon...

A.C. TOURAINE-AZAY-LE-RIDEAU

OVERVIEW: the appellation covers eight villages on both banks of the Indre. The soils are clay with flint ('perruches') and calcareous clay ('aubuis') with patches of eolian sand. Two-thirds of the wines are white. Most of the rosés are made using the direct-to-press method. No red wines are grown here.

WINE STYLES: the white wines, made from Chenin, are delicate, elegant, vigorous, well-balanced and aromatic, with good ageing potential. They have a straw colour and develop fragrances of quince, acacia, verbena and toasted almonds. They can be served with fish in a sauce or cheeses. The rosés, made from Grolleau, Gamay, Cot and Cabernet, can be fresher than Rosé d'Anjou. They are approachable, delicate wines with a pleasant bouquet, a pale, slightly purple-blue hue and floral, fruity notes. Perfect with crudités, cold cuts, poultry terrine and smoked fish.

A.C. TOURAINE-MESLAND

OVERVIEW: the appellation embraces six villages, including Mesland, along the right bank of the Loire in Loir-et-Cher. Production focuses mainly on red wines though there are some whites made from Chenin, augmented with Sauvignon or Chardonnay. The soil make-up comprises sand, clay and flint gravel.

WINE STYLES: the reds are easy-drinking, round, fruity, delicate wines with low tannin content. Wines blended from Cabernet, Cot and Gamay tend to be more robust with medium ageing capacity and fragrances of raspberry, red fruit and spices. Try with perch fillets in red wine, grilled beef or cheeses. The whites are warm, dry, vigorous wines with medium ageing capacity. They develop spring scents and aromas of linden. Try with fish and shellfish.

A.C. TOURAINE NOBLE JOUÉ

OVERVIEW: this tiny 25-hectare appellation is situated in the villages of Chambray-lès-Tours, Esvres, Joué-lès-Tours, Larçay and Saint Avertin in the Indre-et-Loire department. The wines are blended from three varietals: Pinot gris, Pinot Meunier and Pinot noir. They are vinted as 'vin gris', therefore undergoing a short maceration period before being pressed and fermented. Try with grilled fish or cooked cold pork meats.

A.C. VALENCAY

OVERVIEW: this appellation, which was promoted to AC status in 2003, is located on the banks of the Cher and its tributaries (the Fouzon and the Mondon), on the border of Touraine, Sologne and Berry. Red varietals account for 85% of the range and focus primarily on Cabernets, Gamay, Grolleau and Pinot noir. The vines occupy clay silica hillside sites and plateaux with a subsoil dating back to the Senonian and Eocene epochs. Gunflint is one of the soil's most essential components.
WINE STYLES: the reds are only lightly-coloured and display fragrances of cherry and blackberry. They are light, pleasant wines suitable for early drinking. They pair well with veal stew, veal breasts and rabbit with onions. The whites are vigorous, sharp and harmonious wines with character. They display a pale yellow hue and boast characteristic notes of gunflint and floral aromas. Perfect with goats cheeses.

AC ORLÉANAIS

OVERVIEW: from the Middle Ages to the 17th century, Orléans was the most extensive and famous wine region in the whole of the Loire. The appellation is situated on both banks of the Loire and covers 25 towns and villages (19 on the right bank and six on the left). The villages of Olivet, Saint-Hilaire, Saint-Mesman, Mareau-aux-Près, Mézières-les-Cléry and Cléry Saint-André produce 95% of the wines here and they are all on the left bank.

Pinot noir is referred to locally as Auvernat noir, Pinot Meunier as Gris Meunier and Chardonnay as Auvernat blanc. The soils are clay silica and gravel silica.

WINE STYLES: the reds and rosés are pleasant, light, round, well-balanced, lively and fruity and should be drunk young. The most noteworthy wine is made from Gris Meunier. The wines are pale in colour, displaying fragrances of cherry, red currant and wild strawberries with a smoky finish. Try the reds with roast partridge, cooked cold pork meats, mixed salads and fish in a sauce (tuna, pike). For the rosés: poultry terrine, cooked cold pork meats and barbecues.

AC THOUARSAIS

OVERVIEW: this tiny 40-hectare area is split between sixteen villages around Thouars, in the Deux-Sèvres department. Chenin and Chardonnay are grown here for the white wines, and Cabernet Sauvignon and Gamay for the red and rosé wines. The wines are made on a boutique scale, with no more than 20 hectares on-stream for the past few years. Try with fish (whites), cooked cold pork meats (rosés) and meats served in a sauce (reds).

A.C. VOUVRAY

OVERVIEW: vines have been grown here since Roman times though it was Saint-Martin, bishop of Tours, who expanded vine growing in the early Middle Ages. In the 14th century, the wines were popular with the Dutch though also Rabelais, who described them as "pure taffeta wine".

The AC is located upriver from Tours, on the outskirts of the city itself, along the northern banks of the Loire. Between Rochecorbon and Vouvray, the vineyards peer down over the 'tuffeau' cliff faces and subsequently drop down to follow the river Cisseau, as far as Vernou then on to Noizay. The soils are calcareous clay over a 'tuffeau' ('aubuis') or clay silica plateau with occurrences of flint ('perruches'). The site is carved out by the Loire and its tributaries and the soils follow several geological formations: Turonian, Senonian, Eocene. The vines are south-facing and the climate is ocean and continental. Chenin is the grape variety used here.

WINE STYLES: the dry whites are supple, fruity, quaffing wines which can be slightly pungent in their youth. They sport a straw-yellow hue and exhibit aromas of white flower, acacia, linden, apple, citrus fruit, crushed strawberries, peach, quince and lychee. The sweet wines are powerful, unctuous, concentrated and full with delicate, rich aromas: camomile, jasmine, freshly-cut hay, apricot, fig, quince jelly, honey, wax, brioche, dried fruit and occasionally notes of walnut and truffle. All of these wines boast excellent cellaring capacity. The appellation also produces sparkling wines displaying the tell-tale characteristics and slight bitterness of the Chenin grape. With a meal, the dry and medium dry wines sit nicely alongside eel matelote and especially Tours speciality cooked cold pork meats (potted meat, chitterlings sausage, pigs trotters). The sweet wines call for foie gras or mature, flavoursome cheeses.

LOIRE VALLEY

Anjou

DOMAINE DES RICHÈRES +33 2 41 54 10 47

▼ Vintage 2011 Price: ❍ — 88/100

Anjou Villages Brissac

DOMAINE DE HAUTE PERCHE +33 2 41 57 75 65

▼ Vintage 2011 Price: ❍ — 87/100

DOMAINE DE MONTGILET +33 2 41 91 90 48

▼ Les Yvonnais 2011 Price: ❍❍ — 84/100

Bourgueil

DOMAINE DES OUCHES +33 2 47 96 98 77

▼ Côteaux des Ouches 2010 Price: ❍ — 89/100

▼ Igoranda 2012 Price: ❍ — 86/100

DOMAINE DU COUDRAY +33 2 47 97 76 92

▼ Le Coudray la Lande Vieilles Vignes 2011 Price: ❍ — 87/100

DOMAINE DU PETIT BONDIEU +33 2 47 97 33 18

CV▼ Couplets 2010 Price: ❍ — 90/100

CV▼ Petit Mont 2011 Price: ❍ — 87/100

Detailed instructions are featured at the start of the book.

Cabernet d'Anjou

DOMAINE DE MONTGILET +33 2 41 91 90 48

▼ Millésime 2012 Price: ❍ 89/100

DOMAINE DES RICHÈRES +33 2 41 54 10 47

▼ Vintage 2011 Price: ❍ 86/100

Chinon

DOMAINE AUBERT-MONORY +33 2 47 93 33 73

▼ Réserve Familiale 2010 Price: ❍ 89/100

▼ Vieilles Vignes 2010 Price: ❍ 88/100

▼ Vintage 2012 Price: ❍ 86/100

▼ Prestige 2011 Price: ❍ 86/100

DOMAINE DE LA DOZONNERIE +33 2 47 93 16 72

▼ Vintage 2011 Price: ❍ 86/100

MAISON COULY-DUTHEIL +33 2 47 97 20 20

▼ Clos de l'Echo 2010 Price: ❍❍ 91/100

▼ Clos de l'Olive 2010 Price: ❍❍ 90/100

▼ Vintage 2011 Price: ❍❍ 88/100

▼ La Diligence 2011 Price: ❍ 88/100

▼ René Couly 2011 Price: ❍ 87/100

Coteaux de l'Aubance

DOMAINE DE HAUTE PERCHE +33 2 41 57 75 65

▼ Les Fontenelles 2011 Price: ❍❍ 90/100

DOMAINE DE MONTGILET +33 2 41 91 90 48

▼ Les Trois Schistes 2011 Price: ❍❍ 95/100

Coteaux du Giennois

PHILIPPE RAIMBAULT +33 2 48 79 29 54

- ▼ Récolté sur les Coteaux de Saint Père 2012 Price: ❍ 86/100
- ▼ Récolté sur les Coteaux de Saint Père 2012 Price: ❍ 86/100
- ▼ Récolté sur les Coteaux de Saint Père 2010 Price: ❍ 83/100

Crémant de Loire

BOUVET LADUBAY +33 2 41 83 83 83

- ▼ Bouvet Brut rosé Price: ❍ 85/100

Fiefs Vendéens Pissotte

DOMAINE COIRIER +33 2 51 69 40 98

- ▼ Mélusine 2011 Price: ❍❍ 87/100
- ▼ La Petite Groie 2011 Price: ❍❍ 85/100

Menetou-Salon

DOMAINE JEAN-MAX ROGER +33 2 48 54 32 20

- ▼ Le Petit Clos 2012 Price: ❍❍ 86/100

Detailed instructions are featured
at the start of the book.

Muscadet Côtes de Grandlieu

DOMAINE LES HAUTES NOËLLES +33 2 40 31 53 49

CV▼ Vintage 2011 Price: ○ 90/100

CV▼ Vintage 2011 Price: ○ 86/100

Muscadet Sèvre et Maine

CHÂTEAU BOIS BENOIST +33 2 40 33 93 76

▼ La Vigne de Marie 1 Hectare 2010 Price: ○ 89/100

DOMAINE DU GRAND CHÂTELIER +33 2 40 36 40 01

▼ Vieux Moulin 2009 Price: ○ 86/100

DOMAINE POIRON-DABIN +33 2 40 06 56 42

▼ Château-Thébaud Clos des Tabardières 2007 Price: ○○ 90/100

▼ Vignoble Poiron-Dabin Vieilles Vignes 2010 Price: ○○ 87/100

Muscadet Sèvre et Maine sur Lie

CHÂTEAU DE LA CASSEMICHÈRE +33 2 40 06 74 07

▼ Château Cassemichère Cuvée 1601 2010 Price: ○○ 85/100

▼ Château Cassemichère Vintage 2012 Price: ○ 84/100

CHÂTEAU DE LA FERTÉ +33 2 40 86 37 48

▼ Vieilles Vignes 2012 Price: ○ 85/100

DOMAINE DE LA POTARDIÈRE +33 2 40 33 82 50

▼ Domaine de la Potardiere Vintage 2012 Price: ○ 86/100

▼ Domaine de La Potardiere Vintage 2012 Price: ○ 86/100

DOMAINE DES TILLEULS +33 2 40 33 60 04

▼ Les Quatre Chanteaux - Vieilles Vignes 2011 Price: ○ 88/100

▼ Haute Sélection 2012 Price: ○ 86/100

DOMAINE DU GRAND CHÂTELIER +33 2 40 36 40 01

- Haut-Fief 2012 Price: ❍ 87/100

DOMAINE MÉNARD-GABORIT +33 2 40 54 61 06

- Cuvée Prestige Méganome 2011 Price: ❍ 88/100
- Mégalie 2012 Price: ❍ 86/100

DOMAINE POIRON-DABIN +33 2 40 06 56 42

- Clos des Gars d'Bizeux 2012 Price: ❍ 86/100

SARL OLLIVIER FRERES +33 2 28 01 07 07

- Domaine de la Grenaudière Vintage 2012 Price: ❍ 86/100
- Domaine de la Grenaudière La Grenouille 2012 Price: ❍ 86/100
- Domaine des Amoureux Vintage 2012 Price: ❍ 85/100
- Domaine de l'Olivier Vintage 2012 Price: ❍ 84/100

Pouilly-Fumé

DOMAINE CHAUVEAU +33 3 86 39 15 42

- Cuvée Sainte Clélie 2011 Price: ❍ 90/100
- La Charmette 2012 Price: ❍ 89/100
- Les Croqloups 2012 Price: ❍ 87/100

DOMAINE MICHEL DUTARTE +33 3 86 39 13 55

- Vintage 2012 Price: ❍ 88/100

DOMAINE PATRICE MOREUX +33 3 86 39 13 55

- La Loge aux Moines Monopole 2012 Price: ❍❍ 89/100
- Vintage 2012 Price: ❍ 86/100

DOMAINE SERGE DAGUENEAU & FILLES +33 3 86 39 11 18

- La Léontine 2010 Price: ❍❍❍ 91/100
- Clos des Chaudoux 2011 Price: ❍❍ 90/100
- Tradition 2012 Price: ❍❍ 86/100

GITTON PÈRE & FILS +33 2 48 54 38 84

- Péchignolles 2012 Price: ❍❍ 87/100

JEAN PABIOT ET FILS +33 3 86 39 10 25

- Jean Pabiot & Fils Cuvée Séduction 2010 Price: ❍❍ 93/100
- Domaine des Fines Caillottes Vintage 2012 Price: ❍ 91/100

PATRICK COULBOIS +33 3 86 39 15 69

Vintage 2011 Price: ❍ 86/100

PHILIPPE RAIMBAULT +33 2 48 79 29 54

Les Lumeaux 2012 Price: ❍ 93/100

Mosaïque 2012 Price: ❍ 89/100

Quarts de Chaume

DOMAINE DES BAUMARD +33 2 41 78 70 03

Vintage 2009 Price: ❍❍❍ 94/100

Quincy

DOMAINE ADÈLE ROUZÉ +33 2 48 58 93 08

Vintage 2012 Price: ❍ 89/100

DOMAINE TROTEREAU +33 2 48 51 32 23

Vintage 2012 Price: ❍ 85/100

Rosé d'Anjou

BARTON & GUESTIER +33 5 56 95 48 00

Vintage 2011 Price: ❍ 85/100

BOUGRIER SA +33 2 54 32 31 36

Rosé d'Anjou Vintage 2012 Price: ❍ 84/100

DOMAINE DES RICHÈRES +33 2 41 54 10 47

Vintage 2011 Price: ❍ 87/100

Detailed instructions are featured at the start of the book.

Rosé de Loire

ANTOINE SIMONEAU +33 2 54 71 36 14

▼ Vintage 2012 Price: ❍ — 86/100

BOUGRIER SA +33 2 54 32 31 36

▼ Les Caractères Vintage 2012 Price: ❍ — 81/100

Sancerre

ALAIN GIRARD & FILS +33 2 48 79 24 88

▼ Domaine des Brosses Vintage 2012 Price: ❍ — 86/100

DOMAINE DES BROSSES

▼ **Confidence 2011** **87/100**

Brilliant light yellow. Wonderful nose with tropical accents, ripe fruits and vanilla oak. Fleshy, concentrated and nervy palate with refined spice, oak that is still upfront and elegant freshness imparting drive. An enjoyable, ambitious wine.

Price: ❍❍

Serving Temperature: 9-11°C
Ready to drink : 2014

Alain Girard & Fils
Domaine des Brosses - 18300 Veaugues
Tel.: +33 02 48 79 24 88 - Fax: +33 02 48 79 20 49
E-mail: domainedesbrosses@yahoo.fr

CHÂTEAU DE THAUVENAY +33 2 48 79 90 33

▼ Vintage 2012 Price: ❍❍❍ 83/100

DOMAINE DANIEL REVERDY ET FILS +33 2 48 79 33 29

▼ Vintage 2012 Price: ❍ 87/100

DOMAINE HENRY NATTER +33 2 48 69 58 85

▼ François de La Grange de Montigny 2012 Price: ❍ 90/100

▼ Vintage 2012 Price: ❍ 88/100

DOMAINE JEAN-MAX ROGER +33 2 48 54 32 20

▼ Vieilles Vignes 2011 Price: ❍❍ 93/100

▼ Cuvée G.C 2011 Price: ❍❍ 89/100

▼ Cuvée G.C 2012 Price: ❍❍ 87/100

▼ Vieilles Vignes 2009 Price: ❍❍❍ 85/100

▼ La Grande Dîmière 2010 Price: ❍❍ 84/100

DOMAINE LA BARBOTAINE +33 2 48 79 02 32

▼ Vintage 2012 Price: ❍ 88/100

▼ Vintage 2012 Price: ❍ 87/100

▼ Vintage 2012 Price: ❍ 86/100

DOMAINE MATTHIAS ET EMILE ROBLIN +33 2 48 79 48 85

▼ Vintage 2010 Price: ❍❍ 91/100

▼ Vintage 2010 Price: ❍❍ 90/100

▼ Vintage 2011 Price: ❍❍ 89/100

▼ Vintage 2011 Price: ❍❍ 89/100

▼ Vintage 2011 Price: ❍❍ 89/100

▼ Vintage 2010 Price: ❍❍ 86/100

DOMAINE PASCAL ET NICOLAS REVERDY +33 2 48 79 37 31

▼ Les Anges Lots Vieilles Vignes 2011 Price: ❍❍ 93/100

▼ Terre de Maimbray 2012 Price: ❍ 93/100

▼ Terre de Maimbray 2011 Price: ❍ 87/100

DOMAINE PATRICE MOREUX +33 3 86 39 13 55

▼ Vintage 2012 Price: ❍ 84/100

DOMAINE PAUL PRIEUR +33 2 48 79 35 86

▼ Paul Prieur et Fils Vintage 2012 Price: ❍ 89/100

DOMAINE REVERDY DUCROUX +33 2 48 79 31 33

▼ Beau Regard 2011 Price: ❍❍ 87/100

GITTON PÈRE & FILS +33 2 48 54 38 84

- Galinot 2010 Price: ❍❍❍ — 92/100
- Les Romains 2012 Price: ❍❍ — 87/100
- Les Montachins 2012 Price: ❍❍ — 86/100

JEAN PAUL PICARD ET FILS +33 2 48 54 16 13

- Jean Paul Picard Vintage 2011 Price: ❍ — 86/100
- Jean Paul Picard Vintage 2012 Price: ❍ — 85/100

MICHEL VATTAN +33 2 48 79 40 98

- Cuvée Argile 2012 Price: ❍ — 89/100
- Cuvée Calcaire 2012 Price: ❍ — 89/100
- Vintage 2012 Price: ❍ — 88/100

PHILIPPE RAIMBAULT +33 2 48 79 29 54

- Les Chasseignes 2011 Price: ❍❍ — 92/100
- Les Godons 2012 Price: ❍ — 88/100
- Apud Sariacum 2012 Price: ❍ — 88/100
- Apud Sariacum 2012 Price: ❍ — 87/100
- Les Godons 2010 Price: ❍ — 85/100

VINCENT GRALL +33 2 48 78 00 42

- Le Manoir 2012 Price: ❍❍ — 88/100
- Vintage 2012 Price: ❍ — 87/100

Saumur

BOUVET LADUBAY +33 2 41 83 83 83

- Bouvet Brut Trésor 2009 Price: ❍❍ — 90/100
- Brut rosé
Taille Princesse de Gérard Depardieu 2010 Price: ❍❍ — 90/100
- Bouvet Brut Saphir 2010 Price: ❍ — 87/100

DOMAINE DES CLOS MAURICE +33 2 41 38 80 02

- Les Clos Maurice La Licorne des Clos 2011 Price: ❍ — 88/100

Detailed instructions are featured at the start of the book.

Saumur Champigny

DOMAINE DES CLOS MAURICE +33 2 41 38 80 02

▼ Les Clos Maurice La Cabriole des Clos 2010 Price: ❍❍ 88/100

▼ Les Clos Maurice Le Clos de Midi 2011 Price: ❍❍ 87/100

▼ Les Clos Maurice Vieilles Vignes 2011 Price: ❍ 85/100

Savennières

DOMAINE DES BAUMARD +33 2 41 78 70 03

▼ Vintage 2010 Price: ❍❍❍ 91/100

▼ Vintage 2009 Price: ❍❍❍ 90/100

LOÏC MAHÉ +33 6 14 76 66 01

ORG ▼ Les Fougeraies 2011 Price: ❍❍ 88/100

Touraine

ANTOINE SIMONEAU +33 2 54 71 36 14

▼ Vintage 2012 Price: ❍ 86/100

▼ A Simoneau Brut Price: ❍ 86/100

▼ Domaine de la Rablais Vintage 2012 Price: ❍ 86/100

▼ Cabernet Franc 2010 Price: ❍ 86/100

▼ A Simoneau Brut rose Price: ❍ 84/100

BOUGRIER SA +33 2 54 32 31 36

▼ Les Caractères Tradition 2012 Price: ❍ 84/100

DOMAINE DE LA ROCHETTE +33 2 54 71 44 02

▼ Gamay 2012 Price: ❍ 85/100

▼ Sauvignon 2012 Price: ❍ 85/100

▼ Fleur de Printemps 2012 Price: ❍ 83/100

▼ Pineau d'Aunis 2012 Price: ❍ 83/100

DOMAINE DU CLOS DE L'EPINAY +33 2 47 52 61 90

▼ Demi-sec rosé - Cuvée Pauline 2011 Price: ❍ 83/100

DOMAINE FRANÇOIS CARTIER +33 2 54 71 51 54

▼ Vintage 2012 Price: ❍ 84/100

DOMAINE JOËL DELAUNAY +33 2 54 71 45 69

▼ La Voute 2012 Price: ❍ 91/100

▼ Sauvignon 2012 Price: ❍ 90/100

▼ Les Cabotines 2012 Price: ❍ 87/100

DOMAINE MÉRIEAU +33 2 54 32 14 23

▼ Jean François Mérieau Cent Visages 2010 Price: ❍❍ 86/100

FAMILLE GAILLARD +33 2 54 71 45 69

▼ Sauvignon Blanc 2012 Price: ❍ 90/100

VIGNOBLE DES VENDEIGNES +33 2 54 79 52 02

▼ Vignobles des Vendeignes Sauvignon 2012 Price: ❍ 80/100

Touraine Amboise

DOMAINE DUTERTRE +33 2 47 30 10 69

▼ Clos du Pavillon 2011 Price: ❍ 86/100

▼ Cuvée Prestige 2010 Price: ❍ 85/100

Val de Loire

ANTOINE SIMONEAU +33 2 54 71 36 14

▼ Domaine de la Rablais Cuvée St-Georges 2012 Price: ❍ 87/100

Detailed instructions are featured
at the start of the book.

DOMAINE DES TILLEULS +33 2 40 33 60 04

▼ Chardonnay 2012 Price: ❍ 85/100

DOMAINE LES HAUTES NOËLLES +33 2 40 31 53 49

▼ Vintage 2011 Price: ❍ 86/100

CV▼ Vintage 2011 Price: ❍ 84/100

Vouvray

BARTON & GUESTIER +33 5 56 95 48 00

▼ Vintage 2011 Price: ❍ 86/100

CHÂTEAU DE VALMER +33 2 47 52 93 12

▼ Vintage 2005 Price: ❍❍ 91/100

▼ Demi-sec 2012 Price: ❍ 87/100

DOMAINE DES AUBUISIÈRES +33 2 47 52 61 55

▼ Les Girardières - Demi-Sec 2012 Price: ❍ 89/100

▼ Cuvée de Silex 2012 Price: ❍ 88/100

▼ Cuvée de Perruches 2012 Price: ❍ 88/100

DOMAINE DU CLOS DE L'EPINAY +33 2 47 52 61 90

CV▼ Demi-sec 2012 Price: ❍ 90/100

▼ Brut Tête de Cuvée 2009 Price: ❍ 87/100

CV▼ Brut 2010 Price: ❍ 86/100

▼ Demi-sec 2011 Price: ❍ 84/100

VINCENT CARÊME +33 2 47 52 06 40

CV▼ Le Clos 2008 Price: ❍❍ 91/100

ORG▼ L'Ancestrale 2011 Price: ❍❍ 87/100

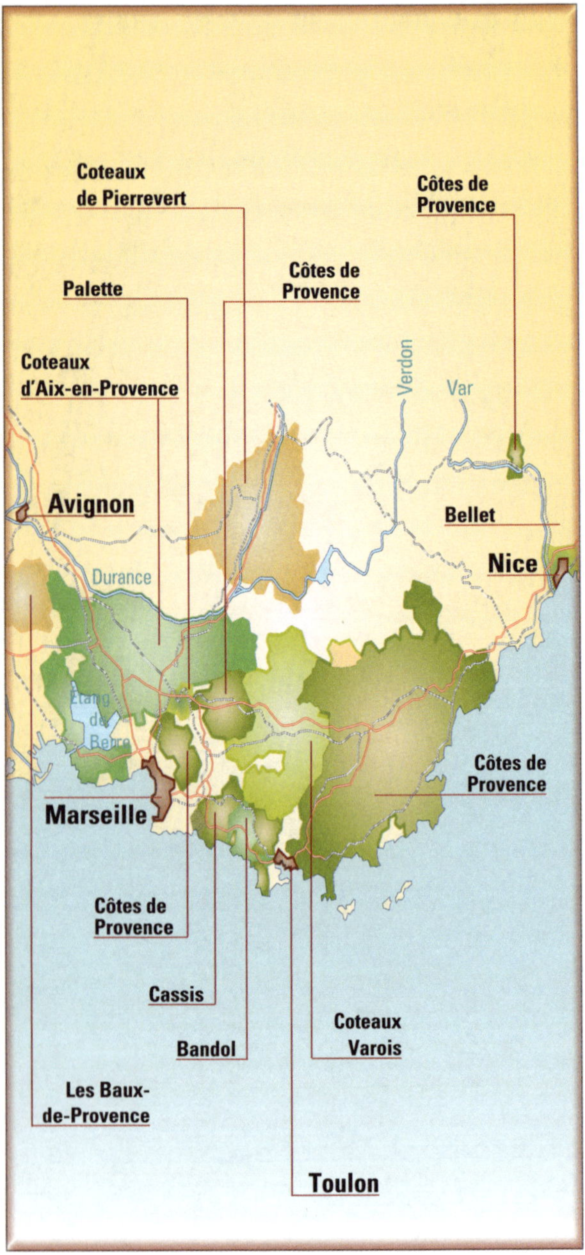

Coteaux de Pierrevert
Côtes de Provence
Palette
Côtes de Provence
Coteaux d'Aix-en-Provence
Verdon
Var
Avignon
Bellet
Nice
Durance
Étang de Berre
Côtes de Provence
Marseille
Côtes de Provence
Cassis
Coteaux Varois
Bandol
Les Baux-de-Provence
Toulon

PROVENCE

MORE THAN JUST ROSÉ

The wine region of Provence begins south of Avignon, on the southern banks of the Durance, and ends up in the hills overlooking Nice. Flanked by the Mediterranean, the entire region basks in the balmy climate of the same name, whose defining characteristic is hot, dry summers. Its size and rugged terrain, however, (due to the nearby Alps) have shaped its diversity. Provence boasts no fewer than 9 appellations, the largest being AC Côtes de Provence spanning three departments: Bouches-du-Rhône, Var and Alpes-Maritimes.

Travelling east, the environment undergoes a series of changes: limestone hillsides around Baux-de-Provence with its distinct Mediter-ranean climate - Montagne-Sainte-Victoire with its more continental climate and sandstone, clay soils yielding robust, idiosyncratic wines - the Beausset basin, between Cassis and Bandol, where the limestone terrain, swept over by sea breezes, produces warm, typically Provençal blends - the sea-influenced coastline where extremely ancient soils formed of shale and granite yield wines with character - the inland valley, north of the Maures mountain range which supplies a large chunk of the region's AC output, producing full-bodied, powerful reds drawn from clay-sand Cambrian soils - and finally, the rolling hills of the highland region, limestone remnants of the Alpine folds, which accounts for a quarter of output. The climate, which is harsh in winter and often extremely hot in summer, produces robust, well-structured yet delicate wines. They can take longer to mature and are more secret wines.

The climate and landscapes of Provence have for a long time attracted holidaymakers and investors from around the globe. The growing tide of pleasure-seeking consumers and a plentiful source of money obviousl y provide the stimulus for advances in quality by giving free rein to initiative. Sleepy wine farms have been given a new lease of life by enterprising, wealthy investors who leave no stone unturned in their quest to fully realise the 'terroir's' potential. Local initiatives also abound, however, and the resultant drive behind Provence is uplifting.

GRAPE VARIETALS: Reds and rosés: Grenache, Syrah, Cinsault, Mourvedre, Carignan, Cabernet, Tibouren and Cabernet-Sauvignon (Coteaux d'Aix); Whites: Rolle, Semillon, Clairette, Ugni Blanc, Sauvignon and Marsanne (the last three are specific to white Cassis).

WINE STYLES: Provence is the world's leading producer of rosé wines. Light, fresh, pleasant wines when young, their quality has improved in leaps and bounds over the past few years. Although some are still enjoyable 'thirst-quenching' wines, others have earned a place on well-set tables, partnering with grilled fish, shellfish, salads or white meat. Their success if reflected in the price tags of the top-flight wines, which can command up to 15 euros. Provence though also produces red wines which are worth seeking out. Although they are made from the same varietal range, they run the gamut in terms of wine styles. A varietal like Carignan can yield superlative wines when the whole grape fermentation process is used. It imparts a host of aromas and freshness though requires early-drinking. Conversely, longer vatting periods for the reds extract more tannins, which are then often perfected by oak ageing; they have greater structure and need to spend a year or two in the bottle to mellow. The better vintages of these deep, complex wines can be laid down. Provence's greatest reds come from Bandol where the dominant varietal is Mourvedre (which is said only to realise its full potential when planted in sight of the sea). Bandol reds are powerful, though well-balanced. They are aged for a minimum of eighteen months (often in oak tuns) before being released, which imparts structure, depth and fullness. In the early years they display fruity, floral (violet) and spicy aromas (pepper, liquorice). As they age, their aromas span an even broader range and their mellow bouquet is occasionally reminiscent of leather, mushroom and undergrowth.

The white wines are produced on a more boutique scale (roughly 5%). They cover a broad aromatic spectrum, ranging from floral, fruity and acidulous to mineral. White wines from Provence flourish around Cassis, within the boundaries of the town which lent its name to the appellation (1936). Their unusual varietal combination imparts a genuine aromatic personality (thyme, sage, wild mint...), and they invariably display a delicious contrast between fat and vigour...

REVIEW OF RECENT VINTAGES

• **2010** • Volumes are generally up on 2009 probably due to rainfall in winter and spring and fairly low temperatures. The mistral wind dried out the vineyards and kept the crop disease-free. A good vintage!

• **2011** • A rainy winter, a hot, dry spring and intermittent storms over the summer: Provence experienced the same weather patterns as other parts of France. No serious damage occurred but the stormy weather led to the region's hallmark disparities from one area to another. Juice yields were often lower than in 2010, particularly in inland areas. Although output was still dominated by rosés, the vintage produced some superlative reds.

• **2012** • The 2012 vintage is quite good, although it varies considerably from one appellation to another, and even more so from one estate to another. Following a mild and very dry winter (just 53 mm of precipitation during the season), the spring was hot, especially from May onwards. During the summer, the drought was detrimental to the development and ripening of the grapes; only after several rains in September did ripening restart.

THE PROVENCE APPELLATIONS

A.C. BANDOL

OVERVIEW: AC Bandol embraces eight villages in the foothills of the Sainte Baume mountain range overlooking the Mediterranean, where soil make-up is formed of calcareous silica, sandstone and sandy marl. This particular site enjoys 3,000 hours of sunshine annually, elevating both the fruitiness and the quality of the wines. Mild winters, early springs and hot summers also factor into this matrix. The reds are vinted traditionally and spend at least 18 months in oak tuns. Drawn from the same varietal range as the reds - namely Mourvedre (at least 50%), Grenache, Cinsault and a tiny proportion of Carignan and Syrah - the rosés are made using the direct to press method. The less common whites come from Bourboulenc, Clairette and Ugni blanc, with a balance of Sauvignon (no more than 40%).

WINE STYLES: Bandol is renowned above all for its reds and rosés. The red wines (which account for 30% of output) exhibit a deep colour, are well-structured, powerful and aromatic (morello cherry, raspberry, violet, blackcurrant, iris, dill); 4 to 5 years down the line, they exude aromas of truffle, undergrowth, liquorice, cinnamon or musk. They boast an outstanding lifespan.

Enjoy with Sisteron lamb, goat meat with garlic or Provençal Banon goat's cheese. The rosés (60% of output) with their extremely pale salmon-pink hue, are well-balanced and conjure up aromas of ripe grapes and morello cherries layered over spices. Enjoy with a courgette tart doused with olive oil, fish or grilled white meat. The straw-yellow colour whites are dry, vigorous and fragrant (citrus fruits, pear, linden and broom). Try them with shellfish, fish and goat's cheeses.

A.C. BELLET

OVERVIEW: Bellet is a minute appellation set in the hills overlooking Nice. Very few wines are actually produced here but their reputation is well-established. Virtually all of them are sold in the hotels along the French Riviera, making them difficult to come by. Vineyard soils are formed of pebbles intermingled with very pale sand and the occasional seam of clay. The site also enjoys an outstanding micro-climate with 2,700 hours of sunshine annually and just the right amount of rainfall. The varietal range is quite unusual: Braquet, Folle noire, Cinsault and Grenache noir for the reds. Rolle, Roussanne, Spagnol as well as Clairette, Bourboulenc, Chardonnay, Pignerol and small-berry Muscat for the whites.

WINE STYLES: Bellet produces equal amounts of white, red and rosé wines. The whites, with their deep, bright hue, are full and suave. They develop aromas of hawthorn, honeysuckle and ripe pear and sit nicely alongside fish in a cream sauce, veal cutlets with mushrooms and Comté cheese. The rosés are soft, lively but not too sharp, with a delicate bouquet (wild rose, pepper). Served with lamb and sweet pepper kebabs, they form an unrivalled match. The reds are rich, elegant and vigorous. They exhibit pleasant aromas of peony, pepper and pine forests. Try them with a grilled leg of lamb with herbs or pork roast with prunes.

A.C. CASSIS

OVERVIEW: the Cassis appellation shares the same boundaries as the town of the same name in the Bouches-du-Rhône department, a few kilometres from Marseilles. Cretaceous limestone and limestone or marl scree are the constituent soil types of this site. The surrounding hillsides deflect the Mistral wind and gentle sea breezes comb through the vines which bask in 3,000 hours of sunshine and receive 670 mm of annual rainfall.

WINE STYLES: AC Cassis produces primarily white wines (70%) blended from a varietal range predominantly formed by Clairette, Marsanne, Sauvignon and Ugni blanc. The wines are dry and heady with a discrete nose (grapefruit, pear, quince, pine resin). They are fat and long on the palate. Pair with Bouillabaisse fish stew with garlic mayonnaise, bass with fennel, anchoïade or anchovy dip, sea urchins and fish served in a cream sauce. The rosés are blended from Barbaroux, Carignan, Cinsault, Grenache and Mourvedre; they are fruity, supple and delicate with a pleasant raspberry-pink colour. The red wines boast a cherry-red hue and display good balance, nice structure and powerful aromas (ripe fruit, havana, liquorice...). Enjoy with wild boar casserole or small game (thrush or lark).

A.C. COTEAUX D'AIX-EN-PROVENCE

OVERVIEW: the Coteaux d'Aix-en-Provence appellation area embraces 49 towns and villages in two departments: Var and Bouches-du-Rhône. The best known of these is, of course, Aix-en-Provence, though also Salon de Provence, Les Baux-de-Provence, (which has also been an appellation in its own right since 1995), Berre-L'Etang, Martigues, Ventabren, Fontvieille, Istres... A variety of soil types can be found here: stony calcareous clay, sand and gravel. The climate is Mediterranean with low rainfall and the vines bask for the most part in generous sunshine.

WINE STYLES: the vast majority of the wines are rosés, blended from Grenache, Cabernet-Sauvignon and Carignan, sometimes augmented with Cinsault, Syrah and Mourvedre. Made using the 'bleeding' technique, they display a pink hue with orangy tints. They are lively, fresh and fruity with good acidity. Try them with olive paste or Mediterranean fish and shellfish. The white wines, made from Ugni Blanc (no more than 40%), Sauvignon and Semillon (30%), Bourboulenc, Clairette, Grenache and Vermentino, are made by the direct to press method. They are light, fresh and delicate (white fruit, floral fragrances) and are a perfect match for grilled fish with herbs (fennel). The red wines, with their delicate tannins, are fruity and well-balanced. They exude aromas of leather, liquorice, black fruit (blackcurrant, prunes) and spicy notes. Enjoy with grilled meat.

A.C. COTEAUX VAROIS

OVERVIEW: entirely surrounded by the Côtes de Provence appellation, Coteaux Varois embraces 28 towns and villages located in the heart of the Var department. The appellation stretches from the Sainte-Baume mountain range to the Bessillons hills around the small town of Brignoles. The vast majority of the vines are planted on calcareous clay soils, for which the Argens river and its tributaries provide drainage. The prevailing climate is, of course, Mediterranean, though semi-continental influences exercise a moderating effect. These climatic conditions promote gradual ripening of the grapes depending on site elevation across the appellation area.

WINE STYLES: the lion's share of Coteaux Varois are rosés (70%) and reds (25%) with interesting potential. They are blended primarily from Grenache noir, Syrah, Mourvedre (at least 70%) though also Cabernet Sauvignon, Carignan and Cinsault. White wines are also made, on a boutique scale (from Rolle, Semillon, Ugni blanc, Clairette and Grenache). The rosés are fresh and fruity and exhibit pleasant aromas of red fruit. The reds, with their vermilion hue, are rustic wines. They are well-structured though often display average concentration. They exude fragrances of violet, liquorice, leather, green pepper and black pepper, and they pair well with lamb kebabs, barbecued meat or an informal buffet lunch. The whites are dry and vigorous and conjure up aromas of citrus fruit (grapefruit). They are equally delicious as appetisers or with fish grilled on a bed of bay leaves.

A.C. COTEAUX-DE-PIERREVERT

OVERVIEW: Coteaux de Pierrevert, which is set in the upper reaches of Provence, gained AC status in 1998. The wines hail from villages nestled amongst the hills which run from Villeneuve and Manosque to Pierrevert and Corbières along the right bank of the Durance river and the southern slopes of the Valensole plateau. Coteaux de Pierrevert are the most northerly of the Provençal wines and are often subsumed into the Rhone Valley appellation system. The soils are predominantly limestone interspersed with patches of sand, loam, stones and sandstone. The area enjoys hot, sunny summers though the frequently high day/night temperature differentials can cause dramatic thunderstorms.

WINE STYLES: Rosés are the predominant wine style here. They are blended from Cinsault, Carignan, Grenache noir, Mourvedre and a balance of Oillade, Petite Syrah and Terret. Deep salmon-pink in colour, they are pleasant, floral, fruity wines (rose, lilac, pear drop). The red wines display a beautiful brilliant crimson hue. On the palate, they combine suppleness with vigour and exhibit aromas of ripe fruit (prune, bilberry), a touch of liquorice and a hint of vanilla. The white wines, blended from Grenache blanc, Marsanne, Picpoul, Ugni blanc and Vermentino exude fragrances of hawthorn, dried flowers and citrus fruit. The wines are made by two co-operative wineries and a dozen independent growers.

A.C. CÔTES DE PROVENCE

OVERVIEW: The winegrowing area of Côtes-de-Provence is extensive. It stretches from Marseille to the department of Alpes-Maritimes, covering 84 districts (68 in the Var, 15 in the Bouches-du-Rhône, and one, Villars-sur-Var, in Alpes-Maritimes). Over such a vast surface area, the terroirs are diverse. The Massif des Maures and the coast form an area composed mainly of granite and schist. From Toulon to Saint-Raphaël, the soils are of sandy clay. The plateaux and hills of Provence consist of limestone. As a whole, the winegrowing region is fragmented, made up of isolated units. Most often, the vines grow up stepped terraces. The region has a Mediterranean climate with long, hot, dry summers, with rain in the spring and autumn. Recently, three new appellations were created: Côtes-de-Provence Sainte-Victoire, to the east of Aix-en-Provence; Côtes-de-Provence La Londe, near Hyères and Bormes-les-Mimosa; and Côtes-de-Provence Fréjus, on the other side of the region, between Saint-Raphaël and Trans-en-Provence. The Côtes de Provence La Londe appellation, near Hyères, was created in 2008.

WINE STYLES: Rosé wines are the predominant style (80%) though red wines (15%) are on the increase. The varietal range comprises Cinsault, Grenache, Mourvedre, Syrah and Tibouren, augmented with Cabernet-Sauvignon and Carignan. The rosés are made primarily using the 'bleeding' process. The initial stages of fermentation lift the pomace and when the right colour has been achieved after 12 to 24 hours of skin contact, part of the juice is run off and then continues to ferment off the pomace. The wines vary in hue from pale pink to very light red. Their defining characteristic is a clean, vigorous attack, a relatively steady body combined with mineral, exotic (mango, passion fruit, pomegranate) and floral fragrances. Pairings include grilled lamb chops. The reds are vinted traditionally and exhibit fine tannic structure. They are often matured in wooden tuns. On the palate, they display complex aromas of ripe fruit, bay, thyme, tobacco, cinnamon and venison. They are becoming increasingly popular. Try with local specialities or grilled ribsteak. The whites are vinted using the direct to press method. They are delicate, gracious, dry and vigorous and depending on the style can display floral, fruity or balsamic fragrances. The ideal partner for grilled red mullet or Bouillabaisse fish stew.

A.C. LES BAUX DE PROVENCE

OVERVIEW: initially subsumed into the Coteaux d'Aix en Provence AC area, the tiny region of Baux de Provence became an appellation in its own right in 1995. Its hot, dry climate, predominantly limestone soils and rugged terrain provide an ideal growing environment for the local grape varieties (Grenache, Syrah, Mourvedre, augmented with Counoise, Carignan and Cabernet-Sauvignon). Only red and rosé wines are made here.

A.C. PALETTE

OVERVIEW: the minute area of Palette is located in close proximity to Aix-en-Provence (Meyreuil, Le Tholonet and Aix-en-Provence) in Bouches-du-Rhône. It is currently one of France's smallest appellations, covering a diminutive thirty hectares or so. The lion's share of the wines are made by two independent growers, including the celebrated Château Simone, whilst the remaining grapes are delivered to the local co-operative. The soil is formed of Langesse lacustrine limestone and the climate is Mediterranean with low rainfall and plenty of sunshine.

WINE STYLES: Mourvedre, Grenache and Cinsault form the backbone of the red and rosé varietal range. The red wines are usually sourced from old vines then matured in oak (rarely new) for at least 18 months. They are dense wines with good cellaring capacity, boasting aromas of raspberry, blackcurrant, old leather and spices. The perfect match for a leg of mutton or game. The rosés are vinted using the 'bleeding' or direct to press method. They are fleshy and well-balanced, fruity and balsamic. The whites undergo classic vinification methods, and are subsequently matured on the lees in oak for at least 8 months. Delicate, elegant, suave wines, they are well-balanced and develop fragrances of spices, quince jelly, fig and hazelnut. Enjoy with foie gras terrine or lamb stew.

• • •

PROVENCE

Alpilles

CHÂTEAU D'ESTOUBLON +33 4 90 54 64 00

ORG▼ Vintage 2009 Price: ○○○ 84/100

Bandol

CHÂTEAU PRADEAUX +33 4 94 32 10 21

▼ Vintage 2008 Price: ○○○ 90/100

DOMAINE DE L'OLIVETTE +33 4 94 985 885

▼ Vintage 2008 Price: ○○ 92/100

▼ Vintage 2012 Price: ○○ 89/100

▼ Vintage 2012 Price: ○○ 88/100

DOMAINE DUPUY DE LÔME +33 4 94 05 22 99

CV▼ Vintage 2010 Price: ○○ 90/100

CV▼ Vintage 2012 Price: ○○ 89/100

CV▼ Vintage 2012 Price: ○○ 87/100

DOMAINE LA SUFFRÈNE +33 4 94 90 09 23

▼ Cuvée Les Lauves 2010 Price: ○○○ 92/100

▼ Vintage 2010 Price: ○○ 89/100

DOMAINES OTT +33 4 94 01 53 50

▼ Château Romassan Vintage 2012 Price: ○○○ 93/100

▼ Château Romassan Vintage 2010 Price: ○○○ 90/100

Coteaux d'Aix en Provence

CAVE DES COTEAUX LANÇON +33 4 90 42 81 09

▼ Vintage 2012 Price: ❍ 83/100

CAVE DES COTEAUX LANÇON

▼ Vintage 2012 **85/100**

Deep crimson with dark purple tints. Fruit-driven nose (redcurrant, blackcurrant, blackberry) with a floral touch. Juicy, svelte and fresh palate with a spicy accent flowing into lots of recurrent fruit revealing crispness. Hint of firmness on the finish.

Price: ❍

Serving Temperature: 15-17°C
Ready to drink : 2014-2015

Cave des Coteaux Lançon
Place du champ de Mars
13680 Lancon Provence
Tel.: +33 04 90 42 81 09
Fax: +33 04 94 53 86 99
E-mail: lacavecoop.lancon@neuf.fr

CHÂTEAU SAINT-HILAIRE +33 4 42 52 10 68

CV▼ Prestige 2012 Price: ❍ 88/100

CV▼ Prestige 2009 Price: ❍❍ 87/100

LES QUATRE TOURS +33 4 42 54 71 11

▼ Les Sentinelles 2012 Price: ❍ 85/100

▼ Signature 2011 Price: ❍ 85/100

▼ Signature 2012 Price: ❍ 85/100

Detailed instructions are featured at the start of the book.

Côtes de Provence

CHÂTEAU BARBEIRANNE +33 4 94 48 84 46

▼ Camille 2012 Price: ○○ 89/100

CHÂTEAU LA MASCARONNE +33 4 94 37 10 64

▼ La Mascaronne Guy Da Nine 2006 Price: ○○○ 90/100

▼ La Mascaronne Vintage 2008 Price: ○○ 88/100

▼ La Mascaronne Quat'saisons 2012 Price: ○○ 87/100

CHÂTEAU LA TOUR DE L'EVÊQUE +33 4 94 28 20 17

ORG▼ Pétale de Rose 2012 Price: ○○ 87/100

ORG▼ Blanc de Blancs 2012 Price: ○○ 86/100

ORG▼ Château Barbeyrolles

Pétale de Rose 2012 Price: ○○ 86/100

CHÂTEAU MALHERBE +33 4 94 64 80 11

CV▼ Vintage 2012 Price: ○○ 89/100

CV▼ Vintage 2010 Price: ○○○ 87/100

CHÂTEAU MONT-REDON +33 4 90 83 72 75

▼ Château Riotor Vintage 2012 Price: ○ 88/100

CHÂTEAUX ET DOMAINES CASTEL +33 5 56 95 54 00

▼ Vintage 2012 Price: ○ 88/100

DOMAINE DE L'ANGUEIROUN +33 4 94 71 11 39

▼ Prestige 2011 Price: ○○ 90/100

DOMAINE DU DRAGON +33 4 98 10 23 00

▼ Cuvée Prestige 2012 Price: ○ 85/100

▼ Perle Noire 2011 Price: ○○ 85/100

DOMAINE PATRICE MOREUX +33 3 86 39 13 55

▼ Château des Vingtinières Vintage 2011 Price: ○ 86/100

▼ Château des Vingtinières Vintage 2012 Price: ○ 85/100

DOMAINES OTT +33 4 94 01 53 50

▼ Clos Mireille Vintage 2012 Price: ○○○ 91/100

▼ Château de Selle Vintage 2012 Price: ○○○ 90/100

GILARDI SA +33 4 98 10 45 45

▼ Domaine de la Vieille Tour Vintage 2012 Price: ○ 86/100

▼ Domaine de Buganay Vintage 2012 Price: ○ 86/100

▼ Bailli de Provence Price: ○ 85/100

Provence - *Côtes de Provence*

LE CERCLE DES VIGNERONS DE PROVENCE +33 4 94 37 21 00

▼ Estandon Légende 2012 Price: ❍ 84/100

LE CLOS DES ROSES +33 4 94 52 80 51

▼ Dame de Coeur 2012 Price: ❍❍ 88/100

▼ Vintage 2012 Price: ❍ 87/100

LES VIGNERONS DE TARADEAU +33 4 94 73 02 03

▼ La Trinité 2010 Price: ❍❍ 89/100

▼ L'Oppidum 2012 Price: ❍ 88/100

▼ L'Oppidum 2011 Price: ❍ 88/100

▼ L'Oppidum 2012 Price: ❍ 88/100

▼ Le Prestige 2011 Price: ❍ 88/100

▼ Le Prestige 2012 Price: ❍ 86/100

PEYRASSOL +33 4 94 69 71 02

▼ Château Peyrassol Vintage 2009 Price: ❍❍ 92/100

▼ Château Peyrassol Vintage 2010 Price: ❍❍ 89/100

▼ Commanderie de Peyrassol Vintage 2011 Price: ❍ 88/100

Côtes de Provence La Londe

DOMAINE DE L'ANGUEIROUN +33 4 94 71 11 39

▼ Prestige 2010 Price: ❍❍ 92/100

▼ Prestige 2012 Price: ❍❍ 89/100

Côtes de Provence Sainte Victoire

DOMAINE DE SAINT SER +33 4 42 66 30 81

▼ Cuvée Prestige 2007 Price: ❍❍ 91/100

▼ Cuvée de l'Ermite 2012 Price: ❍❍ 90/100

▼ Cuvée Prestige 2012 Price: ❍❍ 88/100

Detailed instructions are featured at the start of the book.

Les Baux de Provence

CHÂTEAU D'ESTOUBLON +33 4 90 54 64 00

ORG▼ Vintage 2008 Price: ❍❍ 91/100

CHÂTEAU ROMANIN +33 4 90 92 45 87

BIO▼ Vintage 2007 Price: ❍❍ 93/100

BIO▼ La Chapelle de Romanin Vintage 2010 Price: ❍❍ 90/100

Maures

DOMAINE DE L'ANGLADE +33 4 94 71 10 89

▼ Cuvée Tradition 2012 Price: ❍ 85/100

▼ Grenache - Syrah 2011 Price: ❍ 84/100

▼ Vintage 2010 Price: ❍ 84/100

▼ Le Rosé d'Anna 2012 Price: ❍ 84/100

▼ Vintage 2012 Price: ❍ 84/100

LE CLOS DES ROSES +33 4 94 52 80 51

▼ Mademoiselle Rose 2010 Price: ❍❍ 85/100

Méditerranée

DOMAINE DE L'ATTILON +33 4 90 98 70 04

ORG▼ Merlot 2012 Price: ❍ 85/100

ORG▼ Marselan 2010 Price: ❍ 85/100

ORG▼ Chardonnay 2012 Price: ❍ 85/100

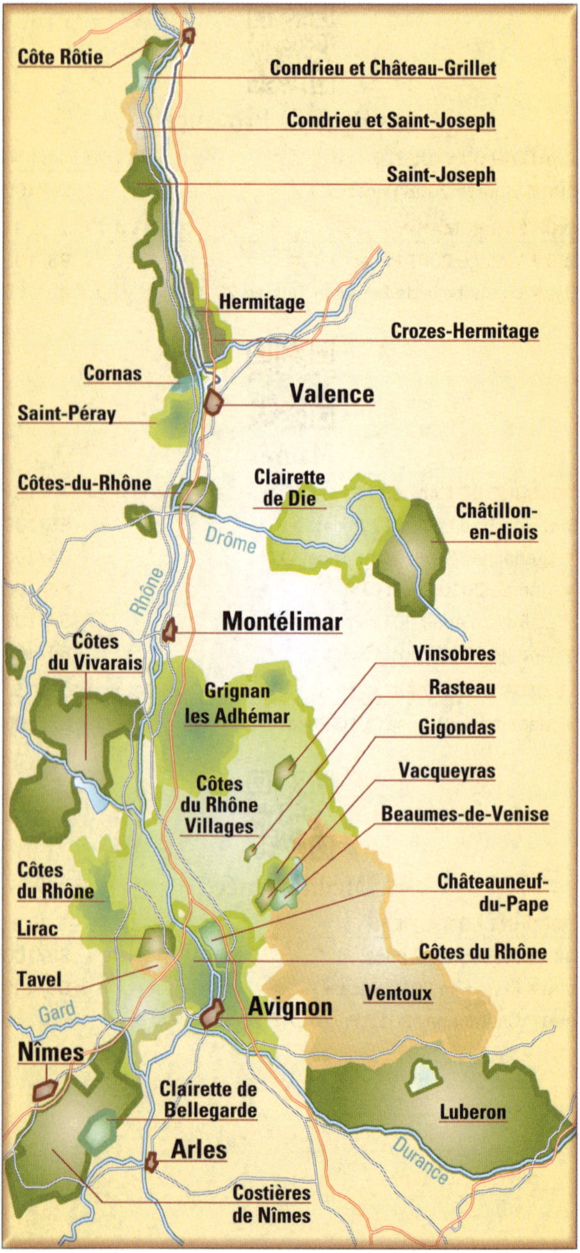
Côte Rôtie
Condrieu et Château-Grillet
Condrieu et Saint-Joseph
Saint-Joseph
Hermitage
Crozes-Hermitage
Cornas
Valence
Saint-Péray
Côtes-du-Rhône
Clairette de Die
Châtillon-en-diois
Drôme
Rhône
Montélimar
Côtes du Vivarais
Vinsobres
Rasteau
Grignan les Adhémar
Gigondas
Vacqueyras
Côtes du Rhône Villages
Beaumes-de-Venise
Côtes du Rhône
Châteauneuf-du-Pape
Lirac
Côtes du Rhône
Tavel
Ventoux
Gard
Avignon
Nîmes
Clairette de Bellegarde
Luberon
Arles
Durance
Costières de Nîmes

RHONE VALLEY

CONTEMPORARY WINES

It has become customary to divide this extensive wine growing region into two completely different parts - the North, where vines grow on a thin strip of land alongside the Rhône, before widening out towards the South. This guide book is no exception. We will review the two parts separately, starting with the North.

NORTHERN CÔTES DU RHÔNE

Unquestionably a fully-fledged member of the world's elite circle of premium quality wines, with a string of household names (Côte Rôtie, Hermitage, Condrieu...). Here, vines cling to the Rhône Valley's steepest inclines, making it sometimes impossible to introduce mechanisation.

In fact, as far back as winegrowers can remember, some sites have never seen a tractor. The only justification for enduring such adverse growing conditions is the quality of the wines (coaxed out of the outstanding 'terroir' and remarkable microclimate). Their reputation stems not only from the 'terroir', though, but also from quality grape varieties and the expertise of the wine growers. The wines are well-structured, robust, aromatic and complex. Both the reds and the whites (probably with the exception of the Viogniers) are suitable for laying down. Low yields and boutique vineyards, where harvesting can often be completed in a day, enable wine growers in the northern Côtes du Rhône to provide an extremely comprehensive range of wines in each appellation.

SOUTHERN CÔTES DU RHÔNE

This region stretches from the southern part of the Drôme department, over half of Vaucluse, the southern tip of Ardèche and along the right bank of Gard. The name 'Côte du Rhône' dates back to the 15th century when it referred to one of two areas around Uzès under the control of a magistrate which was branded onto barrels dispatched from the port of Roquemaure. Unlike its more northerly neighbour, single-crop farming is characteristic of the southern wine region. Many villages are entirely devoted to wine growing. 'Côtes du Rhône' wine is by far the most prevalent and the 'villages' (16 villages are allowed to append their name to the appellation) stand at the pinnacle of the local growths.

Producing vast quantities of wine does not preclude quality, neither at regional AC or Côtes du Rhône Villages level, and of course, even less so for the five local (or growth) appellations - Lirac, Tavel, Vacqueyras, Gigondas and Châteauneuf-du-Pape. Blending (see under varietals) is the norm for these appellations. The rosés (interestingly, Tavel only produces this colour of wine) are made by the 'bleeding' process or the direct-to-press method. Yield restrictions (35 hl/ha in Vaucluse and 42 to 48 hl/ha in Gard for the growths, 42 hl/ha for Côtes du Rhône Villages and 52 hl/ha for regional Côtes du Rhône) are one of the reasons why respectable cellars and restaurants, in France and abroad, stock southern Côtes du Rhône.

THE 'SATELLITE' WINE REGIONS

Five appellation areas are now joined to Côtes du Rhône, even though they are slightly further away from the river:

• DIE: Three appellations including two still wines (Clairette de Die, 88% of output) and Crémant de Die (12%), and one still wine appellation (Châtillon-en-Diois).

• GRIGNAN LES ADHÉMAR: Along the left bank of the Rhône in the Drôme department.

• CÔTES DU VENTOUX: Further south, stretching over 7,500 hectares amongst the foothills of Mont Ventoux, Provence's highest peak.

• CÔTES DU LUBERON: The second-largest area in Vaucluse, this proud 'terroir' growth is set within an area of outstanding natural beauty (the Luberon national park) north of the river Durance.

• COSTIÈRES DE NÎMES: This is the most southerly Rhône valley region, so much so that it borders on Languedoc (Gard department).

VARIETALS

Grenache, Mourvedre, Syrah and Cinsault take centre stage for the reds. The whites use primarily Clairette, Bourboulenc,

Viognier, Roussanne and Marsanne. In Die, Clairette Pointue an d Small Berry Muscat.

Thirteen grape varieties are permitted in Châteauneuf-du-Pape: Clairette, Grenache, Mourvedre, Syrah, Picpoul, Cinsault, Counoise, Muscardin, Terret noir, Vaccarese, Picardan, Roussanne and Bourboulenc. In actual fact, though, few wines nowadays take full advantage of this huge potential.

WINE STYLES

the northern red growths are vigorous, and in some cases (see Châteauneuf-du-Pape) warm. They require several years' cellaring (at least three to five years and more for the likes of Côte Rôtie).

The Côtes du Rhône and Côtes du Rhône-villages are immediately more approachable, except when certain styles of winemaking or ageing are used.

The whites are also heady, fragrant, sunny-clime wines with a framework supported by their acidity. As they age (Châteauneuf-du-Pape again), some scale the heights for complexity and finesse.

REVIEW OF LATEST VINTAGES

• **2010** • Low quantities yet very high quality wines. The reds are dense, aromatic and complex. The white and rosés are pure and show wonderfully refined expression. The reds need to mature but should start to produce some excellent efforts this year. Superlative wines in the north, definitely designed for cellaring.

• **2011** • an extraordinarily inconsistent year, particularly for red wines which account for the bulk of production. Harvesting began in late August, around 10 days early compared with 2010. For Syrah and Mourvèdre, the vintage is generally of an excellent standard with wonderful varietal expression and full, complex wines. Grenache shows clear differences depending on the area, where rainfall and harvest dates have a significant impact. The 2011s show abundant fruit and are similar in style to the 09s with aromas of cherry and prunes, a hint of over-ripeness and a warm edge.

• **2012** • This region experienced incessant rain combined with quite mild temperatures, causing the vines to grow exuberantly. This led to late ripening, which was compensated by uniform development. The reds are dense, with a tight tannic structure. The whites harvested early have retained a good level of acidity. A reasonable vintage.

THE RHÔNE VALLEY APPELLATIONS

A.C. BEAUMES DE VENISE

OVERVIEW: previously subsumed into the Côtes du Rhône Villages appellation, Beaumes de Venise was recently promoted to growth status. The area stretches across the south-eastern face of the Dentelles de Montmiral range (at elevations ranging from 100 to 600m), in four villages in the Vaucluse department. The soil is derived from Oxfordian marl from the Upper Cretaceous series and the Triassic, unique to the Côtes du Rhône. The climate is particularly hot because the landform acts as a buffer against the Mistral wind.

WINE STYLES: Beaumes de Venise produces powerful, mellow red wines which are generous and aromatic. They make suitable partners for meat in a sauce and game.

A.C. CHÂTEAU GRILLET

OVERVIEW: Château Grillet is one of France's smallest appellations, covering just four hectares belonging to a single owner. The area forms an enclave within the Condrieu appellation along the right bank of the Rhône. Only white wines are made here from Viognier. The soils are formed of stony sand on a granite bedrock. The vines grow on sheer, south-facing terraces sheltered from the wind.

WINE STYLES: as the grapes are harvested earlier than for Condrieu, the wines tend to be more austere, less fragrant and heady. Blessed with an attractive pale golden hue and a fresh, delicate bouquet, they are subtle, well-structured wines with a long ageing capacity (10 to 20 years). Principal aromas are lychee and camomile. They can be paired with grilled fish, seafood, shellfish, goats cheese and mi-cuit foie gras.

A.C. CHÂTEAUNEUF-DU-PAPE

OVERVIEW: this area encompasses five towns and villages set in the southern part of the Rhône Valley - Châteauneuf-du-Pape, Bédarrides, Courthézon, Orange and Sorgues. The soil is extremely stony, covered with pebbles interspersed with red clay and sand. This type of soil retains heat during the day which it releases by night. Châteauneuf-du-Pape boasts the driest climate in the region with some 2,800 hours of sunshine annually. The wines are vinted traditionally at controlled temperatures.

The reds are vatted for around three weeks to ensure maximum extraction. The permitted range of grape varieties is extensive, although many are not widely planted. For the reds: Grenache noir, Syrah, Mourvedre, Cinsault, Carignan, Terret noir, Counoise, Muscardin, Vaccarese, Camarese, Calitor and Picpoul noir. For the whites: Clairette, Bourboulenc, Roussanne, Grenache blanc, Picpoul blanc, Picardan, Marsanne, Viognier, Pascal blanc, Ugni blanc and Maccabeo.

WINE STYLES: the appellation produces both red and white wines. The red wines with their intense colour are redolent of red fruit, leather, aniseed, spices and the occasional balsamic note. They are round, unctuous, full and supple with good length on the palate. The white wines sport a translucid pale yellow colour. They are fresh and aromatic (floral notes reminiscent of vine flowers, honeysuckle and daffodils) with good staying power on the palate. The reds pair with game (leg of venison, jugged hare, roast woodpigeon) or cheese. The whites are equally delicious as appetisers or with grilled fish doused with olive oil, shellfish and rosemary-flavoured goats cheese.

A.C. CHÂTILLON-EN-DIOIS

OVERVIEW: a diminutive appellation area (60 hectares) located in the vicinity of Die, in the far eastern portion of the northern Rhône Valley. Although they are grown on the same soil types as Clairette de Die (stony hillsides, calcareous clay), wines from Châtillon-en-Diois come from the cooler zones of the Drôme Valley.

WINE STYLES: the appellation produces light, fruity red wines from Gamay, Pinot noir and Syrah which reward early drinking or pleasant, vigorous still white wines from Chardonnay and Aligoté. The reds can be served with barbecued meats cooked on a wood fire and the whites with grilled fish.

A.C. CLAIRETTE DE DIE

OVERVIEW: this area covers 32 towns and villages dotted along the Drôme Valley. The soils are calcareous clay on stony hillsides. Once the grapes have been pressed, the juice is filtered and chilled and the partially fermented must is then bottled. Alcoholic fermentation continues in the bottle, resulting in a naturally sparkling wine. Sediment is removed at least six months after bottling.

WINE STYLES: Clairette de Die is a light, fruity sparkling wine with a brilliant golden hue. The wines develop aromas of green apple, white fruit and floral notes of rose. They can be served either as appetisers or with desserts, frozen sweets, chocolate or foie gras.

A.C. CONDRIEU

OVERVIEW: the Condrieu area, a producer of white wines, is situated 11 kilometres south of Vienne, on the right bank of the Rhône, just below the red wine appellation area Côte Rôtie. Seven villages feature within the area and the vines are planted on sheer granite slopes enriched with patches of loess. The steep inclines make mechanical harvesting impossible and the crop is therefore hand-picked. Low yields warrant the expensive price tag on these wines which are intended to be drunk in their youth (between two and four years old).

WINE STYLES: the appellation only produces white wines, made from the only permitted grape variety, Viognier. Pale gold in colour, they are heady, yet supple, rich and unctuous with a touch of acidity. Principal aromas are acacia honey, violet, musk, apricot and peach. They can be served with freshwater fish, mi-cuit foie gras, goats cheese, king prawns and duck breast with peaches.

A.C. CORNAS

OVERVIEW: this appellation area is set in the northern half of the Rhône Valley, opposite the town of Valence. The only permitted varietal is Syrah which forms the basis of the area's red wines. Similarly, only one village is entitled to the appellation, Cornas in Ardeche. The vines grow on terraces supported by dry stone walls and enjoy maximum sunshine which promotes good ripening. The neighbouring hills also shield the vines from the wind, resulting in significantly higher temperatures than in Hermitage, just 11 kilometres away. The soil is granite with patches of calcareous clay. At the base of the hills, they are sandy with decomposed granite whilst in the northern part of the appellation, there tends to be more limestone. The only varietal used is Syrah.

WINE STYLES: Cornas is a powerful, robust wine in its early years. Its tannins only begin to mellow several years down the line though even then, the wines remain robust with a dark hue. Strangely, it is unlike any of its northern Rhône Valley neighbours and is often described as rustic or wild. The younger wines display aromas of red fruit and pepper, leading into aromas of truffle, amber, hazelnut and liquorice after five to ten years' ageing. They pair with wild boar in a sauce, venison cutlets marinated in Cornas wine, roast venison or jugged hare.

A.C. COSTIÈRES DE NÎMES

OVERVIEW: an appellation situated between Arles and Nîmes, north of the Camargue. This is the most easterly of the Languedoc appellations although it is officially joined to the Rhône Valley. It covers 24 towns and villages in the Gard department, on ancient alluvial soils formed of pebbles, gravel and sand bordering one of the Rhône's former river beds.

The climate is Mediterranean and the varietal range is traditional. Carignan (40% maximum), Grenache (25% minimum), Syrah and Mourvedre (20% minimum) and Cinsault (40% maximum) for the reds. Clairette, Grenache, Bourboulenc, Ugni blanc (40% maximum), with a 50% maximum supporting range of Marsanne, Roussanne, Maccabeo and Rolle for the whites.

WINE STYLES: the red wines are expressive and well-balanced. They are powerful and robust when sourced in the southern part of the appellation (facing the sea). In the northern zone, they are more supple, fruity wines for quaffing. Their aromas belong to the red fruit, wild berry and small venison range. Try with grilled meat, Sète-style rabbit or small game. The rosés, which are made using the bleeding process, develop aromas of exotic fruit (mango) and citrus fruit. They are lively wines which pair remarkably well with shellfish fritters, squid in a sweet and sour sauce, cooked cold pork meats. Shellfish and fish are a perfect match for the white wines, which are mainly drawn from Grenache blanc and Clairette and are fresh and aromatic.

A.C. CÔTE RÔTIE

OVERVIEW: an appellation set in the far northern part of the Rhône Valley. The vines grow on terraces supported by dry stone walls facing south-east, which provides them with maximum sunshine. Three villages are entitled to the appellation: Ampuis, Saint-Cyr-sur-le-Rhône and Tupin-et-Semons.

The Côte Rôtie area is divided into two parts: Côte Blonde and Côte Brune. Côte Blonde is home to steep granite terraces covered with a layer of siliceous limestone, whilst in Côte Brune the soil is iron oxide-rich clay. The wines are vinted traditionally with relatively long vatting periods (two to three weeks) and aged for 18 to 36 months in oak casks which are often new.

WINE STYLES: these red wines are single varietals made

from Syrah, occasionally augmented with a tiny proportion of Viognier. Their deep red colour with purple tints takes on orangy-yellow tints when they reach 10 to 15 years of age. The wines are extremely well-structured, tannic and unctuous with a characteristic intense bouquet. Wines from Côte Blonde tend not to keep for as long as those from Côte Brune. They display aromas of violet, spices (pepper, vanilla), red fruit (raspberry), black fruit and undergrowth. They pair with water fowl, subtly-flavoured meats (roasted young wild boar), truffles and asparagus.

A.C. COTEAUX DE DIE

OVERVIEW: this is a young appellation set in the Die area, east of the northern Rhône Valley. The soils are primarily calcareous clay and shale marl. The grapes (Clairette) are sent straight to the press, vinted traditionally and then aged for six to eight months.
WINE STYLES: Coteaux de Die are still white wines sporting a golden hue with greenish tints. Usually dry and fresh, they develop fragrances of flowers and green apple. Recommended pairings include fish, shellfish and goats cheese.

A.C. CÔTES DU RHÔNE

OVERVIEW: this is the Rhône Valley's largest appellation (the second-largest in France, after Bordeaux). It covers 163 towns and villages spread over six departments, from Vienne to Avignon - Loire, Rhône, Ardèche, Gard, Drôme and Vaucluse, with most of the area under vine in the last three. The soils are granite in the north and alluvium on limestone in the south. Many areas are also home to gravel from the Alps mountain range.
The climate is Mediterranean with the characteristic Mistral wind. Seasonal rainfall, hot temperatures and outstanding sunshine are all distinctive features of the region. The wines are vinted traditionally at controlled temperatures. Most of the wines are aged in tanks though occasionally oak casks are used. The varietal range is extremely broad. Grenache noir, Syrah, Mourvedre, Cinsault, Carignan, Terret noir, Counoise, Muscardin, Vaccarese, Camarese, Calitor and Picpoul noir for the reds. Clairette, Bou rboulenc, Roussanne, Grenache blanc, Picpoul blanc, Picardan, Marsanne, Viognier, Pascal blanc, Ugni blanc and Maccabeo for the whites.
WINE STYLES: 95% of the wines grown in this appellation area are red and can be divided into two main styles. Some are rich, generous wines with mellow tannins that are intended for cella-

ring. Others are not unlike 'primeur' wines and are light, fruity and vigorous. Predominant aromas are small red and black fruit (red currant, blackcurrant, bilberry, blackberry), spicy and animal notes. Try with Provençal beef stew, leg of mutton with garlic, chicken sauteed with onions… The white and rosé wines, produced on a much smaller scale, are well-balanced and round. The rosés with their fruity bouquet of pear drop and quince paste, pair with barbecues and cooked cold pork meats. The whites exude floral fragrances (linden) or white peach and honey, depending on the varietal. Notes of kiwi and grapefruit may also be present. They are well suited to grilled fish and shellfish.

A.C. CÔTES DU RHÔNE VILLAGES

OVERVIEW: set within the Côtes du Rhône area, this appellation embraces 95 towns and villages spread over the departments of Drôme, Vaucluse, Gard and Ardèche. This takes it either side of the Rhône, from the south of Montélimar to the south of Avignon. Soil types vary from granite in the north, alluvium on a limestone bedrock in the south, both of which often come together in the shape of gravely terraces. The climate is Mediterranean, hot and dry, with the characteristic Mistral wind and maximum sunshine. The term Côtes du Rhône Villages can feature as such on the label or it can be extended with the name of one of 17 villages – Cairanne, Chusclan, Laudun, Puymeras, Roaix, Rochegude, Rousset, Sablet, Saint-Maurice, Saint-Gervais, Saint-Pantaléon, Séguret, Signargues, Valréas and Visan, as well as two site-specific areas: Plan de Dieu and Massif d'Uchaux.

WINE STYLES: AC Côtes du Rhône Villages produces sturdy, heady wines which do not go overboard on tannic astringency and have a silky finish. Principal aromas are fig, stone fruits and liquorice. They pair with cured mountain hams, wild boar stew, bull casserole and cheeses.

A.C. CÔTES DU RHÔNE VILLAGES CAIRANNE

OVERVIEW: Cairanne is situated in the Vaucluse department, in the southern Rhône Valley. Vines grow here on red soil, sandstone, clay terraces and sandy molasse. The appellation produces red, rosé and white wines.

WINE STYLES: the red wines are well-structured, unctuous and spicy with an elegant finish. They display aromas of small black fruit, leather and spices. This type of wine does in fact pair well with spices, Asian or exotic cuisine. The rosé wines are lively and well-balanced. The white wines are round and elegant with floral and vegetal tones (grilled fish).

A.C. CÔTES DU RHÔNE VILLAGES CHUSCLAN

OVERVIEW: an area spread over five villages in Gard. The vines occupy gravely hills and terraces and occasional sandy patches. The appellation produces red and rosé wines.

WINE STYLES: the reds are well-balanced, easy drinking wines with average strength. Try with stew or roast beef. The fleshy, unctuous rosés make good partners for subtly-flavoured cold cuts or barbecued meats.

A.C. CÔTES DU RHÔNE VILLAGES LAUDUN

OVERVIEW: the vines are planted on stony or gravely slopes, terraces formed of pebbles, covering three villages in Gard. Laudun produces red, rosé and white wines.

WINE STYLES: the red wines with their crimson hue are powerful and tannic. They exude aromas of stone fruit and spices. They can be served with meat, game or cheese. The delicate, supple rosé wines display enticing floral aromas. The fat, fruity white wines are buttressed by moorland notes. They pair with shellfish, grilled fish and poultry.

A.C. CÔTES DU RHÔNE VILLAGES MASSIF D'UCHAUX

OVERVIEW: AC Massif d'Uchaux is spread over five villages in Vaucluse. Soil type is mainly siliceous and limestone sandstone at elevations of between 100 and 280m.

WINE STYLES: tightly-woven red wines displaying attractive body and fat are grown here. The standard of quality is excellent and the wines are very consistent.

A.C. CÔTES DU RHÔNE VILLAGES PLAN DE DIEU

OVERVIEW: the area embraces four villages and occupies an extensive alluvial terrace topped with Quaternary limestone stones. Beneath the stones is either blue clay (Pliocene) or sandstone beds which draw up all-important water during the summer months. The name 'Plan de Dieu' is derived from the many local religious foundations which grew vines here over a long period of time.

WINE STYLES: Plan de Dieu produces powerful, well-balanced red wines suited to barbecues and meat served in a sauce.

A.C. CÔTES DU RHÔNE VILLAGES PUYMÉRAS

OVERVIEW: this area extends over five villages set in steep-sided valleys (elevations ranging from 220 to 600 metres) straddling Drôme and Vaucluse. It occupies stony terraces littered with pebbles.

WINE STYLES: Puyméras produces powerful, well-structured red wines.

A.C. CÔTES DU RHÔNE VILLAGES ROAIX

OVERVIEW: the Roaix area is set between Rasteau and Séguret. It stretches over land belonging to the village of the same name, in the Vaucluse department. The vines occupy stony or gravely terraces and decalcified clay slopes. Roaix produces red, rosé and white wines.

WINE STYLES: the reds are supple, delicate and extremely feminine wines with subtle tannins. They display aromas of red fruit and spices. The rosé wines are extremely fruity and refreshing. The white wines are fresh and well-balanced. The reds pair with game and red meat, the rosés barbecues and cooked cold pork meats and the whites, fish.

A.C. CÔTES DU RHÔNE VILLAGES ROCHEGUDE

OVERVIEW: the Rochegude area is spread over a single village of the same name in southern Drôme. It produces red, rosé and white wines.

WINE STYLES: the red wines are supple, round and warm with fragrances of black fruit and peach stone. The rosé wines are powerful and unctuous with a slightly acidulous flavour. They display aromas of red fruit (red currant, raspberry). The whites exhibit tell-tale vegetal flavours and floral tones (honeysuckle).

A.C. CÔTES DU RHÔNE VILLAGES ROUSSET-LES-VIGNES

OVERVIEW: the area covers just one village, Rousset-les-Vignes, in the Drôme department. Sheer hillside sites of sandstone and stone soils are home to the vines.

WINE STYLES: only red wines are grown here. They display a characteristic deep ruby-red hue, compact body, well-integrated tannins and woody flavour. They are suited to cellaring and reward a few years ageing by gaining finesse. They display fragrances of red fruit and are a perfect match for all types of meat.

A.C. CÔTES DU RHÔNE VILLAGES SABLET

OVERVIEW: the entire area is set in just one village, Sablet, which is adjacent to Gigondas in the Vaucluse department. The soils are sandy and clayey. Sablet produces red, rosé and white wines.

WINE STYLES: the red wines are full, round and well-structured, with elegant overtones. They display aromas of red fruit, violet and blackcurrant and pair well with game. The powerful, fat, warm rosés exhibit a fruity bouquet with predominant aromas of raspberry. They are a good match for barbecues. The white wines display well-integrated acidity and fragrances of green apple and freshly-cut hay, evolving over time into aromas of gingerbread. Try with fish and shellfish.

A.C. CÔTES DU RHÔNE VILLAGES SÉGURET

OVERVIEW: the area covers the village of Séguret in the Vaucluse department. Séguret produces red, rosé and white wines on hillside sites and calcareous clay terraces.

WINE STYLES: the red wines are supple and fruity with a fruity bouquet, almond and tobacco tones. They can be served with poultry. The rosés and the whites are delicate and elegant, developing a fruity bouquet brimming with freshness. Try with fish, seafood and cheese.

A.C. CÔTES DU RHÔNE VILLAGES SIGNARGUES

OVERVIEW: this is the most southerly of the Côtes du Rhône Villages appellations with a site specific name. Pebbled terraces, sand or Pliocene marl reddened by iron oxide at an average elevation of 150 metres above the Rhône, provide the context for the wines.

WINE STYLES: Signargues only produces red wines.

A.C. CÔTES DU RHÔNE VILLAGES SAINT-GERVAIS

OVERVIEW: the entire area covers the village of Saint-Gervais in the Gard department. The soils are sandstone on the hillside sites and more stony on the plateau. Saint-Gervais produces red, rosé and white wines.

WINE STYLES: the elegant, well-balanced, unctuous red wines are long on the palate and suitable for cellaring. They display aromas of red and stone fruit and are a good match for game, either roasted or served with a sauce. The rosé wines are elegant, fat and warm with fragrances of raspberry and strawberry. Try them with aubergine caviar, crudités, melon or Parma ham. The white wines are fresh and light with a fresh, floral bouquet. Marry them with grilled fish, prawn kebabs or shellfish.

A.C. CÔTES DU RHÔNE VILLAGES SAINT-MAURICE

OVERVIEW: the entire area covers the village of Saint-Maurice-sur-Eygues in the Drôme department. The soil is calcareous clay, with varying amounts of gravel, and some areas of lighter sandstone. Saint-Maurice produces red, rosé and white wines.

WINE STYLES: the red wines are elegant, not overly powerful, with a distinctively full attack and pleasant finish. They display a bouquet of red fruit leading into woody notes as they age. The rosés are characteristically fresh with a fresh, fruit-forward bouquet. The whites are extremely aromatic with fragrances of peach, apricot and violet.

A.C. CÔTES DU RHÔNE VILLAGES SAINT-PANTALÉON-LES-VIGNES

OVERVIEW: the area covers the village of Saint-Pantaléon, in the southern part of the Drôme department. The vines occupy calcareous clay hillsides with a few sandy patches and produce red and rosé wines.

WINE STYLES: the red wines are well-balanced with supple tannins and good length on the palate. The rosé wines are delicate, with a slight fruit flavour. Both the reds and the rosés display a fruity bouquet. The reds can be served with coq au vin or Provencal-style chicken. Cooked cold pork meats are the perfect match for the rosés.

A.C. CÔTES DU RHÔNE VILLAGES VALRÉAS

OVERVIEW: the are covers the village of Valréas, in the Vaucluse department. Hillside sites and terraces of red clay with varying amounts of stones are home to the vines. Valréas produces red, rosé and white wines.

WINE STYLES: the red wines are moderately powerful and are well-balanced and round. They display aromas of red fruit (raspberry, red currant and blackcurrant). The rosé wines are extremely fruity and acidulous. The white wines are dry, lively and aromatic, fruity with vanilla tones. The reds and the rosés can pair with barbecues and the whites with grilled fish and seafood.

A.C. CÔTES DU RHÔNE VILLAGES VISAN

OVERVIEW: the area covers the village of Visan in the Vaucluse department. The soil is calcareous clay and extremely stony. Visan produces red, rosé and white wines.

WINE STYLES: the red wines are full and supple with elegant tannins. They exhibit a complex bouquet of fruit, vanilla, blackcurrant and truffle. The rosés are elegant and fresh with a slight peppery touch. The whites are unctuous and fruity with fragrances of crushed grapes and lemon peel. All three are the perfect match for truffle-based dishes (scrambled eggs with truffles for example).

A.C. CÔTES DU VIVARAIS

OVERVIEW: situated in the north-western portion of the southern Côtes du Rhône, this area straddles the departments of Ardèche and Gard, with 577 hectares under vine. Of the 14 villages it embraces, only Orgnac, Saint-Remèze and Saint-Montan are entitled to add their name to the appellation. The soils are shallow calcareous clay. Varietals used are Syrah, Grenache, Mourvedre, Cinsault and Carignan.

WINE STYLES: the deeply-coloured red wines are well-balanced and well-structured with a long-lasting finish. Aromas of bell pepper, violet, blackcurrant and raspberry are present. Try them with meat served in a sauce or game. The rosés are harmonious, round and delicious (fragrances of red currant, blackcurrant, raspberry and floral notes) and pair with lamb loin chops. The whites are vigorous and well-balanced on the palate. They develop a floral bouquet (acacia, hawthorn), white fruit (quince, apple, peach) and a touch of hazelnut. Try with fish soup, trout or goats cheese.

A.C. CRÉMANT DE DIE

OVERVIEW: this appellation shares the same boundaries as Clairette de Die. The Clairette varietal forms the backbone of the blend, though a little Aligoté and small berry Muscat can be added. Crémant de Die is vinted traditionally. After pressing and initial must fermentation, secondary fermentation occurs in the bottle after a blend of sugar and yeasts has been added. The sediment (dead yeast deposits) is subsequently removed by disgorging.

WINE STYLES: Crémant de Die is a sparkling white wine with a brilliant, gold-tinted hue and small bubbles. As a rule, it is fresh, dry and soft with good length on the palate. Aromas of fresh flowers and a tell-tale buttery touch are present. Try as an appetiser or with fish.

A.C. CROZES-HERMITAGE

OVERVIEW: this area is set in the northern part of the Rhône Valley. It forms a boundary around Hermitage in the north and south and embraces 11 villages surrounding Tain-l'Hermitage. Soil types vary greatly with primarily granite hillside sites in the north and alluvium and terraces covered with pebbles of various origins in the south. The red wines are made from Syrah, the white wines from Marsanne and Roussanne.

WINE STYLES: the Crozes-Hermitage appellation produces red and white wines. The deeply-coloured red wines are supple and aromatic. They display aromas of blackcurrant, vanilla, cinnamon, liquorice and menthol notes. Try with a rack of lamb or roast chicken. The floral, elegant white wines are supple and fat, displaying fragrances of almond, passion fruit and white flowers. Serve them with eel in a parsley and garlic sauce, fish in a sauce or goats cheese.

A.C. GIGONDAS

OVERVIEW: this area is situated in the southern part of the Rhône valley, in the village of Gigondas (Vaucluse). The soils are formed of stony alluvium rich in red clay, spread over rolling hills or huge terraces. The climate is Mediterranean, characterised by a distinctive period of drought in the summer and the fierce Mistral wind. The vines bask in 2,800 hours of sunshine every year. The wines are vinted traditionally at controlled temperatures. They undergo prolonged vatting and are aged in oak tuns. The red varietal range is comprehensive: Grenache noir, Syrah, Mourvedre, Cinsault, Carignan, Terret noir, Counoise, Muscardin, Vaccarese, Camarese, Calitor and Picpoul noir.

WINE STYLES: the Gigondas appellation produces red and rosé wines. The red wines are robust, well-balanced and powerful though can occasionally be slightly severe in their youth. They are usually wines with a long cellaring capacity, developing finesse and elegance over time. The aromatic range, predominantly red and black fruit and kirsch over the first few years, leads into wilder aromas of undergrowth and animal notes with age. The deeply-coloured rosé wines are heady and generous, although they reward early drinking. They display fragrances of almond and stewed fruit. The reds pair with wild boar stew and the rosés with duck gizzards salad.

A.C. GRIGNAN LES ADHÉMAR

OVERVIEW: the area stretches over the left bank of the Rhône, from south of Montélimar to north of Bollène. It embraces 22 towns and villages in the Drôme department. The soil is formed of extremely stony ancient alluvium and sandy hillside sites. The red grape varieties used are typical of the Rhône: Grenache noir, Syrah, Mourvedre, Cinsault, Carignan, Terret noir, Counoise, Muscardin, Vaccarese, Camarese, Calitor and Picpoul noir.

WINE STYLES: AC Grignan les Adhémar produces red, rosé and white wines, although the latter two are grown more on a boutique scale. The red wines are robust and elegant with a pleasant bouquet, displaying aromas of raspberry, bell pepper and spices. Try with grilled lamb chops or grilled spatchcock. The rosés exhibit an elegant, bright salmon-pink hue. Round and warm, they develop fragrances of flowers (hawthorn) and fresh fruit. Try with pistou soup, tomato omelette or salad niçoise with anchovies. The whites display a bright, pale golden hue and scents of white flowers. They have a rich, full mouthfeel with a pronounced floral character. For shellfish or fish.

A.C. HERMITAGE

OVERVIEW: the appellation area is located in three villages set on the left bank of the Rhône, in the northern portion of the valley. Terraces chiselled into the sheer hillsides are home to the vines here. The soils are predominantly granite though for many years the area was divided into climate-specific sites, each with its own soil make-up. The climate sites situated along the far western end of the hill are formed of gravel and sand on a granite bedrock. On the lower climate sites, clay dominates, whilst calcareous clay occurs on the higher sites. The wines are vinted traditionally at controlled temperatures. Both the red and white wines can be aged either in tanks or oak casks.

WINE STYLES: the Hermitage appellation produces both red and white wines. As in the neighbouring appellations, the red wines are single varietal Syrah. As a rule of thumb, they display a deep red hue evolving into an orangy colour down the years, and an extremely fragrant nose. These wines are opulent, sumptuous, elegant and will keep for twenty to thirty years. Aromas of violet, peony, blackcurrant, raspberry, spices, truffle, leather and prune are present. Try with game served in a sauce, for example. The white wines are drawn from Marsanne, with a small proportion of Roussanne. They exhibit a pretty golden hue, are fat and full with an elegant framework. The best examples come from vineyards set on the highest elevations. They display fragrances of flowers, unroasted coffee, gunflint, vanilla and toasted almonds, leading into notes of honey and wax as they mature. They marry extremely well with lamb curry, pastilla or chicken tajine with lemon confit.

A.C. LIRAC

OVERVIEW: situated in the southern part of the Rhône Valley, this area stretches over four villages in Gard. The vines occupy pebbled terraces rich in loess and sand. The climate is typically Mediterranean with an average 2,700 hours of sunshine every year. The red wines undergo prolonged maceration. The rosés are made by the bleeding method. The varietal range is typically Mediterranean: Grenache noir, Syrah, Mourvedre, Cinsault and Carignan for the reds. Clairette, Grenache blanc, Bourboulenc, Ugni blanc, Marsanne and Roussanne for the whites.

WINE STYLES: the red wines boast an attractive, deep hue and are robust, generous and well-balanced. They reward ageing by becoming full and fleshy. Their aromatic range is dominated by red fruit and spices. Try with red meat or game. The rosé wines, also very popular, are elegant with a full mouthfeel. They marry very well with aioli, mixed salads, courgette or aubergine tart, or subtly-flavoured cold cuts. The white wines are lively and aromatic with good roundness on the palate. They exude floral notes. Enjoyable with grilled Mediterranean fish or seafood.

A.C. LUBERON

The second-largest winegrowing area in the Vaucluse, this proud terroir wine has its origin in a site of extraordinary natural beauty (Luberon Natural Park) north of the Durance River.

OVERVIEW: AC Côtes du Luberon extends over 3,500 hectares situated between Cavaillon and Apt, south-east of Avignon. The appellation area is adjacent to Côtes du Ventoux in the north and Coteaux de Pierrevert in the east. The appellation is divided between thirty-six towns and villages, all set within the Luberon national park. 80% of estates belong to the local co-operative wineries.

Soil types vary from stones on ancient terraces to sand on Miocene molasse and stones of glacial scree. The wines are vinted traditionally at controlled temperatures and most of them are tank aged, though some are aged in casks. Red varietals are Grenache noir, Syrah, Mourvedre, Cinsault and Carignan. White varietals are Grenache blanc, Clairette, Bourboulenc, Ugni blanc and Vermentino.

WINE STYLES: the appellation produces red, rosé and white wines. The red wines, with their crimson hue, are full and racy. They exhibit aromas of blackcurrant, blackberry, bilberry, notes of bell pepper, truffle, leather and undergrowth. Try with red meat and game (wild boar with sage, wild rabbit with savory). The rosés are well-structured and generous with great freshness and fragrances of raspberry and wild strawberry (fish, white meat, cooked cold pork meats). The white wines are harmonious, lively and well-balanced with good length on the palate. They display floral notes (linden, honeysuckle), vine peaches, apricot and unripe quince. They pair well with grilled fish or goats cheese.

A.C. MUSCAT DE BEAUMES DE VENISE

OVERVIEW: the village of Beaumes de Venise is situated in the Vaucluse department, at the foot of the famous Dentelles de Montmirail mountains which act as a natural buffer, deflecting the strong gusts of the Mistral wind. The soil is formed of soft limestone with patches of sandstone. As a whole, it is light with very few stones and the climate is Mediterranean, making it well-suited to the small berry Muscat grape variety.

WINE STYLES: AC Muscat de Beaumes de Venise produces a renowned dessert wine which displays a pretty, limpid, brilliant pale yellow hue with golden tints. On the palate, aromas are reminiscent of the nose, with characteristic scents of passion fruit, apricot and honey. There are also lashings of freshness underscored by notes of peppermint. These wines are generous, rich and should be served chilled when young. They are equally delicious as appetisers or with melon served with a slice of cured ham, fried foie gras or fruit sorbets.

A.C. RASTEAU

OVERVIEW: covering just one village of the same name in Vaucluse, Rasteau owes its reputation to its red and golden dessert wines drawn from the Grenache varietal. Only later was the village promoted to Rasteau appellation for its red wines. Rosés and whites are grown on a very small scale. The soils are limestone on a bedrock of marl or sandstone.

WINE STYLES: the red wines with their deep, brilliant hue are generous and well-balanced with good length on the palate enhanced by aromas of very ripe red fruit, vanilla and pepper. The rosés are heady and the whites fresh and fruity. The reds are a good match for rack of lamb or stew, the rosés for barbecues or mixed salads and the whites as appetisers or with grilled fish and seafood.

A.C. RASTEAU (SWEET WINES)

OVERVIEW: the Rasteau area is situated in the heart of the southern Rhône, north of Séguret and south of Vaison-la-Romaine. Rasteau is a dessert wine, which refers to sweet red and white wines made primarily from the Grenache grape variety. The wines are made by arresting fermentation with spirit ('mutage'). The juice is obtained either by the direct-to-press method or by bleeding. After settling for 24 hours, fermentation begins at a controlled temperature of 18° C. When natural grape sugar content has dropped to around 90g/l, 96% vol. brandy is added to arrest fermentation. Maceration continues for ten days or so after brandy has been added, followed by the ageing phase which lasts for about one year in old casks.

WINE STYLES: the whites display a superb bronze coloured hue with a taste that melts in the mouth and a lingering finish characterised by honey, toasted hazelnut and dried apricot. The reds display a deep red hue. On the palate, they are full and velvety, with overtones of ripe fruit leading into prune and cherries in brandy. The whites can be served with honey cake, fruit salad or orange-flavoured desserts. The reds are delicious either as appetisers or with chocolate-based desserts.

A.C. SAINT-JOSEPH

OVERVIEW: the Saint-Joseph area extends over fifty or so kilometres, along the right bank of the Rhône, between the Condrieu and Cornas appellations. The appellation, which produces red and white wines, embraces 23 towns and villages in Ardèche and three in Loire. The soil is poor (shale and gneiss on a bedrock of granite).

WINE STYLES: Saint-Joseph red wines are fruity and pleasant. The best examples come from Mauves, Tournon, Saint-Jean-de-Mujols, Lemps, Vion and Glun, north of Cornas. They exhibit aromas of raspberry, blackcurrant, black cherry, violet and liquorice and pair well with braised ham or rabbit casserole. The white wines are fresh and relatively robust with good acidity and pleasant fruitiness, with fragrances of peach, apricot, pear, hawthorn, acacia and honey. They pair with rosemary-flavoured goats cheese or turbot in a mustard sauce.

A.C. SAINT-PÉRAY

OVERVIEW: situated on the right bank of the Rhône, south of AC Cornas, this area only produces still and sparkling white wines. Most of the soils are granite though there are also occurrences of limestone scree on the western slopes as well as Quaternary alluvium. The climate in this area is cooler than in other parts of the Valley. The still wines are vinted traditionally at controlled temperatures. The sparkling wines undergo secondary fermentation in the bottle using the traditional method. Marsanne and Roussanne are the two varietals blended to make the wines.

WINE STYLES: Saint-Péray produces primarily sparkling white wines (70%) though also a small amount of still white wines, reminiscent of Saint-Joseph. The sparkling wines are highly distinctive. Sporting a pale golden hue, they usually have better vinosity and lower acidity than other French sparklers. The still wines on the other hand are dry, vigorous and extremely floral. As they mature, they sometimes become more fat and round. They develop aromas of hawthorn, apricot, brioche notes, white fruit, almond and mineral notes. They can be served either as an appetiser or with young guinea-fowl cooked in honey.

A.C. TAVEL

OVERVIEW: situated in the southern part of the Rhône Valley, this area is restricted to a single village, Tavel. The soils are formed of fine sand covered with pebbles, interspersed with fine sandy clay and with limestone in the west. During the wine making process, after cold maceration, the grapes are pressed and the free-run juice is blended with the press juice prior to alcoholic fermentation. Grape varieties used are Grenache noir, Syrah, Cinsault, Clairette, Bourboulenc...

WINE STYLES: Tavel is a rosé wine only appellation boasting a long-standing reputation. Sporting an attractive onion skin colour with ruby-red tints evolving into livelier, more rosé style shades, Tavel is round on the palate with great aromatic power and a spicy finish. It is highly unusual in that it ages well. Tavel wines display fragrances of red fruit leading into notes of stone fruit and toasted almonds. They are suitable partners for fish, white or red meats though also exotic cuisine.

A.C. VACQUEYRAS

OVERVIEW: Vacqueyras covers two villages in Vaucluse, at the foot of the famous Dentelles de Montmirail mountains. The soil make-up is reasonably varied, ranging from stony terraces, to sandy soils on the hillside sites, sandstone, limestone and sandy marl. The climate here is Mediterranean, dry, hot and windy with long sunshine hours. The varietal range is extremely broad-ranging: Grenache noir, Syrah, Mourvedre, Cinsault, Carignan, Terret noir, Counoise, Muscardin, Vaccarese, Camarese, Calitor and Picpoul noir for the reds. Grenache blanc, Clairette, Bourboulenc, Marsanne, Roussanne and Viognier for the whites.

WINE STYLES: the appellation produces red, rosé and white wines. The red wines, with their deep tint, are robust and full, well-balanced and long. They exhibit aromas of fig, ripe stone fruit and black cherry with liquorice notes. As powerful wines, they pair well with game and meats served in a sauce. The full, generous rosés pair with barbecues and aioli. The whites are delicate and floral with their fragrances of honey, dried and acidulous fruit, flowers... Try with fish or shellfish.

A.C. VENTOUX

Farther south, these 7,500 hectares of vineyards stretch to the foothills of Mont Ventoux, the highest point in Provence.

OVERVIEW: 51 towns and villages, all in the Vaucluse department, share this appellation. The area is delineated in the north by Vaison-la-Romaine and by Apt, in the south. There are two distinct 'terroirs': a Rhône-style 'terroir' producing more robust wines and a more southerly-style 'terroir' where the wines are lighter, less concentrated. Eighty-five percent of the wines are made in co-operative wineries, with a balance of independent wineries. Soils vary from hard limestone to Tertiary sediment and scree littered with pebbles. The climate is Mediterranean although it enjoys the moderating influence of Mont Ventoux (harsher winters, wetter summers and cooler nights). Mont Ventoux, which reaches a peak at 1,912 metres, though also the Dentelles de Montmirail and Monts du Vaucluse mountain ranges provide a buffer to the Mistral wind. The varietal range is typical of the Rhône. Grenache noir, Syrah, Mourvedre, Cinsault, Carignan, Counoise, Picpoul noir... for the reds. Clairette, Bourboulenc, Grenache blanc and Roussanne for the whites.

WINE STYLES: although they are well-constituted, red Côtes du Ventoux tend to be less powerful than neighbouring Côtes du Rhône. They boast characteristic fruit (blackcurrant, raspberry) and freshness, particularly in their youth. Fragrances of flowers and spices (pepper, liquorice) are also present. They are served with meat in a sauce, sophisticated dishes with truffles and game. The rosés display a hue ranging from pink with purple tints to salmon-pink. They boast fragrances of fresh fruit and white flowers. On the palate, they are elegant and fruity. The white wines, which are still made on a boutique scale, display an attractive pale yellow hue with greenish tints. They are lively, fresh and elegant with fragrances of flowers and citrus fruit. Try with shellfish or grilled fish.

A.C. VINSOBRES

OVERVIEW: centring on the village of Vinsobres, this area stretches over 7 kilometres of rolling hills in the Drôme department. Vines grow on stony and sandy marl hillsides, and similarly stony terraces. Vinsobres produces red, rosé and white wines.

WINE STYLES: the red wines are reasonably powerful with a certain amount of freshness, they are well-balanced and long on the palate. They can be served with strongly-flavoured meats. The generous rosés are quaffing wines with aromas of ripe fruit and citrus fruit. They are suitable for barbecues. The harmonious white wines are long on the palate and develop a complex bouquet of white flesh fruit (peach, apricot) and exotic notes. Perfect as appetisers or with shellfish.

RHONE VALLEY

Ardèche

DOMAINE DE VIGIER	+33 4 75 88 01 18
▼ Cuvée Mathilde 2011 Price: ❍	89/100
▼ Vintage 2012 Price: ❍	86/100
▼ VO 2011 Price: ❍	86/100
▼ Syrah 2011 Price: ❍	85/100
▼ Cuvée Inès 2011 Price: ❍	85/100

Beaumes de Venise

ARNOUX ET FILS	+33 4 90 65 84 18
▼ Vieux Clocher Les Ravards 2012 Price: ❍	84/100
DOMAINE DES BERNARDINS	+33 4 90 62 94 13
▼ Vintage 2011 Price: ❍	86/100
DOMAINE SAINT AMANT	+33 4 90 62 99 25
▼ Grangeneuve 2011 Price: ❍❍	87/100
VIGNERONS DE BALMA VENITIA - BEAUMES DE VENISE	+33 4 90 12 41 00
▼ Terres du Trias 2011 Price: ❍	89/100
▼ v.i.v.r.e 2011 Price: ❍	89/100
▼ Domaine de la Chêneraie Vintage 2011 Price: ❍	88/100
▼ Vintage 2011 Price: ❍	87/100
▼ Terres de Bel Air 2010 Price: ❍	87/100
▼ Terres des Farisiens 2011 Price: ❍	87/100
▼ Domaine Pied Redon Vintage 2011 Price: ❍	87/100
VIGNOBLES LA COTERIE	+33 4 90 12 41 33
▼ La Coterie Vintage 2011 Price: ❍	87/100

Châteauneuf du Pape

ARNOUX ET FILS +33 4 90 65 84 18

▼ Vieux Clocher Symphonie des Galets 2010 Price: ❍❍ 87/100

CHÂTEAU DE MANISSY +33 4 66 82 86 94

CV▼ Vintage 2011 Price: ❍❍❍ 87/100

CHÂTEAU HUSSON +33 4 90 76 87 76

CV▼ Les Saintes Vierges 2010 Price: ❍❍❍ 91/100

CV▼ Les Saintes Vierges 2009 Price: ❍❍❍ 90/100

CV▼ Les Saumades 2010 Price: ❍❍ 89/100

CHÂTEAU MONT-REDON +33 4 90 83 72 75

▼ Vintage 2010 Price: ❍❍❍ 91/100

▼ Vintage 2012 Price: ❍❍❍ 89/100

DOMAINE DE LA MEREUILLE +33 4 90 34 10 68

▼ Les Baptaurels 2010 Price: ❍❍❍ 89/100

▼ Vintage 2008 Price: ❍❍❍ 89/100

DOMAINE DES 3 CELLIER +33 4 90 02 04 62

▼ Eternelle 2011 Price: ❍❍❍❍ 92/100

▼ Privilège 2011 Price: ❍❍❍ 91/100

▼ Marceau 2011 Price: ❍❍❍ 88/100

▼ Alchimie 2011 Price: ❍❍ 88/100

▼ L'Insolente 2011 Price: ❍❍❍ 88/100

DOMAINE JULIETTE AVRIL +33 4 90 83 72 69

▼ Cuvée Maxence 2011 Price: ❍❍❍ 92/100

▼ Vintage 2011 Price: ❍❍ 89/100

DOMAINE LUCIEN BARROT & FILS +33 4 90 83 70 90

▼ Vintage 2011 Price: ❍❍ 88/100

▼ Vintage 2010 Price: ❍❍❍ 87/100

LE CELLIER DES PRINCES +33 4 90 70 21 44

▼ Le Blason du Prince 2012 Price: ❍❍ 87/100

▼ Vintage 2012 Price: ❍❍ 86/100

VIGNOBLES LA COTERIE +33 4 90 12 41 33

▼ La Coterie Vintage 2007 Price: ○○ 89/100

▼ La Coterie Vintage 2008 Price: ○○ 87/100

Clairette de Die

CAVE MONGE GRANON +33 4 75 21 74 93

▼ Tradition Price: ○ 84/100

Condrieu

CAVE CHIRAT +33 4 74 56 68 92

▼ Vignobles Chirat Vintage 2011 Price: ○○○ 84/100

DOMAINE GILLES FLACHER +33 4 75 34 09 97

▼ Gilles Flacher Les Rouelles 2011 Price: ○○○ 88/100

DOMAINE MOUTON PÈRE ET FILS +33 4 74 87 82 36

▼ Domaine Mouton Côte Chatillon 2011 Price: ○○○ 91/100

DOMAINE NIERO +33 4 74 56 86 99

▼ Rémi Niero Chéry 2011 Price: ○○○ 94/100

▼ Rémi Niero Les Ravines 2011 Price: ○○○ 91/100

JB VINS +33 6 31 20 09 18

▼ Cuvée Petit Bonheur by Josepha 2009 Price: ○○○ 88/100

Costières de Nîmes

CHÂTEAU BEAUBOIS +33 4 66 73 30 59

CV▼ Harmonie 2010 Price: ○○ 89/100

CV▼ Confidence 2011 Price: ○○ 87/100

CV▼ Cuvée Expression 2011 Price: ○ 86/100

CV▼ Elégance 2011 Price: ○ 85/100

Rhone Valley - *Costières de Nîmes*

CHÂTEAU GUIOT +33 4 66 73 30 86

▼ Paulinette 2011 Price: ○○ 89/100

▼ Numa 2010 Price: ○○ 86/100

▼ Vintage 2011 Price: ○ 85/100

▼ Tradition 2012 Price: ○ 85/100

DOMAINES VITICOLES RENOUARD +33 6 15 38 63 07

CV▼ Scamandre 2007 Price: ○○ 89/100

FRANÇOIS COLLARD +33 4 66 59 46 10

CV▼ Château Mourgues du Grès

Capitelles des Mourgues 2011 Price: ○○ 88/100

CV▼ Château la Tour de Béraud Vintage 2012 Price: ○ 84/100

Côte rôtie

DOMAINE BENJAMIN ET DAVID DUCLAUX +33 4 74 59 56 30

▼ Maison Rouge 2011 Price: ○○○ 91/100

▼ La Germine 2011 Price: ○○○ 89/100

DOMAINE DE ROSIERS +33 4 74 56 11 38

▼ Vintage 2011 Price: ○○○ 91/100

JB VINS +33 6 31 20 09 18

▼ Premier Soleil by Josepha 2011 Price: ○○○ 89/100

VIGNOBLES LA COTERIE +33 4 90 12 41 33

▼ Crus des Côtes du Rhône Vintage 2010 Price: ○○ 89/100

VIGNOBLES LEVET +33 4 74 56 15 39

▼ Améthyste 2010 Price: ○○○ 93/100

Côtes du Rhône

ARNOUX ET FILS +33 4 90 65 84 18

▼ Vieux Clocher Vintage 2012 Price: ○ 83/100

CAVE DES VIGNERONS DU CASTELAS +33 4 90 26 62 66

▼ Vintage 2012 Price: ❍ 85/100

▼ Les Mésanges 2012 Price: ❍ 85/100

▼ Vintage 2011 Price: ❍ 84/100

CELLIER DES DAUPHINS +33 4 75 96 20 00

▼ Château de l'Estagnol Vintage 2012 Price: ❍ 84/100

▼ Signature - Vieilli en Fûts de Chêne 2012 Price: ❍ 83/100

▼ Signature - Vieilli en Fûts de Chêne 2012 Price: ❍ 83/100

▼ Signature - Vieilles Vignes 2012 Price: ❍ 83/100

▼ Signature - Grenache - Syrah 2012 Price: ❍ 80/100

CHÂTEAU DE MANISSY +33 4 66 82 86 94

ORG▼ Vintage 2012 Price: ❍ 85/100

CHÂTEAU HAUT MUSIEL +33 4 66 03 69 54

▼ Haut Musiel Vintage 2011 Price: ❍❍ 82/100

CHÂTEAU MONT-REDON +33 4 90 83 72 75

▼ Vintage 2012 Price: ❍ 86/100

▼ Vintage 2012 Price: ❍ 85/100

DOMAINE BERNARD +33 4 90 46 55 76

▼ Cuvée Flora 2012 Price: ❍ 84/100

DOMAINE DE LA MEREUILLE +33 4 90 34 10 68

▼ Vintage 2011 Price: ❍ 83/100

DOMAINE DES ARCHES +33 4 75 27 11 00

▼ Esprit des Arches 2011 Price: ❍ 88/100

DOMAINE DES BERNARDINS +33 4 90 62 94 13

▼ Rosé des Balmes 2012 Price: ❍ 86/100

▼ Les Balmes 2011 Price: ❍ 82/100

DOMAINE DES CARABINIERS +33 4 66 82 62 94

ORG▼ Vintage 2012 Price: ❍ 84/100

DOMAINE DES GRAVENNES +33 4 75 04 84 41

CV▼ Cuvée Marie Louise 2010 Price: ❍❍ 88/100

CV▼ Vintage 2012 Price: ❍ 85/100

Detailed instructions are featured at the start of the book.

DOMAINE NICOLAS CROZE +33 4 75 04 67 11

▼ Coeur de Galets 2010 Price: ❍ 87/100

▼ Les Petits Coins 2011 Price: ❍ 86/100

▼ Vieilles Vignes 2011 Price: ❍ 85/100

▼ Cuvée Fleurie 2011 Price: ❍❍ 85/100

DOMAINE SAINT AMANT +33 4 90 62 99 25

▼ La Borry 2012 Price: ❍ 87/100

▼ Les Trois Roses 2012 Price: ❍❍ 86/100

▼ Les Clapas 2011 Price: ❍ 84/100

DOMAINE SAINT-VINCENT +33 4 75 27 61 10

▼ Vintage 2012 Price: ❍ 84/100

JB VINS +33 6 31 20 09 18

▼ Vintage 2010 Price: ❍ 83/100

LAUDUN CHUSCLAN VIGNERONS +33 4 66 90 53 46

▼ Esprit du Rhône - Réserve 2012 Price: ❍ 84/100

▼ Prieuré St Julien 2012 Price: ❍ 84/100

ORG▼ Terra Vitae 2012 Price: ❍ 83/100

LE CLOS DE CAVEAU +33 4 90 65 85 33

ORG▼ Clos de Caveau Les Bateliers 2012 Price: ❍ 85/100

VIGNERONS DE BALMA VENITIA - BEAUMES DE VENISE +33 4 90 12 41 00

▼ Légende des Toques 2012 Price: ❍ 85/100

▼ Légende des Toques 2012 Price: ❍ 79/100

Côtes du Rhône-Villages

ARNOUX ET FILS +33 4 90 65 84 18

▼ Vieux Clocher Secret de Terroir 2011 Price: ❍ 87/100

CONV▼ Genus Vintage 2011 Price: ❍ 79/100

DOMAINE DE COSTE CHAUDE +33 4 90 41 91 04

▼ Domaine Coste Chaude Madrigal 2010 Price: ❍ 84/100

DOMAINE DES GRAVENNES +33 4 75 04 84 41

CV▼ Vintage 2011 Price: ❍ 86/100

DOMAINE SAINT AMANT	+33 4 90 62 99 25
▼ La Tabardonne 2011 Price: ❍❍	90/100
▼ Roussanne 2011 Price: ❍❍	89/100

DOMAINE SAINT LUC	+33 4 75 98 11 51
▼ L'Escale Serine 2007 Price: ❍	88/100

VINS ET SOLEIL	+33 4 90 12 39 54
▼ Gamme Helios 2010 Price: ❍	87/100

Côtes du Rhône-Villages Chusclan

LAUDUN CHUSCLAN VIGNERONS	+33 4 66 90 53 46
▼ Agapa 2012 Price: ❍	86/100
▼ Excellence 2012 Price: ❍❍	86/100
▼ Les Genêts 2012 Price: ❍	86/100
▼ Les Marians 2012 Price: ❍	86/100
▼ Les Monticauts 2012 Price: ❍	86/100
▼ Domaine de l'Olivette Excellence 2012 Price: ❍	84/100
▼ Prestige des Granges 2012 Price: ❍	84/100
▼ Domaine La Baranière Vintage 2012 Price: ❍	83/100

Côtes du Rhône-Villages Laudun

DOMAINE ROUVRE SAINT LÉGER	+33 6 17 33 80 26
▼ Rouvre Saint Léger Vintage 2011 Price: ❍❍	90/100
▼ Rouvre Saint Léger Vintage 2010 Price: ❍❍	89/100

LAUDUN CHUSCLAN VIGNERONS	+33 4 66 90 53 46
▼ Agapa 2012 Price: ❍	86/100
▼ Les Dolia 2012 Price: ❍	86/100
▼ Les Fontinelles 2012 Price: ❍	85/100
▼ Excellence 2012 Price: ❍	85/100
▼ Camp Romain 2012 Price: ❍	85/100
▼ Clos de Taman 2012 Price: ❍	85/100
ORG▼ Terra Vitae 2012 Price: ❍	83/100

Côtes du Rhône-Villages Plan de Dieu

DOMAINE LES ONDINES +33 4 90 65 86 45

CV▼ Vintage 2011 Price: ❍ 84/100

LES VIGNOBLES DES PASQUIERS +33 4 90 46 83 97

CV▼ Domaine des Pasquiers L'Envy 2010 Price: ❍❍ 90/100

CV▼ Domaine des Pasquiers Vintage 2011 Price: ❍ 87/100

Côtes du Rhône-Villages Puyméras

DOMAINE BERNARD +33 4 90 46 55 76

▼ Cuvée Robin 2010 Price: ❍ 86/100

▼ Vintage 2009 Price: ❍ 85/100

Côtes du Rhône-Villages Sablet

LES VIGNOBLES DES PASQUIERS +33 4 90 46 83 97

CV▼ Domaine des Pasquiers Vintage 2011 Price: ❍ 87/100

Côtes du Rhône-Villages Séguret

DOMAINE DE L'AMAUVE +33 4 90 46 82 81

▼ Les Merrelies 2011 Price: ❍❍ 86/100

VIGNOBLES LA COTERIE +33 4 90 12 41 33

▼ La Coterie Vintage 2010 Price: ❍ 85/100

CAVE DES COTEAUX DU RHÔNE

▼ Panicaut 2011 **85/100**

Young dark purple. Appealing nose of red and black berry fruits with spice undertones. Supple palate boasting elegant stuffing. Restrained heat, delicious young fruit. An endearing Plan de Dieu.

Price: ❍

Wine and food pairing: Roast beef
Serving Temperature: 15-17°C
Ready to drink: From now on

Set in the pretty Mediaeval village of Sérignan-du-Comtat, the winery offers an extensive array of wines. These are grown on limestone-based soils covered with alluvium and the famous Rhone pudding stones. The reds are drawn from the Grenache noir, Syrah, Mourvèdre, Carignan and Cinsault grape varieties and the whites from Grenache blanc, Clairette, Viognier and Roussanne. The winery's Panicaut label is blended from Grenache and Mourvèdre grown on specific sites on the clay-limestone soils of Plan de Dieu renowned for their high stone content, particularly the characteristic pudding stones. The winery shop is open Monday to Saturday from 8.30am - 12.30pm and 2.00pm - 7.00pm. Sundays and bank holidays (from May 2 to August 31) from 9.00am - 12.30pm and 2.30pm - 7.00pm.

Cave les Coteaux du Rhône
Route de Camaret - BP 7 - 84830 Sérignan du Comtat
Tel.: +33 (0)4 90 70 04 22 - Fax: +33 (0)4 90 70 09 23
E-mail: coteau.rhone@wanadoo.fr
Website: http://www.lescoteauxdurhone.com

Côtes du Rhône-Villages Signargues

CAVE DES VIGNERONS DU CASTELAS +33 4 90 26 62 66

▼ Vieilles Vignes 2012 Price: ❍ 84/100

CHÂTEAU HAUT MUSIEL +33 4 66 03 69 54

▼ Haut Musiel Vintage 2009 Price: ❍❍ 82/100

Côtes du Rhône-Villages Visan

DOMAINE DE COSTE CHAUDE +33 4 90 41 91 04

▼ Domaine Coste Chaude La Rocaille 2010 Price: ❍ 87/100

SCEA CLOS DU PÈRE CLÉMENT +33 4 90 41 93 68

CV▼ Cuvée Notre Dame 2009 Price: ❍ 88/100

CV▼ Cuvée Père Clément 2010 Price: ❍ 86/100

VIGNOBLES LA COTERIE +33 4 90 12 41 33

▼ La Coterie Vintage 2009 Price: ❍ 84/100

Côtes du Vivarais

DOMAINE DE VIGIER +33 4 75 88 01 18

▼ Domaine Vigier Vintage 2012 Price: ❍ 86/100

▼ Domaine Vigier L'Intemporel 2011 Price: ❍ 85/100

▼ Domaine Vigier Cuvée Romain 2011 Price: ❍ 84/100

Prices mentioned in this book are guideline and can vary depending on point of sale. The shops, wineries or publisher can in no way be held responsible for this.

Crémant de Die

CAVE MONGE GRANON +33 4 75 21 74 93

▼ Tradition Price: ❍ 83/100

Crozes-Hermitage

ARNOUX ET FILS +33 4 90 65 84 18

▼ Petites Collines 2010 Price: ❍ 83/100

DOMAINE BELLE +33 4 75 08 24 58

▼ Cuvée Louis Belle 2010 Price: ❍❍ 90/100

DOMAINE DES REMIZIÈRES +33 4 75 07 44 28

▼ Cuvée Particulière 2011 Price: ❍ 86/100

DOMAINE DU PAVILLON +33 4 75 07 99 12

▼ Vintage 2011 Price: ❍❍ 87/100

DOMAINE JEAN-CLAUDE MARSANNE +33 4 75 08 86 26

▼ Vintage 2010 Price: ❍❍ 87/100

DOMAINE MUCYN +33 4 75 03 34 52

▼ Vintage 2011 Price: ❍❍ 88/100

VIGNOBLES LA COTERIE +33 4 90 12 41 33

▼ La Coterie Vintage 2011 Price: ❍❍❍ 88/100

Drôme

SCEA CLOS DU PÈRE CLÉMENT +33 4 90 41 93 68

▼ Clos du Père Clément Viognier 2011 Price: ❍ 88/100

Gard

DOMAINES VITICOLES RENOUARD +33 6 15 38 63 07

CV▼ Les Terrasses d'Hortense 2008 Price: ❍ 86/100

Gigondas

ARNOUX ET FILS +33 4 90 65 84 18

▼ Vieux Clocher Nobles Terrasses 2011 Price: ❍❍ 87/100

▼ Seigneur de Lauris Vintage 2011 Price: ❍❍ 85/100

DOMAINE BRUSSET +33 4 90 30 82 16

▼ Tradition Le Grand Montmirail 2011 Price: ❍❍ 91/100

DOMAINE DES FLORETS +33 4 90 40 47 51

▼ 0 2011 Price: ❍❍ 87/100

DOMAINE PALON +33 4 90 62 24 84

▼ Vintage 2011 Price: ❍❍ 84/100

MAS DES RESTANQUES +33 4 90 65 80 87

▼ Vintage 2010 Price: ❍❍ 88/100

VIGNOBLES LA COTERIE +33 4 90 12 41 33

▼ Domaine Chateaubert Vintage 2011 Price: ❍❍ 88/100

▼ La Coterie Vintage 2010 Price: ❍❍ 88/100

Grignan les Adhémar

BARON D'ESCALIN +33 4 75 98 58 40

▼ Domaine Vergobbi Cuvée du Grand V 2011 Price: ❍ 89/100

▼ Domaine Vergobbi Vintage 2011 Price: ❍ 87/100

▼ Domaine Vergobbi Vintage 2012 Price: ❍ 87/100

DOMAINE SAINT LUC +33 4 75 98 11 51

▼ Cuvée Laurine 2012 Price: O 87/100

▼ Cuvée Emiliane 2010 Price: O 82/100

DOMAINES BOUR - DOMAINE DE GRANGENEUVE +33 4 75 98 50 22

▼ Domaine de Grangeneuve
Terre d'Epices 2011 Price: OO 88/100

▼ Domaine de Grangeneuve
Les Dames Blanches du Sud 2012 Price: O 87/100

▼ Domaine de Grangeneuve
Vieilles Vignes 2011 Price: O 86/100

▼ Domaine de La Grange Verte
Tentation de la Marquise 2011 Price: O 85/100

Hermitage

VIGNOBLES LA COTERIE +33 4 90 12 41 33

▼ Blanche de Castille Vintage 2006 Price: OO 85/100

Lirac

CHÂTEAU DE MANISSY +33 4 66 82 86 94

CV▼ Vintage 2011 Price: O 86/100

CHÂTEAU LE DEVOY MARTINE +33 4 66 50 01 23

▼ Via Secreta 2011 Price: O 87/100

CHÂTEAU MONT-REDON +33 4 90 83 72 75

▼ Vintage 2011 Price: OO 88/100

▼ Vintage 2011 Price: OO 88/100

DOMAINE DES CARABINIERS +33 4 66 82 62 94

ORG▼ Vintage 2012 Price: O 86/100

ORG▼ Vintage 2010 Price: O 86/100

Detailed instructions are featured at the start of the book.

LAUDUN CHUSCLAN VIGNERONS +33 4 66 90 53 46

▼ Domaine de Géorand Vintage 2012 Price: ❍ 85/100

▼ Domaine Saint-Nicolas Vintage 2012 Price: ❍ 85/100

Luberon

CHÂTEAU LA CANORGUE - MARGAN +33 4 90 75 81 01

ORG▼ Château la Canorgue Coin Perdu 2011 Price: ❍❍ 87/100

ORG▼ Château la Canorgue Vintage 2011 Price: ❍❍ 86/100

ORG▼ Château la Canorgue Vintage 2012 Price: ❍ 84/100

CHÂTEAU VAL JOANIS +33 4 90 79 20 77

▼ Réserve les Griottes 2009 Price: ❍❍ 89/100

▼ Tradition 2012 Price: ❍ 86/100

▼ Tradition 2009 Price: ❍ 85/100

DOMAINE DE MARIE +33 4 90 72 54 23

▼ 2007 Price: ❍❍ 88/100

Muscat de Beaumes de Venise

DOMAINE DE LA PIERRE DU COQ +33 4 90 62 61 30

▼ Domaine Pierre du Coq Vintage 2012 Price: ❍❍ 86/100

DOMAINE DE LA PIGEADE +33 4 90 62 90 00

▼ Vintage 2012 Price: ❍❍ 87/100

DOMAINE DES BERNARDINS +33 4 90 62 94 13

▼ Hommage - 50 cl Price: ❍❍ 92/100

▼ Vintage 2012 Price: ❍❍ 83/100

VIGNERONS DE BALMA VENITIA - BEAUMES DE VENISE +33 4 90 12 41 00

▼ Château Baroncelli Vintage 2010 Price: ❍❍ 88/100

▼ Bois Doré Vintage 2007 Price: ❍❍ 88/100

▼ Carte Or 2011 Price: ❍❍ 86/100

ORG ▼ Domaine du Paparotier Vintage 2011 Price: ❍❍ 85/100

▼ Carte Rose 2011 Price: ❍❍ 83/100

▼ Tradition Price: ❍ 83/100

Saint-Joseph

ARNOUX ET FILS +33 4 90 65 84 18

▼ Les Echamps Vintage 2010 Price: ❍❍ 90/100

CAVE DE SAINT-DÉSIRAT +33 4 75 34 22 05

▼ Domaine Rochevine

Coeur de Rochevine 2010 Price: ❍❍❍ 90/100

▼ Septentrio 2010 Price: ❍❍ 88/100

DOMAINE DE LA CÔTE SAINTE EPINE +33 4 75 08 85 35

▼ Vieilles Vignes 2011 Price: ❍❍ 89/100

DOMAINE DES REMIZIÈRES +33 4 75 07 44 28

▼ Vintage 2011 Price: ❍❍ 92/100

DOMAINE GILLES FLACHER +33 4 75 34 09 97

▼ Gilles Flacher Cuvée Loess 2011 Price: ❍❍ 90/100

▼ Gilles Flacher Terra Louis 2011 Price: ❍❍ 90/100

▼ Gilles Flacher Les Reines 2011 Price: ❍❍ 89/100

DOMAINE GUY FARGE +33 4 75 06 58 49

▼ Guy Farge Terre de granit 2010 Price: ❍❍ 90/100

▼ Guy Farge Vania 2011 Price: ❍❍ 89/100

DOMAINE JEAN-CLAUDE MARSANNE +33 4 75 08 86 26

▼ Vintage 2010 Price: ❍❍ 90/100

JB VINS +33 6 31 20 09 18

▼ Vintage 2010 Price: ❍❍ 91/100

VIGNOBLES LA COTERIE +33 4 90 12 41 33

▼ Le Muretin Vintage 2011 Price: ❍❍❍ 89/100

Detailed instructions are featured at the start of the book.

Tavel

CHÂTEAU DE MANISSY +33 4 66 82 86 94

ORG▼ Vintage 2012 Price: ❍ 87/100

DOMAINE DES CARABINIERS +33 4 66 82 62 94

ORG▼ Vintage 2012 Price: ❍ 88/100

Vacqueyras

ARNOUX ET FILS +33 4 90 65 84 18

▼ Jean-Marie Arnoux 2011 Price: ❍❍ 88/100

▼ Château Lestours

Clocher Les Pénitents 2011 Price: ❍❍❍ 87/100

▼ Château Lestours

Clocher Saint Barthélémy 2011 Price: ❍❍❍ 87/100

▼ Vieux Clocher Vintage 2012 Price: ❍❍ 87/100

▼ Vieux Clocher Classic 2011 Price: ❍ 86/100

▼ Seigneur de Lauris Vintage 2010 Price: ❍❍ 86/100

DOMAINE CABASSOLE +33 4 90 65 81 21

▼ Alliance 2010 Price: ❍❍ 88/100

▼ Tradition 2010 Price: ❍ 87/100

DOMAINE DE LA PIGEADE +33 4 90 62 90 00

▼ Vintage 2011 Price: ❍❍ 88/100

DOMAINE LES ONDINES +33 4 90 65 86 45

CV▼ Vintage 2011 Price: ❍❍ 84/100

DOMAINE PALON +33 4 90 62 24 84

▼ Vintage 2011 Price: ❍ 85/100

LE CLOS DE CAVEAU +33 4 90 65 85 33

ORG▼ Clos de Caveau Lao Muse 2009 Price: ❍❍❍ 89/100

ORG▼ Clos de Caveau Carmin Brillant 2011 Price: ❍❍ 87/100

ORG▼ Clos de Caveau Fruit Sauvage 2011 Price: ❍❍ 86/100

ORG▼ La Rose du Clos Vintage 2012 Price: ❍ 85/100

ARNOUX ET FILS

▼ 1717 Vintage 2011 **89/100**

Beautiful dark garnet. Enticing nose of mild spices, mild tobacco, mocha and overripe fruits with subtle oak ageing. Suave attack, savoury, profound palate exuding wonderful aromas of spice. Robust, closely-integrated structure. Lively with no heaviness.

Price: OOO

Wine and food pairing: Leg of lamb
Serving Temperature: 16-18°C
Ready to drink: 2014-2016

In 1717, Count François de Castellanne de Lauris de Vassadel de Gérard, Chevalier Marquis d'Ampuis de Lagneroux, the lord of Vacqueyras and its lands, granted a vineyard to an ancestor of the Arnoux family: Pierre Bovis. Since then, the winemaking tradition has been handed down through the generations. In 1936, Aimé Arnoux brought new life to the estate, responding to growing demand by deciding to buy in grapes on top of his own production. Today, the estate covers more than 40 hectares and is managed by Marc and Jean-François Arnoux. Summer opening hours: Monday to Saturday, 9–12 am and 2–7 pm; Winter opening hours: Tuesday to Saturday, 8–12 am and 2–6 pm (closed on Sundays and holidays).

Arnoux et Fils
Le Vieux Clocher
84190 Vacqueyras
Tel.: +33 (0)4 90 65 84 18 - Fax: +33 (0)4 90 65 80 07
E-mail: info@arnoux-vins.com
Website: http://htp://www.arnoux-vins.com

MAS DES RESTANQUES +33 4 90 65 80 87

▼ Vintage 2010 Price: ❍ 88/100

VIGNERONS DE BALMA VENITIA - BEAUMES DE VENISE +33 4 90 12 41 00

▼ Vintage 2012 Price: ❍ 87/100

▼ Vintage 2011 Price: ❍ 85/100

VIGNOBLES LA COTERIE +33 4 90 12 41 33

▼ La Coterie Vintage 2011 Price: ❍ 85/100

▼ Domaine L'Ousteau des Lecques Vintage 2011 Price: ❍ 83/100

VINS ET SOLEIL +33 4 90 12 39 54

▼ Gamme Helios 2011 Price: ❍❍ 86/100

Vaucluse

ARNOUX ET FILS +33 4 90 65 84 18

▼ P'tit Clocher 2012 Price: ❍ 84/100

▼ P'tit Clocher 2012 Price: ❍ 84/100

DOMAINE DE TARA +33 4 90 05 74 87

▼ Terre d'Ocres 2012 Price: ❍ 83/100

DOMAINE SAINT AMANT +33 4 90 62 99 25

▼ Syrah - Grenache 2011 Price: ❍ 83/100

Ventoux

ARNOUX ET FILS +33 4 90 65 84 18

▼ Vieux Clocher Vintage 2012 Price: ❍ 85/100

▼ Vieux Clocher Vintage 2012 Price: ❍ 83/100

CHÂTEAU PESQUIÉ +33 4 90 61 94 08

CV▼ Artemia 2011 Price: ❍❍❍ 87/100

DOMAINE DE LA PIGEADE +33 4 90 62 90 00

▼ Ventoux Classique 2011 Price: ❍ 85/100

DOMAINE DE TARA +33 4 90 05 74 87

▼ Terre d'Ocres 2012 Price: ❍ 85/100

DOMAINE DES ANGES +33 4 90 61 88 78

▼ Séraphin - Vieilles Vignes 2010 Price: ❍❍ 87/100

▼ Archange 2010 Price: ❍❍ 86/100

▼ Archange 2011 Price: ❍❍ 84/100

▼ Vintage 2010 Price: ❍ 84/100

DOMAINE DE TARA +33 4 90 05 74 87

▼ Hautes Pierres 2010 Price: ❍❍ 87/100

▼ Hautes Pierres 2011 Price: ❍❍ 85/100

▼ Terre d'Ocres 2012 Price: ❍ 84/100

DOMAINE DU BON REMÈDE +33 4 90 69 69 76

▼ La Grange Delay 2011 Price: ❍ 86/100

▼ Vignes Rousses 2011 Price: ❍ 81/100

SCEA LE GRAVEYRON +33 4 90 62 31 78

CV▼ Château Juvenal Les Ribes du Vallat 2011 Price: ❍ 87/100

VIGNERONS DE BALMA VENITIA - BEAUMES DE VENISE +33 4 90 12 41 00

▼ Pomelo 2012 Price: ❍ 86/100

▼ Mistral Levant 2011 Price: ❍ 84/100

▼ Mistral Couchant 2011 Price: ❍ 84/100

VIGNOBLES LA COTERIE +33 4 90 12 41 33

▼ La Coterie Vintage 2011 Price: ❍ 85/100

Vinsobres

CELLIER DES DAUPHINS +33 4 75 96 20 00

▼ Signature 2011 Price: ❍ 85/100

DOMAINE JAUME +33 4 75 27 61 01

▼ Clos des Echalas Vintage 2010 Price: ❍❍❍ 92/100

▼ Référence 2011 Price: ❍❍ 89/100

▼ Altitude 420 2011 Price: ❍ 87/100

DOMAINE SAINT-VINCENT +33 4 75 27 61 10

▼ Vintage 2011 Price: ❍❍ 88/100

▼ Vintage 2012 Price: ❍❍ 86/100

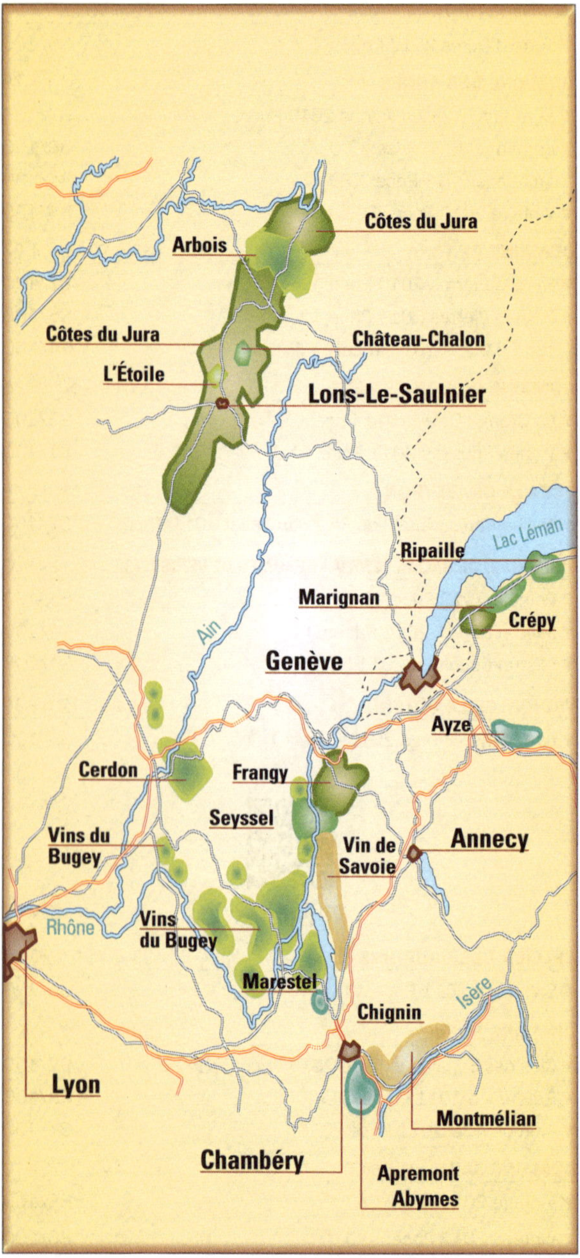

Côtes du Jura
Arbois
Côtes du Jura
Château-Chalon
L'Étoile
Lons-Le-Saulnier
Lac Léman
Ripaille
Marignan
Crépy
Ain
Genève
Ayze
Cerdon
Frangy
Seyssel
Vins du Bugey
Annecy
Vin de Savoie
Rhône
Vins du Bugey
Marestel
Isère
Chignin
Lyon
Montmélian
Chambéry
Apremont
Abymes

SAVOY

A BRAND NEW IMAGE

A land of contrasts is the calling card of this alpine province. Production is centred primarily in Savoie, with 80,000 hectolitres, with a balance of 8,000 hl produced in Haute-Savoie, divided between 30% reds and rosés (truly) and 70% whites. The vines follow the contours of Lake Geneva, stretch southwards alongside the Rhone, circle Lake Bourget and hug the flanks of Savoy Coomb, after occupying the scree slopes of Mount Granier. The diversity of landforms illustrates the determination of Savoy wine producers in the face of such a borderline climate for growing grapes.

There are four ACs in Savoy: Seyssel (still whites or sparkling); Crépy (three villages in Haute-Savoie); Vin de Savoie (perhaps with one of 17 possible growth names attached: Abymes, Apremont, Arbin, Ayze, Char-pignat, Chautagne, Chignin, Chignin-Bergeron or Bergeron, Cruet, Jongieux, Marignan, Marin, Montmélian, Ripaille, Saint-Jean de la Porte, Saint-Jeoire Prieuré, Sainte-Marie), for red or white wines, still, sparkling or semi-sparkling; and Roussette de Savoie (perhaps with one of four possible growth names attached: Frangy, Marestel or Marestel-Altesse, Monterminod and Monthoux) which also refers to red or white wines, still, sparkling or semi-sparkling.

VARIETALS: Reds: Gamay, Pinot noir and Mondeuse plus a small proportion of Cabernets (Franc and Sauvignon), Persan and a few local varieties in Isère. Whites: Aligoté, Roussette (or Altesse), Jacquère, Chasselas, Chardonnay, augmented with some 'secondary' varieties.

WINE STYLES: lively, vigorous, fruity whites, occasionally aged on the lees which gives them their delicious slightly sparkling touch. The best known of these are Roussette and

Apremont. The sparkling wines make excellent appetisers. The reds from Gamay and Pinot noir are fruity and light. The more robust wines from Mondeuse can prove to be excellent laying down wines on a more full-bodied, spicy note.

REVIEW OF RECENT VINTAGES

• **2011** • As a rule, the whites are rich yet crisp and show structure and freshness. The reds and rosés are pleasant and should be drunk whilst still fruit-forward.

• **2012** • This was a difficult year that was mainly rainy and cool apart from a quite mild autumn. These unfavourable conditions caused coulure (dropping of flowers) and millerandage (irregular and stunted grape development), until August when the return of hot weather allowed the grapes to ripen. This vintage does not herald a bad wine, but the volume is very low (the average yield was sometimes as low as 20 hectolitres per hectare!).

THE SAVOY APPELLATIONS

AC BUGEY

OVERVIEW: this 450-hectare area is set on the right bank of the Rhone, between Chanay and Lagnieu, mostly in the Ain department, embracing a total 65 towns and villages. Fifteen or so of these are entitled to a specific growth name: Virieu-le-Grand, Manicle, Machuraz, Montagnieu and Cerdon. Neighbouring Lake Bourget creates a microclimate suitable for vine growing.
White wines from Chardonnay, Altesse (or Roussette), Aligoté, Jacquère, Pinot gris and Molette are made here, as well as sparkling wines, including Cerdon. The red grape varietals used are Gamay, Pinot noir, Poulsard and Mondeuse.
WINE STYLES: the whites are clean, vigorous, lively, fresh and round, with a pleasant bouquet. They are delicate with good length on the palate, developing fragrances of white flowers, citrus fruit and a mineral touch. Try with freshwater fish, fish paté or quenelles. The reds made from Gamay are lively, supple, fruity and light, whilst the Pinots are more delicate and rich. Try with red meat or good Reblochon cheese.

A.C. CRÉPY

OVERVIEW: the Crépy appellation area, covering around 70 ha, is set on the southern-eastern shores of Lake Geneva between

Thonon-les-Bains and Geneva. Three villages in Ain and Isère are entitled to the appellation: Douvaine, Ballaison and Loisin. The soils are formed of limestone scree, mostly moranic in origin, and are littered with stones. Mountain peaks act as a buffer against the cold winds and the reflection off Lake Geneva increases sunlight. Chas-selas, the only varietal grown locally, is also known in Valais as Fendant.

WINE STYLES: these wines are dry white, light, fresh, delicate and lively with a slight sparkle. They are similar to Swiss wines such as Vaud Dorin and Valais Fendant. They reward early drinking although they can be kept for a few years. Their acidity increases their lifespan though as they age they do lose some of their freshness. They display a pale green hue and fragrances of hazelnut, unripe almond, gunflint, violet and hawthorn. They are suitable as appetisers, or with poached crayfish, whitebait, shellfish, trout, calf's brains or Tomme de Savoie cheese.

A.C. ROUSSETTE DE SAVOIE

OVERVIEW: the appellation is situated west of Lake Bourget. The name Roussette is derived from the russset shades the wine acquires as it matures. In Savoy, this grape variety is also called Altesse. Four zones are entitled to growth status: Frangy, north-west of Annecy, Marestel and Monthoux, along the left bank of the Rhone and Monterminod near Chambéry.

WINE STYLES: these white wines are fruity, delicate, racy, full and unctuous with acidulous notes. They can be laid down for a few years. Roussette produces a range of aromas known as 'peacock's fan' because they stretch across the whole palate. The wines display a golden green hue and fragrances of dried fruit, predominantly apricot, almond, honey and hazelnut, enhanced by floral notes. They can be served with lightly poached trout, whitebait, crayfish, white meats...

AC ROUSSETTE DU BUGEY

OVERVIEW: Roussette is the name of a grape variety, also called Altesse. It is usually blended with a small proportion of Chardonnay. Situated in the south-eastern tip of Ain, near the border between Savoie and Haute-Savoie, this area stretches from Bourg-en-Bresse to Belley. The limestone soil marks a boundary between the southern part of Revermont in Jura and the foothills of the Alps.

WINE STYLES: these are distinctive, robust, aromatic white wines, which are delicate, elegant and occasionally soft. Bugey's best Roussette wines hail from six growths: Lagnieu, Montagnieu, Virieu-le-Grand, Arbignieu, Anglefort and Chanay. Suitable for laying down. They display fragrances of peach and apricot, evolving over time into honey and beeswax scents. They can pair with quenelles, grilled freshwater fish or fish in a sauce, fondues, raclette and soft cheeses.

A.C. SEYSSEL

OVERVIEW: Seyssel wines are grown in the twin villages of Seyssel in Haute-Savoie and Seyssel-Corbonod, over 80 or so hectares in Ain. The steep slopes of the upper Rhone valley, where the soil is stony moranic or sandy molasse, provide a foothold for the vines. The best hillside sites are 'Les Michalettes', 'La Tour', 'Les Chênes', 'Les Vérones' and 'La Péclette'. The still and sparkling white wines are made primarily from Altesse and Molette.

WINE STYLES: white Seyssels display a pale hue and a floral bouquet with dominant aromas of violet, bergamot pear and passion fruit. A touch of flint is also present. On the palate, they are light, delicate, soft, dry, racy wines with well-balanced mellowness. They are velvety, supple, refreshing and long on the palate with good acidity. The best examples will keep for a few years. Try with cheeses such as Reblochon, Beaufort and Emmenthal, though also quenelles, poached crayfish, fish (trout, lavaret), raclette or cheese fondue. The sparkling wines have a distinct 'terroir' taste and are suitable as an appetiser or with a dessert.

A.C. VIN DE SAVOIE

OVERVIEW: the production area stretches over 75 km from Thonon-les-Bains to Chambéry. Vineyard sites cover 59 towns and villages: 29 in Savoie, 26 in Haute-Savoie, 2 in Ain and 2 in Isère, totalling just under 2,000 hectares. Most of the vineyards are not contiguous but scattered over the valley floor and along the shores of the lakes. White wines hold a majority share of production. Wines drawn from a single varietal are often labelled as such. The most noteworthy wines are the 17 growths entitled to append their name to that of the appellation.

Soil types are varied, ranging from limestone, to limestone marl, glacial morain, shale and rocky scree. The lakes moderate the effect of the continental climate whilst the mountains form a buffer against the rain fronts. Winters are long and harsh, springs are mild and damp, summers hot and stormy and there are long sunshine hours. Red varietals used: Gamay, Mondeuse, Pinot noir, Persan and Cabernet. For the whites: Jacquère, Altesse, Aligoté, Chardonnay, Malvoisie, Mondeuse blanche, Gringet, Roussette d'Ayze and Chasselas.

WINE STYLES: the whites have an unusual character. They are dry, vigorous and pleasant to drink, developing fragrances of white flowers (hawthorn, honeysuckle). The reds are fresh, pleasant, upfront wines which should be drunk young when they are made from Gamay. Wines made from Mondeuse are more rustic and fruity and improve with age. They display aromas of strawberry, violet and spices. The whites are suitable partners for cheese fondue, raclette, Beaufort soufflé, quenelles and cooked cold pork meats. The reds can pair with potatoes Savoyard, round fillet of veal or game.

SAVOY GROWTHS: 17 of them can add their name to AC Vin de Savoie. Site-specific growing conditions and higher production standards create a point of difference with other local wines. The growths are: Abymes, Apremont, Arbin, Ayze, Charpignat (uncommon), Chautagne, Chignin, Chignin-Bergeron, Cruet, Jongieux, Ma-rignan, Marin, Montmélian, Ripaille, Sainte-Marie-d'Alloix, Saint-Jeoire-Prieuré and Saint-Jean-de-la-Porte.

VIN DE SAVOIE ABYMES: the production area is located in the villages of Mylans and Chapareillan and part of Marches and Apremont. It yields white wines with a crystalline hue tinted with greenish shades. They are dry, light and often slightly sparkling. They display floral fragrances, primarily violet. Made from the Jacquère varietal they should be drunk chilled and young.

VIN DE SAVOIE APREMONT: dry white wines are made here on soils with patches of limestone. The area is 20 km from Chambéry and occupies the slopes of Mount Granier. The wines are light, supple and fruity, conjuring up a touch of gunflint and honeysuckle. They pair with seafood, shellfish and fish.

VIN DE SAVOIE ARBIN: red and white wines are grown here on calcareous clay soils. The wines are grown in the villages of Arbin and Saint-Jean-de-la-Porte. The reds display aromas of blackberry, raspberry and bilberry, with a touch of spice. They are supple wines with good length on the palate. They are served with red meat or cheese. The red wines are made from the Mondeuse varietal.

VIN DE SAVOIE AYZE: this growth is situated in the villages of Ayze, Bonneville and Marignier. It produces sparkling wines from the Gringet, Altesse, Mondeuse blanche and Roussette d'Ayze grape varieties on the south-eastern and south-western flanks of Mount Môle. They can be labelled either as Mousseux de Savoie or Pétillant de Savoie. The soils are formed of glacial alluvium, scree or molasse. The wines are fresh, lively, distinctive, aromatic and supple. They pair best with fish, cheese fondue or desserts.

VIN DE SAVOIE CHAUTAGNE: this growth is situated in north-western Savoy in the villages of Motz, Serrières-en-Chau-tagne, Ruffieux and Chindrieux. Red and white wines are grown on a 10 km strip of land below Mount Gros Foug on the northern tip of Lake Bourget. The soils are formed of glacial scree and alluvium. The well-known red wines with their ruby-red hue are fleshy, solid, well-constituted, complex and tannic with floral and fruity fragrances. They can be savoured with wild boar, venison, cured mountain ham or cheese.

VIN DE SAVOIE CHIGNIN: the vineyards stretch over the villages of Chignin, Francin and Montmélian. The white wines, made from Jacquère, are generous, with a pleasant bouquet and slight sparkle. The reds, made from Gamay or Mondeuse, are flavoursome wines.

VIN DE SAVOIE CHIGNIN-BERGERON: although this wine comes from the same area as Chignin, it is made from the Bergeron varietal, otherwise known as Roussane de l'Hermitage. It is delicate, elegant, aromatic (hazelnut and almond), and capable of withstanding the test of time. It is one of Savoy's finest examples of white wine.

VIN DE SAVOIE CRUET: this area is set on the flanks of Bauges mountain, on calcareous clay soils and stony Jurassic scree. The whites are dry, lively and vigorous with fragrances of exotic fruits. The reds, made from Mondeuse, are delicate.

VIN DE SAVOIE JONGIEUX: this growth occupies the upper reaches of the Monthoux and Marestel appellation areas on calcareous clay soils. Red Jongieux sports a cherry-red hue. It is a supple, light wine with a bouquet of raspberry, strawberry, cherry and blackcurrant. The majority of the wines are red. The rosés are light and pleasant to drink.

VIN DE SAVOIE MARIGNAN: this growth is situated in the villages of Marignan and Sciez. The wines are slightly sparkling, dry and fragrant with predominant aromas of gunflint and hazelnut. The area owes its existence to the single-minded determination of Filly abbey. The wines are made from Chasselas.

VIN DE SAVOIE MARIN: these are dry white wines grown in the most northerly portion of Haute-Savoie, on the edge of Dranse valley. The vineyards enjoy a microclimate and are planted on south-south-west facing slopes. The wines made from Chasselas and are fruity, delicate quaffing wines with aromas of almond.
Vin de Savoie Montmélian: set in the villages of Montmélian and Francin, the vines grow here on limestone scree. The area is well suited to Jacquère and Mondeuse positively thrives here, yielding amazingly full-bodied wines.

VIN DE SAVOIE RIPAILLE: an area located along the shores of Lake Geneva, in the villages of Ripaille and Thonons-les-Bains. The soil is gravely and permeable. It produces fresh, fruity, dry white wines from Chasselas, reminiscent of Crépy.

VIN DE SAVOIE SAINT-JEAN-DE-LA-PORTE: scree and alluvial fans on the north-western flanks of Savoy Coomb provide a foothold for vines here. The reds display a crimson hue. They are rich, aromatic and mature extremely well. Mondeuse is the only permitted grape varietal.

JURA

GREAT DISCOVERIES

This region borders the western edge of the Jura mountain range, adjoining Revermont, a vast, west-facing region of rolling hills overlooking the plains of the Saone. The Franche-Comté wine region boasts some real gems (including «vin de paille» and «vin jaune»). There are six appellations: Côtes du Jura, Arbois, Château Chalon, l'Etoile (only white and «yellow»), Crémant du Jura (sparkling) and Macvin (a liqueur wine). The growths forge their inimitable personalities from their individual terroirs and grape varieties and invariably create a long-lasting impression. «Vin jaune» for instance, (which is a term and not an appellation) is a unique growth which spends six years and three months in casks without being topped up before release. Any other wine would succumb to such shock treatment, not «vin jaune». As it ages, it acquires its famous «yellow taste» prized by wine lovers. Don't tarry, try it !

VARIETALS: Whites: Savagnin (or Na-turé). «Vin jaune» is made entirely from this grape variety, whilst the other appellations can blend in some Chardonnay. Reds and rosés: Poulsard (or Plouss ard), Trousseau and Pinots (noir and gris).

WINE STYLES: the reds and the rosés are powerful though not full-bodied and display intense fruit. The whites are warm. Occasionally they mature in casks used for «vin jaune», which imparts tell-tale aromas of walnut and green apple. Similar aromas for the 'yellow' wines, which boast a huge array of aromas and virtually endless ageing capacity.

REVIEW OF RECENT VINTAGE

• **2012** • his vintage received more rain than any since 1977! Fortunately, the summer brought more sun, but the yield was consequently very low. Despite the low volumes, the wines have a good structure.

THE JURA APPELLATIONS

A.C. ARBOIS

OVERVIEW: the Arbois appellation embraces 12 villages: Abergement-le-Grand, Arbois, Les Arsures, Mathenay, Mesnay, Molamboz, Montigny-les-Arsures, Les Planches-près-Arbois, Pupillin, Saint-Cyr-Montmalin, Vadans and Vilette-lès-Arbois. The soils are clay (lowlands) and limestone (highlands). Most of the wines are red, though there are also rosés, dry whites and of course, the famous 'vin jaune' and 'vin de paille'. The name Pupillin can be appended to the Arbois appellation for wines from the village. INAO decided to allow the additional name in 1970, in recognition of the long-standing reputation of this particular vineyard site which is extremely well-suited to the Poulsard and other grape varieties.

WINE STYLES: the red wines, made from Poulsard, Trousseau, Pinot noir and Pinot gris, usually have little depth of colour. Conversely, the rosés display a deep hue, often tinted with orange, referred to as coral. Both offer delicate aromas of red fruit. They can be served with roast leg of chamois (reds) and cured mountain ham (rosés). The dry white wines are drawn from Chardonnay, Savagnin and Pinot blanc. Wines matured in casks used for 'vin jaune' display aromas of mocha, dried fruit and green apple. Try these lively, intense, fat, sweet wines with morel mushrooms in a creamy sauce, button mushroom fricassee and of course Comté cheese.

'VINS JAUNES': 'vins jaunes' from Arbois display characteristic aromas of unripe walnuts, green apples and spices. Try with Roquefort cheese in puff pastry, chicken cooked with morel mushrooms and 'vin jaune', and walnut cake.

'VINS DE PAILLE': 'vins de Paille' are made from dessicated grapes which have been laid on a bed of straw to dry or hung up in a dry, well-aired room for around three months. The berries, which by now have extremely high sugar concentrations, are pressed at Christmas (100kg of grapes can yield less than 20 litres of must). Fermentation in small casks is a long drawn out process, lasting up to four years. Once the ageing process is over, most 'vins jaunes' have an alcohol content of 15% vol. and are suitable for lengthy bottle ageing. Try with Bresse fatted chicken in a cream sauce or Morbier cheese.

A.C. CHÂTEAU CHALON

OVERVIEW: this prestigious Jura appellation is both the name of a cliff top village and an appellation embracing 4 villages producing 'vin jaune', viz Château Chalon, Menétru, Domblans and Nevy-sur-Seille. The sloping vineyards grow primarily on limestone scree intermingled with Lias marl on the steepest gradients. More consistent black marl type soils are also present. The climate is continental, with extremely cold winters and frequent autumn frosts.

WINE MAKING METHODS: Château Chalon is one of France's greatest white wines, even if the descriptor 'white' is not entirely accurate because Château Chalon is in fact 'yellow'. A ripe crop is a prerequisite for making this type of wine (204g/l of natural sugar at least). Made using conventional wine making techniques, the wines are aged for six years and three months in partly-filled 228-litre oak casks. They are neither racked nor topped up, allowing a kind of yeast veil similar to the flor fungus in Sherry to form on the surface. This yeast veil, which grows during the summer (due to variations in temperature), entices out the characteristic aromas found in the wines. The actual wine making process is in fact extremely tricky as the risk of volatile acidity is very high. As the wines mature, a large proportion of them evaporates, hence the unusual size of the traditional Jura wine bottle. The 62 cl 'clavelin' contains the amount left per litre of matured wine. To maintain high quality standards, growers do not apply for AC approval in years when they consider their wines to be anything less than top notch.

WINE STYLES: Château Chalon only produces 'vin jaune' from Savagnin, a temperamental, low-yielding grape variety which some consider to be on a par with Tokay wines or Sherry. With its inimitable taste of unripe walnuts, green apple and spices (nutmeg, cinnamon), and its deep colour which sometimes turns amber down the years, this wine is extremely well-constituted and rich in alcohol (minimum 12% vol.). It boasts an extensive lifespan (up to 100 years with no deterioration) and shows at its best when it has matured for at least ten to fifteen years. Enjoy with Comté cheese, poultry served in a cream sauce... Drink at room temperature (12-15°C).

A.C. CÔTES DU JURA

OVERVIEW: the Côtes du Jura appellation area covers over 600 hectares divided between 12 villages, with a focal point around Lons-le-Saunier, Poligny and Salins-les-Bains. A full range of soil types is present. At the highest elevations, limestone is interspersed with organic sediment whilst lower down, marl covers stones and on the lowlands, the soil is almost entirely clay. Red varietals used are Pinot noir, Poulsard and Trousseau and white varietals, Chardonnay and Savagnin.

WINE STYLES: red wines made from Trousseau are reasonably tannic. Conversely, Poulsard yields more supple wines with aromas of morello cherry, wild cherry and raspberry. They pair with mountain pork meats and small cuts of venison. The dry whites boast distinctive mocha, dried fruit and green apple aromas, often imparted by the casks they are stored in, previously used for 'vin jaune'.

The 'vins jaunes' themselves develop fragrances of unripe walnut, fir tree honey and bitter almond. The 'vins de paille' display scents of toast, acacia honey, almond, nutmeg and gingerbread.

A.C. CRÉMANT DU JURA

OVERVIEW: Crémant du Jura shares the same appellation area as Côtes du Jura. This fruity wine is made from Savagnin and Chardonnay for the whites and Poulsard, Pinot noir, Pinot gris and Trousseau for the reds. The local climate promotes good acidity in the grapes, making Jura suitable for producing sparkling Crémant wines. This particular type of sparkler undergoes secondary fermentation in the bottle.

WINE STYLES: the wines are sparkling with a pale yellow hue highlighted with greenish tints. They display tiny bubbles and long-lasting aromas of toast, honey, green apple and citrus fruit. Both fruity and floral, they are refreshing on the palate with a hint of pear and hawthorn. They are equally delicious as appetisers or with a dessert.

A.C. L'ETOILE

OVERVIEW: this small appellation area in Jura embraces the villages of l'Etoile, Plainoiseau, Quintigny and Saint-Didier where the soil is black or blue marl from the Lower Jurassic period. The climate is continental, with extremely cold winters and frequent autumn frosts. The white wines are blended from three permitted grape varieties (Chardonnay, Poulsard and Savagnin) and are frequently aged on the lees.

WINE STYLES: the entire regional white range is made here, from white itself to 'yellow', sparkling and 'vin de paille'. The white wines are lively and intense yet also fat and mellow. They pair well with fish and cooked shellfish. 'Vins de paille' are extremely concentrated and syrupy, exhibiting a beautiful amber hue and a rich, smooth taste. The extremely powerful 'vins jaunes' display a clean attack, fine structure and smooth, silky finish. They develop aromas of unripe walnut, fir tree honey and bitter almond.

A.C. MACVIN DU JURA

OVERVIEW: Macvin, previously known as 'Galant des Abbesses', is a liqueur wine made by adding spirit to the grape must to arrest fermentation. Villers-Farlay, Salins, Arbois, Poligny, Sellières, Voiteur, Bletterans, Conliège, Lons-le-Saunier, Beaufort, Saint-Amour and Saint-Julien, are all involved in producing it. The varietal range comprises Poulsard, Trousseau, Pinot noir, Pinot gris, Chardonnay and Savagnin. Macvin is made from the sweetest grapes sourced in prime vineyard sites. It is produced using the 'mutage' technique whereby fermentation is arrested by adding pomace brandy or Franche-Comté brandy made by the grower himself. The ratio is one litre of 50% proof spirit to three litres of must. 'Fine' brandy is not permitted. Macvin is aged in small casks for a year or more and must have an ABV ranging from 16 to 22%.

WINE STYLES: several components factor into the popularity of this liqueur wine: its hue, which can vary from yellow to dark brown depending on its age, its sweet flavour, generous bouquet and length on the palate. Adding brandy to the must preserves full fruit aromas. Several years in casks are required before the grape aromas integrate with the alcohol to produce greater finesse. Macvin can be served either as an appetiser or with a dessert.

• • •

SAVOY-JURA

SAVOY

Roussette de Savoie

DOM. JEAN-PIERRE ET JEAN-FRANÇOIS QUÉNARD +33 4 79 28 08 29

▼ Jean-François Quénard Anne-Sophie 2010 Price: ❍❍ 88/100

PHILIPPE GRISARD +33 4 79 84 30 91

▼ Vintage 2011 Price: ❍ 88/100

Roussette de Savoie Monthoux

JEAN PERRIER & FILS +33 4 79 28 11 45

▼ Jean Perrier Fleur d'Altesse 2011 Price: ❍ 87/100

Seyssel

POLONI DIDIER +33 4 50 56 19 88

▼ Vintage 2010 Price: ❍ 88/100

▼ Vintage 2011 Price: ❍ 86/100

Vin de Savoie

DOMAINE DUPASQUIER +33 4 79 44 02 23

▼ Pinot 2010 Price: ❍ 88/100

JEAN PERRIER & FILS +33 4 79 28 11 45

▼ Pure 2012 Price: ❍ 85/100

Vin de Savoie Apremont

▼ Cuvée Gastronomie 2012 Price: ❍ 86/100

▼ Jean Perrier Cuvée Gastronomique 2011 Price: ❍ 86/100

Vin de Savoie Arbin

PHILIPPE GRISARD +33 4 79 84 30 91

▼ Vintage 2011 Price: ❍ 88/100

Vin de Savoie Chignin

DOM. JEAN-PIERRE ET JEAN-FRANÇOIS QUÉNARD +33 4 79 28 08 29

▼ Jean-François Quénard Vintage 2012 Price: ❍ 87/100

Vin de Savoie Chignin-Bergeron

JEAN PERRIER & FILS +33 4 79 28 11 45

▼ Fleur de Roussane 2012 Price: ❍ 89/100

▼ Fleur de Roussanne 2011 Price: ❍ 88/100

Vin de Savoie Mondeuse

DOMAINE DUPASQUIER +33 4 79 44 02 23

▼ Vintage 2010 Price: ❍❍ 88/100

DOM. JEAN-PIERRE ET JEAN-FRANÇOIS QUÉNARD +33 4 79 28 08 29

▼ Jean-François Quénard Terres Rouges 2012 Price: ❍ 87/100

JEAN PERRIER & FILS +33 4 79 28 11 45

▼ Cuvée Gastronomie 2012 Price: ❍ 85/100

▼ Jean Perrier Cuvée Gastronomique 2011 Price: ❍ 83/100

PHILIPPE GRISARD +33 4 79 84 30 91

▼ Vintage 2011 Price: ❍ 87/100

Vin de Savoie Ripaille

DOMAINE DE RIPAILLE +33 4 50 71 75 12

▼ Château de Ripaille Vintage 2012 Price: ❍ 84/100

JURA

Arbois

DOMAINE JACQUES TISSOT +33 3 84 66 14 27

▼ Jacques Tissot Chardonnay 2009 Price: ❍ 87/100

Château-Chalon

DOMAINE BERTHET-BONDET +33 3 84 44 60 48

▼ Vin Jaune 2006 Price: ❍❍❍ 86/100

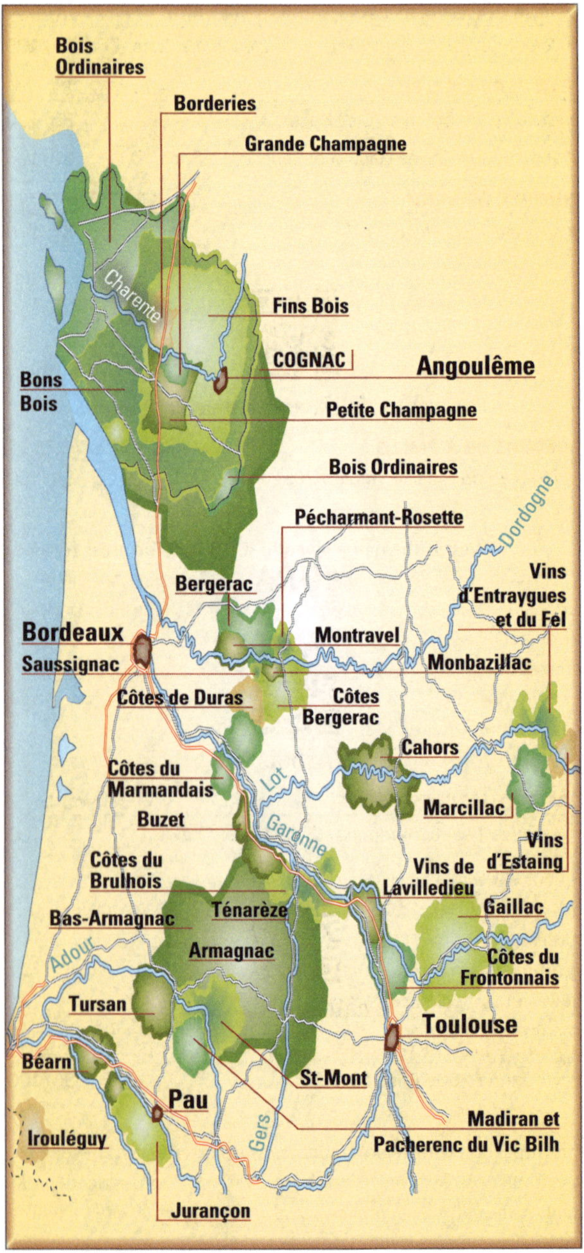
Bois Ordinaires
Borderies
Grande Champagne
Charente
Fins Bois
COGNAC
Angoulême
Bons Bois
Petite Champagne
Bois Ordinaires
Dordogne
Pécharmant-Rosette
Bergerac
Vins d'Entraygues et du Fel
Bordeaux
Montravel
Saussignac
Monbazillac
Côtes de Duras
Côtes Bergerac
Cahors
Côtes du Marmandais
Lot
Marcillac
Buzet
Garonne
Vins d'Estaing
Côtes du Brulhois
Vins de Lavilledieu
Ténarèze
Gaillac
Bas-Armagnac
Armagnac
Adour
Côtes du Frontonnais
Tursan
Toulouse
Béarn
St-Mont
Pau
Madiran et Pacherenc du Vic Bilh
Irouléguy
Gers
Jurançon

SOUTH-WEST

AN IMPRESSIVE LINE-UP OF TALENT

South-West is the name given to a raft of wine areas located in South-Western France, between Bordeaux to the west and Languedoc-Roussillon in the east. Interestingly, although Bordeaux is also located in South-Western France, it is never referred to as such. The South-West is too attached to its own specific qualities to share its name. It thereby protects its internationally-renowned identity.

South-West is the name given to a raft of wine areas located in South-Western France, between Bordeaux to the west and Languedoc-Roussillon in the east. Interestingly, although Bordeaux is also located in South-Western France, it is never referred to as such. The South-West is too attached to its own specific qualities to share its name. It thereby protects its internationally-renowned identity.

It is difficult to sum up the myriad wine styles and diversity of the South-West in just a few lines. In this land of Cockaigne, the choice of gourmet delights is endless: dry or sweet wines, supple or robust reds, rosés for quaffing, sparkling wines, brandies, liqueur wines… This diversity stems from a vast array of 'terroirs' though also from highly individual varietal ranges. Although the Bordeaux varietals (Cabernet-Sauvignon, Merlot, Sauvi-gnon…) are ubiquitous in some areas, elsewhere originality prevails (see the various appellations).

To simplify, the thirty or so appellations can be roughly divided into five different geographical areas:

THE BERGERAC REGION

This important wine region is the eastward extension of Bordeaux, travelling upstream and stretching over the Dordogne department. Although the varietal range and climate differ only slightly from its prestigious neighbour, the soil types change quite significantly: north of the Dordogne river, the soils are Perigordian sand whilst to the south, they are a combination of molasse, marl and limestone. This region is home to red wines (Bergerac, Côtes de Bergerac, Pécharmant), dry whites (Bergerac sec, Montravel) and sweet whites (Monbazillac, Rosette, Côtes de Montravel...).

THE WINE REGIONS OF THE GARONNE AND ITS TRIBUTARIES

These highly diverse regions stretch over the departments of Lot-et-Garonne, Tarn et Garonne, Tarn, Lot and Haute-Garonne. This is red wine territory, and the wines are predominantly dense and robust: Buzet, Côtes de Duras, Marmandais, Gaillac, Fronton, Cahors... some of which are drawn from a highly unusual range of varietals.

THE WINE REGIONS OF AVEYRON

Set in the heart of the Massif Central, these regions cover only a small area and the wines (mostly reds) are drunk locally. Marcillac is the best known.

THE PYRENEAN WINE REGION

This covers Béarn, Gascony and the Basque country, three regions with a strong personality. In the appellation areas of Irouleguy, Tursan, Madiran, Côtes de Saint-Mont and Béarn, growers are proud to produce robust, concentrated wines which can take the first-time drinker aback but are ideal partners for local specialities which abound in preserved meats or meats served with a sauce. At the other end of the spectrum, Jurançon and Pacherenc du Vic Bilh produce the most wonderful sweet wines. Armagnac rounds off the selection with its famous brandies.

THE COGNAC REGION

Although technically it is north of Bordeaux, Cognac belongs to the South-West and is famous the world over for its brandies. An increasing amount of wines labelled as Vin de Pays Charentais are grown there too. Refer to the chapter on 'brandies'.

REVIEW OF RECENT VINTAGES

• **2010** • defying the effects of climate change, harvesting in the region was generally several days later than usual, sometimes more. The wines are off to a promising start, both in terms of fruit and acidity and should produce some great efforts, particularly reds. Watch this space...

• **2011** • after several small crops, the region returned to more normal levels with good quality due to favourable weather patterns. Like other parts of France, weather in the spring was outstanding but July was wet and punctuated by stormy episodes. August and September were absolutely wonderful, providing ideal conditions for harvesting from late August onwards, eight days earlier than usual. Excellent potential, both for the whites (freshness, fruit) and the reds (colour, structure, fruit).
• **2012** • Following a tricky spring, the region experienced a hot, dry summer that impeded the ripening of the berries. The whites suffered, but the reds reached a good level of maturity. Generally a decent vintage, more than likely one that will be ready to drink soon.

THE SOUTH-WEST APPELLATIONS

A.C. BERGERAC

OVERVIEW: the Bergerac appellation area is located in the Dordogne department, on both banks of the river of the same name. 90 towns and villages are entitled to use the appellation. With almost 10,000 hectares under vine, the area has an extremely varied soil make-up, ranging from calcareous clay soils, to Perigordian sand and gravel, molasse... The climate is defined predominantly by the ocean, moderated by the coolness of the Dordogne. Red varietals here are Cabernet-Sauvignon, Cabernet Franc, Merlot, Malbec, Fer Servadou and Merille. White varietals: Semillon, Sauvignon, Muscadelle, augmented with a secondary range of Ondenc, Chenin blanc and Ugni blanc.
WINE STYLES: AC Bergerac produces red, rosés and dry white wines. The red wines are delicate and fruity, supple and elegant. They develop aromas of red fruit (strawberry, blackcurrant) and vanilla notes. They should be drunk within two or three years of being harvested and make a pleasant partner for preserved meats, cooked cold pork meats, poultry and small game birds (quail, thrush...). The rosés, made from Cabernet-Sauvignon, display an attractive salmon-pink hue. They are delicate, supple and extremely fruit-forward with great freshness. They display a fruity (raspberry, banana, blackcurrant) and floral bouquet (violet). Excellent with cooked cold pork meats, grilled meat or fish. The white wines are dry, fresh, with a pleasant bouquet. They boast a distinctively lively attack and good length on the palate. Their

aromas range from toasted, spicy and dried flowers to citrus fruit and vanilla. Try as an appetiser, with fish or shellfish.

A.C. BUZET

OVERVIEW: the Buzet appellation area embraces 27 towns and villages in the Lot-et-Garonne department, along the left bank of the Garonne between Agen and Marmande. Soil types are reasonably varied, ranging from gravel and calcareous clay on hillside sites, to 'boulbènes' (slaked loamy soils) along the plateau and the ridge. Red varietals are: Merlot, Cabernet-Sauvignon, Cabernet Franc and Malbec. For whites: Semillon, Sauvignon and Muscadelle.

WINE STYLES: the appellation produces red, rosé and white wines. With their attractive cherry colour, the reds are powerful, deep, fleshy, tannic wines, reminiscent of wines from Graves. Both wines in fact share virtually identical varietal ranges. Predominant aromas for the reds are ripe red fruit, animal notes and spices. The rosés are fresh and fruity, they are pleasantly nervous without becoming acidic. They exhibit fragrances of small red fruit and pear drops. The white wines are delicate, with a pleasant bouquet, nervous yet well-balanced, they retain freshness. They display floral notes, toasted almonds, ripe fruit (peach). The red wines pair with duck breast, preserved meats, rabbit with prunes. The rosés match with cooked cold pork meats, grilled white or red meats and the whites with foie gras, fish, freshwater whitebait or goats' cheese.

A.C. CAHORS

OVERVIEW: the Cahors region is located in the Lot department. The soils lay on a bed of ancient alluvium shaped into terraces or gently rolling hills. They are meagre, laden with quartz pebbles and siliceous gravel, interspersed with red clay and iron-rich sand. Along the plateau, the soil is more limestone. The valley enjoys an extremely unusual microclimate. The area is prone to some treacherous frost in the winter, though it is not particularly wet and autumn is usually sunny which promotes ripening.

WINE STYLES: Cahors only produces red wines from the Auxerrois grape variety (also known as Cot or Malbec). Occasionally, Merlot is added to the blend to soften the wines. Often dubbed 'black wine' because of its extremely dark hue and highly-present tannins, it is fruity and fleshy when young. Over the first two to three years, it remains closed before subsequently acquiring fullness and roundness. Predominant aromas are mushroom, spices, strawberry, prune, mineral notes and slightly toasted fragrances. In the early years, Cahors pairs extremely well with foie gras, duck confit or a leg of mutton. A few years down the line and it can be enjoyed with truffle croustade, ribsteak with ceps or game.

AC COTEAUX DU QUERCY

OVERVIEW: this 1999-established AOVDQS embraces 15 villages in the Lot department and 18 in Lot-et-Garonne, primarily located between Cahors and Montauban. Cabernet Franc (40% minimum, 60% maximum), though also Cot, Gamay, Merlot and Tannat (which individually must not exceed 20% of the varietal range) are grown here.
WINE STYLES: the red wines, which are relatively robust though less tannic than neighbouring Cahors, sit well alongside local specialities such as preserved meats and cassoulet. The rosés pair with cooked cold pork meats, fish or white meat.

A.C. CÔTES DE BERGERAC

OVERVIEW: the Côtes de Bergerac appellation, which can be applied to different colour wines, shares the same boundaries as AC Bergerac, in the Dordogne department, east of Bordeaux. Soil types are calcareous clay, sand, Perigordian gravel and molasse from several periods, with the climate strongly defined by the ocean.
WINE STYLES: AC Côtes de Bergerac produces red and white wines. The whites range from medium-dry to sweet depending on residual sugar content.
The red wines, with their intense, deep colour, exhibit aromas of crystallised fruit (prune), blackcurrant, spices and vanilla. They are rich, well-structured and fruity with an excellent propensity for ageing. Enjoy with duck or goose confit, duck breasts or cassoulet. The sweet white wines display an attractive golden hue. They combine aromatic freshness (crystallised fruit, honey, citrus fruit, exotic fruit) with roundness on the palate. As they mature they develop a remarkably full mouthfeel. They pair well with foie gras, poultry, white meat, fish served with mousseline sauce, or desserts.

A.C. CÔTES DE DURAS

OVERVIEW: the Côtes de Duras appellation area is situated in Aquitaine. Every style of wine is grown here: reds, rosés, dry and

sweet whites, on soils of molasse and compact clay mixed with various types of limestone.
WINE STYLES: the red wines, drawn from Cabernet Sauvignon, Cabernet Franc, Merlot and Malbec boast an attractive colour. They are powerful, fleshy, round wines displaying aromas of red fruit in brandy and spices. They can be served with garbure soup, black pudding, boiled chicken...
The rosés are made using the 'bleeding' process, and display a floral nose with red fruit (blackcurrant). They are lively, ethereal wines, well-balanced, combining freshness, roundness and fruitiness with a long aromatic finish. They are perfect partners for cooked cold pork meats. The dry white wines (Semillon, Sauvignon, Muscadelle, Chenin blanc, Ugni blanc) are racy and lively (tangerine, lemon, floral notes, hazelnut). Enjoy them with shad in a sorrel sauce or eel in a parsley and garlic sauce.
The sweet white wines, made from overripe grapes, exhibit a brilliant straw-yellow hue. They are unctuous, fat and well-balanced with great aromatic length. Aromas of crystallised fruit, acacia, honey, caramel, prune, crystallised orange... are all present. Perfect with foie gras or desserts.

AC CÔTES DE MILLAU

OVERVIEW: Côtes de Millau is the last region in Aveyron to be granted appellation status (AOVDQS since 1994). The vineyards wend their way along the Tarn river, embracing 17 towns and villages in Aveyron. The soil is calcareous clay on a bed of scree in the east and sandstone to the west. Mediterranean and mountain influences define the climate. Red varietals are: Gamay, Syrah, Cabernet-Sauvignon, Fer Servadou, Duras. White grapes are Chenin and Mauzac.
WINE STYLES: Côtes de Millau can be made as reds, rosés or whites. The red wines are round, well-balanced and harmonious with aromas of wild fruit (blackberry, wild raspberry). In their early years they can be served with cooked cold pork meats or poultry. A little patience allows the tannins to mellow. The rosé wines are fresh and fruity, and the whites well-balanced and supple on the palate.

A.C. CÔTES DE MONTRAVEL AND HAUT MONTRAVEL

OVERVIEW: the Côtes de Montravel and Haut Montravel appellation areas share the same location as Montravel. It is widely held that there is little difference between the two; the only reason there are two names is apparently because of a local feud. The vines are planted on a plateau and calcareous clay hillside sites. The climate is defined predominantly by the ocean, with the moderating influence of the Dordogne. Only white grape varieties are grown here: Semillon, Sauvignon and Muscadelle.

WINE STYLES: both appellations produce sweet or noble-rotted wines which display an unctuous attack, are harmonious, rich, complex and have good cellaring capacity. Some of the them can also be labelled as Bergerac moelleux. Predominant aromas are crystallised fruit, orange peel and lemon. They are suitable as appetisers, with fish served in a sauce and parsley-flavoured cheeses.

AC SAINT-MONT

OVERVIEW: the Saint-Mont region is situated exactly half way between the Atlantic Ocean and the Pyrenees, in the Adour valley. It covers the departments of Gers and Landes, centring on the towns of Saint-Mont, Plaisance, Aignan and Riscle. The soils are gravely (primeur wines), clayey (more distinctive wines) and calcareous clay (the realm of the white wines). The vineyards enjoy the dual climatic influence of the Pyrenees and the ocean. Long sunny days in the summer and autumn promote good ripening. Red varietals are Tannat, Cabernet Sauvignon, Cabernet Franc and Fer Servadou. White varieties are Arrufiac, Clairette, Courbu, Gros Manseng and Petit Manseng.

WINE STYLES: the appellation produces red, rosé and white wines. The red wines are rich, fleshy, fruity and heady, though at the same time elegant (aromas of black fruit, prune, cherry, blackberry, mild spices). The rosés are fresh, fruity and well-constituted with a full mouthfeel. The white wines are full, round and aromatic. The reds can be paired with red meat, poultry, game served with a sauce and cheeses. The rosés are well suited to barbecues (particularly lamb), paella, starters and mixed salads. The whites complement white meat (stuffed veal rolls, chicken Basquaise), shellfish and fish.

AC CÔTES DU BRULHOIS

OVERVIEW: Côtes du Brulhois wines are grown south of the Garonne valley, in an area straddling the departments of Lot-et-Garonne, Tarn-et-Garonne and Gers over 42 towns and villages. The soil is shaped into terraces or spread over stony, gravely and calcareous clay hillsides. The climate is defined both by ocean and Mediterranean influences. The area is home to Cabernet Sauvignon, Cabernet Franc, Merlot, Malbec, Fer Servadou and Tannat.

WINE STYLES: Côtes du Brulhois can be either red or rosé. The red wines, which are described locally as 'black wines', are powerful, full and velvety. They are rustic wines displaying aromas of blackcurrant, cherry, redcurrant, leather, toast and spices. Try with preserved meats, ceps, cassoulet or red meat. The rosé wines are made on a boutique scale and are also powerful and fruity. They should be served at a sit-down meal, with cooked cold pork meats or barbecued meats.

A.C. FRONTON

OVERVIEW: the Fronton wine region (Côtes du Frontonnais prior to 2007) is near Toulouse in the Tarn-et-Garonne and Haute-Garonne departments. The vines are grown on alluvium gravel terraces on a bedrock of molasse. Ocean and Mediterranean-type climates meet here and although the varietal range is varied – Gamay, Merille, Cinsault, Mauzac – the dominant grape is Negrette.

WINE STYLES: Fronton can be either red or rosé. The red wines are powerful with a ruby-red hue. They are well-structured and elegant with aromas of blackcurrant, raspberry, prune, floral notes (peony, violet) and spices (pepper). The rosés are both distinguished and easy-drinking wines. On the palate, they are aromatic with slightly acidulous notes (raspberry, blackcurrant, peach, pear, acacia blossom). The reds pair well with cassoulet, grilled red meats or game. The rosés can be served with fatty fish, barbecues or mixed salads.

A.C. CÔTES DU MARMANDAIS

OVERVIEW: set on the border with Gironde, in Lot-et-Garonne, Côtes du Marmandais is the natural extension of Graves and Entre-deux-Mers. It covers 27 towns and villages, 18 of which are located along the right bank of the Garonne and 9 on the left bank. The soils are gravely and calcareous clay on a bedrock of limestone molasse. The climate is defined primarily by the ocean although it is also influenced by the Pyrenees. The vines enjoy a favourable aspect, with plentiful sunshine, which promotes optimum ripeness. The varietal range embraces Cabernet Sauvignon, Cabernet Franc, Merlot, Abouriou, Cot, Fer, Gamay and Syrah. For the whites: Sauvignon, Semillon, Ugni blanc and Muscadelle.

WINE STYLES: the appellation produces red wines, rosés made predominantly using the 'bleeding' method, and white wines. The red wines are supple and aromatic: stewed fruit (prune, blackcurrant, raspberry) and spices (pepper, vanilla). Try with poultry, leg of lamb, grilled meat, game or cheese. The rosés are fresh, pleasant wines (red fruit, exotic fruit). They combine power with finesse, which makes them the ideal partner for barbecued meats, delicately-flavoured cooked cold pork meats, white meat, or fruit salad. The white wines are dry, aromatic and extremely fruity. They sit nicely alongside shellfish or fish.

A.C. FLOC DE GASCOGNE

OVERVIEW: AC Floc de Gascogne is a liqueur wine blended from grape juice and Armagnac, grown in the Gers, Landes and Lot-et-Garonne departments. The appellation covers an area under vine of 750 hectares and the wines can only be made within the confines of the Armagnac appellation area. Every year, 10% of Armagnac is actually used to make Floc de Gascogne, which is blended from two-thirds fresh grape juice drawn from Gascony grape varieties, and one third young Armagnac. Once the two are blended, the resultant wine then spends the next ten months in the cellar.

WINE STYLES: Floc de Gascogne can be either white or rosé and should be drunk within its first year. The whites are made from the white varietals Colombard, Ugni blanc and Gros Manseng. They are rich, generous and full, with a freshness that provides balance. The rosés are drawn from Cabernet Franc, Cabernet Sauvignon and Merlot. They are soft and extremely aromatic with predominant flavours of kirsch. The whites make perfect appetisers or can be paired with foie gras, melon and desserts (fresh fruit salad for instance). The rosés pair with apple tart, foie gras or melon.

A.C. GAILLAC

OVERVIEW: the Gaillac wine region is situated 50 kilometres from Toulouse in the Tarn department. It stretches northwards along both banks of the river Tarn to the mediaeval walled town of Cordes. Gaillac can be divided into four clear-cut 'terroirs': the terraces along the left banks of the Tarn with their poor gravel soils, the valley floor and its sand and deep gravel, the clay and calcareous clay along the hillocks and the predominantly limestone plateau.

Wet springs and long, dry late autumns are the defining climatic characteristics. The sparkling wines are made either by the hand-crafted method using natural grape sugars or by the traditional method. Either way, secondary fermentation takes place in the bottle. Harnessing the gas produced during alcoholic or malolactic fermentation gives dry whites a slight sparkle.

WINE STYLES: Gaillac wines cover a broad range of styles, from reds to dry whites, sweet whites or sparkling. Red wines are the region's mainstay, with an 80% share, and they are well-balanced, fragrant quaffing wines when they hail from the plateau. The hillside sites produce more robust wines with mellowed tannins and a harmonious finish. Wines grown along the gravel soils of the left bank are powerful with dense body and well-integrated tannins. Aromas of blackcurrant, green pepper and spices (pepper) are present. Try with beef and vegetable stew, duck casserole or rabbit stew.

The dry whites are slightly sparkling, fruity, floral wines with abundant freshness and suppleness. They are perfect with freshwater fish. The Mauzac varietal sweet white wines are rich and mild (musk, apple pips). They pair well with foie gras, roquefort cheese or gateaux. The sparkling wines display characteristic notes of apple, citrus fruit, ripe fruit and honey. Drink as an appetiser.

A.C. IROULEGUY

OVERVIEW: the Irouleguy wine region is located in the Pyrenees-Atlantiques department, in Basque country. The vines grow on siliceous clay and calcareous clay hillside sites with high iron oxide content where they enjoy a favourable aspect and are sheltered from the wind. This allows them to soak up maximum sunshine, particularly in the autumn. The co-operative winery is the region's foremost producer though there are also some independent wineries.

WINE STYLES: the red wines (Cabernet Franc, Cabernet Sauvignon, Tannat) display a bright, deep hue and boast a solid framework. They are often compared to Madiran though possibly have less body, are more rustic and exhibit great fragrance. They display an intense bouquet of wild red and black fruit (bilberries, blackberries) and pepper (Espelette). Try with cooked cold pork meats, roast meats (lamb) or ewe milk cheeses. The rosés, which are lively and quite light, pair well with tomato and pepper omelette, fish or seafood. The white wines (Courbu, Manseng) are fat and well-balanced. Their floral, exotic fruit (mango) and grapefruit tones give their freshness a boost. Perfect with fish and shellfish.

A.C. JURANÇON

OVERVIEW: the Jurançon wine region covers 700 hectares located south and west of Pau, in the foothills of the Pyrenees. Soil types are calcareous clay and siliceous clay and the ground is scattered with pebbles which retain heat during the day and release it by night. The vines grow here in a unique environment. The climate combines ocean influences (well-distributed rainfall) with mountain-type characteristics (risk of spring frosts). The south south-east facing plots enjoy plentiful sunshine and are sheltered from northerly winds. The vines grow at heights of 1.7 m. The Camaralet (15% maximum), Courbu, Gros Manseng, Lauzet (15% maximum) and Petit Manseng thrive in these conditions. A combination of hot daytime temperatures followed by cool nights is highly conducive to the production of sweet wines as it boosts the natural sugar content in the grapes. Fruit for the noble-rotted wines is harvested late in the season (November, or occasionally December).

WINE STYLES: the appellation only produces dry and sweet white wines. The dry white wines are fruity and aromatic (aromas of broom, acacia and passion fruit leading into toasted almond, dried fruit and truffle tones as they age). They can be served with shellfish and fish. The noble-rotted wines are fleshy, silky and harmonious. By and large they boast excellent cellaring capacity. The fruit on the nose is repeated on the palate: honey, white flowers (acacia, wild rose, hawthorn), candied fruit (apricot, orange, quince), fresh, warm bread and spices. Serve with foie gras or Pyrenean cheeses.

AC LAVILLEDIEU

OVERVIEW: the Lavilledieu wine region is situated west of Montauban in the Tarn-et-Garonne department. It covers 13 villages. Soil types are fine loam and silica on a bedrock of large stones or iron-rich hardpan. The climate is defined by both ocean and Mediterranean influences. The wines are aged either in tanks or barrels.

WINE STYLES: Lavilledieu wines can be either red or rosé and are blended from Negrette, Mauzac, Bordelais, Morterille, Chalosse, Gamay, Syrah and Fer Servadou. The red wines are well-constituted with well-integrated tannins. They are delicate and harmonious with aromas of red and black fruit (raspberry, blackcurrant, bilberry, strawberry) and liquorice and vanilla notes. A good match for duck or goose confit. The rosés are light, soft, highly-fragrant quaffing wines (floral and fruity notes, fragrances reminiscent of grenadine and pear drops). They pair well with barbecued meats, cooked cold pork meats and starters.

A.C. MADIRAN

OVERVIEW: Madiran stretches across three departments: Gers, Hautes-Pyrenees and Pyrenees-Atlantiques, embracing 36 towns and villages (27 in Pyrenees-Atlantiques, 6 in Hautes-Pyrenees and 3 in Gers). It shares the same area as the Pacherenc du Vic Bilh appellation where the soils are siliceous clay and calcareous clay. The nearby Atlantic has a moderating influence on the climate, making it slightly milder and wetter.

WINE STYLES: AC Madiran is a red wine only appellation where the primary varietal is Tannat. With their dense, extremely deep garnet-red colour, Madiran wines are rich in tannins, powerful, robust and well-constituted. They have an outstanding capacity to age though as young wines they can be harsh, particularly when Tannat is the mainstay of the blend. Principal aromas are black fruit, roasted coffee and spices. Food pairings include duck confit or breast, meat served with a sauce, lamb and ewe milk cheeses.

A.C. MARCILLAC

OVERVIEW: the Aveyron department is home to this appellation, which stretches over a dozen villages west of Rodez. The soils are made up of clay with high iron oxide content as well as limestone and marl, along the rim of the limestone plateau. The area is blessed with a microclimate conducive to growing vines which enjoy a favourable aspect due to their situation, on extremely steep hillside sites or terraces supported by dry stone walls. The wines are vinted traditionally at controlled temperatures and are aged either in tanks or barrels.

WINE STYLES: Marcillac produces both red wines from the Fer Servadou grape variety and rosés. The red wines are tannic, clean and warm with aromas of red fruit, spices, fern and green pepper. They pair well with sophisticated meat dishes, aligot (a local speciality made from mashed potatoes, fresh cheese and garlic), tripe or Bleu des Causses cheese. The rosés, which in some respects are a reflection of the 'terroir', are a great match for cooked cold pork meats.

A.C. MONBAZILLAC

OVERVIEW: the Monbazillac wine region is located south of Bergerac, along the left bank of the Dordogne. It is France's largest producer of noble-rotted sweet wines (with an average annual production of 50,000 hl). The vines (Semillon, Sauvignon and Muscadelle) are planted on hillside sites and calcareous clay plateaux. A mantle of fog frequently covers the vines on Autumn mornings, lifting during the day to make way for radiant sunshine. This provides ideal conditions for the formation of botrytis cinerea, a prerequisite for producing great sweet wines. As with Sauternes, the grapes are harvested by painstakingly combing through the vineyards time after time as each berry 'roasts'. Once they have been pressed, the resultant juice may have a natural content of up to 20% by volume. The wines are made in the ordinary way and then undergo ageing, usually in barrels, for at least a year.

WINE STYLES: Monbazillac can only produce noble-rotted white wines. They display a golden hue and boast unrivalled fat and unctuousness, bolstered by a touch of nervousness on the finish. They have an excellent propensity for ageing. Principal aromas are honey, acacia, peach, candied fruit. Suitable food pairings include foie gras, fatted chicken in a cream sauce, blue cheese from Auvergne or Roquefort cheese.

A.C. MONTRAVEL

OVERVIEW: the Montravel appellation area sits between Bordeaux and Bergerac. It forms an enclave, surrounded by Côtes-de-Castillon, from which it extends outwards, Entre-deux-Mers and the Sainte-Foy-Bordeaux area. Fifteen villages stretching along the right bank of the Dordogne are entitled to the appellation. The vines grow either on a calcareous clay plateau or on gravely terraces over an Asteries limestone bedrock.

The climate is strongly defined by the ocean and is hot though with the moderating coolness of the Dordogne. Some wines are vinted and aged on the lees which imparts greater structure and roundness.

WINE STYLES: Montravel is a dry white wine drawn from Semillon, Sauvignon and Muscadelle. Boasting a pale yellow hue, they are lively on the palate though not acidic. Growers who choose to do so can label their wines as Bergerac sec. However, red and rosé wines grown within this area are only entitled to the Bergerac or Côtes de Bergerac appellations. The aromas are floral, mineral (gunflint) and blackurrant bud. They can be served with poached trout or pike with melted butter.

A.C. PACHERENC DU VIC BILH

OVERVIEW: the Pacherenc du Vic Bilh appellation shares the same area as Madiran, embracing 36 towns and villages split between three departments: Gers, Hautes-Pyrenees and Pyrenees-Atlantiques. The soils are siliceous clay and calcareous clay. The climate is defined by the ocean and is thus mild and damp.
WINE STYLES: the appellation produces white wine which can range from dry to sweet depending on the weather. It is made from Arrufiac, Courbu, Petit Manseng, Gros Manseng, Sauvignon and Semillon. The dry white wines usually display a lively attack leading into a round mouthfeel. They develop aromas of white flowers and exotic fruits with an extremely pleasant acidulous finish. Try with shellfish or fish in a sauce. The sweet wines are powerful, warm and extremely fragrant (pineapple, orange peel, honey). On the palate, their freshness is unexpected. They are enjoyable as appetisers or with foie gras or ewe milk cheese.

A.C. PINEAU DES CHARENTES

OVERVIEW: Pineau des Charentes is produced in both Charente departments, in the same area as Cognac. It is actually a blend of fresh grape juice and Cognac (mistelle). Once the fruit is pressed, the juice is left for 24 hours in tanks before oak-aged Cognac is added to arrest fermentation. Pineau then matures in oak barrels for at least 1 year before being bottled. These liqueur wines are made from Ugni blanc, Colombard, Folle blanche, Cabernet, Malbec and Merlot. To warrant the appellation, Pineau must comply with stringent regulations. The Cognac must come from the same farm as the fresh grapes and must have an ABV of at least 60%. The resultant Pineau has an ABV of between 16 and 22%.
WINE STYLES: Pineau des Charentes can be either white or rosé. The whites display an amber-yellow colour with golden tints. They are fat, round and aromatic with great length on the palate: dried fruit (walnuts, almonds), honey, quince paste and often slightly oxidised notes, of varying intensity. The rosés display a crimson hue with brick-red tints. They are delicate and extremely fruity, both on the nose and on the palate: red and black fruit (blackberry, blackcurrant, morello cherry). The whites and the rosés can be savoured as appetisers, or partnered with foie gras, fruit-based desserts (melon, tarts, fruit salad) or chocolate.

A.C. ROSETTE

OVERVIEW: Rosette is set in rolling hills near Bergerac in the Dordogne department. Urban sprawl has reduced its area under vine to less than 100 hectares. The vines are planted on gravely clay soils and the climate is defined by the ocean though with a southerly influence. The noble-rotted grapes are picked in stages then pressed, vinted and subsequently aged, primarily in oak.

WINE STYLES: the appellation only produces sweet white wines on a boutique scale, blended from Semillon, Sauvignon and Muscadelle. They are straw-yellow in colour, supple, fat and elegant; their freshness imparts balance. As for aromas, their bouquet is floral and fruity. Rosette can be served as an appetiser, with seafood, mushroom or truffle-based starters or foie gras.

A.C. SAUSSIGNAC

OVERVIEW: Saussignac is grown west of Bergerac, along the left bank of the Dordogne. The area embraces four villages. The soils are calcareous clay or fine grain sandy clay ('boulbènes') which can easily become impermeable. The noble-rotted grapes are picked in stages then pressed in the normal way, vinted and subsequently aged, primarily in oak.

WINE STYLES: the Saussignac appellation produces only sweet white or noble-rotted wines. The sweet whites are supple and well-balanced. The noble-rotted wines are full, rich and fat and will only fully reveal their opulence after a few years' ageing. Predominant aromas for the sweet whites are honey, flower (linden) and citrus fruit (grapefruit), whilst the noble-rotted wines display primarily floral (acacia) and fruit aromas (peach, nectarine). Serve with foie gras, cream soups and desserts.

AC TURSAN

OVERVIEW: the Tursan wine region is situated south-east of Mont-de-Marsan, in the Landes and Gers departments where it embraces 41 towns and villages. The vines occupy rolling hills where the soil make-up is clayey silica, limestone and stones. The region enjoys a mild, temperate ocean climate. A broad range of grape varietals is grown here: Tannat, Bouchy, Cabernet Sauvignon, Cabernet Franc, Fer Servadou and Pinenc for the reds. Baroque, Sauvignon, Petit Manseng, Gros Manseng, Claverie, Cruchinet, Raffiat, Gers Claret and Clairette for the whites.

WINE STYLES: the red wines are powerful, well-constituted and full of finessse (wild fruit and fern notes). They enhance duck or goose breast, wood pigeon casserole, jugged hare, roast beef or foie gras with grapes. The rosés are fresh, fruity quaffing wines which reward early drinking and pair with cooked cold pork meats and mixed salads. The white wines are dry, lively, fruity and pleasing to the palate. They are a particularly good match for oysters, fish (salmon, trout), hors d'ouvre or foie gras.

AC VINS D'ENTRAYGUES ET DU FEL

OVERVIEW: Entraygues et du Fel wines are grown in the departments of Aveyron and Cantal. The area covers around 20 hectares under vine on shale hillsides in Fel and 'barene' type and granite soils in Entraygues. A broad range of grape varietals is grown here: Cabernet Sauvignon, Cabernet Franc, Fer Servadou, Abouriou, Gamay, Jurançon noir, Merlot, Mouyssages, Negrette, Pinot noir, Duras and Castel for the reds. Chenin blanc, Roussellou and Mauzac for the whites.

WINE STYLES: the wines of Entraygues et du Fel can be either red, rosé or white. The red wines are sturdy and bear the hallmark characteristics of their 'terroir'. Occasionally they are described as rough though they can also be approachable quaffing wines intended for early drinking. Try with tripe, Auvergne-style stew or lamb. The rosés are aromatic (red fruit and almond notes), racy and velvety. They pair well with cooked cold pork meats and barbecued meat. The white wines are dry, vigorous and extremely fragrant (broom, acacia, linden, gunflint, citrus fruit). On the palate, they reveal aromas of apple and almond. Try with shellfish.

AC VINS D'ESTAING

OVERVIEW: AOVDQS Estaing wines are grown in the departments of Cantal and Aveyron. The shale or calcareous clay soils provide a foothold for the vines along the abrupt hillsides overlooking the Lot valley.

WINE STYLES: Estaing wines can be either red or white. The red wines are delicate and fruity (red fruit, green pepper) and reward early drinking with roast meat and game (jugged hare, leg of venison...). The white wines are dry and fruity with an after-taste of gunflint. They are good partners for fish and seafood.

• • •

SOUTH-WEST

Bergerac

CHÂTEAU DE FAYOLLE +33 5 53 74 32 02

▼ Vintage 2011 Price: ❍ 86/100

▼ Vintage 2011 Price: ❍ 83/100

CHÂTEAU GRINOU +33 5 53 58 46 63

ORG ▼ Tradition - Sauvignon blanc - Sémillon 2012 Price: ❍ 82/100

CHÂTEAU PIQUE-SÈGUE +33 5 53 58 52 52

▼ Vintage 2009 Price: ❍ 88/100

▼ Vintage 2012 Price: ❍ 83/100

DOMAINE DE MOULIN-POUZY +33 5 53 58 41 20

▼ La Cuvée 2010 Price: ❍❍ 85/100

▼ Vintage 2011 Price: ❍ 85/100

▼ Vintage 2012 Price: ❍ 85/100

VIGNOBLES VALLETTE +33 5 53 24 77 98

▼ Château Roque-Peyre Elégance 2011 Price: ❍ 84/100

▼ Château Riffaud Elégance 2011 Price: ❍ 83/100

▼ Château Riffaud Fraîcheur 2012 Price: ❍ 82/100

▼ Château Roque-Peyre Fraîcheur 2012 Price: ❍ 82/100

Bergerac sec

CHÂTEAU DE PANISSEAU +33 5 53 58 40 03

▼ Divin 2009 Price: ❍❍ 88/100

DOMAINE DE MOULIN-POUZY +33 5 53 58 41 20

▼ Vintage 2012 Price: ❍ 85/100

▼ Moulin-Pouzy Optimum 2011 Price: ❍❍ 83/100

Cahors

BLADINIÈRES LIORIT +33 5 65 22 41 85

▼ Mas des Etoiles Une étoile est née... 2009 Price: ❍❍ 92/100

CHÂTEAU EUGÉNIE +33 5 65 30 73 51

▼ Haute Collection 2010 Price: ❍❍❍ 93/100

▼ Cuvée Réservée de l'Aïeul 2010 Price: ❍❍ 91/100

▼ Pierre Le Grand 2010 Price: ❍ 88/100

CHÂTEAU FAMAEY +33 5 65 30 59 42

▼ Cuvée X 2009 Price: ❍❍ 90/100

CHÂTEAU GAUTOUL +33 5 65 30 84 17

▼ Vieilli en Fûts de Chêne 2011 Price: ❍ 88/100

CHÂTEAU NOZIÈRES +33 5 65 36 52 73

▼ Ambroise de l'Her - Elevé en Fûts de Chêne 2010 Price: ❍ 88/100

▼ L'Elégance - Malbec 2010 Price: ❍❍ 88/100

▼ Vintage 2010 Price: ❍ 84/100

CHÂTEAU PINERAIE +33 5 65 30 82 07

▼ L'Authentique 2010 Price: ❍❍❍ 93/100

▼ Vintage 2010 Price: ❍ 90/100

DOMAINE DU SOULEILLAN +33 5 65 35 61 72

▼ Phénix - Elevé en fût de chêne 2009 Price: ❍ 88/100

▼ Phénix 2009 Price: ❍ 86/100

DUROU ET FILS +33 5 65 36 52 93

▼ Château de Gaudou Réserve Caillau 2011 Price: ❍❍❍ 92/100

▼ Château de Gaudou Renaissance 2011 Price: ❍❍ 89/100

▼ Château de Gaudou Grande Lignée 2011 Price: ❍ 88/100

▼ Château de Gaudou La Colombe 2011 Price: ❍ 86/100

▼ Château de Gaudou Tradition 2012 Price: ❍ 85/100

Detailed instructions are featured at the start of the book.

Côtes de Bergerac

CHÂTEAU BÉLINGARD +33 5 53 58 28 03

- ▼ Cuvée Blanche de Bosredon 2011 Price: ❍ 93/100
- ▼ Ortus 2010 Price: ❍❍ 91/100
- ▼ Cuvée Blanche de Bosredon 2010 Price: ❍ 89/100

CHÂTEAU DE PANISSEAU +33 5 53 58 40 03

- ▼ Mademoiselle Jane 2007 Price: ❍❍ 85/100

CHÂTEAU PIQUE-SÈGUE +33 5 53 58 52 52

- ▼ Château Dauzan la Vergne Vintage 2008 Price: ❍ 88/100

Côtes de Bergerac moelleux

CHÂTEAU GRINOU +33 5 53 58 46 63

- ORG ▼ Tradition - Sémillon 2012 Price: ❍ 82/100

DOMAINE DE MOULIN-POUZY +33 5 53 58 41 20

- ▼ Vintage 2012 Price: ❍ 82/100

Côtes de Gascogne

CHÂTEAU BARRÉJAT +33 5 62 69 74 92

- ▼ Denis Capmartin Colombard - Ugni blanc 2011 Price: ❍ 84/100

DOMAINE CHIROULET +33 5 62 28 02 21

- ▼ Soleil d'Automne 2012 Price: ❍ 89/100
- ▼ Terroir Gascon 2011 Price: ❍ 88/100
- ▼ Le Temps des Fleurs 2012 Price: ❍ 87/100
- ▼ Terres Blanches 2012 Price: ❍ 85/100

DOMAINE DE JOŸ +33 5 62 09 03 20

- ▼ Attitude 2010 Price: ❍❍ 88/100
- ▼ Saint André 2012 Price: ❍ 84/100
- ▼ L'Etoile 2012 Price: ❍ 83/100

DOMAINE DE MAGNAUT +33 5 62 29 45 40

▼ Colombard 2012 Price: ❍ — 85/100

Côtes de Montravel

CHÂTEAU PIQUE-SÈGUE +33 5 53 58 52 52

▼ Vintage 2009 Price: ❍ — 84/100

VIGNOBLES VALLETTE +33 5 53 24 77 98

▼ Château Roque-Peyre Douceur 2012 Price: ❍ — 84/100

▼ Château Riffaud Douceur 2012 Price: ❍ — 84/100

Côtes du Lot

CHÂTEAU GAUTOUL +33 5 65 30 84 17

▼ Malbec 2011 Price: ❍ — 84/100

DOMAINE DE BELFORT +33 6 87 72 18 35

CV▼ Tour de Belfort Cuvée Classique 2012 Price: ❍❍ — 86/100

CV▼ Tour de Belfort Cuvée Classique 2012 Price: ❍❍ — 85/100

DUROU ET FILS +33 5 65 36 52 93

▼ Gaudou Premier Grain 2012 Price: ❍ — 86/100

Côtes du Tarn

DOMAINE D\'EN SÉGUR +33 5 63 58 09 45

▼ Grande Réserve 2008 Price: ❍❍ — 85/100

▼ Le Rosé 2012 Price: ❍ — 83/100

▼ Cuvée Madeleine 2011 Price: ❍ — 82/100

▼ Sauvignon Blanc 2012 Price: ❍ — 82/100

DOMAINE DU COMTE DE THUN +33 5 63 56 14 02

▼ Comte de Thun La Tarabelle 2007 Price: ❍❍❍ 89/100

▼ Comte de Thun La Maze 2008 Price: ❍❍❍ 88/100

▼ Comte de Thun La Parrazal 2007 Price: ❍❍ 87/100

Fronton

DOMAINE ROUMAGNAC +33 6 80 95 34 08

▼ O Grand R 2011 Price: ❍ 87/100

▼ Authentique 2011 Price: ❍ 83/100

▼ Authentique 2012 Price: ❍ 82/100

LE FRONTON NEZ +33 5 61 82 93 29

▼ Château Cassin 2009 Price: ❍ 87/100

Gaillac

CHÂTEAU DE MAYRAGUES +33 5 63 33 94 08

ORG▼ Vintage 2011 Price: ❍❍ 85/100

CHÂTEAU LECUSSE +33 5 63 33 90 09

▼ Grande Cuvée Prestige - Fer servadou 2010 Price: ❍ 88/100

▼ Vieilli en fûts de chêne 2009 Price: ❍ 88/100

▼ Vieilli en fûts de chêne 2010 Price: ❍ 87/100

▼ Extra Brut 2009 Price: ❍ 86/100

▼ Grande Cuvée Prestige - Syrah 2010 Price: ❍ 86/100

▼ Grande Cuvée Prestige - Duras 2010 Price: ❍ 86/100

DOMAINE DE PIALENTOU +33 5 63 57 17 99

ORG▼ Les Gentilles Pierres
Elevé en fûts de chêne 2007 Price: ❍❍ 87/100

ORG▼ Mauzac 2012 Price: ❍ 86/100

ORG▼ Nuance de Cocagne 2012 Price: ❍ 84/100

Haut-Montravel

CHÂTEAU PIQUE-SÈGUE +33 5 53 58 52 52

▼ Château Dauzan la Vergne Vintage 1996 Price: ○○ 95/100

Jurançon

DOMAINE BRU-BACHÉ +33 5 59 21 36 34

ORG▼ L'Eminence 2010 Price: ○○○○ 95/100

ORG▼ La Quintessence 2010 Price: ○○○ 90/100

ORG▼ Les Casterasses 2010 Price: ○○ 86/100

DOMAINE NIGRI +33 5 59 21 42 01

CV▼ Toute une Histoire 2011 Price: ○○ 91/100

CV▼ Pas de Deux 2011 Price: ○ 86/100

Jurançon sec

DOMAINE BRU-BACHÉ +33 5 59 21 36 34

ORG▼ Les Casterasses 2010 Price: ○○ 87/100

DOMAINE NIGRI +33 5 59 21 42 01

CV▼ Pierre de Lune 2011 Price: ○ 88/100

CV▼ Confluence 2012 Price: ○ 86/100

> Prices mentioned in this book are guideline and can vary depending on point of sale. The shops, wineries or publisher can in no way be held responsible for this.

Madiran

CHÂTEAU BARRÉJAT +33 5 62 69 74 92

▼ Cuvée de l'Extrême
Élevé en fûts de chêne neufs 2010 Price: ❍❍ — 94/100

▼ Cuvée des Vieux Ceps 2010 Price: ❍ — 88/100

▼ Séduction - élevé en fûts de chêne 2010 Price: ❍ — 86/100

DOMAINE DES BORIES +33 5 59 68 16 24

▼ Grande Réserve 2011 Price: ❍❍ — 89/100

▼ Tradition 2011 Price: ❍ — 86/100

▼ Réserve 2010 Price: ❍ — 86/100

Marcillac

DOMAINE LAURENS +33 5 65 72 69 37

▼ Cuvée de Flars 2011 Price: ❍ — 87/100

▼ Vintage 2012 Price: ❍ — 86/100

▼ Vintage 2011 Price: ❍ — 85/100

Monbazillac

CHÂTEAU VIEUX TOURON +33 5 53 58 21 16

▼ Vintage 2009 Price: ❍ — 86/100

DOMAINE DE MOULIN-POUZY +33 5 53 58 41 20

▼ Moulin-Pouzy Optimum 2010 Price: ❍❍❍ — 94/100

▼ La Cuvée 2010 Price: ❍❍ — 93/100

▼ Vintage 2011 Price: ❍❍ — 85/100

Montravel

CHÂTEAU MASBUREL +33 5 53 24 77 73

▼ Vintage 2008 Price: ❍❍ 90/100

CHÂTEAU PIQUE-SÈGUE +33 5 53 58 52 52

▼ Terre de Pique-Sègue Anima Vitis 2005 Price: ❍❍ 90/100

▼ Vintage 2012 Price: ❍ 86/100

VIGNOBLES VALLETTE +33 5 53 24 77 98

▼ Château Riffaud Subtilité 2012 Price: ❍ 86/100

▼ Château Roque-Peyre Subtilité 2012 Price: ❍ 86/100

Pacherenc du Vic Bilh

DOMAINE DES BORIES +33 5 59 68 16 24

▼ Vintage 2011 Price: ❍ 89/100

Pineau des Charentes

PINEAU ROUSSILLE +33 5 45 91 05 18

▼ Roussille Extra Vieux - rosé Price: ❍❍ 88/100

▼ Roussille Price: ❍ 86/100

ENTRY LEVEL TABLE WINES

Vin de France

ANTOINE SIMONEAU +33 2 54 71 36 14

▼ A Simoneau Rouge Price: ❍ 81/100

CAVE COOPÉRATIVE AGHIONE +33 4 95 56 60 20

▼ Cuvée Napoléon Bonaparte 2008 Price: ❍ 83/100

CHÂTEAU GUIOT +33 4 66 73 30 86

▼ L'Enclos de la Chance Extrafragance 2011 Price: ❍❍❍ 87/100

DENOIS +33 4 68 31 39 12

CV▼ Vintage 2011 Price: ❍ 86/100

DOMAINE DES RICHÈRES +33 2 41 54 10 47

▼ Vintage 2011 Price: ❍ 86/100

DOMAINE RICHEAUME +33 4 42 66 31 27

▼ Cuvée Columelle 2010 Price: ❍❍❍ 90/100

DUROU ET FILS +33 5 65 36 52 93

▼ Gaudou Exception 2012 Price:❍ 82/100

VILLA DELORT +33 6 74 94 14 75

▼ VD 2010 Price: ❍❍❍ 88/100

Vin Mousseux (Brut)

DENOIS +33 4 68 31 39 12

▼ Brut Price: ❍❍ 86/100

Vin Mousseux (Demi-Sec)

CAVE COOPÉRATIVE AGHIONE +33 4 95 56 60 20

▼ Casanova - Muscatu Frizante Price:❍ 82/100

BRANDIES

Calvados Domfrontais

LES CHAIS DU VERGER NORMAND +33 2 33 38 53 96

▼ Comte Louis de Lauriston 1973 Price:○○○○○ 92/100

▼ Comte Louis de Lauriston 1993 Price:○○○○ 89/100

▼ Comte Louis de Lauriston Réserve Price:○○○ 86/100

▼ Comte Louis de Lauriston 1963 Price:○○○○○ 94/100

Calvados Pays d'Auge

CALVADOS CHRISTIAN DROUIN +33 2 31 64 30 05

▼ Vintage 1993 Price:○○○○ 91/100

▼ 25 ans Price:○○○○○ 90/100

▼ X.O. Price:○○○○ 88/100

▼ Vintage 1963 Price:○○○○○ 94/100

Cognac

PINEAU ROUSSILLE +33 5 45 91 05 18

▼ Roussille V.S.O.P. Price:○○○ 86/100

COGNAC GODET +33 5 46 41 10 66

▼ Antarctica - Icy Cognac Price:○ 86/100

PINEAU ROUSSILLE +33 5 45 91 05 18

▼ Roussille X.O. Price:○○○ 89/100

Detailed instructions are featured at the start of the book.

Cognac Fine Champagne

COGNAC GODET +33 5 46 41 10 66

▼ Gastronome Price:○ 88/100

Cognac Grande Champagne (See also page 404)

COGNAC FRAPIN +33 5 45 83 40 03

▼ Multi vintage 1982 - 1986 - 1989 Price:○○○○○ 94/100

PASCAL DUMONT +33 5 45 81 69 16

▼ XO Price:○○○○○ 90/100

PIERRE FERRAND +33 5 45 36 62 50

▼ 1er Cru Sélection des Anges Price:○○○○○ 92/100

Cognac Petite Champagne

COGNAC GODET +33 5 46 41 10 66

▼ Vintage 1972 Price:○ 93/100

WINE SCORES:

95-100/100: an outstanding wine, when a great 'terroir' meets exceptional winemaking expertise.

90-94/100: a superlative wine combining finesse, complexity and remarkable winemaking.

85-89/100:a wine of extremely high standard, which we enjoyed for its typicity and character.

80-84/100: a quality wine combining balance, structure and neatness for a pleasurable wine drinking experience.

75-79/100: a wine deemed acceptable.

***Note:** wines scoring less than 75/100 are not included in our publications.*

COGNAC FRAPIN

▼ Carafe Plume **99/100**

Deeply-coloured with mahogany. The nose is complex yet subtle and evolving with floral notes leading into spice tones, dried flowers and prunes. Extraordinary roundness on the palate and an endless explosion of aromas. Remarkable.

Price: OOOOO

Cognac and food pairing: After an exceptional dinner
Serving Temperature: 14-16°C
Ready to drink: From now on

Plume Frapin is a Cognac that pays tribute to the writer François Rabelais, the son of Anne-Catherine Frapin, the illustrious ancestor of this family that has been established in southwestern France since 1270. It is created from a blend of some 20 different eaux-de-vie, all produced from Ugni Blanc grapes grown in the 240 hectares of vineyards surrounding Château Fontpinot. This very old Grande Champagne Cognac has been patiently aged for more than 60 years in 100-year-old casks. An exceptional eau-de-vie, it comes in an exclusive, elegant decanter decorated with the House's signature feather and topped with two entwined pewter feathers gilded with 18-carat pink gold. The House's terroir, artful blending, patience and respect for the environment make Plume Frapin an exceptional Cognac, produced in a limited series of 500 numbered bottles.

Cognac Frapin
1 rue Pierre Frapin
16130 Segonzac
Tel.: +33 (0)5 45 83 40 03 - Fax: +33 (0)5 45 83 33 67
E-mail: info@cognac-frapin.com
Website: http://www.cognac-frapin.com

COGNAC FRAPIN

▼ Château Fontpinot XO **93/100**

Very deep orange with fiery highlights. Delightful nose marrying citrus, orange peel and spice. Great purity from point of entry onwards. More of the same very endearing fragrance. Long, spicy finish displaying a certain character.

Price: OOOOO

Cognac and food pairing: Chocolates desserts
Serving Temperature: 13-15°C
Ready to drink: From now on

The Frapin family settled in Charente around 1270, but the House as it exists today was founded by Pierre Frapin at the end of the 19th century. Located on the hillsides of Segonzac in the Grande Champagne appellation, the estate extends over more than 316 hectares around the Château Fontpinot. It produces a Cognac made exclusively from grapes from its own vineyards, officially classified as Premier Cru de Cognac. The eaux-de-vie are made using double distillation and then matured in Limousin oak casks. This is a superior House, producing top-notch Cognacs that we have been following for some time. To visit (by appointment only), take the N141 to Angoulême in the direction of Cognac. After Saint-Yrieix-sur-Charente, take the D736 towards Segonzac.

Cognac Frapin
1 rue Pierre Frapin - 16130 Segonzac
Tel.: +33 (0)5 45 83 40 03 - Fax: +33 (0)5 45 83 33 67
E-mail: info@cognac-frapin.com
Website: http://www.cognac-frapin.com

WINES OF THE WORLD

ARGENTINA

Argentina

MARKS & SPENCER FRANCE +33 01 47 30 10 35

▼ Balbi Shiraz - Viognier 2011 Price: O — 80/100

AUSTRALIA

South Eastern Australia

MARKS & SPENCER FRANCE +33 01 47 30 10 35

▼ Riverina Shiraz 2011 Price: O — 83/100

South Australia

Barossa Valley

MARKS & SPENCER FRANCE +33 01 47 30 10 35

▼ Marananga Dam Old Wines
Grenache - Shiraz - Mourvèdre 2009 Price: OO — 91/100

▼ Barosa Shiraz 2010 Price: OO — 91/100

Prices mentioned in this book are guideline and can vary depending on point of sale. The shops, wineries or publisher can in no way be held responsible for this.

CHILE

Casablanca (Cile)

Casablanca

MARKS & SPENCER FRANCE +33 01 47 30 10 35

▼ Tierra y Hombre Pinot Noir 2011 Price: O 85/100

Coquimbo

Valle de Limari

MARKS & SPENCER FRANCE +33 01 47 30 10 35

▼ Joya del Limari Sauvignon blanc 2011 Price: OO 88/100

Valle Central

Valle Central

MARKS & SPENCER FRANCE +33 01 47 30 10 35

▼ Paradiso Sauvignon blanc 2011 Price: O 86/100

CHINA

Vin de Chine

GREAT RIVER HILL WINERY

▼ Château Nine Peaks Reserva 2011 Price: OOO 90/100

▼ Château Nine Peaks Vintage 2011 Price: OOO 85/100

Detailed instructions are featured at the start of the book.

ITALIA

Apulia

Primitivo di Manduria D.O.C.

MASSERIA DI ALTEMURA +39 831740485

▼ Vintage 2010 Price: ❍ 91/100

Salento I.G.T

MASSERIA DI ALTEMURA +39 831740485

▼ Sasseo 2011 Price: ❍ 88/100

CASTELLO MONACI +39 831665700

▼ Artas 2010 Price: ❍❍ 89/100

MASSERIA DI ALTEMURA +39 831740485

▼ Fiano 2012 Price: ❍ 89/100

Salice Salentino D.O.C.

CASTELLO MONACI +39 831665700

▼ Aiace 2009 Price: ❍❍ 89/100

THE COLOUR OF THE WINES :

■ Red wine	▲ Sparkling brut
■ Dry white wine	▲ Sparkling brut rose
■ Rose wine	◆ Brandy
● Sweet white wine	● Liqueur wine

Campania

Campagna I.G.P.

AZIENDA AGRICOLA LE VIGNE DI RAITO DI PATRIZIA MAL +39 3288651452

CV▼ Ragis rosso 2009 Price: OO 87/100

Fiano di Avellino D.O.C.G

CANTINE COLLE DI SAN DOMENICO +39 825985423

▼ Vintage 2012 Price: O 85/100

Greco di Tufo D.O.C.G

CANTINE COLLE DI SAN DOMENICO +39 825985423

▼ Vintage 2012 Price: O 85/100

Taurasi D.O.C.G

CANTINE COLLE DI SAN DOMENICO +39 825985423

▼ Riserva 2007 Price: OO 90/100

▼ Riserva 2006 Price: O 90/100

Terre del Volturno I.G.P.

TERRE DEL PRINCIPE +39 823867126

CV▼ Le Sèrole 2011 Price: OO 88/100

▼ Centomoggia 2010 Price: OOO 84/100

CV▼ Ambruco 2010 Price: OOO 87/100

Emilia-Romagna

Albana di Romagna D.O.C.G.

TENUTE D'ITALIA +39 542641194

▼ Santerno 2010 Price: O 87/100

Lambrusco Grasparossa di Castelvetro D.O.C

AZIENDA AGRICOLA MANICARDI +39 59799000

- ▼ Manicardi Az. Agr. Castrum Vetus 2012 Price: ❍ 84/100
- ▼ Manicardi Az. Agr. Vigna ca' del fiore 2012 Price: ❍ 85/100

Rubicone I.G.T.

DREI DONA' TENUTA LA PALAZZA +39 543769371

- ▼ Notturno 2011 Price: ❍ 86/100
- ▼ Magnificat Single Vineyard 2008 Price: ❍❍❍ 87/100

Sangiovese di Romagna D.O.C.

DREI DONA' TENUTA LA PALAZZA +39 543769371

- ▼ Pruno Single Vineyard 2009 Price: ❍❍❍ 89/100

Vino spumante

AZIENDA AGRICOLA MANICARDI +39 59799000

- ▼ Manicardi Az. Agr. Rosé Brut 2012 Price: ❍ 85/100

Detailed instructions are featured at the start of the book.

Friuli - Venezia Giulia

Alto Livenza I.G.T

TENUTE TOMASELLA +39 042 28 50 043

- ▼ Rigole Brut 2011 Price: ❍ 85/100
- ▼ Rosso di Rigole 2010 Price: ❍ 84/100
- ▼ Rigole rosso 2011 Price: ❍ 81/100
- ▼ Rigole bianco 2011 Price: ❍ 87/100

Carso D.O.C.

PAROVEL +39 3467590953

- ▼ Vinja Barde - Malvasia Istriana 2008 Price: ❍❍ 89/100
- ▼ Vinja Barde - Malvasia Istriana 2011 Price: ❍❍ 89/100
- ▼ Vinja Barde - Vitovska 2011 Price: ❍❍ 87/100
- ▼ Vinja Barde - Malvasia Istriana 2009 Price: ❍❍ 87/100
- ▼ Vinja Barde - Matos Nonet 2008 Price: ❍❍ 91/100

Colli Orientali del Friuli D.O.C

AZIENDA AGRICOLA LA BUSE DAL LOF DI MICHELE PAVAN +39 374 642197

- ▼ Chardonnay 2012 Price: ❍ 87/100

AZIENDA AGRICOLA LA TUNELLA S.S. +39 432716030

- ▼ Biancosesto 2011 Price: ❍ 87/100

AZIENDA AGRICOLA SPECOGNA LEONARDO S.S. +39 432755840

- ▼ Friulano 2012 Price: ❍ 87/100

ARZENTON MARIO AZIENDA AGRICOLA +39 432716139

- ▼ Pinot Nero 2010 Price: ❍ 86/100

LA VIARTE AZIENDA AGRICOLA DI CESCHIN GIULIO +39 432759458

▼ Friulano 2012 Price: ❍❍ 86/100

AZIENDA AGRICOLA LA BUSE DAL LOF DI MICHELE PAVAN +39 374 642197

▼ Cabernet Franc 2011 Price: ❍ 84/100

COLLAVINI - EUGENIO COLLAVINI VITICULTORI +39 432753222

▼ Turian Ribolla Gialla 2012 Price: ❍ 83/100

ARZENTON MARIO AZIENDA AGRICOLA +39 432716139

▼ Sauvignon 2012 Price: ❍ 89/100

▼ Friulano 2012 Price: ❍ 87/100

AZIENDA AGRICOLA LA BUSE DAL LOF DI MICHELE PAVAN +39 374 642197

▼ Pinot Grigio 2012 Price: ❍ 89/100

▼ Schioppettino di Prepotto 2009 Price: ❍❍ 88/100

▼ Ribolla Gialla 2012 Price: ❍ 84/100

AZIENDA AGRICOLA LA TUNELLA S.S. +39 432716030

▼ Col Matiss Sauvignon 2011 Price: ❍ 90/100

▼ Col Livius Friulano 2011 Price: ❍ 90/100

AZIENDA AGRICOLA RONCO MARGHERITA +39 427949809

▼ Pinot grigio 2012 Price: ❍ 87/100

▼ Ovalis 2009 Price: ❍ 83/100

AZIENDA AGRICOLA SPECOGNA LEONARDO S.S. +39 432755840

▼ Sauvignon duality 2009 Price: ❍❍❍ 93/100

▼ Pignolo 2008 Price: ❍❍ 87/100

AZIENDA CANTARUTTI ALFIERI SOCIETA" AGRICOLA +39 432756317

▼ Pinot grigio 2012 Price: ❍ 89/100

▼ Bianco 2011 Price: ❍ 87/100

CADIBON AZ. AGR. +39 432759316

▼ Bontaj Friulano 2012 Price: ❍ 91/100

COLLAVINI - EUGENIO COLLAVINI VITICULTORI +39 432753222

▼ Turian Schioppettino 2006 Price: ❍ 89/100

▼ Forresco rosso 2006 Price: ❍ 85/100

ERMACORA DARIO E LUCIANO AZIENDA AGRICOLA +39 0432 716439 -

▼ Vintage 2012 Price: ❍ 87/100

▼ Vintage Pinot grigio 2012 Price: ❍ 82/100

IL RONCAL AZIENDA AGRICOLA +39 432730138

▼ Pinot grigio 2012 Price: ❍ 89/100

▼ Sauvignon 2012 Price: ❍ 87/100

LA VIARTE AZIENDA AGRICOLA DI CESCHIN GIULIO +39 432759458

▼ Sium dolce 2007 Price: ❍❍❍ 92/100

▼ Schiopettino di Prepotto 2009 Price: ❍❍ 87/100

LIVIO FELLUGA S.R.L. +39 48160203

▼ Friulano 2012 Price: ❍❍ 88/100

▼ Illivio 2011 Price: ❍❍ 83/100

PIZZULIN DENIS +39 432713425

▼ Sauvignon 2011 Price: ❍ 88/100

▼ Friulano 2011 Price: ❍ 86/100

ROBERTO SCUBLA AZ.AGR. +39 3356919043

▼ Verduzzo Friulano 2009 Price: ❍❍❍ 91/100

RONCO DEI PINI DI NOVELLO +39 432713239

▼ Schiopettino 2010 Price: ❍❍ 89/100

▼ Friulano 2012 Price: ❍ 87/100

RONCSORELI +39 432713005

▼ Sauvignon Dei Peschi 2011 Price: ❍❍ 90/100

▼ Pinot Grigio Ramato dei Melograni 2011 Price: ❍❍ 88/100

TALIS WINE +39 3285393920

▼ Refosco Peduncolo Rosso 2009 Price: ❍ 86/100

TOBLAR S.R.L. +39 432755840

▼ Toblar Refosco dal P.R. 2011 Price: ❍ 85/100

VIGNA PETRUSSA DI HILDE PETRUSSA +39 432713021

▼ Vintage 2009 Price: ❍❍ 88/100

Collio D.O.C.

RUSSIZ SUPERIORE +39 0481 80328 - 92237

▼ Sauvignon Riserva 2009 Price: ❍❍ 89/100

AZIENDA AGRICOLA RONCO BLANCHIS +39 48180519

▼ Collio Bianco 2012 Price: ❍ 86/100

CONTI FORMENTINI	+39.0481.88.41.31
▼ Chardonnay 2012 Price: OO	85/100
▼ Raiade 2012 Price: OO	84/100

LA REGUTA	+39 432779175
▼ Cabernet Sauvignon 2011 Price: O	84/100

PRIMOSIC S.R.L.	+39 481535153
▼ Ribolla gialla di Oslavia 2009 Price: OO	83/100

AZIENDA AGRICOLA CODELLI SNC	+39 481809285
▼ Friulano 2012 Price: O	86/100

AZIENDA AGRICOLA DRAGA DI MIKLUS MILANO & C.	+39 481884182
▼ Sauvignon 2010 Price: OO	86/100
▼ Pinot grigio 2011 Price: O	86/100

AZIENDA AGRICOLA GRADIS'CIUTTA	+39 481390237
▼ Bràtinis 2011 Price: OO	88/100

AZIENDA AGRICOLA RONCO BLANCHIS	+39 48180519
▼ Friulano 2012 Price: O	88/100
▼ Pinot Grigio 2012 Price: O	86/100

PIGHIN DI FERNANDO PIGHIN

▼ Sauvignon 2012 **90/100**

Light yellow. Intense, open nose dominated by very upfront vegetal perfumes of tomato stem and sage. Fresh palate echoing the nose aromatics. A long wine showing real archetypal features though perhaps an acquired taste. Serve with tomato-based dishes.

Price: OO

Serving Temperature: 8-10°C - Ready to drink : From now on

Pighin di Fernando Pighin & Fligi Soc. Agr. a r.l.
Viale Grado, 1 - 33050 Pavia di Udine
Tel.: +39 0 432 675 444 - Fax: +39 0 432 675 999
E-mail: info@pighin.com
Website: http://www.pighin.com

COLLAVINI - EUGENIO COLLAVINI VITICULTORI +39 432753222

- Broy 2012 Price: ❍ — 89/100
- Merlot dal Pic 2006 Price: ❍ — 85/100

CONTI FORMENTINI +39.0481.88.41.31

- Caligo 2012 Price: ❍❍ — 89/100
- Friulano 2012 Price: ❍❍ — 88/100
- Pinot griggio 2012 Price: ❍❍ — 84/100

LA REGUTA +39 432779175

- Ribolla gialla 2012 Price: ❍ — 89/100
- Pinot grigio 2012 Price: ❍ — 86/100

MARCO FELLUGA +39 48199164

- Molamatta 2011 Price: ❍❍ — 89/100
- Mongris Riserva 2010 Price: ❍❍ — 88/100

PIGHIN DI FERNANDO PIGHIN & FLIGI SOC. AGR. A R.L. +39 432675444

- Chardonnay 2012 Price: ❍ — 88/100

PRIMOSIC S.R.L. +39 481535153

- Chardonnay Gmajne 2010 Price: ❍❍ — 89/100
- Sauvignon Gmajne 2011 Price: ❍❍ — 88/100
- Klin Collio bianco 2009 Price: ❍❍ — 84/100

RONCO DEI PINI DI NOVELLO +39 432713239

- Pinot grigio 2012 Price: ❍ — 85/100

RUSSIZ SUPERIORE +39 0481 80328 - 92237

- Pinot Bianco Riserva 2007 Price: ❍❍ — 92/100

TENUTA VILLANOVA S.R.L. +39 481889311

- Refosco del Peduncolo Rosso 2010 Price: ❍ — 87/100
- Pinot Grigio Ronco Cucco 2012 Price: ❍ — 82/100

TERCIC MATJAZ +39 481884920

- Pinot Grigio 2011 Price: ❍ — 87/100

VIDUSSI GESTIONI AGRICOLE +39 48180072

- Ribolla gialla 2012 Price: ❍ — 86/100

VILLA RUSSIZ +39 48180047

- Sauvignon de la Tour 2012 Price: ❍❍❍ — 93/100
- Pinot bianco 2012 Price: ❍❍❍ — 89/100

ZUANI SOC. AGRIC. DI FELLUGA PATRIZIA E FIGLI S.S +39 481391432

- Riserva 2010 Price: ❍ 85/100
- Vigne bianco 2012 Price: ❍ 84/100

Friuli Aquileia D.O.C

TENUTA CA BOLANI +39 0444 640111

- Aquilis 2012 Price: ❍❍ 88/100

Grave del Friuli D.O.C

FOSSA MALA SOCIETA' AGRICOLA +39 434957997

- Fossa Mala Societa' Agricola Re Fossa 2009 Price: ❍ 88/100

LE MONDE SOC.AGR. +39 0434 622087

- Sauvignon 2012 Price: ❍ 88/100

LE DUE TORRI AZIENDA AGRICOLA +39 432759150

- Vintage 2009 Price: ❍ 86/100

SAN SIMONE DI BRISOTTO S.R.L. +39 434578633

- Refosco del Peduncolo Rosso 2011 Price: ❍ 84/100

LE MONDE SOC.AGR. +39 0434 622087

- Refosco del Peduncolo rosso 2011 Price: ❍ 83/100

PITARS AZIENDA AGRICOLA +39 43488078

- Pitars Brumal 2010 Price: ❍ 83/100

TENUTE TOMASELLA +39 042 28 50 043

- Friulano 2012 Price: ❍ 82/100
- Le bastie rosso 2007 Price: ❍❍ 81/100
- Cabernet franc 2011 Price: ❍ 81/100

LE MONDE SOC.AGR. +39 0434 622087

- Pinot grigio 2012 Price: ❍ 80/100

TENUTE TOMASELLA +39 042 28 50 043

- Merlot 2011 Price: ❍ 76/100

FOSSA MALA SOCIETA' AGRICOLA +39 434957997

▼ Traminer Aromatico 2012 Price: ❍ 89/100

LE DUE TORRI AZIENDA AGRICOLA +39 432759150

▼ Vintage 2011 Price: ❍ 92/100

▼ Vintage 2009 Price: ❍ 85/100

LE MONDE SOC.AGR. +39 0434 622087

▼ Friulano 2012 Price: ❍ 89/100

▼ Cabernet Franc 2011 Price: ❍ 85/100

PIGHIN DI FERNANDO PIGHIN & FLIGI SOC. AGR. A R.L. +39 432675444

▼ Riserva 2009 Price: ❍ 87/100

▼ Pinot grigio 2012 Price: ❍ 85/100

PITARS AZIENDA AGRICOLA +39 43488078

▼ Pitars Séris 2011 Price: ❍ 90/100

▼ Pitars Braida Santa Cecilia 2012 Price: ❍ 85/100

SAN SIMONE DI BRISOTTO S.R.L. +39 434578633

▼ Friulano 2012 Price: ❍ 85/100

▼ Pinot grigio Case Sugan 2012 Price: ❍ 84/100

TENUTE TOMASELLA +39 042 28 50 043

▼ Le bastie bianco 2007 Price: ❍❍ 92/100

▼ Le bastie rosso 2007 Price: ❍ 83/100

VINI DELLA DELIZIA - VITICOLTORI FRIULANI LA DELIZ +39 434869564

▼ Friulano Vignal 2012 Price: ❍ 86/100

▼ Refosco dal Peduncolo rosso 2011 Price: ❍ 84/100

Isonzo D.O.C

TENUTA LUISA EDDI AZIENDA AGRICOLA +39 48169680

▼ Sauvignon 2012 Price: ❍ 87/100

AZIENDA AGRICOLA LORENZO ENZO - I FEUDI DI ROMANS +39 48176445

▼ Pinot Grigio 2012 Price: ❍ 85/100

▼ Refosco dal Peduncolo Rosso 2011 Price: ❍ 84/100

▼ Sauvignon Blanc 2012 Price: ❍ 88/100

TENUTA LUISA EDDI AZIENDA AGRICOLA +39 48169680

▼ I Ferretti Friulano 2011 Price: OO 88/100

VENICE JULIA SRL +39 48176445

▼ Pinot grigio 2012 Price: O 87/100

Isonzo del Friuli D.O.C

LIS NERIS AGRICOLA +39 48180105

▼ Lis Neris Lis 2008 Price: OOO 93/100

▼ Lis Neris Tal Lùc 2008 Price: OOOO 89/100

▼ Lis Neris Gris - Pinot Grigio 2010 Price: OO 88/100

VIE DI ROMANS AZIENDA AGRICOLA DI GALLO GIANFRANCO +39 48169600

▼ Flors di Vis 2011 Price: OO 90/100

▼ Chardonnay 2011 Price: OO 90/100

▼ Piere Sauvignon 2011 Price: OO 89/100

▼ Flors di Vis 2010 Price: OO 89/100

MASUT DA RIVE DI GALLO FABRIZIO E MARCO +39 48169200

▼ Pinot nero 2011 Price: OO 86/100

TENUTA VILLANOVA S.R.L. +39 481889311

▼ Merlot 2011 Price: O 83/100

BLASON AZIENDA AGRICOLA DI GIOVANNI BLASON +39 48192414

▼ Blason Pinot Grigio 2012 Price: OO 87/100

▼ Blason Friulano 2012 Price: OO 86/100

DRIUS MAURO AZIENDA AGRICOLA +39 48160998

▼ Vignis di Siris 2010 Price: O 87/100

FERLAT SILVANO +39 34048161367

▼ Sauvignon 2012 Price: O 90/100

▼ Merlot 2011 Price: O 88/100

▼ Cabernet Franc 2011 Price: O 87/100

▼ Friulano 2012 Price: O 86/100

▼ Grame 2011 Price: O 85/100

LIS NERIS AGRICOLA +39 48180105

- ▼ Lis Neris Confini 2009 Price: ❍❍❍ — 94/100
- ▼ Lis Neris Picol Sauvignon Blanc 2011 Price: ❍❍ — 92/100
- ▼ Lis Neris Jurosa - Chardonnay 2010 Price: ❍❍ — 90/100
- ▼ Lis Neris La Vila - Friulano 2011 Price: ❍❍ — 88/100

MASUT DA RIVE DI GALLO FABRIZIO E MARCO +39 48169200

- ▼ Sauvignon blanc 2012 Price: ❍ — 90/100
- ▼ Chardonnay 2012 Price: ❍ — 88/100
- ▼ Semidis 2009 Price: ❍❍ — 87/100

TENUTA VILLANOVA S.R.L. +39 481889311

- ▼ Pinot Grigio 2012 Price: ❍ — 87/100
- ▼ Malvasia 2012 Price: ❍ — 86/100

VIE DI ROMANS AZIENDA AGRICOLA DI GALLO GIANFRANCO +39 48169600

- ▼ Chardonnay 2010 Price: ❍❍ — 92/100
- ▼ Piere Sauvignon 2010 Price: ❍❍ — 92/100
- ▼ Vieris Sauvignon 2010 Price: ❍❍❍ — 90/100
- ▼ Vieris Sauvignon 2011 Price: ❍❍❍ — 88/100

Prosecco D.O.C. (FR)

PITARS AZIENDA AGRICOLA +39 43488078

- ▼ Pitars Extra dry Price: ❍ — 84/100

TENUTE TOMASELLA +39 042 28 50 043

- ▼ Osè 2011 Price: ❍ — 83/100
- ▼ Prò 2012 Price: ❍ — 83/100

Venezia Giulia I.G.T

LIVON VINI DEL COLLIO +39 432757173

- ▼ Solarco 2012 Price: ❍❍ — 86/100

TOBLAR

Sauvignon 2012 **89/100**

Straw-yellow. Expressive nose with vegetal accents, redcurrants, white flowers and a menthol touch. Fresh, clearly-defined palate flowing into savoury spring-like notes. A harmonious style pairing well with finely-sliced vegetables.

Price: ❍

Wine and food pairing: Grilled fish
Serving Temperature: 8-10°C
Ready to drink: 2013-2014

Established in 2000, Toblâr is firmly rooted in the traditions and local growing environment of the Friuli region. The property is run by the enterprising and energetic Paolo Duri and Michele Specogna. The vineyards are centred primarily on the DOC Colli Orientali but Toblâr is also present in the Ramandolo and Isonzo areas. Conditions are particularly well suited to the production of white wines such as Pinot Grigio, Sauvignon, Friulano and Ramandolo. Some extremely worthwhile reds however are also produced on a boutique scale, including the highly uncommon Refosco, a native grape of Friuli, and the extremely aromatic Schioppettino which draws abundant flavour from the rich soils. Offering an unusual array of wines, the Cantina is well worth discovering.

Toblâr S.r.l.
Via Ramandolo, 17 - 33045 Nimis
Tel.: +39 0432 755 840 - Fax: +39 0432 752 235
E-mail: info@toblar.it
Website: http://www.toblar.it

TOBLAR

▼ Pinot grigio 2012 **86/100**

Coppery hue. The nose opens up to perfumes of dried white flowers and herbs (mint, fennel). Fresh, fruity palate displaying good volume and a vegetal touch. Warm, savoury palate. Serve with food.

Price: ❍

Wine and food pairing: White meat
Serving Temperature: 8-10°C
Ready to drink: 2013-2014

Chicken fricassee with chanterelle mushrooms

4 chicken legs, 600g chanterelle mushrooms, 100g of smoked lardons, 1 onion, 75cl of chicken stock, 3 tbsp double cream, 30g butter, 3 tbsp oil, salt and pepper.

Method: *Clean the chanterelle mushrooms by rinsing them briefly in cold water. Brown the chicken legs in oil in a casserole dish. Remove and fry the chopped onion in the casserole dish with the butter. Add the lardons and ¼ of the chanterelles. Cook for 5 min. Add the chicken pieces and pour over the stock. Season, cover and cook on a low heat for 40 min. Meanwhile, brown the remaining chanterelles in a pan with a knob of butter. Remove the chicken legs and add the cream to the casserole dish. Mix with the pan-fried chanterelles. Serve hot.*

Toblâr S.r.l.
Via Ramandolo, 17 - 33045 Nimis
Tel.: +39 0432 755 840 - Fax: +39 0432 752 235
E-mail: info@toblar.it
Website: http://www.toblar.it

AZIENDA AGRICOLA CODELLI SNC	+39 481809285
▼ Merlot Ronchi della Vallisella 2011 Price: ❍	83/100

AZIENDA AGRICOLA SPECOGNA LEONARDO S.S.	+39 432755840
▼ Oltre 2009 Price: ❍❍❍	85/100

BLASON AZIENDA AGRICOLA DI GIOVANNI BLASON	+39 48192414
▼ Blason Malvasia 2012 Price: ❍❍	87/100

LIVON VINI DEL COLLIO	+39 432757173
▼ Braide Alte 2011 Price: ❍❍❍	87/100

PAROVEL	+39 3467590953
▼ Vinja Barde - Refosco 2008 Price: ❍❍	87/100

PECORARI PIERPAOLO AZIENDA AGRICOLA	+39 481808775
▼ Kolaus Sauvignon 2011 Price: ❍❍	86/100

PITARS AZIENDA AGRICOLA	+39 43488078
▼ Pitars Tureis 2010 Price: ❍❍	89/100
▼ Pitars Angelo 2009 Price: ❍❍❍	85/100

RONCSORELI	+39 432713005
▼ Ottolustri 2010 Price: ❍❍❍	92/100

VENICE JULIA SRL	+39 48176445
▼ Rosso del Doge 2011 Price: ❍	85/100

VIGNA PETRUSSA DI HILDE PETRUSSA	+39 432713021
▼ Richenza 2010 Price: ❍❍	88/100

Venezie I.G.T

LE DUE TORRI AZIENDA AGRICOLA	+39 432759150
▼ Malvasia 2012 Price: ❍	87/100

TENUTA LUISA EDDI AZIENDA AGRICOLA	+39 48169680
▼ I Ferretti Desiderium 2011 Price: ❍❍	83/100

TENUTE TOMASELLA	+39 042 28 50 043
▼ Chinomoro Price: ❍	83/100

VINI DELLA DELIZIA - VITICOLTORI FRIULANI LA DELIZ	+39 434869564
▼ Vignal 2012 Price: ❍	84/100

Vino aromatizzato

TENUTE TOMASELLA +39 042 28 50 043

▼ Chinomoro 2010 Price: OO 84/100

Vino Spumante

AZIENDA AGRICOLA RONCO MARGHERITA +39 427949809

▼ Ribolla Gialla Brut 2012 Price: O 82/100

COLLAVINI - EUGENIO COLLAVINI VITICULTORI +39 432753222

▼ Brut 2009 Price: O 85/100

LE DUE TORRI AZIENDA AGRICOLA +39 432759150

▼ Vintage 2012 Price: O 85/100

SAN SIMONE DI BRISOTTO S.R.L. +39 434578633

▼ Blanc de Blancs extra-brut 2011 Price: O 84/100

TENUTA CA BOLANI +39 0444 640111

▼ Brut Price: O 85/100

Lombardy

Curtefranca D.O.C

CA' DEL BOSCO S.R.L. - SOCIETA' AGRICOLA +39 307766111

▼ Rosso 2009 Price: OO 88/100

▼ Bianco 2012 Price: OO 85/100

▼ Chardonnay 2010 Price: OOOO 86/100

Franciacorta D.O.C.G

CA' DEL BOSCO S.R.L. - SOCIETA' AGRICOLA +39 307766111

▼ Cuvée Anna Maria Clementi Brut 2005 Price: OOOO 93/100

LO SPARVIERE GUSSALI BERETTA AZIENDA AGRICOLA +39 30652382

▼ Lo Sparviere Gussali Beretta Azienda Agricola Extra-brut Millesimato 2007 Price: ❍❍ 91/100

VILLA FRANCIACORTA +39 30652329

▼ Brut Selezione 2004 Price: ❍ 91/100

SOCIETA' AGRICOLA LA FIOCA +39 309826313

▼ La Fioca Brut 2006 Price: ❍❍ 90/100

VILLA FRANCIACORTA +39 30652329

▼ Extra Brut Extra blu 2007 Price: ❍ 89/100

▼ Rosé Demi-sec Price: ❍ 89/100

LA BOSCAIOLA AZIENDA AGRICOLA +39 307156386

▼ La Capinera Cuvée Cenci Brut Price: ❍ 89/100

SOCIETA' AGRICOLA LA FIOCA +39 309826313

▼ La Fioca Dosaggio zero Price: ❍ 89/100

BERSI SERLINI SOCIETA' AGRICOLA S.R.L. +39 309823338

▼ Brut Price: ❍ 88/100

VILLA FRANCIACORTA

▼ **Emozione Brut 2009** **90/100**

Golden hue with a fine, persistent effervescence. Open nose intermixing plum with orange and melted chocolate. Fresh, clean and well-structured palate with a long, savoury finish. Drink with swordfish steak.

Price: ❍❍❍

Serving Temperature: 9-11°C
Ready to drink : From now on

Villa Franciacorta
Via Villa 12
25040 Monticelli Brusati
Tel.: +39 030 65 23 29 - Fax: +39 030 68 52 585
E-mail: info@villafranciacorta.it
Website: http://www.villafranciacorta.it

CA' DEL BOSCO S.R.L. - SOCIETA' AGRICOLA +39 307766111

▼ Vintage collection Satèn 2008 Price: ❍❍❍ 88/100

GUIDO BERLUCCHI & C. S.P.A. +39 30984381

▼ Berlucchi Guido Cellarius rosé 2008 Price: ❍❍ 88/100

VEZZOLI UGO AZIENDA AGRICOLA +39 30738018

▼ Brut Price: ❍❍ 88/100

LE MARCHESINE S.S. DI BIATTA G. AZIENDA AGRICOLA +39 30657005

▼ Brut Nature 2007 Price: ❍❍❍ 87/100

▼ Le Marchesine S.S. Blanc de Noirs 2009 Price: ❍❍❍ 85/100

BERSI SERLINI SOCIETA' AGRICOLA S.R.L. +39 309823338

▼ Brut 2008 Price: ❍ 87/100

CA' DEL BOSCO S.R.L. - SOCIETA' AGRICOLA +39 307766111

▼ Vintage collection dosage zéro 2008 Price: ❍❍❍ 87/100

GUIDO BERLUCCHI & C. S.P.A. +39 30984381

▼ Berlucchi Guido Cellarius Brut 2008 Price: ❍❍ 87/100

MONTENISA DI ALBIERA ALLEGRA E ALESSIA ANTINORI +39 307750838

▼ Montenisa Satèn 2006 Price: ❍❍ 87/100

SOCIETA' AGRICOLA LA FIOCA +39 309826313

▼ La Fioca Brut rosé Price: ❍❍ 87/100

VEZZOLI UGO AZIENDA AGRICOLA +39 30738018

▼ Brut 2009 Price: ❍❍ 87/100

CA' DEL BOSCO S.R.L. - SOCIETA' AGRICOLA +39 307766111

▼ Cuvée prestige Price: ❍❍❍ 86/100

LA BOSCAIOLA AZIENDA AGRICOLA +39 307156386

▼ Nelson Cenci Vigneti Cenci Extra-Brut Price: ❍ 86/100

AZ. AGR. FRANCA CONTEA S.S. +39 307451217

▼ Brut 2009 Price: ❍❍ 85/100

CORTEBIANCA +39 30983293

▼ Extra-brut Price: ❍❍ 85/100

LA MONTINA S.R.L. +39 30653278

▼ Aurum Brut 2007 Price: ❍ 85/100

MONTENISA DI ALBIERA ALLEGRA E ALESSIA ANTINORI +39 307750838

▼ Montenisa Rosé Price: ❍❍ 85/100

ANTICA FRATTA S.P.A. +39 30652068

▼ Essence Rosé 2009 Price: ❍❍ 84/100

LANTIERI DE PARATICO AZIENDA AGRICOLA +39 30736151

- Rosé Arcadia Price: ❍❍ 84/100

MONTE ROSSA S.R.L. +39 30725066

- Cabochon Brut 2008 Price: ❍❍❍ 84/100

RICCI CURBASTRO AZIENDA AGRICOLA +39 30736094

- Non dosato 2007 Price: ❍❍❍ 84/100

AMBROSINI TENUTA SOCIETA AGRICOLA SRL +39 0339 690 24 44

- Rosé Price: ❍❍ 89/100
- Satèn Price: ❍❍ 88/100

ANTICA FRATTA S.P.A. +39 30652068

- Brut Price: ❍❍ 90/100
- Essence Satèn 2009 Price: ❍❍ 87/100
- Quintescence Extra-brut 2006 Price: ❍❍❍ 85/100

ARCIPELAGO MURATORI +39 307451051

- Frattelli Muratori Dosaggio zero Riserva Villa Crespia Francesco Iacone 2006 Price: ❍❍❍ 88/100

AZ. AGR. FRANCA CONTEA S.S. +39 307451217

- Primus Price: ❍ 91/100
- Satèn 2009 Price: ❍❍ 87/100

BERSI SERLINI SOCIETA' AGRICOLA S.R.L. +39 309823338

- Riserva Extra-Brut 2006 Price: ❍ 89/100
- Anniversario Brut Price: ❍ 89/100
- Nuvola Demi-sec Price: ❍ 88/100
- Satèn Brut Price: ❍ 87/100
- Rosa rosae Brut Price: ❍ 85/100

CA' DEL BOSCO S.R.L. - SOCIETA' AGRICOLA +39 307766111

- Cuvée Anna Maria Clementi rosé Extra-Brut 2005 Price: ❍❍❍❍❍ 93/100
- Cuvée prestige rosé Price: ❍❍❍ 87/100
- Vintage collection brut 2008 Price: ❍❍❍ 85/100

CORNALETO S.R.L. SOCIETA' AGRICOLA +39 307450507

- Satèn Brut Price: ❍❍ 90/100

CORTEBIANCA +39 30983293

- Satèn Brut 2009 Price: ❍❍ 86/100
- Rosé Extra-Brut 2009 Price: ❍❍ 86/100

GUIDO BERLUCCHI & C. S.P.A.	+39 30984381
▼ Cellarius Pas Dosé 2007 Price: ❍❍	88/100
▼ Palazzo lana extreme riserva 2006 Price: ❍	88/100
LA BOSCAIOLA AZIENDA AGRICOLA	+39 307156386
▼ Satèn Price: ❍	90/100
▼ Brut Price: ❍	89/100
LA MONTINA S.R.L.	+39 30653278
▼ Satèn Brut Argens 2008 Price: ❍	92/100
▼ Riserva Extra-brut 2006 Price: ❍	88/100
LANTIERI DE PARATICO AZIENDA AGRICOLA	+39 30736151
▼ Arcadia 2009 Price: ❍❍	88/100
▼ Satèn Price: ❍❍	86/100
LE MARCHESINE S.S. DI BIATTA G. AZIENDA AGRICOLA	+39 30657005
▼ Le Marchesine S.S. Saten 2009 Price: ❍❍❍	89/100
▼ Le Marchesine S.S. Extra Brut Price: ❍❍	87/100
▼ Le Marchesine S.S. Rosé Brut 2008 Price: ❍❍❍	84/100
LO SPARVIERE GUSSALI BERETTA AZIENDA AGRICOLA	+39 30652382
▼ Lo Sparviere Gussali Beretta Azienda Agricola Millesimato Dosaggio Zero 2006 Price: ❍❍❍	92/100
MONTE ROSSA S.R.L.	+39 30725066
▼ Coupé non dosato Price: ❍❍	87/100
▼ Sansevé Satèn Brut Price: ❍❍	87/100
MONTENISA DI ALBIERA ALLEGRA E ALESSIA ANTINORI	+39 307750838
▼ Montenisa Cuvée spéciale Brut Price: ❍❍	89/100
▼ Montenisa Blanc de Blancs Dizero Price: ❍❍	87/100
▼ Montenisa Brut Price: ❍❍	85/100
RICCI CURBASTRO AZIENDA AGRICOLA	+39 30736094
▼ Musuem release extra-brut 2005 Price: ❍❍	89/100
▼ Extra-brut 2009 Price: ❍❍	86/100
▼ Vintage 2009 Price: ❍❍	85/100
SOCIETA' AGRICOLA LA FIOCA	+39 309826313
▼ La Fioca Satèn Riserva 2005 Price: ❍❍	93/100
▼ La Fioca Brut 2008 Price: ❍❍	90/100

VEZZOLI UGO AZIENDA AGRICOLA +39 30738018

▼ Satèn Price: ○○ 89/100

▼ Rosé Price: ○○ 87/100

VILLA FRANCIACORTA +39 30652329

▼ Satèn Brut 2009 Price: ○ 92/100

▼ Diamant Pas Dosé 2006 Price: ○ 90/100

Sebino I.G.T

CA' DEL BOSCO S.R.L. - SOCIETA' AGRICOLA +39 307766111

▼ Maurizio Zanella 2007 Price: ○○○ 87/100

▼ Pinéro 2009 Price: ○○○○ 88/100

Terre di Franciacorta D.O.C.

SOCIETA' AGRICOLA LA FIOCA +39 309826313

▼ La Fioca Rosso del diavolo allegro 2008 Price: ○ 87/100

Valtellina Superiore D.O.C.G

NINO NEGRI +39 342485211

▼ Sfursat 5 stelle 2009 Price: ○○○ 93/100

▼ Inferno Carlo Negri 2009 Price: ○○ 89/100

▼ Vigneto Fracia 2009 Price: ○○○ 89/100

Vino da Tavola

CA' DEL BOSCO S.R.L. - SOCIETA' AGRICOLA +39 307766111

▼ Carmenero 2007 Price: ○○○ 89/100

Piedmont

Barbaresco D.O.C.G.

MARCHESI DI BAROLO +39 173564400

▼ Vintage 2009 Price: ○○○ 91/100

Barbera d'Asti D.O.C.G

CASTELLO IL POGGIO

▼ Masareu 2006 Price: ❍ 87/100

Barolo D.O.C.G.

FENOCCHIO GIACOMO AZIENDA AGRICOLA S.S. +39 17378675

▼ Villero 2009 Price: ❍ 89/100

MARCHESI DI BAROLO +39 173564400

▼ Sarmassa 2009 Price: ❍❍❍ 88/100

FENOCCHIO GIACOMO AZIENDA AGRICOLA S.S. +39 17378675

▼ Bussia 2009 Price: ❍❍❍ 95/100

MARCHESI DI BAROLO +39 173564400

▼ Cannubi 2009 Price: ❍❍❍ 93/100

Sicilia

Etna D.O.C.

AZIENDA VITIVINICOLA COSTANTINO FABIO VINCENZO+39 95434288

ORG▼ DeAetnA 2012 Price: ❍❍ 88/100

ORG▼ DeAetnA 2011 Price: ❍❍ 87/100

ORG▼ DeAetnA 2010 Price: ❍❍ 88/100

Moscato di Siracusa D.O.C

ENOFANUSA SRL CANTINE GULINO +39 931721218

▼ Don Nuzzo 2012 Price: ❍❍ 87/100

Detailed instructions are featured at the start of the book.

Sicilia I.G.T

ENOFANUSA SRL CANTINE GULINO +39 931721218

- ▼ Jaraya 2012 Price: ❍❍ — 93/100
- ▼ Fania 2012 Price: ❍ — 90/100
- ▼ Drus 2011 Price: ❍❍ — 90/100

TENUTE GALFANO +39 923723311

- ▼ Giùva Fabbri 2012 Price: ❍❍❍ — 88/100
- ▼ Grillo 2012 Price: ❍❍ — 88/100

TENUTA RAPITALÀ +39 457235772

- ▼ Solinero 2010 Price: ❍❍❍ — 86/100

TENUTE GALFANO +39 923723311

- ▼ Frappato 2011 Price: ❍ — 86/100

ENOFANUSA SRL CANTINE GULINO +39 931721218

- ▼ Fanus 2012 Price: ❍ — 84/100
- ▼ Pretiosa 2012 Price: ❍❍ — 88/100
- ▼ Saliens 2011 Price: ❍❍ — 86/100

FEUDO PRINCIPI DI BUTERA +39 934347726

- ▼ Deliella 2011 Price: ❍ — 91/100

TENUTA RAPITALÀ +39 457235772

- ▼ Chardonnay Grand Cru 2011 Price: ❍❍ — 91/100
- ▼ Hugonis 2010 Price: ❍❍❍ — 87/100

TENUTE GALFANO +39 923723311

- ▼ Giuvà Alessà 2010 Price: ❍❍❍ — 91/100
- ▼ Nero d'Avola 2011 Price: ❍❍ — 89/100
- ▼ Nero d'Avola 2010 Price: ❍ — 84/100

Trentino

Teroldego Rotaliano D.O.C.

ENDRIZZI +39 461650129

- ▼ Riserva 2009 Price: ❍❍ — 82/100

Trento Spumante D.O.C.

FERRARI F.LLI LUNELLI S.P.A. +39 046 19 72 386

▼ Ferrari F.lli Lunelli SpA Rosé Price: OO — 89/100

ENDRIZZI +39 461650129

▼ Pian Castello Rosé Brut 2006 Price: O — 88/100

FERRARI F.LLI LUNELLI S.P.A. +39 046 19 72 386

▼ Ferrari F.lli Lunelli SpA Brut Price: OO — 88/100

ENDRIZZI +39 461650129

▼ Pian Castello Brut Price: O — 91/100

FERRARI F.LLI LUNELLI S.P.A. +39 046 19 72 386

▼ Ferrari F.lli Lunelli SpA Perlé noir 2007 Price: OO — 92/100

▼ Riserva Lunelli 2006 Price: O — 91/100

Vigneti delle Dolomiti I.G.T

ENDRIZZI +39 461650129

▼ Gran Masetto 2009 Price: OOO — 90/100

▼ Masetto nero 2009 Price: OO — 88/100

Tuscany

Brunello di Montalcino D.O.C.G.

TENUTA GREPPO - FRANCO BIONDI SANTI +39 577848087

▼ Annata 2008 Price: OOOO — 95/100

▼ Riserva 2007 Price: OOOOO — 97/100

Carmignano D.O.C.G.

TENUTA DI CAPEZZANA +39 558706005

CV▼ Trefiano Riserva 2008 Price: OO 89/100

CV▼ Vinsanto Capezzana 2006 Price: OO 93/100

Chianti Classico D.O.C.G.

TENUTA LA NOVELLA +39 558337749

▼ Riserva 2008 Price: OOO 89/100

IL MOLINO DI GRACE +39 558561010

▼ Vintage 2011 Price: O 87/100

TENUTA DI BIBBIANO +39 057 77 43 065

ORG▼ Bibbiano 2011 Price: OO 87/100

CASTELLO VICCHIOMAGGIO +39 55854078

▼ San Jacopo da Vicchiomaggio 2010 Price: O 86/100

BORGO SCOPETO +39 577322729

▼ Riserva Vigna misiano 2008 Price: O 85/100

MELINI +39 577998511

▼ Granaio 2011 Price: OO 85/100

FATTORIA LAVACCHIO +39 558317472

▼ Fattoria Lavacchio Cedro Rufina Riserva 2008 Price: O 84/100

FATTORIA LORNANO +39 577309059

▼ Lornano 2010 Price: O 84/100

BORGO SCOPETO +39 577322729

▼ Vintage 2010 Price: O 83/100

CANDIALLE +39 55852201

▼ Vintage 2009 Price: OO 89/100

▼ La misse 2011 Price: O 86/100

CASTELLINUZZA E PIUCA +39 558549033

▼ Vintage 2010 Price: ❍ 92/100

CASTELLO D ALBOLA +39 577738019

▼ Riserva 2008 Price: ❍ 92/100

▼ Vintage 2009 Price: ❍ 91/100

CASTELLO DI MELETO +39 577749217

▼ Vintage 2010 Price: ❍ 85/100

CASTELLO DI MONSANTO +39 558059000

▼ Riserva 2010 Price: ❍ 91/100

▼ Riserva Vigneto il Poggio 2009 Price: ❍❍❍ 88/100

CASTELLO DI VOLPAIA

▼ Riserva 2009 Price: ❍ 93/100

CASTELLO VICCHIOMAGGIO +39 55854078

▼ Vigna la prima 2010 Price: ❍❍ 90/100

▼ Riserva Vigna La Prima 2008 Price: ❍ 89/100

FATTORIA CASALOSTE +39 55852725

▼ Casaloste 2010 Price: ❍ 87/100

FATTORIA DI MONTEMAGGIO +39 577738323

▼ Riserva 2008 Price: ❍❍❍ 88/100

FATTORIA LAVACCHIO +39 558317472

▼ Fattoria Lavacchio Cedro Rufina 2010 Price: ❍❍ 87/100

▼ Fattoria Lavacchio Puro 2012 Price: ❍ 85/100

FATTORIA LORNANO +39 577309059

▼ Lornano Le Bandite riserva 2009 Price: ❍ 93/100

▼ Lornano Riserva 2009 Price: ❍ 91/100

FATTORIA MONTECCHIO +39 558072907

▼ Chianti Classico 2009 Price: ❍ 87/100

FATTORIA TREGOLE +39 577740991

▼ Riserva 2010 Price: ❍ 93/100

FELSINA +39 577355117

▼ Rancia Riserva 2010 Price: ❍❍❍ 92/100

Detailed instructions are featured at the start of the book.

▼ Vintage 2011 Price: ❍ 89/100

IL MOLINO DI GRACE +39 558561010

▼ Riserva Il Margone 2009 Price: ❍❍ 90/100

▼ Vintage 2009 Price: ❍ 89/100

LE MICCINE +39 577749526

▼ Riserva 2010 Price: ❍❍ 90/100

▼ Vintage 2010 Price: ❍ 84/100

LOSI QUERCIAVALLE AZIENDA AGRICOLA +39 577356842

▼ Millenium Riserva 2007 Price: ❍❍ 91/100

MELINI +39 577998511

▼ Vigneti la Selvanella 2010 Price: ❍❍❍ 88/100

▼ Granaio 2010 Price: ❍❍ 86/100

PODERE L'AIA +39 577738089

▼ Podere l'Aja 2008 Price: ❍ 88/100

POGGIO BONELLI +39 577355382

▼ Chianti Classico 2010 Price: ❍ 85/100

QUERCIA AL POGGIO +39 558075278

ORG▼ 2009 Price: ❍ 93/100

ROCCA DELLE MACIE S.P.A. +39 3905777321

▼ Riserva 2010 Price: ❍❍ 86/100

RUFFINO +39 5583605

▼ Riserva ducale oro 2008 Price: ❍❍ 87/100

TENUTA DI BIBBIANO +39 057 77 43 065

CV▼ Vigna del Capannino 2009 Price: ❍❍❍ 91/100

ORG▼ Montornello 2011 Price: ❍❍ 88/100

TENUTA LA NOVELLA +39 558337749

▼ Riserva 2006 Price: ❍❍❍ 94/100

▼ Casa di Colombo 2009 Price: ❍❍ 91/100

TERRABIANCA +39 0577 540 29

▼ Scassino 2010 Price: ❍❍ 87/100

VILLA CALCINAIA +39 55854008

▼ Riserva Conti Capponi 2009 Price: ❍❍ 86/100

▼ Conti Capponi 2010 Price: ❍❍ 85/100

VILLA VIGNAMAGGIO +39 55854661

▼ Riserva 2010 Price: ❍ 89/100

▼ Cabernet Franc 2010 Price: ❍ 87/100

Chianti Colli senesi D.O.C.G.

AZ AG LE BERTILLE +39 578758330

▼ Le Bertille 2009 Price: ❍❍ 87/100

AZIENDA AGRICOLA ANTICO COLLE +39 578707828

▼ Vintage 2011 Price: ❍ 82/100

Chianti D.O.C.G.

MELINI +39 577998511

▼ San Lorenzo 2011 Price: ❍ 87/100

CASTELLO DI SELVOLE +39 577322662

▼ Vintage 2011 Price: ❍ 86/100

MELINI +39 577998511

▼ San Lorenzo 2012 Price: ❍ 88/100

▼ Governo All'uso Toscano 2011 Price: ❍❍ 86/100

Cortona D.O.C

BALDETTI ALFONSO AZ. AGR. +39 57567077

▼ Marius 2010 Price: ❍ 86/100

SOC. AGR. I VICINI +39 5 75 67 85 07

▼ Laudario Merlot 2010 Price: ❍ 85/100

AZIENDA AGRICOLA STEFANIA MEZZETTI +39 575678528

▼ Mezzetti Az. agricola Dardano 2009 Price: ❍❍ 88/100

BALDETTI ALFONSO AZ. AGR. +39 57567077

▼ Crano 2010 Price: ❍❍ 87/100

BILLI EDDA AZ. GR. +39 3395406901

▼ Vintage 2010 Price: ❍❍ 89/100

FABRIZIO DIONISIO +39 06 3223541

▼ Il castagno 2010 Price: ❍❍ 89/100

FATTORIA LA BRACCESCA +39 578724252

▼ Bramasole 2009 Price: ❍❍❍ 87/100

GIANNONI FABBRI +39 3475883939

▼ Amato 2010 Price: ❍ 86/100

SOC. AGR. I VICINI +39 5 75 67 85 07

▼ Laudario Syrah 2010 Price: ❍❍ 92/100

▼ Laudario Cabernet Sauvignon 2010 Price: ❍ 85/100

Maremma Toscana I.G.T.

ROCCA DI MONTEMASSI +39 564579700

▼ Vintage 2010 Price: ❍ 89/100

CASTELLO DI VOLPAIA

▼ Prelius 2010 Price: ❍ 88/100

ROCCA DI MONTEMASSI +39 564579700

▼ Sassabruna 2010 Price: ❍ 90/100

Montescudaio D.O.C.

PAGANI DE MARCHI +39 586652835

▼ Principe Guerriero 2009 Price: ❍❍ 89/100

Orcia D.O.C

LUNADORO - AZIENDA AGRICOLA LA BANDITA E LUNADORO +39 578748154

▼ Eclisse 2011 Price: ❍ 84/100

Rosso di Montalcino D.O.C.

TENUTA GREPPO - FRANCO BIONDI SANTI +39 577848087

▼ Vintage 2009 Price: ❍❍ 89/100

Rosso di Montepulciano D.O.C.

AZ AG LE BERTILLE +39 578758330

▼ Le Bertille 2011 Price: ❍ 85/100

AZIENDA AGRICOLA ANTICO COLLE +39 578707828

▼ Antico colle di Frangiosa Andrea Az. Agr. 2011 Price: ❍ 81/100

AZIENDA AGRICOLA CANNETO +39 578757737

▼ Canneto 2011 Price: ❍ 84/100

BINDELLA SRL. +39 578767777

▼ Bindella Srl Fossolupaio 2012 Price: ❍ 85/100

CANTINE DEI +39 578716878

▼ Dei 2011 Price: ❍ 87/100

LUNADORO - AZIENDA AGRICOLA LA BANDITA E LUNADORO +39 578748154

▼ 2010 Price: ❍ 85/100

▼ Primo senso 2011 Price: ❍ 84/100

PODERI BOSCARELLI +39 578767277

▼ Prugnolo 2011 Price: ❍ 89/100

Toscana I.G.T.

CENNATOIO INTER VINEAS +39 558963230

▼ Sogno dell'uva 2008 Price: ❍❍❍ 87/100

AGRICOLA LE QUERCE +39 565846535

▼ Il maestrale 2012 Price: ❍ 85/100

COLLE SAN MUSTIOLA AZ. AGR. +39 57820525

▼ Vigna Flavia 2009 Price: ❍❍ 85/100

AGRICOLA LE QUERCE +39 565846535

▼ Il Libeccio 2012 Price: ❍ 84/100

JACOPO BIONDI SANTI CASTELLO DI MONTEPO +39 577848238

▼ Vintage 2010 Price: ❍ 84/100

PODERE LA REGOLA S.S. DI LUCA E FLAVIO NUTI +39 586698145

▼ Vallino 2008 Price: ❍❍ 83/100

▼ La Regola 2008 Price: ❍❍❍ 82/100

AGRICOLA LE QUERCE +39 565846535

▼ Terre di Paola 2012 Price: ❍ 88/100

▼ Calviolo 2010 Price: ❍ 84/100

BADIA DI MORRONA +39 0587 656013

▼ N'antia 2009 Price: ❍❍ 88/100

▼ Vignalta 2009 Price: ❍❍ 88/100

BINDELLA SRL. +39 578767777

▼ Bindella Srl Antenata 2010 Price: ❍❍❍ 85/100

▼ Bindella Srl Gemella 2012 Price: ❍ 85/100

BORGO SCOPETO +39 577322729

▼ Borgonero 2010 Price: ❍ 85/100

CASTELLARE DI CASTELLINA +39 577742903

▼ I sodi di San Niccolò 2009 Price: ❍❍❍ 90/100

CASTELLO VICCHIOMAGGIO +39 55854078

▼ Ripa delle mandorle 2012 Price: ❍ 88/100

▼ Ripa delle more 2010 Price: ❍❍ 87/100

CENNATOIO INTER VINEAS +39 558963230

▼ Mammolo 2008 Price: ❍❍❍ 89/100

▼ Etrusco 2007 Price: ❍❍❍ 89/100

COLLE SAN MUSTIOLA AZ. AGR. +39 57820525

▼ Poggio Ai Chiari 2006 Price: ❍❍ 94/100

▼ Kernos 2012 Price: ❍ 87/100

ENDRIZZI +39 461650129

▼ Meria 2008 Price: ❍❍ 86/100

▼ Serpaiolo 2011 Price: ❍ 84/100

FATTORIA DI MAGLIANO	+39 5645933040
▼ Poggio bestiale 2009 Price: ❍	86/100
▼ Perenzo 2009 Price: ❍	85/100
FATTORIA DI MONTEMAGGIO	+39 577738323
▼ Torre di Montemaggio 2009 Price: ❍❍❍	81/100
FELSINA	+39 577355117
▼ Fontalloro 2010 Price: ❍❍❍	90/100
IL MOLINO DI GRACE	+39 558561010
▼ Gratius 2008 Price: ❍❍	92/100
▼ Il volano 2010 Price: ❍	86/100
JACOPO BIONDI SANTI CASTELLO DI MONTEPO	+39 577848238
▼ Morione 2006 Price: ❍❍❍❍❍	93/100
▼ Sassoalloro 2009 Price: ❍❍	88/100
▼ Braccale Rosato 2011 Price: ❍	87/100
LE MICCINE	+39 577749526
▼ Carduus 2010 Price: ❍❍❍	85/100
LUNADORO - AZIENDA AGRICOLA LA BANDITA E LUNADORO	+39 578748154
▼ Rosato Dispetto 2012 Price: ❍	87/100
▼ Bianco 2012 Price: ❍	86/100
MELINI	+39 577998511
▼ I coltri 2011 Price: ❍	85/100
PAGANI DE MARCHI	+39 586652835
▼ Casa Nocera 2008 Price: ❍❍❍	87/100
PODERE L'AIA	+39 577738089
▼ Podere l'Aja L'ingegnere 2009 Price: ❍❍	88/100
PODERE LA REGOLA S.S. DI LUCA E FLAVIO NUTI	+39 586698145
▼ Strido 2008 Price: ❍❍❍❍	85/100
▼ Vintage 2011 Price: ❍❍	84/100
PODERI BOSCARELLI	+39 578767277
▼ De Ferrari 2012 Price: ❍	91/100
▼ Vintage 2007 Price: ❍❍❍	88/100
POGGIO BONELLI	+39 577355382
▼ Vintage 2008 Price: ❍❍	87/100

ROCCA DELLE MACIE S.P.A.	+39 905777321
▼ Sergioveto 2010 Price: OOO	88/100
TENUTA DI CAPEZZANA	+39 558706005
CV▼ Ghiaie Della Furba 2008 Price: OO	90/100
TERRABIANCA	+39 0577 540 29
▼ Il tesoro 2007 Price: OOO	86/100
▼ Cuvée rosé 2012 Price: OO	85/100
TORRACIA DI PRESURA SOC. AGR. S.R.L.	+39 5 58 58 86 56
▼ Arcante 2008 Price: OO	88/100
▼ Lucciolaio 2008 Price: OO	86/100
TUSCANY LUXURY	+39 35464848
▼ Dè Ré 2010 Price: OO	87/100

Vernaccia di San Giminiano D.O.C.G

TENUTE GUICCIARDINI STROZZI	+39 577950028
▼ Vintage 2010 Price: O	90/100

Vin Santo del Chianti Classico D.O.C.G.

CASTELLO DI SELVOLE	+39 577322662
▼ 1995 Price: OO	93/100

Vin Santo di Montepulciano D.O.C.G

BINDELLA SRL.	+39 578767777
▼ Bindella Srl Dolce sinfonia - Occhio di Pernice 2004 Price: OOO	90/100
▼ Bindella Srl Dolce Sinfonia 2008 Price: OO	92/100

Prices mentioned in this book are guideline and can vary depending on point of sale. The shops, wineries or publisher can in no way be held responsible for this.

Vino Nobile de Montepulciano D.O.C.G

CANTINE DEI +39 578716878

▼ Dei 2010 Price: ❍ — 91/100

PODERI BOSCARELLI +39 578767277

▼ Nocio 2009 Price: ❍ — 91/100

AZ AG LE BERTILLE +39 578758330

▼ Le Bertille 2009 Price: ❍ — 89/100

AZIENDA AGRICOLA ANTICO COLLE +39 578707828

▼ Vintage 2010 Price: ❍ — 85/100

▼ Riserva 2007 Price: ❍❍ — 85/100

AZIENDA AGRICOLA CANNETO +39 578757737

▼ Canneto Riserva 2009 Price: ❍❍ — 89/100

▼ Canneto 2010 Price: ❍❍ — 88/100

BINDELLA SRL. +39 578767777

▼ Bindella Srl I Quadri 2010 Price: ❍❍ — 90/100

▼ Bindella Srl 2010 Price: ❍ — 88/100

CANTINE DEI +39 578716878

▼ Dei Riserva Bossona 2008 Price: ❍❍ — 94/100

FATTORIA LA BRACCESCA +39 578724252

▼ Vigneto Santa Pia 2007 Price: ❍❍ — 93/100

▼ 2010 Price: ❍ — 90/100

LUNADORO - AZIENDA AGRICOLA LA BANDITA E LUNADORO +39 578748154

▼ Riserva Quercione 2009 Price: ❍ — 88/100

▼ Tradizionale 2010 Price: ❍ — 87/100

PODERI BOSCARELLI +39 578767277

▼ Riserva 2008 Price: ❍❍❍ — 94/100

▼ 2010 Price: ❍❍ — 92/100

▼ Riserva 2009 Price: ❍ — 88/100

Detailed instructions are featured at the start of the book.

Umbria

Colli Martani D.O.C

ARNALDO CAPRAI +39 742378802

▼ Grecante 2012 Price: ❍ — 84/100

CANTINA PLANI ARCHE +39 742720487

▼ Grechetto 2012 Price: ❍ — 84/100

DI FILIPPO +39 742731242

▼ Sassi d'Arenaria 2011 Price: ❍ — 84/100

Montefalco D.O.C.

TENUTA CASTELBUONO +39 742361670

▼ Rosso 2010 Price: ❍ — 84/100

ARNALDO CAPRAI +39 742378802

▼ 2011 Price: ❍❍ — 86/100

AZIENDA AGRICOLA SCACCIADIAVOLI +39 742371210

▼ Vintage 2010 Price: ❍ — 89/100

▼ Vintage 2011 Price: ❍ — 85/100

BOCALE +39 742399233

▼ Vintage 2011 Price: ❍ — 84/100

CANTINA COLLE CIOCCO - AGRICOLA SPACCHETTI SS +39 742379859

▼ Vintage 2009 Price: ❍ — 90/100

FATTORIA COLSANTO +39 432757173

▼ Vintage 2010 Price: ❍ — 87/100

SOC. AGR. PERTICAIA +39 07 42 37 90 14

▼ Vintage 2010 Price: ❍ — 86/100

TENUTA CASTELBUONO +39 742361670

▼ Rosso riserva 2008 Price: ❍❍ — 87/100

▼ Vintage 2008 Price: ❍ — 86/100

Montefalco Sagrantino D.O.C.G

ANTONELLI SAN MARCO +39 742379158

- Chiusa di pannone 2007 Price: ❍ 86/100
- Vintage 2008 Price: ❍ 89/100
- Passito 2008 Price: ❍ 86/100

ARNALDO CAPRAI +39 742378802

- 25 Anni 2009 Price: ❍❍❍ 87/100
- Collepiano 2009 Price: ❍❍❍ 86/100

AZIENDA AGRICOLA SCACCIADIAVOLI +39 742371210

- Vintage 2008 Price: ❍❍ 90/100

AZIENDA AGRICOLA MONTIONI +39 742379214

- Vintage 2009 Price: ❍❍❍ 86/100

BOCALE +39 742399233

- Vintage 2010 Price: ❍❍ 85/100

CANTINA COLLE CIOCCO - AGRICOLA SPACCHETTI SS +39 742379859

- Vintage 2007 Price: ❍❍ 88/100
- Passito 2008 Price: ❍❍ 87/100

CANTINA FRATELLI PARDI +39 742379023

- Vintage 2008 Price: ❍❍❍ 87/100

CANTINA PLANI ARCHE +39 742720487

- Montefalco Sagrantino 2007 Price: ❍❍ 89/100

CANTINA TUDERNUM +39 075 89 89 403

- Cantina Tudernum sca Colle nobile 2008 Price: ❍❍ 87/100

COLLE DEL SARACENO AZ. AGR. +39 742379500

- Vintage 2008 Price: ❍❍ 86/100
- Passito 2008 Price: ❍❍❍ 85/100

DI FILIPPO +39 742731242

- Etnico 2009 Price: ❍❍ 87/100

FATTORIA COLSANTO +39 432757173

- Vintage 2009 Price: ❍❍ 86/100

IL GHEPPIO. S.A. +39 9413382935020

▼ Il Gheppio Soc. Agr. 2009 Price: ○○ 85/100

▼ Il Gheppio Soc. Agr. Passito 2009 Price: ○○ 84/100

SOC. AGR. PERTICAIA +39 07 42 37 90 14

▼ Vintage 2007 Price: ○○ 86/100

TENUTA BELLAFONTE SOC. AGR. +39 0742 710018/9

▼ Vintage 2009 Price: ○○○ 87/100

TENUTA CASTELBUONO +39 742361670

▼ Vintage 2007 Price: ○○ 87/100

▼ Sagrantino 2008 Price: ○○ 87/100

Todi D.O.C

AZIENDA AGRICOLA SCACCIADIAVOLI +39 742371210

▼ Grechetto dell'Umbria 2012 Price: ○ 80/100

CANTINA TUDERNUM +39 075 89 89 403

▼ Cantina Tudernum sca Colle nobile 2012 Price: ○ 82/100

Umbria I.G.T.

ANTONELLI SAN MARCO +39 742379158

▼ Trebiano spoletino 2011 Price: ○ 85/100

CANTINA FRATELLI PARDI +39 742379023

▼ Trebbiano spoletino 2012 Price: ○ 86/100

SOC. AGR. PERTICAIA +39 07 42 37 90 14

▼ Trebiano Spoletino 2012 Price: ○ 85/100

Venetian

Amarone della Valpolicella D.O.C.G

AGRICOLA F.ILI TEDESCHI S.R.L. +39 457701487

CV▼ Tedeschi Capitel Monte Olmi 2008 Price: ○○○○ 92/100

Amarone Valpolicella Classico D.O.C.

BOLLA S.P.A

▼ Le Origini 2007 Price: ❍ 87/100

Colli Asolani D.O.C.G

MONTELVINI SPA +39 4238777

▼ Prosecco superiore millesimato 2012 Price: ❍ 89/100

▼ Luna storta 2010 Price: ❍ 86/100

▼ Prosecco superiore 2012 Price: ❍ 87/100

Colli Trevigiani I.G.T.

AZIENDA AGRICOLA CONTE COLLALTO DI ISABELLA COLLAL +39 438738241

▼ Conte Collalto Wildbacher 2010 Price: ❍ 84/100

Lison classico DOCG

CANTINA S. OSVALDO S.R.L. +39 0422 864 012/4 R.A.

▼ Raboso di Bibi 2008 Price: ❍❍ 88/100

Lison-Pramaggiore D.O.C.

CANTINA S. OSVALDO S.R.L. +39 0422 864 012/4 R.A.

▼ Vintage 2012 Price: ❍ 86/100

Piave D.O.C.

AZIENDA AGRICOLA CONTE COLLALTO DI ISABELLA COLLAL+39 438738241

▼ Conte Collalto Vinciguerra I 2007 Price: ❍ 81/100

Prosecco D.O.C (VE)

VINI DELLA DELIZIA - VITICOLTORI FRIULANI LA DELIZ +39 434869564

▼ Vignal Extra-dry 2012 Price: ❍ 83/100

Prosecco di Conegliano-Valdobbiadene D.O.C.

AZIENDA AGRICOLA CONTE COLLALTO DI ISABELLA COLLAL +39 438738241

▼ Conte Collalto Spumante Extra Dry 2012 Price: ❍ 89/100

Prosecco Treviso D.O.C.

BELLENDA S.A.S. DI CASAGRANDE COSMO UMBERTO & C. +39 438920025

▼ Millesimato oro Extra-Dry Col di Luna 2012 Price: ❍ 83/100

Soave D.O.C

CORTE ADAMI AZIENDA VITIVINICOLA DI ANDREA ADAMI +39 457680423

▼ E 2012 Price: ❍ 86/100

▼ Vigna della Corte 2011 Price: ❍❍ 88/100

Soave DOC Classico

BOLLA S.P.A

▼ Tufaie 2011 Price: ❍ 89/100

Terradeiforti D.O.C

AZIENDA AGRICOLA ROENO DI FUGATT R. & C. +39 457230110

▼ Roeno Soc. Agr. Enantio Riserva 2009 Price: ❍❍❍❍ 89/100

Prices mentioned in this book are guideline and can vary depending on point of sale. The shops, wineries or publisher can in no way be held responsible for this.

Valdobbiadene Prosecco Superiore D.O.C.G.

AZIENDA AGRICOLA MALIBRAN DI FAVREL MAURIZIO +39 3332119461

▼ Extra-dry Gorio 2012 Price: O 88/100

BORTOLOMIOL S.P.A. +39 423974911

▼ Ius naturae Brut 2012 Price: OO 87/100

AZIENDA AGRICOLA BORTOLIN ANGELO +39 423900125

▼ Bortolin Angelo Brut 2012 Price: O 86/100

CARPENE MALVOLTI SPA +39 438364611

▼ 1868 Dry 2012 Price: O 86/100

DEA AZIENDA AGRICOLA +39 423971017

▼ Incontri Rivalta Extra-dry 2012 Price: O 86/100

ZARDETTO +39 438394969

▼ Le Rive di Ogliano Brut Tre venti 2012 Price: O 86/100

BORTOLOMIOL S.P.A. +39 423974911

▼ Banda rossa extra-dry 2012 Price: O 85/100

CARPENE MALVOLTI SPA +39 438364611

▼ 1868 Extra-dry 2012 Price: O 85/100

AZIENDA AGRICOLA ANDREOLA +39 438989379

▼ Andreola az.agr. Mas de fer extra-dry 2012 Price: O 84/100

VAL D'OCA S.R.L. +39 423982070

▼ Vintage 2012 Price: O 84/100

VIGNE MATTE AZIENDA AGRICOLA +39 438975798

▼ Vigne matte Az. agricola Brut cuvée 2012 Price: O 83/100

AZIENDA AGRICOLA ALTHEA DI DRUSIAN MARIKA +39 438560511

▼ Extra-dry 2012 Price: O 89/100

▼ Brut 2012 Price: O 83/100

AZIENDA AGRICOLA ANDREOLA +39 438989379

▼ Andreola az.agr. Vigneto Dirupo Brut 2012 Price: O 87/100

▼ Andreola az.agr. Dry 2012 Price: O 85/100

AZIENDA AGRICOLA BORTOLIN ANGELO +39 423900125

▼ Bortolin Angelo Extra-dry 2012 Price: O 88/100

▼ Bortolin Angelo Dry desiderio 2012 Price: OO 87/100

AZIENDA AGRICOLA DRUSIAN FRANCESCO +39 423982151

- Drusian Francesco Az. Agr. Extra-dry 2012 Price: ❍ 85/100
- Drusian Francesco Az. Agr. Brut 2012 Price: ❍ 84/100

AZIENDA AGRICOLA MALIBRAN DI FAVREL MAURIZIO +39 3332119461

- Brut Ruio 2012 Price: ❍ 88/100

BELLENDA S.A.S. DI CASAGRANDE COSMO UMBERTO & C. +39 438920025

- Sei uno fermentazione in bottiglia Price: ❍ 85/100
- Brut San Fermo 2012 Price: ❍ 84/100

BORTOLOMIOL S.P.A. +39 423974911

- Cartizze Dry 2012 Price: ❍❍ 92/100
- Prior Brut 2012 Price: ❍ 89/100
- Senior extra-dry Price: ❍ 85/100

CA' VITTORIA DI FAVERO LORENZO +39 43860751

- Riva dei ciliegi Extra-dry 2012 Price: ❍ 86/100
- Dry 2012 Price: ❍ 84/100

CANEVEL SPUMANTI +39 423975940

- Extra-dry 2012 Price: ❍ 90/100
- Brut 2012 Price: ❍ 86/100

CANTINA S. OSVALDO S.R.L. +39 0422 864 012/4 R.A.

- Vintage Price: ❍ 85/100

CARPENE MALVOLTI SPA +39 438364611

- 1868 Cartizze 2012 Price: ❍ 89/100
- 1868 Brut 2012 Price: ❍ 85/100

CASA VINICOLA CANELLA S.P.A. +39 0421 5 24 46

- Canella Extra-dry 2012 Price: ❍ 84/100

DEA AZIENDA AGRICOLA +39 423971017

- Convivio Rivalta Brut 2012 Price: ❍ 89/100
- Solitario Rivalta 2012 Price: ❍ 88/100

LA TORDERA AZIENDA AGRICOLA +39 042 39 85 362

- La Tordera Az.Agr. Cru del Tittoni dry 2012 Price: ❍ 85/100

LE BERTOLE +39 423975332

- Dry supreme 2012 Price: ❍ 88/100
- Brut 2012 Price: ❍ 84/100

LE COLTURE AZIENDA AGRICOLA +39 423900192

▼ Le Colture Dry Cruner 2012 Price: ❍ 90/100

▼ Le Colture Brut Fagher 2012 Price: ❍ 86/100

SAN GIUSEPPE AZIENDA AGRICOLA +39 438450526

▼ San Giuseppe Extra-dry 2012 Price: ❍ 84/100

SOC. AGR. VALDELLOVO +39 3355710188

▼ Anno zero Extra-dry 2012 Price: ❍ 86/100

TANORE AZIENDA AGRICOLA +39 423975770

▼ Tanorè Azienda agricola Extra-dry 2013 Price: ❍ 88/100

▼ Tanorè Azienda agricola Brut 2013 Price: ❍ 88/100

TOFFOLI OCIETA' AGRICOLA S.S. +39 438978204

▼ Rive di Refrontolo Brut 2012 Price: ❍ 88/100

▼ Rive di Refrontolo Extra-dry 2012 Price: ❍ 84/100

VAL D'OCA S.R.L. +39 423982070

▼ Rive di San Pietro di Barbozza Brut 2012 Price: ❍ 89/100

▼ Extra-dry 2012 Price: ❍ 88/100

▼ Brut 2012 Price: ❍ 85/100

VIGNE MATTE AZIENDA AGRICOLA +39 438975798

▼ Extra-dry cuvée 2012 Price: ❍ 88/100

▼ Dry cuvée 2012 Price: ❍ 86/100

VINICOLA SERENA +39 4382011

▼ Ville d'Arfanta 2012 Price: ❍ 88/100

▼ Terra Serena 2012 Price: ❍ 87/100

ZARDETTO +39 438394969

▼ Brut Refosso 2012 Price: ❍ 87/100

▼ Extra-dry Molin 2012 Price: ❍ 86/100

Valpolicella D.O.C.

AGRICOLA F.ILI TEDESCHI S.R.L. +39 457701487

CV▼ Tedeschi La Fabriseria 2010 Price: ❍❍❍ 91/100

Valpolicella Ripasso D.O.C

BOLLA S.P.A

▼ Le Poiane 2010 Price: ❍❍ 89/100

CANTINE GIACOMO MONTRESOR +39 45913399

▼ Primo Ripasso Castelliere delle Guaite 2009 Price: ❍ 89/100

CORTE ADAMI AZIENDA VITIVINICOLA DI ANDREA ADAMI +39 457680423

▼ E 2011 Price: ❍ 82/100

Veneto I.G.T.

AZIENDA AGRICOLA CONTE COLLALTO DI ISABELLA COLLAL +39 438738241

▼ Spumante Rosé Manzoni Moscato 2012 Price: ❍ 88/100

LEBANON

Békaa

Békaa-Ouest

CHÂTEAU KSARA +961 1 200 715

▼ Cuvée du Troisième Millénaire 2009 Price: ❍❍❍ 85/100

DOMAINE DES TOURELLES, P. L BRUN +961 8 540 114

CV▼ Domaine des Tourelles Vintage 2010 Price: ❍ 83/100

CHÂTEAU KSARA +961 1 200 715

▼ Réserve du Couvent 2011 Price: ❍ 81/100

▼ Le Souverain 2009 Price: ❍❍❍ 90/100

▼ Blanc de Blancs 2012 Price: ❍ 84/100

CHÂTEAU NAKAD +96 18540191

▼ Château des Coteaux 2005 Price: ❍❍ 77/100

CHATEAU QANAFAR +961 1 398 782

▼ Château Qanafar Vintage 2010 Price: ❍❍ 89/100

DOMAINE DES TOURELLES, P. L BRUN +961 8 540 114

CV▼ Grande Cuvée - Syrah du Liban 2009 Price: ❍❍❍ 91/100

CV▼ Marquis des Beys

Grande Cuvée Pierre L. Brun 2009 Price: ❍❍❍ 88/100

Detailed instructions are featured at the start of the book.

Zahlé

CHÂTEAU ST THOMAS +961 8 500 812

- ▼ Les Emirs 2010 Price: ❍ — 82/100
- ▼ Vintage 2009 Price: ❍❍ — 84/100

Lebanon (all regions)

Vin du Liban

CHÂTEAU FAKRA +961 9 635 111

- ▼ Blanc de Blancs 2012 Price: ❍ — 84/100
- ▼ Pinacle 2010 Price: ❍ — 82/100
- ▼ La Fleur 2012 Price: ❍ — 79/100
- ▼ Collection Privée 2009 Price: ❍❍ — 87/100

North

Batroun

ATIBAIA +961 3 363 941

- ▼ Vintage 2009 Price: ❍❍❍ — 91/100

NEW ZEALAND

South Island

Marlborough

MARKS & SPENCER FRANCE +33 6 46 11 55 62

- ▼ Clocktower Pinot Noir 2010 Price: ❍❍ — 89/100
- ▼ Kaituna Hills Blue - Sauvignon Blanc 2011 Price: ❍ — 88/100
- ▼ Marlborough Sauvignon Blanc 2011 Price: ❍ — 88/100
- ▼ Kaituna Hills Pinot Grigio 2011 Price: ❍ — 83/100

SLOVAKIA

All Appellations

ZITAVSKE VINICE +421 911659199

- ▼ Chardonnay 41 2011 Price: OOO 88/100
- ▼ Shiraz 2011 Price: OOO 85/100
- ▼ Cabernet sauvignon 2009 Price: OOO 85/100
- ▼ Dunaj 2011 Price: OOO 84/100
- ▼ Irsai Oliver 29 2011 Price: OO 83/100
- ▼ Palava 28 2011 Price: OO 82/100
- ▼ Cabernet Sauvignon 2010 Price: OO 75/100
- ▼ Veltinske Zelené 46 2011 Price: OOO 89/100

SOUTH AFRICA

Coastal Region

Stellenbosch W.O.

MARKS & SPENCER FRANCE +33 01 47 30 10 35

- ▼ Crow's Fountain Chenin blanc 2012 Price: O 81/100
- ▼ Crow's Fountain Sauvignon blanc 2012 Price: OO 86/100

South Africa (all regions)

South African Wine

MARKS & SPENCER FRANCE +33 01 47 30 10 35

- ▼ Rockridge Cabernet Sauvignon 2011 Price: O 83/100

Detailed instructions are featured at the start of the book.

SPAIN

Canarian Islands

Lanzarote D.O.

BODEGAS STRATVS +34 928809977

▼ Sratvs Tinto crianza 2012 Price: ❍❍ 87/100

▼ Sratvs Malvasía seco 2012 Price: ❍❍ 90/100

Castile - La Mancha

Almansa D.O.

BODEGAS CASA ROJO +34 968151520

▼ Cavalls 2010 Price: ❍ 84/100

La Mancha D.O.

AYUSO S.L., BODEGAS(2)

▼ Estola Gran Reserva 2004 Price: ❍ 84/100

▼ Estola Reserva 2008 Price: ❍ 85/100

BIO MANCHA

Sí.▼ Almenara 2008 Price: ❍ 89/100

VINOS Y BODEGAS SA +34 926531067

▼ Vinos Real bodega crianza 2009 Price: ❍ 84/100

> Prices mentioned in this book are guideline and can vary depending on point of sale. The shops, wineries or publisher can in no way be held responsible for this.

Manchuela D.O.

BODEGA PARDO TOLOSA

▼ **Senda de las Rochas 2008** **85/100**

Subtle, complex nose of black fruits, cherry, pepper, coffee, snuff and a mineral dimension. Upfront acidity and fairly firm tannins impart personality on the palate. The finish displays a subtle trace of sourness.

Price: ❍

Serving Temperature: 15-17°C
Ready to drink : 2013-2015

Bodega Pardo Tolosa
c/. Villatoya 26
2215 Alborea
Tel.: +34 96 351 70 67 - Fax: +34 96 351 70 91
E-mail: mj.veses@bodegapardotolosa.com

Valdepenas D.O.

BODEGAS CASA ROJO +34 968151520

▼ Balthasar Gran Reserva 2002 Price: ❍ 84/100

Vino de Pago Calzadilla D.O.

PAGO DE CALZADILLA (BODEGAS Y VIÑEDOS URIBES MADERO)

▼ Calzadilla Classic 2007 Price: ❍❍ 89/100

▼ Calzadilla Allegro 2007 Price: ❍❍ 90/100

VT Castilla

VERUM S.L., BODEGAS Y VIÑEDOS +34 926511404

▼ Merlot 2009 Price: ❍ 90/100

NEBBIA WINES +34 925167493

▼ Tempranillo 22 meses 2009 Price: ❍ 88/100

▼ Verdejo 2012 Price: ❍ 87/100

ORGANIC SIGNATURE WINES +34 967472503

ORG▼ Finca Lastonar Price: ❍❍ 87/100

VERUM S.L., BODEGAS Y VIÑEDOS +34 926511404

▼ Terra Verum - Airén de pie franco 2012 Price: ❍ 87/100

ALENUR

▼ Blanco 2012 Price: ❍ 86/100

ORGANIC SIGNATURE WINES +34 967472503

ORG▼ Franchete Barrique 2005 Price: ❍❍ 86/100

VINOS Y BODEGAS SA +34 926531067

▼ Vinos Tantra Premium 2008 Price: ❍ 83/100

▼ RO Reserva de Oro 2007 Price: ❍ 82/100

ALENUR

▼ Alenur Roble 2012 Price: ❍ 88/100

▼ Olé Tempranillo 2011 Price: ❍ 87/100

AURUM RED +34 967160464

▼ Aurum Red Edición Plata 2012 Price: ❍ 97/100

▼ Aurum Red White 2012 Price: ❍ 96/100

BODEGA ABAXTERRA

▼ Tempranillo - Syrah 2011 Price: ❍ 87/100

BODEGAS ARÚSPIDE +34 926347075

▼ Autor de Arúspide 2008 Price: ❍ 88/100

▼ El Linze 2008 Price: ❍ 88/100

BODEGAS CASA ROJO +34 968151520

▼ Musso 2010 Price: ❍ 83/100

BODEGAS VILLAVID - DULCE NOMBRE DE JESUS S.COOP	+34 962189006
▼ Secret Bubbles of Villavid Price: ❍	88/100

ENCOMIENDA DE CERVERA	+34 926102089
▼ Poker de Tempranillos 2010 Price: ❍	90/100

NEBBIA WINES	+34 925167493
▼ Tempranillo dulce 2009 Price: ❍	89/100
▼ Moscatel dulce 2011 Price: ❍	89/100
▼ Tempranillo 16 meses 2010 Price: ❍	87/100

ORGANIC SIGNATURE WINES	+34 967472503
ORG▼ Franchete Cabernet Sauvignon 2007 Price: ❍	88/100
ORG▼ Franchete Assemblage 2011 Price: ❍	87/100

VERUM S.L., BODEGAS Y VIÑEDOS	+34 926511404
▼ Tempranillo Reserva Familiar 2009 Price: ❍❍	90/100
▼ Sauvignon blanc - gewurztraminer 2012 Price: ❍	89/100
▼ Verum 2010 Price: ❍	89/100

VINOS Y BODEGAS SA	+34 926531067
▼ Vinos Amelasio Sauvignon blanc 2012 Price: ❍❍	84/100
▼ Vinos Templum tempranillo 2011 Price: ❍❍	83/100

Castile and Leon

Ribera del Duero D.O.

MARQUÉS DE VARGAS, S.A., BODEGAS Y VIÑEDOS+34 941261401

▼ Grupo Varma Conde de San Cristobal 2010 Price: ❍❍
89/100

Rueda D.O.

BODEGA PAGO TRASLAGARES S.L	+34 983667023
▼ 2012 Price: ❍	87/100

Toro D.O.

BODEGA DOMINIO DEL BENDITO, S.L. +34 980693306

ORG▼ El Primer Paso 2010 Price: ○○ 95/100

ORG▼ El Titán del Bendito 2009 Price: ○○○ 92/100

BODEGA DOMINIO DEL BENDITO, S.L.

▼ Las Sabías 2008 94/100

ORG Brilliant garnet-red. The nose shows pronounced spice (black pepper), forest fruits, black plum and refined, well-integrated oak notes. Mouth-coating with a lovely tannic framework that is very dense yet subtle. Elegant coffee note on the finish.

Price: ○○

Serving Temperature: 16-18°C
Ready to drink : 2014-2016

Bodega Dominio del Bendito, S.L.
Plaza Santo Domingo, 8 - 49800 Toro
Tel.: +34 980 693 306 - Fax: +34 980 694 991
E-mail: info@bodegadominiodelbendito.es
Website: http://www.bodegadominiodelbendito.com/

Catalonia

Cava D.O.

ANTONIO MASCARO, S.L. +34 938901628

▼ Reserva Brut Nigrum Price: ○ 90/100

▼ Brut Rosé Rubor Aurorae Price: ○○ 89/100

▼ Reserva Brut Nature Pure Price: ○○ 89/100

Costers del Segre D.O.

LAGRAVERA SLU (ARNÓ AGRÍCOLA SLU)

▼ Ónra. MontaHonra tinto 2009 Price: ○ — 88/100

MAS BLANCH I JOVÉ SL

▼ Saó Expressiu 2008 Price: ○○ — 86/100

▼ Petit Saó 2010 Price: ○ — 85/100

LAGRAVERA SLU (ARNÓ AGRÍCOLA SLU)

▼ Ónra. MontaHonra blanc 2011 Price: ○ — 90/100

MAS BLANCH I JOVÉ SL

▼ Saó Abrivat 2009 Price: ○○ — 86/100

▼ Saó Blanc 2011 Price: ○○ — 86/100

Priorato D.O.

BODEGAS CASA ROJO +34 968151520

▼ Fauno de Casa Rojo 2009 Price: ○○ — 89/100

Spirits

ANTONIO MASCARO, S.L. +34 938901628

▼ Ego Rare XO Brandy Price: ○○○ — 89/100

▼ Gin 9 London Dry Gin Price: ○○○ — 91/100

Galicia

Rias Baixas D.O.

BODEGAS SANTIAGO ROMA, S.L. +34 986718477

▼ Albariño Selección 2012 Price: ○ — 90/100

▼ Colleita de Martis 2012 Price: ○ — 87/100

▼ Albariño 2012 Price: ○ — 88/100

MARQUÉS DE VARGAS, S.A., BODEGAS Y VIÑEDOS +34 941261401

▼ Grupo Varma Pazo San Mauro 2012 Price: OO 89/100

Ribeiro D.O.

BODEGAS EL PARAGUAS +34 636161479

▼ El Paraguas 2012 Price: OO 89/100

La Rioja

Rioja D.O.Ca.

CASTILLO DE CUZCURRITA, S.L. +34 941328022

▼ Cerrado del Castillo 2008 Price: O 94/100

▼ Señorío de Cuzcurrita 2007 Price: O 92/100

MARQUÉS DE VARGAS, S.A., BODEGAS Y VIÑEDOS +34 941261401

▼ Marqués de Vargas Reserva 2008 Price: OO 89/100

VALENCISO, S.A. CÍA. BODEGAS DE +34 941304724

▼ Valenciso blanco 2012 Price: O 90/100

▼ Reserva 2006 Price: O 89/100

Madrid

Madrid D.O.

BODEGA BERNABELEVA +34 915091909

ORG▼ Cantocuerdas 2011 Price: OO 92/100

▼ Viña Bonita 2010 Price: OOO 92/100

▼ Navarreros Garnacha 2010 Price: OO 92/100

Detailed instructions are featured at the start of the book.

Murcie

Jumilla D.O.

BODEGAS PIO DEL RAMO NUÑEZ

▼ Tinto Crianza 2010 Price: ❍ 87/100

EGO BODEGAS +34 968964326

▼ Talento 2012 Price: ❍ 87/100

BODEGAS CARCHELO +34 968435137

▼ Altico syrah 2011 Price: ❍ 89/100

BODEGAS CASA ROJO +34 968151520

▼ Casa del Rojo 2007 Price: ❍❍ 87/100

BODEGAS PIO DEL RAMO NUÑEZ

▼ Tinto Roble 2011 Price: ❍ 88/100

EGO BODEGAS +34 968964326

▼ Fuerza 2009 Price: ❍❍ 90/100

▼ Gorú 2012 Price: ❍ 87/100

Valence

Utiel-Requena D.O.

CHOZAS CARRASCAL +34 963410395

ORG▼ El Cabernet Franc
de Chozas Carrascal 2010 Price: ❍❍❍ 93/100

ORG▼ Las 2 CES 2011 Price: ❍ 90/100

ORG▼ Las Ocho 2010 Price: ❍❍ 92/100

Valencia D.O.

MURVIEDRO BODEGAS +34 962329003

▼ Murviedro crianza 2010 Price: ❍ 88/100

▼ Murviedro reserva 2009 Price: ❍ 89/100

USA

California

Alexander Valley

ALEXANDER VALLEY VINEYARDS +1 7074337209

- ▼ Alexander School Reserve Cabernet 2009 Price: ○○○ 90/100
- ▼ Cabernet Sauvignon Estate 2010 Price: ○○○ 88/100
- ▼ Sin Zin Zinfandel 2010 Price: ○○○ 88/100
- ▼ Merlot Estate 2010 Price: ○○○ 87/100
- ▼ Chardonnay Estate 2011 Price: ○○ 86/100
- ▼ Cyrus 2009 Price: ○○○○ 91/100

ARBIOS CELLARS +1 7075395641

- ▼ Cabernet Sauvignon 2006 Price: ○○○ 91/100

PRAXIS CELLARS +1 707-539-5642

- ▼ Merlot 2009 Price: ○○○ 87/100

Anderson Valley

HANDLEY CELLARS WINERY +1 7078953876

- ▼ Pinot Noir 2009 Price: ○○○ 94/100
- ▼ Gewurztraminer 2011 Price: ○○ 89/100
- ▼ Vineyard Chardonnay 2011 Price: ○○○ 90/100

Carneros (Los Carneros)

SCHUG CARNEROS ESTATE WINERY +1 7079399363

- ▼ Schug Carneros Estate Chardonnay 2011 Price: ○○○ 86/100
- ▼ Schug Carneros Estate Pinot Noir 2010 Price: ○○○ 89/100

El Dorado

CRYSTAL BASIN CELLARS	+1 5306471767
▼ Zinfandel Reserve 2010 Price: OOO	81/100
▼ Syrah Reserve 2010 Price: OOO	80/100
▼ Cabernet Sauvignon Reserve 2009 Price: OOO	80/100

Russian River Valley

RUSSIAN HILL ESTATE WINERY	+1 7075759428
▼ Tara Vineyard Pinot noir 2009 Price: OOOO	87/100
▼ Pinot Noir 2009 Price: OOO	87/100
▼ Estate Vineyards Pinot Noir 2009 Price: OOO	84/100

DUTTON GOLDFIELD WINERY	+1 7078233887
▼ Dutton Ranch Chardonnay 2011 Price: OOO	92/100
▼ Pinot noir 2011 Price: OOO	85/100

RUSSIAN HILL ESTATE WINERY	+1 7075759428
▼ Estate Vineyards Syrah 2009 Price: OOO	89/100
▼ Top Block Syrah 2007 Price: OOO	87/100
▼ Viognier 2011 Price: OOO	85/100

New York

Finger Lakes

FOX RUN VINEYARDS	+1 3155364616
▼ Lake Dana Vineyard Riesling 12 2010 Price: OOO	87/100
▼ Chardonnay Reserve 2009 Price: OO	87/100
▼ Blanc de Blancs 2010 Price: OOO	86/100
▼ Cabernet Franc Reserve 2010 Price: OOO	89/100

INDEX OF WINES AND PRODUCERS

Wine or producer .... Pages

A

B

C

D

E

F

G

H

I

J

K

L

M

N

O

P

Q

R

S

T

U

V

Y

Z

INDEX OF APPELLATIONS

A

B

C

D

E

F

G

H

I

J

L

M

N

O

P

Q

R

S

T

U

V

Z

Publisher: Vinipresse - 7 Parc des Fontenelles 78870 Bailly - FRANCE

Publishing managers: François Gilbert & Philippe Gaillard
Editor: Sylvain Patard

ISBN 978 2 919184 11-8

With the collaboration of:
FRANCE: Frédéric Comet, Annick Delauneux, Olivier Delorme, Michèle Huyard, Emma Rakotomalala, Nicolas Sanseigne and James Turnbull.
USA: Jamal Rayyis
ITALY: Francesca Bassetti
PORTUGAL AND SPAIN: Diego Bonnel and Santiago Bosch

Translation: Elise Bradbury, Sharon Nagel.

Distributed in the United States by
BookMasters Distribution Services, Inc.
30 Amberwood Parkway - Ashland, OH 44805

Distributed in Canada by
BookMasters Distribution Services, Inc.
c/o Jacqueline Gross Associates - 165 Dufferin Street
Toronto, Ontario, Canada M6K 3H6

Distributed in UK, Ireland, East Europa and Asia by:
Vinehouse Distribution Ltd
The Old Mill House, Mill Lane, Uckfield, East Sussex - TN22 5AA
Phone: 01825 767396
email: sales@vinehouseuk.co.uk

Printed by La Tipografica Varese S.p.A. (Varese - Italy)
Copyright: November 2013